THE OXFORD
ILLUSTRATED DICKENS

AMERICAN NOTES

AND

PICTURES FROM ITALY

THE OXFORD ILLUSTRATED DICKENS

Charles John Huffham Dickens was born on 7 February 1812 at Landport near Portsmouth, where his father was a Navy pay clerk. His family moved to London in 1815 and in 1817 to Chatham, where Dickens spent the happiest time of his boyhood. This was followed by a period of misery during which his father was imprisoned for debt in the Marshalsea and Dickens was withdrawn from school and, at the age of 12, sent to work in a blacking warehouse. These experiences deeply affected him and his future work. He returned to school, and left at 15 to become a clerk, a shorthand reporter in the law courts, and a reporter of debates in the Commons. In 1833 he began contributing articles to periodicals, which were later reprinted as *Sketches by Boz* (1836–7); these led to an approach from publishers, resulting in the creation of Mr Pickwick and the publication in monthly numbers of *The Posthumous Papers of the Pickwick Club* (1836–7). In 1836 he married Catherine Hogarth; they had ten children over the next 16 years. Dickens began to publish *Oliver Twist* in 1837 in *Bentley's Miscellany*, a periodical of which he was the first editor. *Nicholas Nickleby* followed in 1838–9. *The Old Curiosity Shop* (1840–1) and *Barnaby Rudge* (1841) were intended for *Master Humphrey's Clock*, a weekly written by Dickens, but he eventually abandoned 'Master Humphrey'.

Dickens's visit to America in 1842 resulted in *American Notes* (1842) and an American section in *Martin Chuzzlewit* (1843–4). He lost readership with the latter but regained it with 'A Christmas Carol' (1843), the first of his five *Christmas Books*. In 1844 he visited Italy, and contributed 'Pictures from Italy' (1846) to the *Daily News*, a paper he founded. *Dombey and Son* appeared in 1846–8 and *David Copperfield* in 1849–50. In 1850 Dickens began the weekly journal *Household Words*, incorporated in 1859 into *All The Year Round*, which he edited until his death. In these appeared essays later issued as *Reprinted Pieces* (1858) and *The Uncommercial Traveller* (1861), and his *Christmas Stories*. *A Child's History of England* was published in 1851–3, *Bleak House* in 1852–3, *Hard Times* in 1854, *Little Dorrit* in 1855–7, *A Tale of Two Cities* in 1859, *Great Expectations* in 1860–1, and *Our Mutual Friend* in 1864–5. In 1856 Dickens bought a country house, Gad's Hill Place, near Rochester, and in 1858 he and his wife separated. He threw himself into public readings of his works, which were greatly successful but draining. His last work, *The Mystery of Edwin Drood*, was left unfinished when he died suddenly on 9 June 1870.

The 'Britannia'

AMERICAN NOTES
AND
PICTURES FROM ITALY

By
CHARLES DICKENS

With Twelve Illustrations by Marcus Stone
Samuel Palmer and Clarkson Stanfield
and an Introduction by
SACHEVERELL SITWELL

OXFORD   NEW YORK   TORONTO   MELBOURNE
OXFORD UNIVERSITY PRESS

Oxford University Press, Walton Street, Oxford OX2 6DP

Oxford New York Toronto
Delhi Bombay Calcutta Madras Karachi
Petaling Jaya Singapore Hong Kong Tokyo
Nairobi Dar es Salaam Cape Town
Melbourne Auckland

and associated companies in
Berlin Ibadan

Oxford is a trade mark of Oxford University Press

American Notes was first published in 1842 in two volumes. *Pictures from Italy* appeared serially in the *Daily News* and was first published as one volume in 1846.

The illustrations for *American Notes* have been taken from the Cheap Edition, 1850, and the Illustrated Library Edition, 1862–8; those for *Pictures from Italy* from the first edition, 1846, and from the Illustrated Library Edition.

In the Oxford Illustrated Dickens (known before 1966 as The New Oxford Illustrated Dickens) this volume was first published in 1957, and reprinted in 1966, 1970, 1974, 1978, 1982, 1987, 1989.

Published in the United States by Oxford University Press, USA

This volume: ISBN 0 19 254519 1
21-volume set: ISBN 0 19 254522 1

Printed in the United States of America

INTRODUCTION

By SACHEVERELL SITWELL

American Notes and *Pictures from Italy* are two minor works
of one of our greatest writers but we must not be misled by
this into thinking that they are short in length. No literary
work in mid-Victorian times was little in respect of number
of lines or pages. The tendency, if anything, was for the
lesser works to be as long as major ones. This seems to be
true in every field of mid-nineteenth-century life; in painting, music, as well as in the writing of books. We have only
to think of the immense length of some of the lesser works by
Dumas *père*. How many readers of our day know 'Il Carri-
colo', the book which Dumas *père* dictated, we can only
imagine, on Neapolitan life ? Or another extraordinary work
by him—his book on New Zealand whaling ? In all of these
the pages go by the hundred; and it is the same with these
two books of Dickens; they total 460 pages. *American Notes*
opens, naïvely, with the voyage on the Britannia steam
packet, 1,200 tons, to Halifax and Boston, and Dickens's
remarks on sea sickness are not unusual. He gives an excellent description of coming up on deck and staring into
the grey blankness of the ocean, nearly unconscious with
exhaustion, and then crawling down again to his cabin.
What is more interesting if we are searching for details of
Victorian life is his account of dinner at 5 p.m., a feature one
always notices in old advertisements of *table d'hôtes* in hotels
abroad.

The greyness is relieved, however, when he gets to Boston,
of which he gives a charming description, everything looking
gay and beautiful after imprisonment on board ship. 'When
I got into the streets upon this Sunday morning, the air was
so clear, the houses were so bright and gay; the signboards
were painted in such gaudy colours; the gilded letters were
so very golden; the bricks were so very red, the stone was so
very white; the blinds and area railings were so very green,
the knobs and plates upon the street doors so marvellously
bright and twinkling.' And he goes on to say that the boards

in front of the houses covered with inscriptions seemed about
to change into something else, reminding him of the harle-
quinade, so that he was on the look-out for Clown and Pantaloon around the corner, and Columbine.

On arrival in a new town Dickens's instinct led him at once,
as one might expect, to the poor house, prison, and lunatic
asylum. I am reminded, myself, of reaching Dublin for the
first time after a bad night crossing, hiring a taxi to drive
round the town and being taken, still half-conscious, to the
slaughter house. Perhaps it was not only Dickens's own individuality that took him to these places, but a part of the
Victorian mentality of the time. At Boston he visits an
Asylum for the Blind and gives a touching account of a
young girl called Laura Bridgman, who seems to have been
saved from the abyss of darkness rather in the same manner
as Helen Keller. His account is wonderful reading for its
understanding of the darkness from which this poor child
was saved.

Next, we find him on the American railroad. And it is
perhaps a little surprising to hear that 'there is usually a
stove fed with charcoal or anthracite coal in the centre of
the carriage and it is, for the most part, red-hot'. No wonder
railway travel was dangerous in those days. Here again the
sensation of newness comes over him as in the pantomime
streets of Boston. 'A large hotel, whose walls and colonnades were so crisp, and thin, and slight, that it had exactly
the appearance of being built with cards ... fresh buildings,
of bright red brick and painted wood ... the golden pestles
and mortars fixed as signs upon the sunblind frames outside
the Druggists, appear to have been just turned out of the
U.S. Mint.'

A few moments after this we are in New York with
Dickens, and we hear of Broadway swarming with hogs.
'They are the city scavengers, these pigs ... at this hour,
just as evening is closing in, you will see them roaming towards bed by scores, eating their way to the last. Occasionally, some youth among them who has over-eaten himself, or
has been worried by dogs, trots shrinkingly homeward, like
a prodigal son.' He is at his best in speaking of the oyster-
cellars; but the tone becomes quite different when he goes
into the Tombs Prison, where, he tells us of the gaoler
making, as he goes, 'a kind of iron castanet of the key and

stair rail'. Coming out of the Tombs Prison he comments, 'but how quiet the streets are', and it is evident that New York was a very different city from what it is now. He is writing in 1842. How curious to think that Lorenzo da Ponte, the librettist of *Figaro* and *Don Giovanni*, and friend of Casanova, had only died in New York five years before this! The rather level monotony of style is enlivened, as only Dickens could do, in his inspired moments, as when he tells of being rowed by a crew of prisoners in a boat belonging to the Island Gaol, 'who were dressed in striped uniforms of black and buff, in which they looked like faded tigers'.

The best part of *American Notes* by far, is his account of the appalling Eastern Penitentiary in Philadelphia; a place of horror of which it is difficult to speak in moderate tones. I would refer readers to the dreadful talk with a prisoner on page 102. Immediately on arrival in this awful place a black hood was drawn over the head and face of a criminal and he was led to his cell, never to come out again, until his sentence was expired; never hearing of wife and children, home or friends. The insensate brutality of the silent system, as it was called, passes comprehension. In 1818, the Legislature of Pennsylvania resolved to construct a penitentiary for enforced solitary confinement, without even work. Solitude was all that mattered, and it was to be no luxury of idleness for the solitary confinement was in darkness. At another prison, a trial of solitary confinement was made upon 80 convicts. In 1822 they were shut up for 10 months, each in a little cell 7 feet long by $3\frac{1}{2}$ feet broad, and were not allowed to leave it at any time or for any purpose. At the end of this time the experiment could only be called a partial success. More than half of the convicts were insane. In Maine, the prisoners were kept alone in underground cells which were veritable pits entered only by a ladder. In the Eastern Penitentiary the prisoner, on being received, passed through three rooms in his initiation. In the first he was undressed; in the second he was cleaned by a warm bath; and in the third he was attired in prison garb and his face was covered by the dreadful hood. But, to continue with the ceremony of his induction, he was led through, blindfolded, into the presence of a prison warden who admonished him and prepared him for his doom. He was then taken to his cell and left in solitude. The cell was 12 feet by 7 feet, and elongated with a peculiar effect of horror into a funnel-like height of 16 feet at the top of which a small grated window let in a little light. The prisoners in the cells of the upper storey never went out at all. The successive symbolism of the three rooms to be passed through by each prisoner was a stroke of dramatic genius on the part of its inventor. The casting off of the clothes or trappings of ordinary life; the cleansing or purification by water; the investiture with the felon's distinctive dress, the hiding of the face in a cowl or mask; the speech from the governor or king of this underworld; and then the years of silence, of misery and meditation.

The accounts of Cincinnati, Louisville, and St. Louis make interesting reading. Cincinnati was already a city of fifty thousand inhabitants when Dickens saw it, and although on the edge of the civilized world, a place of some culture and refinement, as all will agree who have visited the Taft mansion, one of its old houses, full of pictures and furniture in Biedermeier and delayed Empire style. It is only a pity that Dickens's journey did not take him to Kentucky for he would have seen much to delight him in Lexington and the surrounding district, which much resembles another Co. Kildare taken over bodily to America and left there in 1840, which is about the date that he made his tour. The Mississippi was then the frontier, and the Western Steamboats are described in full, but, unfortunately, not a showboat for this is just before their time. Dickens did not like the river. 'The hideous waters . . . that intolerable river' . . . and he trusts never to see it again except in nightmares. It is obvious, too, that he hated the Niagara Falls; and after a brisk account of some Canadian cities, appropriately disapproving remarks on slavery, and a visit to the Shakers, he is on board ship again bound for a Victorian homecoming.

Pictures from Italy is an account of a tour of two years later, made in 1844. It must have been one of the last opportunities of making a journey by diligence through France. On reaching the Mediterranean this master hand at writing of the poorer quarters of London is quite flabbergasted, and rendered almost speechless by the bright colours and mingled tawdriness and squalor of Genoa. A strange and unexpected conjunction soon after this is that of Dickens and Correggio. The cathedral at Parma 'is odorous with the rotting of his frescoes. Heaven knows how beautiful they may have been at one time,' he continues, adding that such heaps and labyrinths of arms and legs, 'no operative surgeon, gone mad, could imagine in his wildest delirium.' Correggio and Charles Dickens were not made to appreciate one another. It is only extraordinary that their paths should ever have crossed at all. Who would have thought to meet the creator of *Oliver Twist* and *Dombey and Son* in Parma! But the writer emerges again in Modena, the next town, when coming out of the dark Romanesque cathedral which cannot have been to his liking, he hears a shrill trumpet and an equestrian company from Paris ' comes tearing round the corner'. First, 'a stately nobleman with a great deal of hair, and no hat', bearing a banner on which was inscribed Mazeppa! To-night! Then, a Mexican chief; and six or eight chariots, each holding a lady in pink tights, amid a shower of handbills.

It is curious to think that a longer span of time lies between ourselves and Dickens in Venice than lay between him and the Venetian Carnival. That is to say, he is writing a hundred and ten, and more, years ago ; and a like interval would have brought him to Venice in 1730, in the time of Goldoni and Tiepolo and Guardi. Surely, then, he would have discovered much to interest him! But he finds Venice so dead that he has to describe it in a dream, shows more interest in the Doges' Prison than in either St. Mark's or the Doges' Palace ; and hurries off to Mantua which he finds almost as dead as he found Ferrara. And my own memories of first visiting those two cities more than thirty years ago points to how much deader they may have been a hundred years before.

Dickens in Rome is memorable for just his description of the Carnival, which is what he missed in Venice but could have seen, had he been but a generation older. Buildings, old or new (which is to say of the age of Bernini), do not interest him, and off he goes to witness a beheading, writing excellently of it so that the scene stays in the memory like a Goya drawing. The Washing of the Feet by the Pope (Pio Nono) in St. Peter's is another wonderful passage, with the English tourist saying from the back: 'Can any gentleman, in front there, see mustard on the table? Sir, will you oblige me? Do you see a Mustard-Pot ?'

In Naples it is typical of his genius that he should describe a galley-slave in chains dictating a letter to a public letter-writer, under the portico of the great theatre of San Carlo. And, meanwhile, the sentinel leans against the wall waiting for the galley-slave to finish, and cracking nuts! And, of course, Dickens loves Pompeii, though, somehow, it is unexpected to find him looking up at Vesuvius, the burning mountain. It is the unlikeliness that makes *Pictures from Italy* interesting; as it would be to find Hokusai at a bull-fight, or Goya in Japan. In the last sentence of the book he writes that 'the wheel of Time is rolling for an end, and that the world is, in all great essentials, better, gentler, more forbearing, and more hopeful, as it rolls'. There, alas! few persons in this generation would agree with him. That the hopelessness of many hundreds of thousands has improved; that there is no little Oliver asking for more; all this, and much more, is true, but we are overshadowed by other dangers of which he can have had no inkling. H. G. Wells, who had as little feeling for works of art as had Dickens, lived to see the peril in the mechanical age that he had prophesied and helped to bring on, as we know from his last despairing writings. Wells's reputation is now blowing about in the doldrums, the pause, or lull, that nearly always follows a writer's death. But it is the measure of Dickens's genius that he has never lacked readers for with Shakespeare he is the one universal writer of our race. The two lesser works, here presented, show the sparks of his talent, and if they do not enhance, still less do they tarnish his great name.

PREFACE

My readers have opportunities of judging for themselves whether the influences and tendencies which I distrusted in America, had, at that time, any existence but in my imagination. They can examine for themselves whether there has been anything in the public career of that country since, at home or abroad, which suggests that those influences and tendencies really did exist. As they find the fact, they will judge me. If they discern any evidences of wrong-going, in any direction that I have indicated, they will acknowledge that I had reason in what I wrote. If they discern no such indications, they will consider me altogether mistaken—but not wilfully.

Prejudiced, I am not, and never have been, otherwise than in favour of the United States. I have many friends in America, I feel a grateful interest in the country, I hope and believe it will successfully work out a problem of the highest importance to the whole human race. To represent me as viewing AMERICA with ill-nature, coldness, or animosity, is merely to do a very foolish thing: which is always a very easy one.

CONTENTS

LIST OF ILLUSTRATIONS

CHAPTER I

GOING AWAY

I SHALL never forget the one-fourth serious and three-fourths comical astonishment, with which, on the morning of the third of January eighteen-hundred-and-forty-two, I opened the door of, and put my head into, a "state-room" on board the "Britannia" steam-packet, twelve hundred tons burthen per register, bound for Halifax and Boston, and carrying Her Majesty's mails.

That this state-room had been specially engaged for "Charles Dickens, Esquire, and Lady," was rendered sufficiently clear even to my scared intellect by a very small manuscript, announcing the fact, which was pinned on a very flat quilt, covering a very thin mattress, spread like a surgical plaster on a most inaccessible shelf. But that this was the state-room concerning which Charles Dickens, Esquire, and Lady, had held daily and nightly conferences for at least four months preceding: that this could by any possibility be that small snug chamber of the imagination, which Charles Dickens, Esquire, with the spirit of prophecy strong upon him, had always foretold would contain at least one little sofa, and which his lady, with a modest yet most magnificent sense of its limited dimensions, had from the first opined would not hold more than two enormous portmanteaus in some odd corner out of sight (portmanteaus which could now no more be got in at the door, not to say stowed away, than a giraffe could be persuaded or forced into a flower-pot): that this utterly impracticable, thoroughly hopeless, and pro-

foundly preposterous box, had the remotest reference to, or connexion with, those chaste and pretty, not to say gorgeous little
bowers, sketched by a masterly hand, in the highly varnished
lithographic plan hanging up in the agent's counting-house
in the city of London; that this room of state, in short,
could be anything but a pleasant fiction and cheerful jest of
the captain's, invented and put in practice for the better
relish and enjoyment of the real state-room presently to be
disclosed:—these were truths which I really could not, for
the moment, bring my mind at all to bear upon or comprehend. And I sat down upon a kind of horsehair slab, or
perch, of which there were two within; and looked, without
any expression of countenance whatever, at some friends who
had come on board with us, and who were crushing their
faces into all manner of shapes by endeavouring to squeeze
them through the small doorway.

We had experienced a pretty smart shock before coming
below, which, but that we were the most sanguine people
living, might have prepared us for the worst. The imagina-
tive artist to whom I have already made allusion, has
depicted in the same great work, a chamber of almost interminable perspective, furnished, as Mr. Robins would say, in
a style of more than Eastern splendour, and filled (but not
inconveniently so) with groups of ladies and gentlemen, in
the very highest state of enjoyment and vivacity. Before
descending into the bowels of the ship, we had passed from
the deck into a long narrow apartment, not unlike a gigantic
hearse with windows in the sides; having at the upper end
a melancholy stove, at which three or four chilly stewards
were warming their hands; while on either side, extending
down its whole dreary length, was a long, long table, over
each of which a rack, fixed to the low roof, and stuck full of
drinking-glasses and cruet-stands, hinted dismally at rolling
seas and heavy weather. I had not at that time seen the
ideal presentment of this chamber which has since gratified
me so much, but I observed that one of our friends who had
made the arrangements for our voyage, turned pale on entering, retreated on the friend behind him, smote his forehead
involuntarily, and said below his breath, "Impossible! it
cannot be!" or words to that effect. He recovered himself
however by a great effort, and after a preparatory cough or
two, cried, with a ghastly smile which is still before me,
looking at the same time round the walls, "Ha! the break-

fast-room, steward—eh?" We all foresaw what the answer must be: we knew the agony he suffered. He had often spoken of *the saloon;* had taken in and lived upon the pictorial idea; had usually given us to understand, at home, that to form a just conception of it, it would be necessary to multiply the size and furniture of an ordinary drawing-room by seven, and then fall short of the reality. When the man in reply avowed the truth; the blunt, remorseless, naked truth; "This is the saloon, Sir"—he actually reeled beneath the blow.

In persons who were so soon to part, and interpose between their else daily communication the formidable barrier of many thousand miles of stormy space, and who were for that reason anxious to cast no other cloud, not even the passing shadow of a moment's disappointment or discomfiture, upon the short interval of happy companionship that yet remained to them—in persons so situated, the natural transition from these first surprises was obviously into peals of hearty laughter, and I can report that I, for one, being still seated upon the slab or perch before mentioned, roared outright until the vessel rang again. Thus, in less than two minutes after coming upon it for the first time, we all by common consent agreed that this state-room was the pleasantest and most facetious and capital contrivance possible; and that to have had it one inch larger, would have been quite a disagreeable and deplorable state of things. And with this; and with showing how,—by very nearly closing the door, and twining in and out like serpents, and by counting the little washing slab as standing-room,—we could manage to insinuate four people into it, all at one time; and entreating each other to observe how very airy it was (in dock), and how there was a beautiful port-hole which could be kept open all day (weather permitting), and how there was quite a large bull's-eye just over the looking-glass which would render shaving a perfectly easy and delightful process (when the ship didn't roll too much); we arrived, at last, at the unanimous conclusion that it was rather spacious than otherwise: though I do verily believe that, deducting the two berths, one above the other, than which nothing smaller for sleeping in was ever made except coffins, it was no bigger than one of those hackney cabriolets which have the door behind, and shoot their fares out, like sacks of coals, upon the pavement.

Having settled this point to the perfect satisfaction of all parties, concerned and unconcerned, we sat down round the fire in the ladies' cabin—just to try the effect. It was rather dark, certainly; but somebody said, "of course it would be light, at sea," a proposition to which we all assented; echoing "of course, of course;" though it would be exceedingly difficult to say why we thought so. I remember, too, when we had discovered and exhausted another topic of consolation in the circumstance of this ladies' cabin, adjoining our state-room, and the consequently immense feasibility of sitting there at all times and seasons, and had fallen into a momentary silence, leaning our faces on our hands and looking at the fire, one of our party said, with the solemn air of a man who had made a discovery, "What a relish mulled claret will have down here!" which appeared to strike us all most forcibly; as though there were something spicy and high-flavoured in cabins, which essentially improved that composition, and rendered it quite incapable of perfection anywhere else.

There was a stewardess, too, actively engaged in producing clean sheets and table-cloths from the very entrails of the sofas, and from unexpected lockers, of such artful mechanism, that it made one's head ache to see them opened one after another, and rendered it quite a distracting circumstance to follow her proceedings, and to find that every nook and corner and individual piece of furniture was something else besides what it pretended to be, and was a mere trap and deception and place of secret stowage, whose ostensible purpose was its least useful one.

God bless that stewardess for her piously fraudulent account of January voyages! God bless her for her clear recollection of the companion passage of last year, when nobody was ill, and everybody dancing from morning to night, and it was "a run" of twelve days, and a piece of the purest frolic, and delight, and jollity! All happiness be with her for her bright face and her pleasant Scotch tongue, which had sounds of old Home in it for my fellow-traveller; and for her predictions of fair winds and fine weather (all wrong, or I shouldn't be half so fond of her); and for the ten thousand small fragments of genuine womanly tact, by which, without piecing them elaborately together, and patching them up into shape and form and case and pointed application, she nevertheless did plainly show that all young mothers on one side of the Atlantic were near and close at hand to their little children left upon the other; and that what seemed to the uninitiated a serious journey, was, to those who were in the secret, a mere frolic, to be sung about and whistled at! Light be her heart, and gay her merry eyes, for years!

The state-room had grown pretty fast; but by this time it had expanded into something quite bulky, and almost boasted a bay-window to view the sea from. So we went upon deck again in high spirits; and there, everything was in such a state of bustle and active preparation, that the blood quickened its pace, and whirled through one's veins on that clear frosty morning with involuntary mirthfulness. For every gallant ship was riding slowly up and down, and every little boat was splashing noisily in the water; and knots of people stood upon the wharf, gazing with a kind of "dread delight" on the far-famed fast American steamer; and one party of men were "taking in the milk," or, in other words, getting the cow on board; and another were filling the icehouses to the very throat with fresh provisions; with butchers'-meat and garden-stuff, pale sucking-pigs, calves' heads in scores, beef, veal, and pork, and poultry out of all proportion; and others were coiling ropes and busy with oakum yarns; and others were lowering heavy packages into the hold; and the purser's head was barely visible as it loomed in a state of exquisite perplexity from the midst of a vast pile of passengers' luggage; and there seemed to be nothing going on anywhere, or uppermost in the mind of anybody, but preparations for this mighty voyage. This, with the bright cold sun, the bracing air, the crisply-curling water, the thin white crust of morning ice upon the decks which crackled with a sharp and cheerful sound beneath the lightest tread, was irresistible. And when, again upon the shore, we turned and saw from the vessel's mast her name signalled in flags of joyous colours, and fluttering by their side the beautiful American banner with its stars and stripes,—the long three thousand miles and more, and, longer still, the six whole months of absence, so dwindled and faded, that the ship had gone out and come home again, and it was broad spring already in the Coburg Dock at Liverpool.

I have not inquired among my medical acquaintance, whether Turtle, and cold Punch, with Hock, Champagne,

and Claret, and all the slight et cetera usually included in an
unlimited order for a good dinner—especially when it is left
to the liberal construction of my faultless friend, Mr. Radley,
of the Adelphi Hotel—are peculiarly calculated to suffer
a sea-change; or whether a plain mutton-chop, and a glass
or two of sherry, would be less likely of conversion into
foreign and disconcerting material. My own opinion is, that
whether one is discreet or indiscreet in these particulars,
on the eve of a sea-voyage, is a matter of little consequence;
and that, to use a common phrase, "it comes to very much
the same thing in the end." Be this as it may, I know
that the dinner of that day was undeniably perfect; that
it comprehended all these items, and a great many more;
and that we all did ample justice to it. And I know too,
that, bating a certain tacit avoidance of any allusion to
to-morrow; such as may be supposed to prevail between
delicate-minded turnkeys, and a sensitive prisoner who is
to be hanged next morning; we got on very well, and, all
things considered, were merry enough.

When the morning—*the* morning—came, and we met at
breakfast, it was curious to see how eager we all were to
prevent a moment's pause in the conversation, and how
astoundingly gay everybody was: the forced spirits of each
member of the little party having as much likeness to his
natural mirth, as hot-house peas at five guineas the quart,
resemble in flavour the growth of the dews, and air, and rain
of Heaven. But as one o'clock, the hour for going aboard,
drew near, this volubility dwindled away by little and little,
despite the most persevering efforts to the contrary, until at
last, the matter being now quite desperate, we threw off all
disguise; openly speculated upon where we should be this
time to-morrow, this time next day, and so forth; and
entrusted a vast number of messages to those who intended
returning to town that night, which were to be delivered at
home and elsewhere without fail, within the very shortest
possible space of time after the arrival of the railway train
at Euston Square. And commissions and remembrances do
so crowd upon one at such a time, that we were still busied
with this employment when we found ourselves fused, as
it were, into a dense conglomeration of passengers and
passengers' friends and passengers' luggage, all jumbled
together on the deck of a small steamboat, and panting
and snorting off to the packet, which had worked out of

dock yesterday afternoon and was now lying at her moorings
in the river.

And there she is! all eyes are turned to where she lies,
dimly discernible through the gathering fog of the early
winter afternoon; every finger is pointed in the same
direction; and murmurs of interest and admiration—as
"How beautiful she looks!" "How trim she is!"—are
heard on every side. Even the lazy gentleman with his
hat on one side and his hands in his pockets, who has
dispensed so much consolation by inquiring with a yawn
of another gentleman whether he is "going across"—as
if it were a ferry—even he condescends to look that way,
and nod his head, as who should say, "No mistake about
that:" and not even the sage Lord Burleigh in his nod,
included half so much as this lazy gentleman of might who
has made the passage (as everybody on board has found out
already; it's impossible to say how) thirteen times without
a single accident! There is another passenger very much
wrapped-up, who has been frowned down by the rest, and
morally trampled upon and crushed, for presuming to inquire
with a timid interest how long it is since the poor President
went down. He is standing close to the lazy gentleman,
and says with a faint smile that he believes She is a very
strong Ship; to which the lazy gentleman, looking first in
his questioner's eye and then very hard in the wind's,
answers unexpectedly and ominously, that She need be.
Upon this the lazy gentleman instantly falls very low in
the popular estimation, and the passengers, with looks of
defiance, whisper to each other that he is an ass, and
an impostor, and clearly don't know anything at all
about it.

But we are made fast alongside the packet, whose huge
red funnel is smoking bravely, giving rich promise of
serious intentions. Packing-cases, portmanteaus, carpet-bags,
and boxes, are already passed from hand to hand, and
hauled on board with breathless rapidity. The officers,
smartly dressed, are at the gangway handing the passengers
up the side, and hurrying the men. In five minutes' time,
the little steamer is utterly deserted, and the packet is beset
and over-run by its late freight, who instantly pervade the
whole ship, and are to be met with by the dozen in every
nook and corner: swarming down below with their own
baggage, and stumbling over other people's; disposing

themselves comfortably in wrong cabins, and creating a most horrible confusion by having to turn out again; madly bent upon opening locked doors, and on forcing a passage into all kinds of out-of-the-way places where there is no thoroughfare; sending wild stewards, with elfin hair, to and fro upon the breezy decks on unintelligible errands, impossible of execution: and in short, creating the most extraordinary and bewildering tumult. In the midst of all this, the lazy gentleman, who seems to have no luggage of any kind—not so much as a friend, even—lounges up and down the hurricane deck, coolly puffing a cigar; and, as this unconcerned demeanour again exalts him in the opinion of those who have leisure to observe his pro-ceedings, every time he looks up at the masts, or down at the decks, or over the side, they look there too, as wondering whether he sees anything wrong anywhere, and hoping that, in case he should, he will have the goodness to mention it.

What have we here? The captain's boat! and yonder the captain himself. Now, by all our hopes and wishes, the very man he ought to be! A well-made, tight-built, dapper little fellow; with a ruddy face, which is a letter of invitation to shake him by both hands at once; and with a clear, blue honest eye, that it does one good to see one's sparkling image in. "Ring the bell!" "Ding, ding, ding!" the very bell is in a hurry. "Now for the shore—who's for the shore?"—"These gentlemen, I am sorry to say." They are away, and never said, Good b'ye! Ah! now they wave it from the little boat. "Good b'ye! Good b'ye!" Three cheers from them; three more from us; three more from them: and they are gone.

To and fro, to and fro, to and fro again a hundred times! This waiting for the latest mail-bags is worse than all. If we could have gone off in the midst of that last burst, we should have started triumphantly: but to lie here, two hours and more in the damp fog, neither staying at home nor going abroad, is letting one gradually down into the very depths of dulness and low spirits. A speck in the mist, at last! That's something. It is the boat we wait for! That's more to the purpose. The captain appears on the paddle-box with his speaking trumpet; the officers take their stations; all hands are on the alert; the flagging hopes of the passengers revive; the cooks pause in their savoury work, and look out with

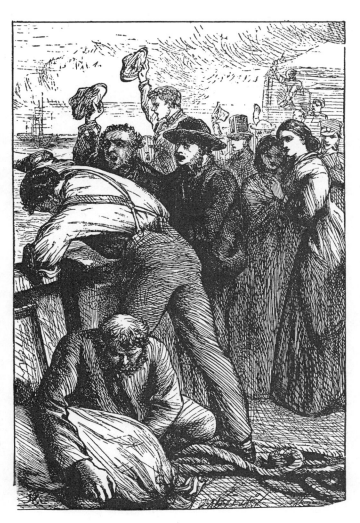

Emigrants

faces full of interest. The boat comes alongside; the bags are dragged in anyhow, and flung down for the moment any-where. Three cheers more: and as the first one rings upon our ears, the vessel throbs like a strong giant that has just received the breath of life; the two great wheels turn fiercely round for the first time; and the noble ship, with wind and tide astern, breaks proudly through the lashed and foaming water.

CHAPTER II

We all dined together that day; and a rather formidable party we were: no fewer than eighty-six strong. The vessel being pretty deep in the water, with all her coals on board and so many passengers, and the weather being calm and quiet, there was but little motion; so that before the dinner was half over, even those passengers who were most distrustful of themselves plucked up amazingly; and those who in the morning had returned to the universal question, "Are you a good sailor?" a very decided negative, now either parried the inquiry with the evasive reply, "Oh! I suppose I'm no worse than anybody else;" or, reckless of all moral obligations, answered boldly "Yes:" and with some irritation too, as though they would add, "I should like to know what you see in *me*, Sir, particularly, to justify suspicion!"

Notwithstanding this high tone of courage and confidence, I could not but observe that very few remained long over their wine; and that everybody had an unusual love of the open air; and that the favourite and most coveted seats were invariably those nearest to the door. The tea-table, too, was by no means as well attended as the dinner-table; and there was less whist-playing than might have been expected. Still, with the exception of one lady, who had retired with some precipitation at dinner-time, immediately after being assisted to the finest cut of a very yellow boiled leg of mutton with very green capers, there were no invalids as yet; and walking, and smoking, and drinking of brandy-and-water (but always in the open air), went on with unabated spirit, until eleven o'clock or thereabouts, when "turning in"—no sailor of seven hours' experience talks of going to bed—became the order of the night. The perpetual tramp of boot-heels on the decks gave place to a heavy silence, and the whole human freight was stowed away below, excepting a very few stragglers, like myself, who were probably, like me, afraid to go there.

To one unaccustomed to such scenes, this is a very striking time on shipboard. Afterwards, and when its novelty had long worn off, it never ceased to have a peculiar interest and charm for me. The gloom through which the great black mass holds its direct and certain course ; the rushing water, plainly heard, but dimly seen ; the broad, white, glistening track, that follows in the vessel's wake ; the men on the look-out forward, who would be scarcely visible against the dark sky, but for their blotting out some score of glistening stars ; the helmsman at the wheel, with the illuminated card before him, shining, a speck of light amidst the darkness, like something sentient and of Divine intelligence ; the melancholy sighing of the wind through block, and rope, and chain ; the gleaming forth of light from every crevice, nook, and tiny piece of glass about the decks, as though the ship were filled with fire in hiding, ready to burst through any outlet, wild with its resistless power of death and ruin. At first, too, and even when the hour, and all the objects it exalts, have come to be familiar, it is difficult, alone and thoughtful, to hold them to their proper shapes and forms. They change with the wandering fancy; assume the semblance of things left far away; put on the well-remembered aspect of favourite places dearly loved; and even people them with shadows. Streets, houses, rooms ; figures so like their usual occupants, that they have startled me by their reality, which far exceeded, as it seemed to me, all power of mine to conjure up the absent ; have, many and many a time, at such an hour, grown suddenly out of objects with whose real look, and use, and purpose, I was as well acquainted as with my own two hands.

My own two hands, and feet likewise, being very cold, however, on this particular occasion, I crept below at midnight. It was not exactly comfortable below. It was decidedly close: and it was impossible to be unconscious of the presence of that extraordinary compound of strange smells, which is to be found nowhere but on board ship, and which is such a subtle perfume that it seems to enter at every pore of the skin, and whisper of the hold. Two passengers' wives (one of them my own) lay already in silent agonies on the sofa ; and one lady's maid (*my* lady's) was a mere bundle on the

B

floor, execrating her destiny, and pounding her curl-papers among the stray boxes. Everything sloped the wrong way : which in itself was an aggravation scarcely to be borne. I had left the door open, a moment before, in the bosom of a gentle declivity, and, when I turned to shut it, it was on the summit of a lofty eminence. Now every plank and timber creaked, as if the ship were made of wicker-work ; and now crackled, like an enormous fire of the driest possible twigs. There was nothing for it but bed ; so I went to bed.

It was pretty much the same for the next two days. with a tolerably fair wind and dry weather. I read in bed (but to this hour I don't know what) a good deal; and reeled on deck a little ; drank cold brandy-and-water with an unspeakable disgust, and ate hard biscuit perseveringly : not ill, but going to be.

It is the third morning. I am awakened out of my sleep by a dismal shriek from my wife, who demands to know whether there's any danger. I rouse myself, and look out of bed. The water-jug is plunging and leaping like a lively dolphin ; all the smaller articles are afloat, except my shoes, which are stranded on a carpet-bag, high and dry, like a couple of coal-barges. Suddenly I see them spring into the air, and behold the looking-glass, which is nailed to the wall, sticking fast upon the ceiling. At the same time the door entirely disappears, and a new one is opened in the floor. Then I begin to comprehend that the state-room is standing on its head.

Before it is possible to make any arrangement at all compatible with this novel state of things, the ship rights. Before one can say "Thank Heaven !" she wrongs again. Before one can cry she *is* wrong, she seems to have started forward, and to be a creature actually running of its own accord, with broken knees and failing legs, through every variety of hole and pitfall, and stumbling constantly. Before one can so much as wonder, she takes a high leap into the air. Before she has well done that, she takes a deep dive into the water. Before she has gained the surface, she throws a summerset. The instant she is on her legs, she rushes backward. And so she goes on staggering, heaving, wrestling, leaping, diving, jumping, pitching. throbbing, rolling, and rocking : and going through all these movements, sometimes by turns, and sometimes altogether : until one feels disposed to roar for mercy.

A steward passes. "Steward!" "Sir?" "What *is* the matter? what *do* you call this?" "Rather a heavy sea on, Sir, and a head-wind."

A head-wind! Imagine a human face upon the vessel's prow, with fifteen thousand Samsons in one bent upon driving her back, and hitting her exactly between the eyes whenever she attempts to advance an inch. Imagine the ship herself, with every pulse and artery of her huge body swollen and bursting under this maltreatment, sworn to go on or die. Imagine the wind howling, the sea roaring, the rain beating : all in furious array against her. Picture the sky both dark and wild, and the clouds, in fearful sympathy with the waves, making another ocean in the air. Add to all this, the clattering on deck and down below; the tread of hurried feet ; the loud hoarse shouts of seamen ; the gurgling in and out of water through the scuppers; with, every now and then, the striking of a heavy sea upon the planks above, with the deep, dead, heavy sound of thunder heard within a vault ;— and there is the head-wind of that January morning.

I say nothing of what may be called the domestic noises of the ship: such as the breaking of glass and crockery, the tumbling down of stewards, the gambols, overhead, of loose casks and truant dozens of bottled porter, and the very remarkable and far from exhilarating sounds raised in their various state-rooms by the seventy passengers who were too ill to get up to breakfast. I say nothing of them : for although I lay listening to this concert for three or four days, I don't think I heard it for more than a quarter of a minute, at the expiration of which term, I lay down again, excessively sea-sick.

Not sea-sick, be it understood, in the ordinary acceptation of the term : I wish I had been : but in a form which I have never seen or heard described, though I have no doubt it is very common. I lay there, all the day long, quite coolly and contentedly ; with no sense of weariness, with no desire to get up, or get better, or take the air ; with no curiosity, or care, or regret, of any sort or degree, saving that I think I can remember, in this universal indifference, having a kind of lazy joy—of fiendish delight, if anything so lethargic can be dignified with the title—in the fact of my wife being too ill to talk to me. If I may be allowed to illustrate my state of mind by such an example, I should say that I was exactly in the condition of the elder Mr. Willet, after the incursion of the rioters into his bar at Chigwell.   Nothing would have surprised me.   If, in the momentary illumination of any ray of intelligence that may have come upon me in the way of thoughts of Home, a goblin postman, with a scarlet coat and bell, had come into that little kennel before me, broad awake in broad day, and, apologising for being damp through walking in the sea, had handed me a letter directed to my-self, in familiar characters, I am certain I should not have felt one atom of astonishment : I should have been perfectly satisfied.   If Neptune himself had walked in, with a toasted shark on his trident, I should have looked upon the event as one of the very commonest everyday occurrences.

Once—once—I found myself on deck.   I don't know how I got there, or what possessed me to go there, but there I was ; and completely dressed too, with a huge pea-coat on, and a pair of boots such as no weak man in his senses could ever have got into.   I found myself standing, when a gleam of consciousness came upon me, holding on to something.   I don't know what.   I think it was the boatswain : or it may have been the pump : or possibly the cow.   I can't say how long I had been there ; whether a day or a minute.   I recol-lect trying to think about something (about anything in the whole wide world, I was not particular) without the smallest effect.   I could not even make out which was the sea, and which the sky, for the horizon seemed drunk, and was flying wildly about in all directions.   Even in that incapable state, however, I recognised the lazy gentleman standing before me: nautically clad in a suit of shaggy blue, with an oilskin hat. But I was too imbecile, although I knew it to be he, to sepa-rate him from his dress ; and tried to call him, I remember, *Pilot.*   After another interval of total unconsciousness, I found he had gone, and recognised another figure in his place. It seemed to wave and fluctuate before me as though I saw it reflected in an unsteady looking-glass ; but I knew it for the captain ; and such was the cheerful influence of his face, that I tried to smile : yes, even then I tried to smile.   I saw by his gestures that he addressed me ; but it was a long time before I could make out that he remonstrated against my standing up to my knees in water—as I was; of course I don't know why.   I tried to thank him, but couldn't.   I could only point to my boots—or wherever I supposed my boots to be—and say in a plaintive voice, "Cork soles : " at the same time endeavouring, I am told, to sit down in the pool. Finding that I was quite insensible, and for the time a maniac, he humanely conducted me below.

There I remained until I got better: suffering, whenever I was recommended to eat anything, an amount of anguish only second to that which is said to be endured by the apparently drowned, in the process of restoration to life. One gentleman on board had a letter of introduction to me from a mutual friend in London. He sent it below with his card, on the morning of the head-wind; and I was long troubled with the idea that he might be up, and well, and a hundred times a day expecting me to call upon him in the saloon. I imagined him one of those cast-iron images—I will not call them men—who ask, with red faces, and lusty voices, what sea-sickness means, and whether it really is as bad as it is represented to be. This was very torturing indeed; and I don't think I ever felt such perfect gratification and gratitude of heart, as I did when I heard from the ship's doctor that he had been obliged to put a large mustard poultice on this very gentleman's stomach. I date my recovery from the receipt of that intelligence.

It was materially assisted though, I have no doubt, by a heavy gale of wind, which came slowly up at sunset, when we were about ten days out, and raged with gradually increasing fury until morning, saving that it lulled for an hour a little before midnight. There was something in the unnatural repose of that hour, and in the after-gathering of the storm, so inconceivably awful and tremendous, that its bursting into full violence was almost a relief.

The labouring of the ship in the troubled sea on this night I shall never forget. "Will it ever be worse than this?" was a question I had often heard asked, when everything was sliding and bumping about, and when it certainly did seem difficult to comprehend the possibility of anything afloat being more disturbed, without toppling over and going down. But what the agitation of a steam-vessel is, on a bad winter's night in the wild Atlantic, it is impossible for the most vivid imagination to conceive. To say that she is flung down on her side in the waves, with her masts dipping into them, and that, springing up again, she rolls over on the other side, until a heavy sea strikes her with the noise of a hundred great guns, and hurls her back—that she stops, and staggers, and shivers, as though stunned, and then, with a violent throbbing at her heart, darts onward like a monster goaded into madness, to be beaten down, and battered, and crushed, and leaped on by the angry sea—that thunder, lightning, hail, and rain, and wind, are all in fierce contention for the mastery—that every plank has its groan, every nail its shriek, and every drop of water in the great ocean its howling voice —is nothing. To say that all is grand, and all appalling and horrible in the last degree, is nothing. Words cannot express it. Thoughts cannot convey it. Only a dream can call it up again, in all its fury, rage, and passion.

And yet, in the very midst of these terrors, I was placed in a situation so exquisitely ridiculous, that even then I had as strong a sense of its absurdity as I have now, and could no more help laughing than I can at any other comical incident, happening under circumstances the most favourable to its enjoyment. About midnight we shipped a sea, which forced its way through the skylights, burst open the doors above, and came raging and roaring down into the ladies' cabin, to the unspeakable consternation of my wife and a little Scotch lady—who, by-the-way, had previously sent a message to the captain by the stewardess, requesting him, with her compliments, to have a steel conductor immediately attached to the top of every mast, and to the chimney, in order that the ship might not be struck by lightning. They and the handmaid before-mentioned, being in such ecstasies of fear that I scarcely knew what to do with them, I naturally bethought myself of some restorative or comfortable cordial; and nothing better occurring to me, at the moment, than hot brandy-and-water, I procured a tumblerful without delay. It being impossible to stand or sit without holding on, they were all heaped together in one corner of a long sofa—a fixture extending entirely across the cabin—where they clung to each other in momentary expectation of being drowned. When I approached this place with my specific, and was about to administer it with many consolatory expressions to the nearest sufferer, what was my dismay to see them all roll slowly down to the other end! And when I staggered to that end, and held out the glass once more, how immensely baffled were my good intentions by the ship giving another lurch, and their all rolling back again! I suppose I dodged them up and down this sofa for at least a quarter of an hour, without reaching them once; and by the time I did catch them, the brandy-and-water was diminished, by constant spilling, to a teaspoonful. To complete the group, it is necessary to recognise in this disconcerted dodger, an individual very pale from sea-sickness, who had shaved his beard and brushed his hair, last, at Liverpool: and whose only articles of dress (linen not included) were a pair of dreadnought trousers; a blue jacket, formerly admired upon the Thames at Richmond; no stockings; and one slipper.

Of the outrageous antics performed by that ship next-morning; which made bed a practical joke, and getting up, by any process short of falling out, an impossibility; I say nothing. But anything like the utter dreariness and desolation that met my eyes when I literally "tumbled up" on deck at noon, I never saw. Ocean and sky were all of one dull, heavy, uniform, lead colour. There was no extent of prospect even over the dreary waste that lay around us, for the sea ran high, and the horizon encompassed us like a large black hoop. Viewed from the air, or some tall bluff on shore, it would have been imposing and stupendous, no doubt; but seen from the wet and rolling decks, it only impressed one giddily and painfully. In the gale of last night the lifeboat had been crushed by one blow of the sea like a walnut-shell; and there it hung dangling in the air: a mere faggot of crazy boards. The planking of the paddle-boxes had been torn sheer away. The wheels were exposed and bare; and they whirled and dashed their spray about the decks at random. Chimney, white with crusted salt; topmasts struck; storm-sails set; rigging all knotted, tangled, wet, and drooping: a gloomier picture it would be hard to look upon.

I was now comfortably established by courtesy in the ladies' cabin, where, besides ourselves, there were only four other passengers. First, the little Scotch lady before-mentioned, on her way to join her husband at New York, who had settled there three years before. Secondly and thirdly, an honest young Yorkshireman, connected with some American house; domiciled in that same city, and carrying thither his beautiful young wife to whom he had been married but a fortnight, and who was the fairest specimen of a comely English country girl I have ever seen. Fourthly, fifthly, and lastly, another couple: newly married too, if one might judge from the endearments they frequently interchanged: of whom I know no more than that they were rather a mysterious, runaway kind of couple; that the lady had great personal attractions also; and that the gentleman carried more guns with him

than Robinson Crusoe, wore a shooting-coat, and had two
great dogs on board. On further consideration, I remember
that he tried hot roast pig and bottled ale as a cure for sea-
sickness ; and that he took these remedies (usually in bed)
day after day, with astonishing perseverance. I may add,
for the information of the curious, that they decidedly
failed.

The weather continuing obstinately and almost unprece-
dentedly bad, we usually straggled into this cabin, more or
less faint and miserable, about an hour before noon, and lay
down on the sofas to recover ; during which interval, the
captain would look in to communicate the state of the wind,
the moral certainty of its changing to-morrow (the weather
is always going to improve to-morrow, at sea), the vessel's
rate of sailing, and so forth. Observations there were
none to tell us of, for there was no sun to take them by.
But a description of one day will serve for all the rest.
Here it is.

The captain being gone, we compose ourselves to read, if
the place be light enough ; and if not, we doze and talk
alternately. At one, a bell rings, and the stewardess comes
down with a steaming dish of baked potatoes, and another
of roasted apples ; and plates of pig's face, cold ham, salt
beef ; or perhaps a smoking mess of rare hot collops. We
fall to upon these dainties ; eat as much as we can (we have
great appetites now) ; and are as long as possible about it.
If the fire will burn (it *will* sometimes) we are pretty cheerful.
If it won't, we all remark to each other that it's very cold,
rub our hands, cover ourselves with coats and cloaks, and lie
down again to doze, talk, and read (provided as aforesaid),
until dinner-time. At five, another bell rings, and the
stewardess reappears with another dish of potatoes—boiled
this time—and store of hot meat of various kinds: not forgetting the roast pig, to be taken medicinally. We sit down
at table again (rather more cheerfully than before) ; prolong
the meal with a rather mouldy dessert of apples, grapes, and
oranges ; and drink our wine and brandy-and-water. The
bottles and glasses are still upon the table, and the oranges
and so forth are rolling about according to their fancy and
the ship's way, when the doctor comes down, by special
nightly invitation, to join our evening rubber : immediately
on whose arrival we make a party at whist, and as it is
a rough night and the cards will not lie on the cloth, we put

the tricks in our pockets as we take them. At whist we remain with exemplary gravity (deducting a short time for tea and toast) until eleven o'clock, or thereabouts ; when the captain comes down again, in a sou'-wester hat tied under his chin, and a pilot-coat : making the ground wet where he stands. By this time the card-playing is over, and the bottles and glasses are again upon the table ; and after an hour's pleasant conversation about the ship, the passengers, and things in general, the captain (who never goes to bed, and is never out of humour) turns up his coat collar for the deck again ; shakes hands all round ; and goes laughing out into the weather as merrily as to a birthday party.

As to daily news, there is no dearth of that commodity. This passenger is reported to have lost fourteen pounds at Vingt-et-un in the saloon yesterday ; and that passenger drinks his bottle of champagne every day, and how he does it (being only a clerk), nobody knows. The head engineer has distinctly said that there never was such times—meaning weather—and four good hands are ill, and have given in, dead beat. Several berths are full of water, and all the cabins are leaky. The ship's cook, secretly swigging damaged whiskey, has been found drunk ; and has been played upon by the fire-engine until quite sober. All the stewards have fallen downstairs at various dinner-times, and go about with plasters in various places. The baker is ill, and so is the pastry-cook. A new man, horribly indisposed, has been required to fill the place of the latter officer ; and has been propped and jammed up with empty casks in a little house upon deck, and commanded to roll out pie-crust, which he protests (being highly bilious) it is death to him to look at. News ! A dozen murders on shore would lack the interest of these slight incidents at sea.

Divided between our rubber and such topics as these, we were running (as we thought) into Halifax Harbour, on the fifteenth night, with little wind and a bright moon—indeed, we had made the Light at its outer entrance, and put the pilot in charge—when suddenly the ship struck upon a bank of mud. An immediate rush on deck took place of course : the sides were crowded in an instant ; and for a few minutes we were in as lively a state of confusion as the greatest lover of disorder would desire to see. The passengers, and guns, and water-casks, and other heavy matters, being all huddled together aft, however, to lighten her in the head, she was soon got off; and after some driving on towards an uncomfortable line of objects (whose vicinity had been announced very early in the disaster by a loud cry of "Breakers ahead!") and much backing of paddles, and heaving of the lead into a constantly decreasing depth of water, we dropped anchor in a strange outlandish-looking nook which nobody on board could recognise, although there was land all about us, and so close that we could plainly see the waving branches of the trees.

It was strange enough, in the silence of midnight, and the dead stillness that seemed to be created by the sudden and unexpected stoppage of the engine which had been clanking and blasting in our ears incessantly for so many days, to watch the look of blank astonishment expressed in every face: beginning with the officers, tracing it through all the passengers, and descending to the very stokers and furnacemen, who emerged from below, one by one, and clustered together in a smoky group about the hatchway of the engine-room, comparing notes in whispers. After throwing up a few rockets and firing signal guns in the hope of being hailed from the land, or at least of seeing a light—but without any other sight or sound presenting itself—it was determined to send a boat on shore. It was amusing to observe how very kind some of the passengers were, in volunteering to go ashore in this same boat: for the general good, of course: not by any means because they thought the ship in an unsafe position, or contemplated the possibility of her heeling over in case the tide were running out. Nor was it less amusing to remark how desperately unpopular the poor pilot became in one short minute. He had had his passage out from Liverpool, and during the whole voyage had been quite a notorious character, as a teller of anecdotes and cracker of jokes. Yet here were the very men who had laughed the loudest at his jests, now flourishing their fists in his face, loading him with imprecations, and defying him to his teeth as a villain!

The boat soon shoved off, with a lantern and sundry blue lights on board; and in less than an hour returned; the officer in command bringing with him a tolerably tall young tree, which he had plucked up by the roots, to satisfy certain distrustful passengers whose minds misgave them that they were to be imposed upon and shipwrecked, and who would on no other terms believe that he had been ashore, or had done anything but fraudulently row a little way into the mist, specially to deceive them and compass their deaths. Our captain had foreseen from the first that we must be in a place called the Eastern passage ; and so we were. It was about the last place in the world in which we had any business or reason to be, but a sudden fog, and some error on the pilot's part, were the cause. We were surrounded by banks, and rocks, and shoals of all kinds, but had happily drifted, it seemed, upon the only safe speck that was to be found thereabouts. Eased by this report, and by the assurance that the tide was past the ebb, we turned in at three o'clock in the morning.

I was dressing about half-past nine next day, when the noise above hurried me on deck. When I had left it overnight, it was dark, foggy, and damp, and there were bleak hills all around us. Now, we were gliding down a smooth, broad stream, at the rate of eleven miles an hour : our colours flying gaily ; our crew rigged out in their smartest clothes ; our officers in uniform again ; the sun shining as on a brilliant April day in England ; the land stretched out on either side, streaked with light patches of snow ; white wooden houses ; people at their doors ; telegraphs working ; flags hoisted ; wharfs appearing ; ships ; quays crowded with people ; distant noises ; shouts ; men and boys running down steep places towards the pier : all more bright and gay and fresh to our unused eyes than words can paint them. We came to a wharf, paved with uplifted faces ; got alongside, and were made fast, after some shouting and straining of cables ; darted, a score of us along the gangway, almost as soon as it was thrust out to meet us, and before it had reached the ship—and leaped upon the firm glad earth again !

I suppose this Halifax would have appeared an Elysium, though it had been a curiosity of ugly dulness. But I carried away with me a most pleasant impression of the town and its inhabitants, and have preserved it to this hour. Nor was it without regret that I came home, without having found an opportunity of returning thither, and once more shaking hands with the friends I made that day.

It happened to be the opening of the Legislative Council and General Assembly, at which ceremonial the forms observed on the commencement of a new Session of Parliament in England were so closely copied, and so gravely presented on a small scale, that it was like looking at Westminster through the wrong end of a telescope. The governor, as her Majesty's representative, delivered what may be called the Speech from the Throne. He said what he had to say manfully and well. The military band outside the building struck up "God save the Queen" with great vigour before his Excellency had quite finished ; the people shouted ; the in's rubbed their hands ; the out's shook their heads ; the Government party said there never was such a good speech ; the Opposition declared there never was such a bad one ; the Speaker and members of the House of Assembly withdrew from the bar to say a great deal among themselves and do a little ; and, in short, everything went on, and promised to go on, just as it does at home upon the like occasions.

The town is built on the side of a hill, the highest point being commanded by a strong fortress, not yet quite finished. Several streets of good breadth and appearance extend from its summit to the water-side, and are intersected by cross streets running parallel with the river. The houses are chiefly of wood. The market is abundantly supplied ; and provisions are exceedingly cheap. The weather being unusually mild at that time for the season of the year, there was no sleighing : but there were plenty of those vehicles in yards and by-places, and some of them, from the gorgeous quality of their decorations, might have "gone on" without alteration as triumphal cars in a melodrama at Astley's. The day was uncommonly fine ; the air bracing and healthful ; the whole aspect of the town cheerful, thriving, and industrious.

We lay there seven hours, to deliver and exchange the mails. At length, having collected all our bags and all our passengers (including two or three choice spirits, who, having indulged too freely in oysters and champagne, were found lying insensible on their backs in unfrequented streets), the engines were again put in motion, and we stood off for Boston.

Encountering squally weather again in the Bay of Fundy, we tumbled and rolled about as usual all that night and all next day. On the next afternoon, that is to say, on Saturday, the twenty-second of January, an American pilot-boat came alongside, and soon afterwards the "Britannia" steam-packet, from Liverpool, eighteen days out, was telegraphed at Boston.

The indescribable interest with which I strained my eyes, as the first patches of American soil peeped like molehills from the green sea, and followed them, as they swelled, by slow and almost imperceptible degrees, into a continuous line of coast, can hardly be exaggerated. A sharp keen wind blew dead against us; a hard frost prevailed on shore; and the cold was most severe. Yet the air was so intensely clear, and dry, and bright, that the temperature was not only endurable, but delicious.

How I remained on deck, staring about me, until we came alongside the dock, and how, though I had had as many eyes as Argus, I should have had them all wide open, and all employed on new objects—are topics which I will not prolong this chapter to discuss. Neither will I more than hint at my foreigner-like mistake in supposing that a party of most active persons, who scrambled on board at the peril of their lives as we approached the wharf, were newsmen, answering to that industrious class at home; whereas, despite the leathern wallets of news slung about the necks of some, and the broad sheets in the hands of all, they were Editors, who boarded ships in person (as one gentleman in a worsted comforter informed me), "because they liked the excitement of it." Suffice it in this place to say, that one of these invaders, with a ready courtesy for which I thank him here most gratefully, went on before to order rooms at the hotel; and that when I followed, as I soon did, I found myself rolling through the long passages with an involuntary imitation of the gait of Mr. T. P. Cooke, in a new nautical melodrama.

"Dinner, if you please," said I to the waiter.

"When?" said the waiter.

"As quick as possible," said I.

"Right away?" said the waiter.

After a moment's hesitation, I answered "No," at hazard.

"*Not* right away?" cried the waiter, with an amount of surprise that made me start.

I looked at him doubtfully, and returned, "No; I would rather have it in this private room. I like it very much."

At this, I really thought the waiter must have gone out of his mind: as I believe he would have done, but for the interposition of another man, who whispered in his ear, "Directly."

"Well! and that's a fact!" said the waiter, looking helplessly at me: "Right away."

I saw now that "Right away" and "Directly" were one and the same thing. So I reversed my previous answer, and sat down to dinner in ten minutes afterwards; and a capital dinner it was.

The hotel (a very excellent one) is called the Tremont House. It has more galleries, colonnades, piazzas, and passages than I can remember, or the reader would believe.

CHAPTER III

BOSTON

In all the public establishments of America, the utmost courtesy prevails. Most of our Departments are susceptible of considerable improvement in this respect, but the Custom-house above all others would do well to take example from the United States and render itself somewhat less odious and offensive to foreigners. The servile rapacity of the French officials is sufficiently contemptible; but there is a surly boorish incivility about our men, alike disgusting to all persons who fall into their hands, and discreditable to the nation that keeps such ill-conditioned curs snarling about its gates.

When I landed in America, I could not help being strongly impressed with the contrast their Custom-house presented, and the attention, politeness and good humour with which its officers discharged their duty.

As we did not land at Boston, in consequence of some detention at the wharf, until after dark, I received my first impressions of the city in walking down to the Custom-house on the morning after our arrival, which was Sunday. I am afraid to say, by the way, how many offers of pews and seats in church for that morning were made to us, by formal note of invitation, before we had half finished our first dinner in America, but if I may be allowed to make a moderate guess, without going into nicer calculation, I should say that at least as many sittings were proffered us, as would have accommodated a score or two of grown-up families. The number of creeds and forms of religion to which the pleasure of our company was requested, was in very fair proportion.

Not being able, in the absence of any change of clothes, to go to church that day, we were compelled to decline these kindnesses, one and all; and I was reluctantly obliged to forego the delight of hearing Dr. Channing, who happened to preach that morning for the first time in a very long interval. I mention the name of this distinguished and accomplished man (with whom I soon afterwards had the pleasure of becoming personally acquainted), that I may have the gratification of recording my humble tribute of admiration and respect for his high abilities and character; and for the bold philanthropy with which he has ever opposed himself to that most hideous blot and foul disgrace—Slavery.

To return to Boston. When I got into the streets upon this Sunday morning, the air was so clear, the houses were so bright and gay; the signboards were painted in such gaudy colours; the gilded letters were so very golden; the bricks were so very red, the stone was so very white, the blinds and area railings were so very green, the knobs and plates upon the street doors so marvellously bright and twinkling; and all so slight and unsubstantial in appearance—that every thoroughfare in the city looked exactly like a scene in a pantomime. It rarely happens in the business streets that a tradesman, if I may venture to call anybody a tradesman, where everybody is a merchant, resides above his store; so that many occupations are often carried on in one house, and the whole front is covered with boards and inscriptions. As I walked along, I kept glancing up at these boards, confidently expecting to see a few of them change into something; and I never turned a corner suddenly without looking out for the clown and pantaloon, who, I had no doubt, were hiding in a doorway or behind some pillar close at hand. As to Harlequin and Columbine, I discovered immediately that they lodged (they are always looking after lodgings in a pantomime) at a very small clockmaker's one story high, near the hotel; which, in addition to various symbols and devices, almost covering the whole front, had a great dial hanging out—to be jumped through, of course.

The suburbs are, if possible, even more unsubstantial-looking than the city. The white wooden houses (so white that it makes one wink to look at them), with their green jalousie blinds, are so sprinkled and dropped about in all directions, without seeming to have any root at all in the ground; and the small churches and chapels are so prim, and bright, and highly varnished; that I almost believed the whole affair could be taken up piecemeal like a child's toy, and crammed into a little box.

The city is a beautiful one, and cannot fail, I should

imagine, to impress all strangers very favourably. The private dwelling-houses are, for the most part, large and elegant; the shops extremely good; and the public buildings handsome. The State House is built upon the summit of a hill, which rises gradually at first, and afterwards by a steep ascent, almost from the water's edge. In front is a green enclosure, called the Common. The site is beautiful: and from the top there is a charming panoramic view of the whole town and neighbourhood. In addition to a variety of commodious offices, it contains two handsome chambers; in one the House of Representatives of the State hold their meetings: in the other, the Senate. Such proceedings as I saw here, were conducted with perfect gravity and decorum; and were certainly calculated to inspire attention and respect.

There is no doubt that much of the intellectual refinement and superiority of Boston, is referable to the quiet influence of the University of Cambridge, which is within three or four miles of the city. The resident professors at that university are gentlemen of learning and varied attainments; and are, without one exception that I can call to mind, men who would shed a grace upon, and do honour to, any society in the civilised world. Many of the resident gentry in Boston and its neighbourhood, and I think I am not mistaken in adding, a large majority of those who are attached to the liberal professions there, have been educated at this same school. Whatever the defects of American universities may be, they disseminate no prejudices; rear no bigots; dig up the buried ashes of no old superstitions; never interpose between the people and their improvement; exclude no man because of his religious opinions; above all, in their whole course of study and instruction, recognise a world, and a broad one too, lying beyond the college walls.

It was a source of inexpressible pleasure to me to observe the almost imperceptible, but not less certain effect, wrought by this institution among the small community of Boston; and to note at every turn the humanising tastes and desires it has engendered; the affectionate friendships to which it has given rise; the amount of vanity and prejudice it has dispelled. The golden calf they worship at Boston is a pigmy compared with the giant effigies set up in other parts of that vast counting-house which lies beyond the Atlantic; and the almighty dollar sinks into something comparatively insignificant, amidst a whole Pantheon of better gods.

Above all, I sincerely believe that the public institutions and charities of this capital of Massachusetts are as nearly perfect, as the most considerate wisdom, benevolence, and humanity, can make them. I never in my life was more affected by the contemplation of happiness, under circumstances of privation and bereavement, than in my visits to these establishments.

It is a great and pleasant feature of all such institutions in America, that they are either supported by the State or assisted by the State; or (in the event of their not needing its helping hand) that they act in concert with it, and are emphatically the people's. I cannot but think, with a view to the principle and its tendency to elevate or depress the character of the industrious classes, that a Public Charity is immeasurably better than a Private Foundation, no matter how munificently the latter may be endowed. In our own country, where it has not, until within these latter days, been a very popular fashion with governments to display any extraordinary regard for the great mass of the people or to recognise their existence as improvable creatures, private charities, unexampled in the history of the earth, have arisen, to do an incalculable amount of good among the destitute and afflicted. But the government of the country, having neither act nor part in them, is not in the receipt of any portion of the gratitude they inspire; and, offering very little shelter or relief beyond that which is to be found in the workhouse and the jail, has come, not unnaturally, to be looked upon by the poor rather as a stern master, quick to correct and punish, than a kind protector, merciful and vigilant in their hour of need.

The maxim that out of evil cometh good, is strongly illustrated by these establishments at home; as the records of the Prerogative Office in Doctors' Commons can abundantly prove. Some immensely rich old gentleman or lady, surrounded by needy relatives, makes, upon a low average, a will a-week. The old gentleman or lady, never very remarkable in the best of times for good temper, is full of aches and pains from head to foot; full of fancies and caprices; full of spleen, distrust, suspicion, and dislike. To cancel old wills, and invent new ones, is at last the sole business of such a testator's existence; and relations and friends (some of whom have been bred up distinctly to inherit a large share of the property, and have been, from their cradles, specially disqualified from devoting themselves to any useful pursuit, on that account) are so often and so unexpectedly and summarily cut off, and reinstated, and cut off again, that the whole family, down to the remotest cousin, is kept in a perpetual fever. At length it becomes plain that the old lady or gentleman has not long to live ; and the plainer this becomes, the more clearly the old lady or gentleman perceives that everybody is in a conspiracy against their poor old dying relative ; wherefore the old lady or gentleman makes another last will—positively the last this time—conceals the same in a china teapot, and expires next day. Then it turns out, that the whole of the real and personal estate is divided between half-a-dozen charities ; and that the dead and gone testator has in pure spite helped to do a great deal of good, at the cost of an immense amount of evil passion and misery.

The Perkins Institution and Massachusetts Asylum for the Blind, at Boston, is superintended by a body of trustees who make an annual report to the corporation. The indigent blind of that state are admitted gratuitously. Those from the adjoining state of Connecticut, or from the states of Maine, Vermont, or New Hampshire, are admitted by a war-rant from the state to which they respectively belong ; or, failing that, must find security among their friends, for the payment of about twenty pounds English for their first year's board and instruction, and ten for the second. "After the first year," say the trustees, "an account current will be opened with each pupil ; he will be charged with the actual cost of his board, which will not exceed two dollars per week ;" a trifle more than eight shillings English ; "and he will be credited with the amount paid for him by the state, or by his friends ; also with his earnings over and above the cost of the stock which he uses ; so that all his earnings over one dollar per week will be his own. By the third year it will be known whether his earnings will more than pay the actual cost of his board ; if they should, he will have it at his option to remain and receive his earnings, or not. Those who prove unable to earn their own livelihood will not be retained ; as it is not desirable to convert the establishment into an almshouse, or to retain any but working bees in the hive. Those who by physical or mental imbecility are dis-qualified from work, are thereby disqualified from being members of an industrious community ; and they can be better provided for in establishments fitted for the infirm."

I went to see this place one very fine winter morning: an
Italian sky above, and the air so clear and bright on every
side, that even my eyes, which are none of the best, could
follow the minute lines and scraps of tracery in distant
buildings.   Like most other public institutions in America,
of the same class, it stands a mile or two without the town,
in a cheerful healthy spot; and is an airy, spacious, handsome edifice.   It is built upon a height, commanding the
harbour.   When I paused for a moment at the door, and
marked how fresh and free the whole scene was—what sparkling bubbles glanced upon the waves, and welled up every
moment to the surface, as though the world below, like that
above, were radiant with the bright day, and gushing over
in its fulness of light: when I gazed from sail to sail away
upon a ship at sea, a tiny speck of shining white, the only
cloud upon the still, deep, distant blue—and, turning, saw
a blind boy with his sightless face addressed that way, as
though he too had some sense within him of the glorious
distance: I felt a kind of sorrow that the place should be so
very light, and a strange wish that for his sake it were
darker.   It was but momentary, of course, and a mere fancy,
but I felt it keenly for all that.

The children were at their daily tasks in different rooms,
except a few who were already dismissed, and were at play.
Here, as in many institutions, no uniform is worn; and I
was very glad of it, for two reasons.   Firstly, because I am
sure that nothing but senseless custom and want of thought
would reconcile us to the liveries and badges we are so fond
of at home.   Secondly, because the absence of these things
presents each child to the visitor in his or her own proper
character, with its individuality unimpaired; not lost in a
dull, ugly, monotonous repetition of the same unmeaning
garb: which is really an important consideration.   The
wisdom of encouraging a little harmless pride in personal
appearance even among the blind, or the whimsical absurdity
of considering charity and leather breeches inseparable companions, as we do, requires no comment.

Good order, cleanliness, and comfort, pervaded every
corner of the building.   The various classes, who were
gathered round their teachers, answered the questions put
to them with readiness and intelligence, and in a spirit of
cheerful contest for precedence which pleased me very much.
Those who were at play, were gleesome and noisy as other

children. More spiritual and affectionate friendships appeared to exist among them, than would be found among other young persons suffering under no deprivation; but this I expected and was prepared to find. It is a part of the great scheme of Heaven's merciful consideration for the afflicted.

In a portion of the building, set apart for that purpose, are workshops for blind persons whose education is finished, and who have acquired a trade, but who cannot pursue it in an ordinary manufactory because of their deprivation. Several people were at work here; making brushes, mattresses, and so forth; and the cheerfulness, industry, and good order discernible in every other part of the building, extended to this department also.

On the ringing of a bell, the pupils all repaired, without any guide or leader, to a spacious music-hall, where they took their seats in an orchestra erected for that purpose, and listened with manifest delight to a voluntary on the organ, played by one of themselves. At its conclusion, the performer, a boy of nineteen or twenty, gave place to a girl; and to her accompaniment they all sang a hymn, and afterwards a sort of chorus. It was very sad to look upon and hear them, happy though their condition unquestionably was; and I saw that one blind girl, who (being for the time deprived of the use of her limbs, by illness) sat close beside me with her face towards them, wept silently the while she listened.

It is strange to watch the faces of the blind, and see how free they are from all concealment of what is passing in their thoughts; observing which, a man with eyes may blush to contemplate the mask he wears. Allowing for one shade of anxious expression which is never absent from their countenances, and the like of which we may readily detect in our own faces if we try to feel our way in the dark, every idea, as it rises within them, is expressed with the lightning's speed and nature's truth. If the company at a rout, or drawing-room at court, could only for one time be as unconscious of the eyes upon them as blind men and women are, what secrets would come out, and what a worker of hypocrisy this sight, the loss of which we so much pity, would appear to be!

The thought occurred to me as I sat down in another room, before a girl, blind, deaf, and dumb; destitute of smell; and nearly so of taste: before a fair young creature with every

human faculty, and hope, and power of goodness and affection, inclosed within her delicate frame, and but one outward
sense—the sense of touch. There she was, before me; built
up, as it were, in a marble cell, impervious to any ray of light,
or particle of sound; with her poor white hand peeping
through a chink in the wall, beckoning to some good man
for help, that an Immortal soul might be awakened.

Long before I looked upon her, the help had come. Her
face was radiant with intelligence and pleasure. Her hair,
braided by her own hands, was bound about a head, whose
intellectual capacity and development were beautifully expressed in its graceful outline, and its broad open brow; her
dress, arranged by herself, was a pattern of neatness and
simplicity; the work she had knitted, lay beside her; her
writing-book was on the desk she leaned upon.—From the
mournful ruin of such bereavement, there had slowly risen
up this gentle, tender, guileless, grateful-hearted being.

Like other inmates of that house, she had a green ribbon
bound round her eyelids. A doll she had dressed lay near
upon the ground. I took it up, and saw that she had made
a green fillet such as she wore herself, and fastened it about
its mimic eyes.

She was seated in a little enclosure, made by school-desks
and forms, writing her daily journal. But soon finishing
this pursuit, she engaged in an animated communication
with a teacher who sat beside her. This was a favourite
mistress with the poor pupil. If she could see the face of
her fair instructress, she would not love her less, I am sure.

I have extracted a few disjointed fragments of her history,
from an account, written by that one man who has made her
what she is. It is a very beautiful and touching narrative;
and I wish I could present it entire.

Her name is Laura Bridgman. "She was born in Hanover,
New Hampshire, on the twenty-first of December, 1829.
She is described as having been a very sprightly and pretty
infant, with bright blue eyes. She was, however, so puny
and feeble until she was a year and a half old, that her
parents hardly hoped to rear her. She was subject to severe
fits, which seemed to rack her frame almost beyond her
power of endurance: and life was held by the feeblest
tenure: but when a year and a half old, she seemed to
rally; the dangerous symptoms subsided; and at twenty
months old, she was perfectly well.

"Then her mental powers, hitherto stinted in their growth, rapidly developed themselves ; and during the four months of health which she enjoyed, she appears (making due allowance for a fond mother's account) to have displayed a considerable degree of intelligence.

"But suddenly she sickened again ; her disease raged with great violence during five weeks, when her eyes and ears were inflamed, suppurated, and their contents were discharged. But though sight and hearing were gone for ever, the poor child's sufferings were not ended. The fever raged during seven weeks ; for five months she was kept in bed in a darkened room ; it was a year before she could walk unsupported, and two years before she could sit up all day. It was now observed that her sense of smell was almost entirely destroyed ; and, consequently, that her taste was much blunted.

"It was not until four years of age that the poor child's bodily health seemed restored, and she was able to enter upon her apprenticeship of life and the world.

"But what a situation was hers ! The darkness and the silence of the tomb were around her : no mother's smile called forth her answering smile, no father's voice taught her to imitate his sounds :—they, brothers and sisters, were but forms of matter which resisted her touch, but which differed not from the furniture of the house, save in warmth, and in the power of locomotion ; and not even in these respects from the dog and the cat.

"But the immortal spirit which had been implanted within her could not die, nor be maimed nor mutilated ; and though most of its avenues of communication with the world were cut off, it began to manifest itself through the others. As soon as she could walk, she began to explore the room, and then the house ; she became familiar with the form, density, weight, and heat, of every article she could lay her hands upon. She followed her mother, and felt her hands and arms, as she was occupied about the house ; and her disposition to imitate, led her to repeat everything herself. She even learned to sew a little, and to knit."

The reader will scarcely need to be told, however, that the opportunities of communicating with her, were very, very limited ; and that the moral effects of her wretched state soon began to appear. Those who cannot be enlightened by reason, can only be controlled by force ; and this, coupled

with her great privations, must soon have reduced her to
a worse condition than that of the beasts that perish, but for
timely and unhoped-for aid.

"At this time, I was so fortunate as to hear of the child,
and immediately hastened to Hanover to see her. I found
her with a well-formed figure ; a strongly-marked, nervous-
sanguine temperament; a large and beautifully-shaped head ;
and the whole system in healthy action. The parents were
easily induced to consent to her coming to Boston, and
on the 4th of October, 1837, they brought her to the
Institution.

"For a while, she was much bewildered ; and after waiting about two weeks, until she became acquainted with her
new locality, and somewhat familiar with the inmates, the
attempt was made to give her knowledge of arbitrary signs,
by which she could interchange thoughts with others.

"There was one of two ways to be adopted : either to go
on to build up a language of signs on the basis of the natural
language which she had already commenced herself, or to
teach her the purely arbitrary language in common use:
that is, to give her a sign for every individual thing, or to
give her a knowledge of letters by combination of which she
might express her idea of the existence, and the mode and
condition of existence, of any thing. The former would
have been easy, but very ineffectual ; the latter seemed very
difficult, but, if accomplished, very effectual. I determined
therefore to try the latter.

"The first experiments were made by taking articles in
common use, such as knives, forks, spoons, keys, &c., and
pasting upon them labels with their names printed in raised
letters. These she felt very carefully, and soon, of course,
distinguished that the crooked lines *s p o o n*, differed as much
from the crooked lines *k e y*, as the spoon differed from the
key in form.

"Then small detached labels, with the same words printed
upon them, were put into her hands ; and she soon observed
that they were similar to the ones pasted on the articles.
She showed her perception of this similarity by laying the
label *k e y* upon the key, and the label *s p o o n* upon the
spoon. She was encouraged here by the natural sign of
approbation, patting on the head.

"The same process was then repeated with all the articles
which she could handle ; and she very easily learned to place

the proper labels upon them. It was evident, however, that the only intellectual exercise was that of imitation and memory. She recollected that the label *book* was placed upon a book, and she repeated the process first from imitation, next from memory, with only the motive of love of approbation, but apparently without the intellectual perception of any relation between the things.

"After a while, instead of labels, the individual letters were given to her on detached bits of paper : they were arranged side by side so as to spell *book, key,* &c. ; then they were mixed up in a heap and a sign was made for her to arrange them herself so as to express the words *book, key,* &c. ; and she did so.

"Hitherto, the process had been mechanical, and the success about as great as teaching a very knowing dog a variety of tricks. The poor child had sat in mute amazement, and patiently imitated everything her teacher did ; but now the truth began to flash upon her : her intellect began to work : she perceived that here was a way by which she could herself make up a sign of anything that was in her own mind, and show it to another mind ; and at once her countenance lighted up with a human expression : it was no longer a dog, or parrot : it was an immortal spirit, eagerly seizing upon a new link of union with other spirits ! I could almost fix upon the moment when this truth dawned upon her mind, and spread its light to her countenance ; I saw that the great obstacle was overcome ; and that henceforward nothing but patient and persevering, but plain and straightforward, efforts were to be used.

"The result thus far, is quickly related, and easily conceived ; but not so was the process ; for many weeks of apparently unprofitable labour were passed before it was effected.

"When it was said above, that a sign was made, it was intended to say, that the action was performed by her teacher, she feeling his hands, and then imitating the motion.

"The next step was to procure a set of metal types, with the different letters of the alphabet cast upon their ends ; also a board, in which were square holes, into which holes she could set the types ; so that the letters on their ends could alone be felt above the surface.

"Then, on any article being handed to her, for instance a pencil, or a watch, she would select the component letters.

and arrange them on her board, and read them with apparent pleasure.

"She was exercised for several weeks in this way, until her vocabulary became extensive ; and then the important step was taken of teaching her how to represent the different letters by the position of her fingers, instead of the cumbrous apparatus of the board and types. She accomplished this speedily and easily, for her intellect had begun to work in aid of her teacher, and her progress was rapid.

"This was the period, about three months after she had commenced, that the first report of her case was made, in which it was stated that 'she has just learned the manual alphabet, as used by the deaf mutes, and it is a subject of delight and wonder to see how rapidly, correctly, and eagerly, she goes on with her labours. Her teacher gives her a new object, for instance, a pencil, first lets her examine it, and get an idea of its use, then teaches her how to spell it by making the signs for the letters with her own fingers : the child grasps her hand, and feels her fingers, as the different letters are formed ; she turns her head a little on one side like a person listening closely ; her lips are apart; she seems scarcely to breathe ; and her countenance, at first anxious, gradually changes to a smile, as she comprehends the lesson. She then holds up her tiny fingers, and spells the word in the manual alphabet ; next, she takes her types and arranges her letters ; and last, to make sure that she is right, she takes the whole of the types composing the word, and places them upon or in contact with the pencil, or whatever the object may be.'

The whole of the succeeding year was passed in gratifying her eager inquiries for the names of every object which she could possibly handle ; in exercising her in the use of the manual alphabet ; in extending in every possible way her knowledge of the physical relations of things ; and in proper care of her health.

"At the end of the year a report of her case was made, from which the following is an extract.

" 'It has been ascertained beyond the possibility of doubt, that she cannot see a ray of light, cannot hear the least sound, and never exercises her sense of smell, if she have any. Thus her mind dwells in darkness and stillness, as profound as that of a closed tomb at midnight. Of beautiful sights, and sweet sounds, and pleasant odours, she has no conception ; nevertheless, she seems as happy and playful as a bird or a lamb ; and the employment of her intellectual faculties, or the acquirement of a new idea, gives her a vivid pleasure, which is plainly marked in her expressive features. She never seems to repine, but has all the buoyancy and gaiety of childhood. She is fond of fun and frolic, and when playing with the rest of the children, her shrill laugh sounds loudest of the group.

" 'When left alone, she seems very happy if she have her knitting or sewing, and will busy herself for hours ; if she have no occupation, she evidently amuses herself by imaginary dialogues, or by recalling past impressions ; she counts with her fingers, or spells out names of things which she has recently learned, in the manual alphabet of the deaf mutes. In this lonely self-communion she seems to reason, reflect, and argue ; if she spell a word wrong with the fingers of her right hand, she instantly strikes it with her left, as her teacher does, in sign of disapprobation ; if right, then she pats herself upon the head, and looks pleased. She sometimes purposely spells a word wrong with the left hand, looks roguish for a moment and laughs, and then with the right hand strikes the left, as if to correct it.

" 'During the year she has attained great dexterity in the use of the manual alphabet of the deaf mutes ; and she spells out the words and sentences which she knows, so fast and so deftly, that only those accustomed to this language can follow with the eye the rapid motions of her fingers.

" 'But wonderful as is the rapidity with which she writes her thoughts upon the air, still more so is the ease and accuracy with which she reads the words thus written by another ; grasping their hands in hers, and following every movement of their fingers, as letter after letter conveys their meaning to her mind. It is in this way that she converses with her blind playmates, and nothing can more forcibly show the power of mind in forcing matter to its purpose than a meeting between them. For if great talent and skill are necessary for two pantomimes to paint their thoughts and feelings by the movements of the body, and the expression of the countenance, how much greater the difficulty when darkness shrouds them both, and the one can hear no sound.

" 'When Laura is walking through a passage-way, with her hands spread before her, she knows instantly every one she meets, and passes them with a sign of recognition : but if it be a girl of her own age, and especially if it be one of her favourites, there is instantly a bright smile of recognition, a twining of arms, a grasping of hands, and a swift telegraphing upon the tiny fingers ; whose rapid evolutions convey the thoughts and feelings from the outposts of one mind to those of the other. There are questions and answers, exchanges of joy or sorrow, there are kissings and partings, just as between little children with all their senses.'

"During this year, and six months after she had left home, her mother came to visit her, and the scene of their meeting was an interesting one.

"The mother stood some time, gazing with overflowing eyes upon her unfortunate child, who, all unconscious of her presence, was playing about the room. Presently Laura ran against her, and at once began feeling her hands, examining her dress, and trying to find out if she knew her ; but not succeeding in this, she turned away as from a stranger, and the poor woman could not conceal the pang she felt, at finding that her beloved child did not know her.

"She then gave Laura a string of beads which she used to wear at home, which were recognised by the child at once, who, with much joy, put them around her neck, and sought me eagerly to say she understood the string was from her home.

"The mother now sought to caress her, but poor Laura repelled her, preferring to be with her acquaintances.

"Another article from home was now given her, and she began to look much interested ; she examined the stranger much closer, and gave me to understand that she knew she came from Hanover ; she even endured her caresses, but would leave her with indifference at the slightest signal. The distress of the mother was now painful to behold ; for, although she had feared that she should not be recognised, the painful reality of being treated with cold indifference by a darling child, was too much for woman's nature to bear.

"After a while, on the mother taking hold of her again, a vague idea seemed to flit across Laura's mind, that this could not be a stranger ; she therefore felt her hands very eagerly, while her countenance assumed an expression of intense interest ; she became very pale ; and then suddenly red ; hope seemed struggling with doubt and anxiety, and never were contending emotions more strongly painted upon the human face : at this moment of painful uncertainty, the mother drew her close to her side, and kissed her fondly, when at once the truth flashed upon the child, and all mistrust and anxiety disappeared from her face, as with an expression of exceeding joy she eagerly nestled to the bosom of her parent, and yielded herself to her fond embraces.

"After this, the beads were all unheeded ; the playthings which were offered to her were utterly disregarded ; her playmates, for whom but a moment before she gladly left the stranger, now vainly strove to pull her from her mother ; and though she yielded her usual instantaneous obedience to my signal to follow me, it was evidently with painful reluctance.   She clung close to me, as if bewildered and fearful ; and when, after a moment, I took her to her mother, she sprang to her arms, and clung to her with eager joy.

"The subsequent parting between them, showed alike the affection, the intelligence, and the resolution of the child.

"Laura accompanied her mother to the door, clinging close to her all the way, until they arrived at the threshold, where she paused, and felt around, to ascertain who was near her. Perceiving the matron, of whom she is very fond, she grasped her with one hand, holding on convulsively to her mother with the other ; and thus she stood for a moment ; then she dropped her mother's hand ; put her handkerchief to her eyes ; and turning round, clung sobbing to the matron ; while her mother departed, with emotions as deep as those of her child.

*   *   *   *   *   *

"It has been remarked in former reports, that she can distinguish different degrees of intellect in others, and that she soon regarded, almost with contempt, a new-comer, when, after a few days, she discovered her weakness of mind. This unamiable part of her character has been more strongly developed during the past year.

"She chooses for her friends and companions, those children who are intelligent, and can talk best with her ; and she evidently dislikes to be with those who are deficient in intellect, unless, indeed, she can make them serve her purposes, which she is evidently inclined to do.   She takes advantage of them, and makes them wait upon her, in a manner that she knows she could not exact of others ; and in various ways shows her Saxon blood.

"She is fond of having other children noticed and caressed

by the teachers, and those whom she respects ; but this must not be carried too far, or she becomes jealous. She wants to have her share, which, if not the lion's, is the greater part ; and if she does not get it, she says, ' *My mother will love me.*'

"Her tendency to imitation is so strong, that it leads her to actions which must be entirely incomprehensible to her, and which can give her no other pleasure than the gratification of an internal faculty. She has been known to sit for half an hour, holding a book before her sightless eyes, and moving her lips, as she has observed seeing people do when reading.

"She one day pretended that her doll was sick ; and went through all the motions of tending it, and giving it medicine; she then put it carefully to bed, and placed a bottle of hot water to its feet, laughing all the time most heartily. When I came home, she insisted upon my going to see it, and feel its pulse ; and when I told her to put a blister on its back, she seemed to enjoy it amazingly, and almost screamed with delight.

"Her social feelings, and her affections, are very strong ; and when she is sitting at work, or at her studies, by the side of one of her little friends, she will break off from her task every few moments, to hug and kiss them with an earnestness and warmth that is touching to behold.

"When left alone, she occupies and apparently amuses herself, and seems quite contented ; and so strong seems to be the natural tendency of thought to put on the garb of language, that she often soliloquizes in the *finger language*, slow and tedious as it is. But it is only when alone, that she is quiet: for if she becomes sensible of the presence of any one near her, she is restless until she can sit close beside them, hold their hand, and converse with them by signs.

"In her intellectual character it is pleasing to observe an insatiable thirst for knowledge, and a quick perception of the relations of things. In her moral character, it is beautiful to behold her continual gladness, her keen enjoyment of existence, her expansive love, her unhesitating confidence, her sympathy with suffering, her conscientiousness, truthfulness, and hopefulness."

Such are a few fragments from the simple but most interesting and instructive history of Laura Bridgman. The name of her great benefactor and friend, who writes it, is Dr. Howe. There are not many persons, I hope and believe, who, after reading these passages, can ever hear that name with indifference.

A further account has been published by Dr. Howe, since the report from which I have just quoted. It describes her rapid mental growth and improvement during twelve months more, and brings her little history down to the end of last year. It is very remarkable, that as we dream in words, and carry on imaginary conversations, in which we speak both for ourselves and for the shadows who appear to us in those visions of the night, so she, having no words, uses her finger alphabet in her sleep. And it has been ascertained that when her slumber is broken, and is much disturbed by dreams, she expresses her thoughts in an irregular and confused manner on her fingers : just as we should murmur and mutter them indistinctly, in the like circumstances.

I turned over the leaves of her Diary, and found it written in a fair legible square hand, and expressed in terms which were quite intelligible without any explanation. On my saying that I should like to see her write again, the teacher who sat beside her, bade her, in their language, sign her name upon a slip of paper, twice or thrice. In doing so, I observed that she kept her left hand always touching, and following up, her right, in which, of course, she held the pen. No line was indicated by any contrivance, but she wrote straight and freely.

She had, until now, been quite unconscious of the presence of visitors ; but, having her hand placed in that of the gentleman who accompanied me, she immediately expressed his name upon her teacher's palm. Indeed her sense of touch is now so exquisite, that having been acquainted with a person once, she can recognise him or her after almost any interval. This gentleman had been in her company, I believe, but very seldom, and certainly had not seen her for many months. My hand she rejected at once, as she does that of any man who is a stranger to her. But she retained my wife's with evident pleasure, kissed her, and examined her dress with a girl's curiosity and interest.

She was merry and cheerful, and showed much innocent playfulness in her intercourse with her teacher. Her delight on recognising a favourite playfellow and companion—herself a blind girl—who silently, and with an equal enjoyment of the coming surprise, took a seat beside her, was beautiful to

witness. It elicited from her at first, as other slight circumstances did twice or thrice during my visit, an uncouth noise
which was rather painful to hear. But on her teacher
touching her lips, she immediately desisted, and embraced
her laughingly and affectionately.

I had previously been into another chamber, where a
number of blind boys were swinging, and climbing, and
engaged in various sports. They all clamoured, as we
entered, to the assistant-master, who accompanied us, " Look
at me, Mr. Hart! Please, Mr. Hart, look at me ! " evincing,
I thought, even in this, an anxiety peculiar to their condition,
that their little feats of agility should be *seen*. Among them
was a small laughing fellow, who stood aloof, entertaining
himself with a gymnastic exercise for bringing the arms and
chest into play ; which he enjoyed mightily ; especially when,
in thrusting out his right arm, he brought it into contact
with another boy. Like Laura Bridgman, this young child
was deaf, and dumb, and blind.

Dr. Howe's account of this pupil's first instruction is so
very striking, and so intimately connected with Laura herself,
that I cannot refrain from a short extract. I may premise
that the poor boy's name is Oliver Caswell; that he is thirteen
years of age ; and that he was in full possession of all his
faculties, until three years and four months old. He was
then attacked by scarlet fever ; in four weeks became deaf;
in a few weeks more, blind ; in six months, dumb. He
showed his anxious sense of this last deprivation, by often
feeling the lips of other persons when they were talking, and
then putting his hand upon his own, as if to assure himself
that he had them in the right position.

" His thirst for knowledge," says Dr. Howe, " proclaimed
itself as soon as he entered the house, by his eager examination of everything he could feel or smell in his new location.
For instance, treading upon the register of a furnace, he
instantly stooped down, and began to feel it, and soon
discovered the way in which the upper plate moved upon
the lower one ; but this was not enough for him, so lying
down upon his face, he applied his tongue first to one, then
to the other, and seemed to discover that they were of
different kinds of metal.

" His signs were expressive: and the strictly natural
language, laughing, crying, sighing, kissing, embracing, &c.,
was perfect.

"Some of the analogical signs which (guided by his faculty of imitation) he had contrived, were comprehensible; such as the waving motion of his hand for the motion of a boat, the circular one for a wheel, &c.

"The first object was to break up the use of these signs and to substitute for them the use of purely arbitrary ones.

"Profiting by the experience I had gained in the other cases, I omitted several steps of the process before employed, and commenced at once with the finger language. Taking, therefore, several articles having short names, such as key, cup, mug, &c., and with Laura for an auxiliary, I sat down, and taking his hand, placed it upon one of them, and then with my own, made the letters *key*. He felt my hands eagerly with both of his, and on my repeating the process, he evidently tried to imitate the motions of my fingers. In a few minutes he contrived to feel the motions of my fingers with one hand, and holding out the other he tried to imitate them, laughing most heartily when he succeeded. Laura was by, interested even to agitation; and the two presented a singular sight: her face was flushed and anxious, and her fingers twining in among ours so closely as to follow every motion, but so lightly as not to embarrass them; while Oliver stood attentive, his head a little aside, his face turned up, his left hand grasping mine, and his right held out: at every motion of my fingers his countenance betokened keen attention; there was an expression of anxiety as he tried to imitate the motions; then a smile came stealing out as he thought he could do so, and spread into a joyous laugh the moment he succeeded, and felt me pat his head, and Laura clap him heartily upon the back, and jump up and down in her joy.

"He learned more than a half-dozen letters in half an hour, and seemed delighted with his success, at least in gaining approbation. His attention then began to flag, and I commenced playing with him. It was evident that in all this he had merely been imitating the motions of my fingers, and placing his hand upon the key, cup, &c., as part of the process, without any perception of the relation between the sign and the object.

"When he was tired with play I took him back to the table, and he was quite ready to begin again his process of imitation. He soon learned to make the letters for *key, pen, pin*; and by having the object repeatedly placed in his

C

hand, he at last perceived the relation I wished to establish between them. This was evident, because, when I made the letters *p i n*, or *p e n*, or *c u p*, he would select the article.

"The perception of this relation was not accompanied by that radiant flash of intelligence, and that glow of joy, which marked the delightful moment when Laura first perceived it. I then placed all the articles on the table, and going away a little distance with the children, placed Oliver's fingers in the positions to spell *key*, on which Laura went and brought the article : the little fellow seemed much amused by this, and looked very attentive and smiling. I then caused him to make the letters *b r e a d*, and in an instant Laura went and brought him a piece : he smelled at it ; put it to his lips ; cocked up his head with a most knowing look ; seemed to reflect a moment ; and then laughed outright, as much as to say, 'Aha ! I understand now how something may be made out of this.'

"It was now clear that he had the capacity and inclination to learn, that he was a proper subject for instruction, and needed only persevering attention. I therefore put him in the hands of an intelligent teacher, nothing doubting of his rapid progress."

Well may this gentleman call that a delightful moment, in which some distant promise of her present state first gleamed upon the darkened mind of Laura Bridgman. Throughout his life, the recollection of that moment will be to him a source of pure, unfading happiness ; nor will it shine less brightly on the evening of his days of Noble Usefulness.

The affection which exists between these two—the master and the pupil—is as far removed from all ordinary care and regard, as the circumstances in which it has had its growth, are apart from the common occurrences of life. He is occupied now, in devising means of imparting to her, higher knowledge ; and of conveying to her some adequate idea of the Great Creator of that universe in which, dark and silent and scentless though it be to her, she has such deep delight and glad enjoyment.

Ye who have eyes and see not, and have ears and hear not ; ye who are as the hypocrites of sad countenances, and disfigure your faces that ye may seem unto men to fast ; learn healthy cheerfulness, and mild contentment, from the deaf, and dumb, and blind ! Self-elected saints with gloomy brows, this sightless, earless, voiceless child may teach you lessons you will do well to follow. Let that poor hand of hers lie gently on your hearts; for there may be something in its healing touch akin to that of the Great Master whose precepts you misconstrue, whose lessons you pervert, of whose charity and sympathy with all the world, not one among you in his daily practice knows as much as many of the worst among those fallen sinners, to whom you are liberal in nothing but the preachment of perdition!

As I rose to quit the room, a pretty little child of one of the attendants came running in to greet its father. For the moment, a child with eyes, among the sightless crowd, impressed me almost as painfully as the blind boy in the porch had done, two hours ago. Ah! how much brighter and more deeply blue, glowing and rich though it had been before, was the scene without, contrasting with the darkness of so many youthful lives within!

At SOUTH BOSTON, as it is called, in a situation excellently adapted for the purpose, several charitable institutions are clustered together. One of these, is the State Hospital for the insane; admirably conducted on those enlightened principles of conciliation and kindness, which twenty years ago would have been worse than heretical, and which have been acted upon with so much success in our own pauper Asylum at Hanwell. "Evince a desire to show some confidence, and repose some trust, even in mad people," said the resident physician, as we walked along the galleries, his patients flocking round us unrestrained. Of those who deny or doubt the wisdom of this maxim after witnessing its effects, if there be such people still alive, I can only say that I hope I may never be summoned as a Juryman on a Commission of Lunacy whereof they are the subjects; for I should certainly find them out of their senses, on such evidence alone.

Each ward in this institution is shaped like a long gallery or hall, with the dormitories of the patients opening from it on either hand. Here they work, read, play at skittles, and other games; and when the weather does not admit of their taking exercise out of doors, pass the day together. In one of these rooms, seated, calmly, and quite as a matter of course, among a throng of madwomen, black and white, were the physician's wife and another lady, with a couple of children.

These ladies were graceful and handsome; and it was not difficult to perceive at a glance that even their presence there, had a highly beneficial influence on the patients who were grouped about them.

Leaning her head against the chimneypiece, with a great assumption of dignity and refinement of manner, sat an elderly female, in as many scraps of finery as Madge Wildfire herself. Her head in particular was so strewn with scraps of gauze and cotton and bits of paper, and had so many queer odds and ends stuck all about it, that it looked like a bird's-nest. She was radiant with imaginary jewels; wore a rich pair of undoubted gold spectacles; and gracefully dropped upon her lap, as we approached, a very old greasy newspaper, in which I dare say she had been reading an account of her own presentation at some Foreign Court.

I have been thus particular in describing her, because she will serve to exemplify the physician's manner of acquiring and retaining the confidence of his patients.

"This," he said aloud, taking me by the hand, and advancing to the fantastic figure with great politeness—not raising her suspicions by the slightest look or whisper, or any kind of aside, to me : "This lady is the hostess of this mansion, Sir. It belongs to her. Nobody else has anything whatever to do with it. It is a large establishment, as you see, and requires a great number of attendants. She lives, you observe, in the very first style. She is kind enough to receive my visits, and to permit my wife and family to reside here; for which it is hardly necessary to say, we are much indebted to her. She is exceedingly courteous, you perceive," on this hint she bowed condescendingly, "and will permit me to have the pleasure of introducing you : a gentleman from England, ma'am : newly arrived from England, after a very tempestuous passage : Mr. Dickens,—the lady of the house !"

We exchanged the most dignified salutations with profound gravity and respect, and so went on. The rest of the madwomen seemed to understand the joke perfectly (not only in this case, but in all the others, except their own), and be highly amused by it. The nature of their several kinds of insanity was made known to me in the same way, and we left each of them in high good humour. Not only is a thorough confidence established, by those means, between the physician and patient, in respect of the nature and extent of their hallucinations, but it is easy to understand that opportunities are afforded for seizing any moment of reason, to startle them by placing their own delusion before them in its most incongruous and ridiculous light.

Every patient in this asylum sits down to dinner every day with a knife and fork; and in the midst of them sits the gentleman, whose manner of dealing with his charges, I have just described.   At every meal, moral influence alone restrains the more violent among them from cutting the throats of the rest; but the effect of that influence is reduced to an absolute certainty, and is found, even as a means of restraint, to say nothing of it as a means of cure, a hundred times more efficacious than all the strait-waistcoats, fetters, and handcuffs, that ignorance, prejudice, and cruelty have manufactured since the creation of the world.

In the labour department, every patient is as freely trusted with the tools of his trade as if he were a sane man.   In the garden, and on the farm, they work with spades, rakes, and hoes.   For amusement, they walk, run, fish, paint, read, and ride out to take the air in carriages provided for the purpose. They have among themselves a sewing society to make clothes for the poor, which holds meetings, passes resolutions, never comes to fisticuffs or bowie-knives as sane assemblies have been known to do elsewhere; and conducts all its proceedings with the greatest decorum.   The irritability, which would otherwise be expended on their own flesh, clothes, and furniture, is dissipated in these pursuits.   They are cheerful, tranquil, and healthy.

Once a week they have a ball, in which the Doctor and his family, with all the nurses and attendants, take an active part.   Dances and marches are performed alternately, to the enlivening strains of a piano; and now and then some gentleman or lady (whose proficiency has been previously ascertained) obliges the company with a song: nor does it ever degenerate, at a tender crisis, into a screech or howl; wherein, I must confess, I should have thought the danger lay.   At an early hour they all meet together for these festive purposes; at eight oclock refreshments are served; and at nine they separate.

Immense politeness and good breeding are observed throughout.   They all take their tone from the Doctor; and he moves a very Chesterfield among the company.   Like other assemblies, these entertainments afford a fruitful topic

of conversation among the ladies for some days; and the
gentlemen are so anxious to shine on these occasions, that
they have been sometimes found " practising their steps " in
private, to cut a more distinguished figure in the dance.

It is obvious that one great feature of this system, is the
inculcation and encouragement, even among such unhappy
persons, of a decent self-respect. Something of the same
spirit pervades all the Institutions at South Boston.

There is the House of Industry. In that branch of it,
which is devoted to the reception of old or otherwise helpless paupers, these words are painted on the walls: " WOR-
THY OF NOTICE. SELF-GOVERNMENT, QUIETUDE, AND PEACE,
ARE BLESSINGS." It is not assumed and taken for granted
that being there they must be evil-disposed and wicked people, before whose vicious eyes it is necessary to flourish
threats and harsh restraints. They are met at the very
threshold with this mild appeal. All within-doors is very
plain and simple, as it ought to be, but arranged with a view
to peace and comfort. It costs no more than any other plan
of arrangement, but it speaks an amount of consideration for
those who are reduced to seek a shelter there, which puts
them at once upon their gratitude and good behaviour. Instead of being parcelled out in great, long, rambling wards,
where a certain amount of weazen life may mope, and pine,
and shiver, all day long, the building is divided into separate
rooms, each with its share of light and air. In these, the
better kind of paupers live. They have a motive for exertion and becoming pride, in the desire to make these little
chambers comfortable and decent.

I do not remember one but it was clean and neat, and had
its plant or two upon the window-sill, or row of crockery
upon the shelf, or small display of coloured prints upon the
whitewashed wall, or, perhaps, its wooden clock behind the
door.

The orphans and young children are in an adjoining building; separate from this, but a part of the same Institution.
Some are such little creatures, that the stairs are of Liliputian measurement, fitted to their tiny strides. The same
consideration for their years and weakness is expressed in
their very seats, which are perfect curiosities, and look like
articles of furniture for a pauper doll's-house. I can imagine
the glee of our Poor Law Commissioners at the notion of
these seats having arms and backs; but small spines being

of older date than their occupation of the Board-room at
Somerset House, I thought even this provision very merciful
and kind.

Here again, I was greatly pleased with the inscriptions on the
wall, which were scraps of plain morality, easily remembered and understood : such as " Love one another "—" God remembers the smallest creature in His creation : " and straightforward advice of that nature. The books and tasks of these
smallest of scholars, were adapted, in the same judicious
manner, to their childish powers. When we had examined
these lessons, four morsels of girls (of whom one was blind)
sang a little song, about the merry month of May, which I
thought (being extremely dismal) would have suited an English November better. That done, we went to see their sleep-
ing-rooms on the floor above, in which the arrangements
were no less excellent and gentle than those we had seen
below. And after observing that the teachers were of a class
and character well suited to the spirit of the place, I took
leave of the infants with a lighter heart than ever I have
taken leave of pauper infants yet.

Connected with the House of Industry, there is also an
Hospital, which was in the best order, and had, I am glad
to say, many beds unoccupied. It had one fault, however,
which is common to all American interiors : the presence of
the eternal, accursed, suffocating, red-hot demon of a stove,
whose breath would blight the purest air under Heaven.

There are two establishments for boys in this same neighbourhood. One is called the Boylston school, and is an
asylum for neglected and indigent boys who have committed
no crime, but who in the ordinary course of things would
very soon be purged of that distinction if they were not
taken from the hungry streets and sent here. The other is
a House of Reformation for Juvenile Offenders. They are
both under the same roof, but the two classes of boys never
come in contact.

The Boylston boys, as may be readily supposed, have very
much the advantage of the others in point of personal appearance. They were in their school-room when I came upon
them, and answered correctly, without book, such questions
as where was England ; how far was it ; what was its population ; its capital city ; its form of government ; and so forth.
They sang a song too, about a farmer sowing his seed : with
corresponding action at such parts as " 'tis thus he sows,"

"he turns him round," "he claps his hands;" which gave it greater interest for them, and accustomed them to act together, in an orderly manner. They appeared exceedingly well-taught, and not better taught than fed; for a more chubby-looking full-waistcoated set of boys, I never saw.

The juvenile offenders had not such pleasant faces by a great deal, and in this establishment there were many boys of colour. I saw them first at their work (basket-making, and the manufacture of palm-leaf hats), afterwards in their school, where they sang a chorus in praise of Liberty: an odd, and, one would think, rather aggravating, theme for prisoners. These boys are divided into four classes, each denoted by a numeral, worn on a badge upon the arm. On the arrival of a new-comer, he is put into the fourth or lowest class, and left, by good behaviour, to work his way up into the first. The design and object of this Institution is to reclaim the youthful criminal by firm but kind and judicious treatment; to make his prison a place of purification and improvement, not of demoralisation and corruption; to impress upon him that there is but one path, and that one sober industry, which can ever lead him to happiness; to teach him how it may be trodden, if his footsteps have never yet been led that way; and to lure him back to it if they have strayed: in a word, to snatch him from destruction, and restore him to society a penitent and useful member. The importance of such an establishment, in every point of view, and with reference to every consideration of humanity and social policy, requires no comment.

One other establishment closes the catalogue. It is the House of Correction for the State, in which silence is strictly maintained, but where the prisoners have the comfort and mental relief of seeing each other, and of working together. This is the improved system of Prison Discipline which we have imported into England, and which has been in successful operation among us for some years past.

America, as a new and not over-populated country, has in all her prisons, the one great advantage, of being enabled to find useful and profitable work for the inmates; whereas, with us, the prejudice against prison labour is naturally very strong, and almost insurmountable, when honest men who have not offended against the laws are frequently doomed to seek employment in vain. Even in the United States, the principle of bringing convict labour and free labour into a competition which must obviously be to the disadvantage of the latter, has already found many opponents, whose number is not likely to diminish with access of years.

For this very reason though, our best prisons would seem at the first glance to be better conducted than those of America. The treadmill is conducted with little or no noise; five hundred men may pick oakum in the same room, without a sound; and both kinds of labour admit of such keen and vigilant superintendence, as will render even a word of personal communication amongst the prisoners almost impossible. On the other hand, the noise of the loom, the forge, the carpenter's hammer, or the stonemason's saw, greatly favour those opportunities of intercourse—hurried and brief no doubt, but opportunities still—which these several kinds of work, by rendering it necessary for men to be employed very near to each other, and often side by side, without any barrier or partition between them, in their very nature present. A visitor, too, requires to reason and reflect a little, before the sight of a number of men engaged in ordinary labour, such as he is accustomed to out of doors, will impress him half as strongly as the contemplation of the same persons in the same place and garb would, if they were occupied in some task, marked and degraded everywhere as belonging only to felons in jails. In an American state prison or house of correction, I found it difficult at first to persuade myself that I was really in a jail: a place of ignominious punishment and endurance. And to this hour I very much question whether the humane boast that it is not like one, has its root in the true wisdom or philosophy of the matter.

I hope I may not be misunderstood on this subject, for it is one in which I take a strong and deep interest. I incline as little to the sickly feeling which makes every canting lie or maudlin speech of a notorious criminal a subject of newspaper report and general sympathy, as I do to those good old customs of the good old times which made England, even so recently as in the reign of the Third King George, in respect of her criminal code and her prison regulations, one of the most bloody-minded and barbarous countries on the earth. If I thought it would do any good to the rising generation, I would cheerfully give my consent to the disinterment of the bones of any genteel highwayman (the more genteel, the more cheerfully), and to their exposure, piece-

meal, on any sign-post, gate, or gibbet, that might be deemed
a good elevation for the purpose. My reason is as well
convinced that these gentry were as utterly worthless and
debauched villains, as it is that the laws and jails hardened
them in their evil courses, or that their wonderful escapes
were effected by the prison-turnkeys who, in those admirable
days, had always been felons themselves, and were, to the
last, their bosom-friends and pot-companions. At the same
time I know, as all men do or should, that the subject of
Prison Discipline is one of the highest importance to any
community ; and that in her sweeping reform and bright
example to other countries on this head, America has shown
great wisdom, great benevolence, and exalted policy. In
contrasting her system with that which we have modelled
upon it, I merely seek to show that with all its drawbacks,
ours has some advantages of its own.

The House of Correction which has led to these remarks,
is not walled, like other prisons, but is palisaded round about
with tall rough stakes, something after the manner of an
enclosure for keeping elephants in, as we see it represented
in Eastern prints and pictures. The prisoners wear a parti-
coloured dress ; and those who are sentenced to hard labour,
work at nail-making, or stone-cutting. When I was there,
the latter class of labourers were employed upon the stone
for a new custom-house in course of erection at Boston. They
appeared to shape it skilfully and with expedition, though
there were very few among them (if any) who had not
acquired the art within the prison gates.

The women, all in one large room, were employed in
making light clothing, for New Orleans and the Southern
States. They did their work in silence like the men ; and
like them were overlooked by the person contracting for
their labour, or by some agent of his appointment. In
addition to this, they are every moment liable to be visited
by the prison officers appointed for that purpose.

The arrangements for cooking, washing of clothes, and so
forth, are much upon the plan of those I have seen at home.
Their mode of bestowing the prisoners at night (which is of
general adoption) differs from ours, and is both simple and
effective. In the centre of a lofty area, lighted by windows
in the four walls, are five tiers of cells, one above the other ;
each tier having before it a light iron gallery, attainable by
stairs of the same construction and material : excepting the

lower one, which is on the ground. Behind these, back to back with them and facing the opposite wall, are five corresponding rows of cells, accessible by similar means : so that supposing the prisoners locked up in their cells, an officer stationed on the ground, with his back to the wall, has half their number under his eye at once ; the remaining half being equally under the observation of another officer on the opposite side ; and all in one great apartment. Unless this watch be corrupted or sleeping on his post, it is impossible for a man to escape ; for even in the event of his forcing the iron door of his cell without noise (which is exceedingly improbable), the moment he appears outside, and steps into that one of the five galleries on which it is situated, he must be plainly and fully visible to the officer below. Each of these cells holds a small truckle bed, in which one prisoner sleeps; never more. It is small, of course ; and the door not being solid, but grated, and without blind or curtain, the prisoner within is at all times exposed to the observation and inspection of any guard who may pass along that tier at any hour or minute of the night. Every day, the prisoners receive their dinner, singly, through a trap in the kitchen wall ; and each man carries his to his sleeping cell to eat it, where he is locked up, alone, for that purpose, one hour. The whole of this arrangement struck me as being admirable ; and I hope that the next new prison we erect in England may be built on this plan.

I was given to understand that in this prison no swords or fire-arms, or even cudgels, are kept ; nor is it probable that, so long as its present excellent management continues, any weapon, offensive or defensive, will ever be required within its bounds.

Such are the Institutions at South Boston ! In all of them, the unfortunate or degenerate citizens of the State are carefully instructed in their duties both to God and man ; are surrounded by all reasonable means of comfort and happiness that their condition will admit of ; are appealed to, as members of the great human family, however afflicted, indigent, or fallen ; are ruled by the strong Heart, and not by the strong (though immeasurably weaker) Hand. I have described them at some length ; firstly, because their worth demanded it ; and secondly, because I mean to take them for a model, and to content myself with saying of others we may come to, whose design and purpose are the same, that in this or that respect they practically fail, or differ.

I wish by this account of them, imperfect in its execution,
but in its just intention, honest, I could hope to convey to
my readers one-hundredth part of the gratification, the sights
I have described, afforded me.

To an Englishman, accustomed to the paraphernalia of
Westminster Hall, an American Court of Law, is as odd a
sight as, I suppose, an English Court of Law would be to
an American.   Except in the Supreme Court at Washington
(where the judges wear a plain black robe), there is no such
thing as a wig or gown connected with the administration of
justice.   The gentlemen of the bar being barristers and
attorneys too (for there is no division of those functions as
in England) are no more removed from their clients than
attorneys in our Court for the Relief of Insolvent Debtors
are, from theirs.   The jury are quite at home, and make
themselves as comfortable as circumstances will permit.
The witness is so little elevated above, or put aloof from,
the crowd in the court, that a stranger entering during a
pause in the proceedings would find it difficult to pick him
out from the rest.   And if it chanced to be a criminal trial,
his eyes, in nine cases out of ten, would wander to the dock
in search of the prisoner, in vain ; for that gentleman would
most likely be lounging among the most distinguished ornaments of the legal profession, whispering suggestions in his
counsel's ear, or making a toothpick out of an old quill with
his penknife.

I could not but notice these differences, when I visited the
courts at Boston.   I was much surprised at first, too, to
observe that the counsel who interrogated the witness under
examination at the time, did so *sitting*.   But seeing that he
was also occupied in writing down the answers, and remembering that he was alone and had no "junior," I quickly
consoled myself with the reflection that law was not quite
so expensive an article here, as at home ; and that the
absence of sundry formalities which we regard as indispensable, had doubtless a very favourable influence upon
the bill of costs.

In every Court, ample and commodious provision is made
for the accommodation of the citizens.   This is the case all
through America.   In every Public Institution, the right of
the people to attend, and to have an interest in the pro-

ceedings, is most fully and distinctly recognised. There are no grim doorkeepers to dole out their tardy civility by the sixpenny-worth ; nor is there, I sincerely believe, any insolence of office of any kind. Nothing national is exhibited for money ; and no public officer is a showman. We have begun of late years to imitate this good example. I hope we shall continue to do so ; and that in the fulness of time, even deans and chapters may be converted.

In the civil court an action was trying, for damages sustained in some accident upon a railway. The witnesses had been examined, and counsel was addressing the jury. The learned gentleman (like a few of his English brethren) was desperately long-winded, and had a remarkable capacity of saying the same thing over and over again. His great theme was "Warren the ĕn*gine* driver," whom he pressed into the service of every sentence he uttered. I listened to him for about a quarter of an hour ; and, coming out of court at the expiration of that time, without the faintest ray of enlightenment as to the merits of the case, felt as if I were at home again.

In the prisoner's cell, waiting to be examined by the magistrate on a charge of theft, was a boy. This lad, instead of being committed to a common jail, would be sent to the asylum at South Boston, and there taught a trade ; and in the course of time he would be bound apprentice to some respectable master. Thus, his detection in this offence, instead of being the prelude to a life of infamy and a miserable death, would lead, there was a reasonable hope, to his being reclaimed from vice, and becoming a worthy member of society.

I am by no means a wholesale admirer of our legal solemnities, many of which impress me as being exceedingly ludicrous. Strange as it may seem too, there is undoubtedly a degree of protection in the wig and gown—a dismissal of individual responsibility in dressing for the part—which encourages that insolent bearing and language, and that gross perversion of the office of a pleader for The Truth, so frequent in our courts of law. Still, I cannot help doubting whether America, in her desire to shake off the absurdities and abuses of the old system, may not have gone too far into the opposite extreme ; and whether it is not desirable, especially in the small community of a city like this, where each man knows the other, to surround the administration

of justice with some artificial barriers against the "Hail
fellow, well met" deportment of everyday life. All the aid
it can have in the very high character and ability of the
Bench, not only here but elsewhere, it has, and well deserves
to have; but it may need something more: not to impress
the thoughtful and the well-informed, but the ignorant and
heedless; a class which includes some prisoners and many
witnesses. These institutions were established, no doubt,
upon the principle that those who had so large a share in
making the laws, would certainly respect them. But experience has proved this hope to be fallacious; for no men know
better than the Judges of America, that on the occasion of
any great popular excitement the law is powerless, and
cannot, for the time, assert its own supremacy.

The tone of society in Boston is one of perfect politeness,
courtesy, and good breeding. The ladies are unquestionably
very beautiful—in face: but there I am compelled to stop.
Their education is much as with us; neither better nor
worse. I had heard some very marvellous stories in this
respect; but not believing them, was not disappointed. Blue
ladies there are, in Boston; but like philosophers of that
colour and sex in most other latitudes, they rather desire
to be thought superior than to be so. Evangelical ladies
there are, likewise, whose attachment to the forms of religion,
and horror of theatrical entertainments, are most exemplary.
Ladies who have a passion for attending lectures are to be
found among all classes and all conditions. In the kind of
provincial life which prevails in cities such as this, the Pulpit
has great influence. The peculiar province of the Pulpit in
New England (always excepting the Unitarian Ministry)
would appear to be the denouncement of all innocent and
rational amusements. The church, the chapel, and the
lecture-room, are the only means of excitement excepted;
and to the church, the chapel, and the lecture-room, the
ladies resort in crowds.

Wherever religion is resorted to, as a strong drink, and as
an escape from the dull monotonous round of home, those of
its ministers who pepper the highest will be the surest to
please. They who strew the Eternal Path with the greatest
amount of brimstone, and who most ruthlessly tread down
the flowers and leaves that grow by the wayside, will be
voted the most righteous; and they who enlarge with the
greatest pertinacity on the difficulty of getting into heaven,

will be considered by all true believers certain of going there : though it would be hard to say by what process of reasoning this conclusion is arrived at. It is so at home, and it is so abroad. With regard to the other means of excitement, the Lecture, it has at least the merit of being always new. One lecture treads so quickly on the heels of another, that none are remembered ; and the course of this month may be safely repeated next, with its charm of novelty unbroken, and its interest unabated.

The fruits of the earth have their growth in corruption. Out of the rottenness of these things, there has sprung up in Boston a sect of philosophers known as Transcendentalists. On inquiring what this appellation might be supposed to signify, I was given to understand that whatever was unintelligible would be certainly transcendental. Not deriving much comfort from this elucidation, I pursued the inquiry still further, and found that the Transcendentalists are followers of my friend Mr. Carlyle, or I should rather say, of a follower of his, Mr. Ralph Waldo Emerson. This gentleman has written a volume of Essays, in which, among much that is dreamy and fanciful (if he will pardon me for saying so), there is much more that is true and manly, honest and bold. Transcendentalism has its occasional vagaries (what school has not?), but it has good healthful qualities in spite of them ; not least among the number a hearty disgust of Cant, and an aptitude to detect her in all the million varieties of her everlasting wardrobe. And therefore if I were a Bostonian, I think I would be a Transcendentalist.

The only preacher I heard in Boston was Mr. Taylor, who addresses himself peculiarly to seamen, and who was once a mariner himself. I found his chapel down among the shipping, in one of the narrow, old, water-side streets, with a gay blue flag waving freely from its roof. In the gallery opposite to the pulpit were a little choir of male and female singers, a violoncello, and a violin. The preacher already sat in the pulpit, which was raised on pillars, and ornamented behind him with painted drapery of a lively and somewhat theatrical appearance. He looked a weather-beaten hard-featured man, of about six or eight and fifty ; with deep lines graven as it were into his face, dark hair, and a stern, keen eye. Yet the general character of his countenance was pleasant and agreeable. The service commenced with a hymn, to which succeeded an extemporary prayer. It had the fault of frequent repetition, incidental to all such prayers; but it was plain and comprehensive in its doctrines, and breathed a tone of general sympathy and charity, which is not so commonly a characteristic of this form of address to the Deity as it might be. That done he opened his discourse, taking for his text a passage from the Songs of Solomon, laid upon the desk before the commencement of the service by some unknown member of the congregation: "Who is this coming up from the wilderness, leaning on the arm of her beloved?"

He handled his text in all kinds of ways, and twisted it into all manner of shapes; but always ingeniously, and with a rude eloquence, well adapted to the comprehension of his hearers. Indeed if I be not mistaken, he studied their sympathies and understandings much more than the display of his own powers. His imagery was all drawn from the sea, and from the incidents of a seaman's life; and was often remarkably good. He spoke to them of "that glorious man, Lord Nelson," and of Collingwood; and drew nothing in, as the saying is, by the head and shoulders, but brought it to bear upon his purpose, naturally, and with a sharp mind to its effect. Sometimes, when much excited with his subject, he had an odd way—compounded of John Bunyan, and Balfour of Burley—of taking his great quarto Bible under his arm and pacing up and down the pulpit with it; looking steadily down, meantime, into the midst of the congregation. Thus, when he applied his text to the first assemblage of his hearers, and pictured the wonder of the church at their presumption in forming a congregation among themselves, he stopped short with his Bible under his arm in the manner I have described, and pursued his discourse after this manner:

"Who are these—who are they—who are these fellows? where do they come from? Where are they going to?— Come from! What's the answer?"—leaning out of the pulpit, and pointing downward with his right hand: "From below!"—starting back again, and looking at the sailors before him: "From below, my brethren. From under the hatches of sin, battened down above you by the evil one. That's where you came from!"—a walk up and down the pulpit: "and where are you going"—stopping abruptly: "where are you going? Aloft!"—very softly, and pointing upward: "Aloft!"—louder: "aloft!"—louder still: "That's where you are going—with a fair wind,—all taut and trim, steering direct for Heaven in its glory, where there are no storms or foul weather, and where the wicked cease from troubling, and the weary are at rest."—Another walk: "That's where you're going to, my friends. That's it. That's the place. That's the port. That's the haven. It's a blessed harbour—still water there, in all changes of the winds and tides; no driving ashore upon the rocks, or slipping your cables and running out to sea, there: Peace—Peace—Peace —all peace!"—Another walk, and patting the Bible under his left arm: "What! These fellows are coming from the wilderness, are they? Yes. From the dreary, blighted wilderness of Iniquity, whose only crop is Death. But do they lean upon anything—do they lean upon nothing, these poor seamen?"—Three raps upon the Bible: "Oh yes.—Yes. —They lean upon the arm of their Beloved"—three more raps: "upon the arm of their Beloved"—three more, and a walk: "Pilot, guiding-star, and compass, all in one, to all hands—here it is"—three more: "Here it is. They can do their seaman's duty manfully, and be easy in their minds in the utmost peril and danger, with this"—two more: "They can come, even these poor fellows can come, from the wilderness leaning on the arm of their Beloved, and go up— up—up!"—raising his hand higher, and higher, at every repetition of the word, so that he stood with it at last stretched above his head, regarding them in a strange, rapt manner, and pressing the book triumphantly to his breast, until he gradually subsided into some other portion of his discourse.

I have cited this, rather as an instance of the preacher's eccentricities than his merits, though taken in connexion with his look and manner, and the character of his audience, even this was striking. It is possible, however, that my favourable impression of him may have been greatly influenced and strengthened, firstly, by his impressing upon his hearers that the true observance of religion was not inconsistent with a cheerful deportment and an exact discharge of the duties of their station, which, indeed, it scrupulously required of them; and secondly, by his cautioning them not to set up any monopoly in Paradise and its mercies. I never heard these two points so wisely touched (if indeed I have ever heard them touched at all), by any preacher of that kind before.

Having passed the time I spent in Boston, in making myself acquainted with these things, in settling the course I should take in my future travels, and in mixing constantly with its society, I am not aware that I have any occasion to prolong this chapter. Such of its social customs as I have not mentioned, however, may be told in a very few words.

The usual dinner-hour is two o'clock. A dinner party takes place at five; and at an evening party, they seldom sup later than eleven; so that it goes hard but one gets home, even from a rout, by midnight. I never could find out any difference between a party at Boston and a party in London, saving that at the former place all assemblies are held at more rational hours; that the conversation may possibly be a little louder and more cheerful; and a guest is usually expected to ascend to the very top of the house to take his cloak off; that he is certain to see, at every dinner, an unusual amount of poultry on the table; and at every supper, at least two mighty bowls of hot stewed oysters, in any one of which a half-grown Duke of Clarence might be smothered easily.

There are two theatres in Boston, of good size and construction, but sadly in want of patronage. The few ladies who resort to them, sit, as of right, in the front rows of the boxes.

The bar is a large room with a stone floor, and there people stand and smoke, and lounge about, all the evening: dropping in and out as the humour takes them. There too the stranger is initiated into the mysteries of Gin-sling, Cocktail, Sangaree, Mint Julep, Sherry-cobbler, Timber Doodle, and other rare drinks. The house is full of boarders, both married and single, many of whom sleep upon the premises, and contract by the week for their board and lodging: the charge for which diminishes as they go nearer the sky to roost. A public table is laid in a very handsome hall for breakfast, and for dinner, and for supper. The party sitting down together to these meals will vary in number from one to two hundred: sometimes more. The advent of each of these epochs in the day is proclaimed by an awful gong, which shakes the very window-frames as it reverberates through the house, and horribly disturbs nervous foreigners. There is an ordinary for ladies, and an ordinary for gentlemen.

In our private room the cloth could not, for any earthly

consideration, have been laid for dinner without a huge glass dish of cranberries in the middle of the table ; and breakfast would have been no breakfast unless the principal dish were a deformed beef-steak with a great flat bone in the centre, swimming in hot butter, and sprinkled with the very blackest of all possible pepper. Our bedroom was spacious and airy, but (like every bedroom on this side of the Atlantic) very bare of furniture, having no curtains to the French bedstead or to the window. It had one unusual luxury, however, in the shape of a wardrobe of painted wood, something smaller than an English watch-box ; or if this comparison should be insufficient to convey a just idea of its dimensions, they may be estimated from the fact of my having lived for fourteen days and nights in the firm belief that it was a shower-bath.

CHAPTER IV

AN AMERICAN RAILROAD. LOWELL AND ITS FACTORY SYSTEM

BEFORE leaving Boston, I devoted one day to an excursion to Lowell. I assign a separate chapter to this visit; not because I am about to describe it at any great length, but because I remember it as a thing by itself, and am desirous that my readers should do the same.

I made acquaintance with an American railroad, on this occasion, for the first time. As these works are pretty much alike all through the States, their general characteristics are easily described.

There are no first and second class carriages as with us; but there is a gentlemen's car and a ladies' car: the main distinction between which is that in the first, everybody smokes; and in the second, nobody does. As a black man never travels with a white one, there is also a negro car; which is a great blundering clumsy chest, such as Gulliver put to sea in, from the kingdom of Brobdingnag. There is a great deal of jolting, a great deal of noise, a great deal of wall, not much window, a locomotive engine, a shriek, and a bell.

The cars are like shabby omnibuses, but larger: holding thirty, forty, fifty, people. The seats, instead of stretching from end to end, are placed crosswise. Each seat holds two persons. There is a long row of them on each side of the caravan, a narrow passage up the middle, and a door at both ends. In the centre of the carriage there is usually a stove, fed with charcoal or anthracite coal; which is for the most part red-hot. It is insufferably close; and you see the hot air fluttering between yourself and any other object you may happen to look at, like the ghost of smoke.

In the ladies' car, there are a great many gentlemen who have ladies with them. There are also a great many ladies who have nobody with them: for any lady may travel alone, from one end of the United States to the other, and be certain of the most courteous and considerate treatment everywhere. The conductor or check-taker, or guard, or whatever he may be, wears no uniform. He walks up and down the car, and in and out of it, as his fancy dictates ; leans against the door with his hands in his pockets and stares at you, if you chance to be a stranger ; or enters into conversation with the passengers about him. A great many newspapers are pulled out, and a few of them are read. Everybody talks to you, or to anybody else who hits his fancy. If you are an Englishman, he expects that that railroad is pretty much like an English railroad. If you say "No," he says "Yes?" (interrogatively), and asks in what respect they differ. You enumerate the heads of differ-ence, one by one, and he says "Yes?" (still interrogatively) to each. Then he guesses that you don't travel faster in England ; and on your replying that you do, says, "Yes?" again (still interrogatively), and it is quite evident, don't believe it. After a long pause he remarks, partly to you, and partly to the knob on the top of his stick, that "Yankees are reckoned to be considerable of a go-ahead people too ;" upon which *you* say "Yes," and then *he* says "Yes" again (affirma-tively this time) ; and upon your looking out of window, tells you that behind that hill, and some three miles from the next station, there is a clever town in a smart lo-ca-tion, where he expects you have concluded to stop. Your answer in the negative naturally leads to more questions in reference to your intended route (always pronounced rout) ; and wherever you are going, you invariably learn that you can't get there without immense difficulty and danger, and that all the great sights are somewhere else.

If a lady take a fancy to any male passenger's seat, the gentleman who accompanies her gives him notice of the fact, and he immediately vacates it with great politeness. Politics are much discussed, so are banks, so is cotton. Quiet people avoid the question of the Presidency, for there will be a new election in three years and a half, and party feeling runs very high : the great constitutional feature of this institution being, that directly the acrimony of the last election is over, the acrimony of the next one begins ; which is an unspeakable comfort to all strong politicians and true lovers of their country : that is to say, to ninety-nine men and boys out of every ninety-nine and a quarter.

Except when a branch road joins the main one, there is

seldom more than one track of rails ; so that the road is very narrow, and the view, where there is a deep cutting, by no means extensive. When there is not, the character of the scenery is always the same. Mile after mile of stunted trees : some hewn down by the axe, some blown down by the wind, some half fallen and resting on their neighbours, many mere logs half hidden in the swamp, others mouldered away to spongy chips. The very soil of the earth is made up of minute fragments such as these ; each pool of stagnant water has its crust of vegetable rottenness ; on every side there are the boughs, and trunks, and stumps of trees, in every possible stage of decay, decomposition, and neglect. Now you emerge for a few brief minutes on an open country, glittering with some bright lake or pool, broad as many an English river, but so small here that it scarcely has a name ; now catch hasty glimpses of a distant town, with its clean white houses and their cool piazzas, its prim New England church and school-house ; when whir-r-r-r ! almost before you have seen them, comes the same dark screen : the stunted trees, the stumps, the logs, the stagnant water—all so like the last that you seem to have been transported back again by magic.

The train calls at stations in the woods, where the wild impossibility of anybody having the smallest reason to get out, is only to be equalled by the apparently desperate hopelessness of there being anybody to get in. It rushes across the turnpike road, where there is no gate, no policeman, no signal : nothing but a rough wooden arch, on which is painted "WHEN THE BELL RINGS, LOOK OUT FOR THE LOCOMOTIVE." On it whirls headlong, dives through the woods again, emerges in the light, clatters over frail arches, rumbles upon the heavy ground, shoots beneath a wooden bridge which intercepts the light for a second like a wink, suddenly awakens all the slumbering echoes in the main street of a large town, and dashes on haphazard, pell-mell, neck-or-nothing, down the middle of the road. There—with mechanics working at their trades, and people leaning from their doors and windows, and boys flying kites and playing marbles, and men smoking, and women talking, and children crawling, and pigs burrowing, and unaccustomed horses plunging and rearing, close to the very rails—there—on, on, on—tears the mad dragon of an engine with its train of cars ; scattering in all directions a shower of burning sparks from its wood fire ; screeching, hissing, yelling, panting ; until at last the thirsty monster stops beneath a covered way to drink, the people cluster round, and you have time to breathe again.

I was met at the station at Lowell by a gentleman intimately connected with the management of the factories there; and gladly putting myself under his guidance, drove off at once to that quarter of the town in which the works, the object of my visit, were situated. Although only just of age —for if my recollection serve me, it has been a manufacturing town barely one-and-twenty years—Lowell is a large, populous, thriving place. Those indications of its youth which first attract the eye, give it a quaintness and oddity of character which, to a visitor from the old country, is amusing enough. It was a very dirty winter's day, and nothing in the whole town looked old to me, except the mud, which in some parts was almost knee-deep, and might have been deposited there, on the subsiding of the waters after the Deluge. In one place, there was a new wooden church, which, having no steeple, and being yet unpainted, looked like an enormous packing-case without any direction upon it. In another there was a large hotel, whose walls and colonnades were so crisp, and thin, and slight, that it had exactly the appearance of being built with cards. I was careful not to draw my breath as we passed, and trembled when I saw a workman come out upon the roof, lest with one thoughtless stamp of his foot he should crush the structure beneath him, and bring it rattling down. The very river that moves the machinery in the mills (for they are all worked by water power), seems to acquire a new character from the fresh buildings of bright red brick and painted wood among which it takes its course; and to be as light-headed, thoughtless, and brisk a young river, in its murmurings and tumblings, as one would desire to see. One would swear that every "Bakery," "Grocery," and "Bookbindery," and other kind of store, took its shutters down for the first time, and started in business yesterday. The golden pestles and mortars fixed as signs upon the sun-blind frames outside the Druggists', appear to have been just turned out of the United States' Mint; and when I saw a baby of some week or ten days old in a woman's arms at a street corner, I found myself unconsciously wondering where it came from : never supposing for an instant that it could have been born in such a young town as that.

There are several factories in Lowell, each of which belongs to what we should term a Company of Proprietors, but what

they call in America a Corporation. I went over several of
these ; such as a woollen factory, a carpet factory, and a cotton
factory : examined them in every part ; and saw them in their
ordinary working aspect, with no preparation of any kind, or
departure from their ordinary everyday proceedings. I may
add that I am well acquainted with our manufacturing towns
in England, and have visited many mills in Manchester and
elsewhere in the same manner.

I happened to arrive at the first factory just as the dinner
hour was over, and the girls were returning to their work ;
indeed the stairs of the mill were thronged with them as I
ascended. They were all well dressed, but not to my thinking
above their condition ; for I like to see the humbler classes
of society careful of their dress and appearance, and even, if
they please, decorated with such little trinkets as come within the compass of their means. Supposing it confined within reasonable limits, I would always encourage this kind of
pride, as a worthy element of self-respect, in any person I
employed ; and should no more be deterred from doing so,
because some wretched female referred her fall to a love of
dress, than I would allow my construction of the real intent
and meaning of the Sabbath to be influenced by any warning
to the well-disposed, founded on his backslidings on that
particular day, which might emanate from the rather doubtful authority of a murderer in Newgate.

These girls, as I have said, were all well dressed : and that
phrase necessarily includes extreme cleanliness. They had
serviceable bonnets, good warm cloaks, and shawls ; and were
not above clogs and pattens. Moreover, there were places in
the mill in which they could deposit these things without
injury ; and there were conveniences for washing. They were
healthy in appearance, many of them remarkably so, and
had the manners and deportment of young women : not of
degraded brutes of burden. If I had seen in one of those
mills (but I did not, though I looked for something of this
kind with a sharp eye), the most lisping, mincing, affected,
and ridiculous young creature that my imagination could
suggest, I should have thought of the careless, moping,
slatternly, degraded, dull reverse (I *have* seen that), and
should have been still well pleased to look upon her.

The rooms in which they worked, were as well ordered as
themselves. In the windows of some, there were green
plants, which were trained to shade the glass ; in all, there

was as much fresh air, cleanliness, and comfort, as the
nature of the occupation would possibly admit of. Out of
so large a number of females, many of whom were only
then just verging upon womanhood, it may be reasonably
supposed that some were delicate and fragile in appearance:
no doubt there were. But I solemnly declare, that from all
the crowd I saw in the different factories that day, I cannot
recall or separate one young face that gave me a painful
impression; not one young girl whom, assuming it to be
matter of necessity that she should gain her daily bread by
the labour of her hands, I would have removed from those
works if I had had the power.

They reside in various boarding-houses near at hand. The
owners of the mills are particularly careful to allow no persons
to enter upon the possession of these houses, whose characters
have not undergone the most searching and thorough inquiry.
Any complaint that is made against them, by the boarders,
or by any one else, is fully investigated; and if good ground
of complaint be shown to exist against them, they are
removed, and their occupation is handed over to some more
deserving person. There are a few children employed in
these factories, but not many. The laws of the State forbid
their working more than nine months in the year, and require
that they be educated during the other three. For this
purpose there are schools in Lowell; and there are churches
and chapels of various persuasions, in which the young
women may observe that form of worship in which they
have been educated.

At some distance from the factories, and on the highest
and pleasantest ground in the neighbourhood, stands their
hospital, or boarding-house for the sick: it is the best house
in those parts, and was built by an eminent merchant for
his own residence. Like that institution at Boston, which I
have before described, it is not parcelled out into wards, but
is divided into convenient chambers, each of which has all
the comforts of a very comfortable home. The principal
medical attendant resides under the same roof; and were
the patients members of his own family, they could not be
better cared for, or attended with greater gentleness and
consideration. The weekly charge in this establishment for
each female patient is three dollars, or twelve shillings
English; but no girl employed by any of the corporations
is ever excluded for want of the means of payment. That

they do not very often want the means, may be gathered from the fact, that in July, 1841, no fewer than nine hundred and seventy-eight of these girls were depositors in the Lowell Savings Bank: the amount of whose joint savings was estimated at one hundred thousand dollars, or twenty thousand English pounds.

I am now going to state three facts, which will startle a large class of readers on this side of the Atlantic, very much.

Firstly, there is a joint-stock piano in a great many of the boarding-houses. Secondly, nearly all these young ladies subscribe to circulating libraries. Thirdly, they have got up among themselves a periodical called THE LOWELL OFFERING, " A repository of original articles, written exclusively by females actively employed in the mills,"—which is duly printed, published, and sold ; and whereof I brought away from Lowell four hundred good solid pages, which I have read from beginning to end.

The large class of readers, startled by these facts, will exclaim, with one voice, "How very preposterous !" On my deferentially inquiring why, they will answer, " These things are above their station." In reply to that objection, I would beg to ask what their station is.

It is their station to work. And they *do* work. They labour in these mills, upon an average, twelve hours a day, which is unquestionably work, and pretty tight work too. Perhaps it is above their station to indulge in such amusements, on any terms. Are we quite sure that we in England have not formed our ideas of the "station" of working people, from accustoming ourselves to the contemplation of that class as they are, and not as they might be ? I think that if we examine our own feelings, we shall find that the pianos, and the circulating libraries, and even the Lowell Offering, startle us by their novelty, and not by their bearing upon any abstract question of right or wrong.

For myself, I know no station in which, the occupation of to-day cheerfully done and the occupation of to-morrow cheerfully looked to, any one of these pursuits is not most humanising and laudable. I know no station which is rendered more endurable to the person in it, or more safe to the person out of it, by having ignorance for its associate. I know no station which has a right to monopolise the means of mutual instruction, improvement, and rational entertainment; or which has ever continued to be a station very long, after seeking to do so.

Of the merits of the Lowell Offering as a literary production, I will only observe, putting entirely out of sight the fact of the articles having been written by these girls after the arduous labours of the day, that it will compare advantageously with a great many English Annuals. It is pleasant to find that many of its Tales are of the Mills and of those who work in them; that they inculcate habits of self-denial and contentment, and teach good doctrines of enlarged benevolence. A strong feeling for the beauties of nature, as displayed in the solitudes the writers have left at home, breathes through its pages like wholesome village air; and though a circulating library is a favourable school for the study of such topics, it has very scant allusion to fine clothes, fine marriages, fine houses, or fine life. Some persons might object to the papers being signed occasionally with rather fine names, but this is an American fashion. One of the provinces of the state legislature of Massachusetts is to alter ugly names into pretty ones, as the children improve upon the tastes of their parents. These changes costing little or nothing, scores of Mary Annes are solemnly converted into Bevelinas every session.

It is said that on the occasion of a visit from General Jackson or General Harrison to this town (I forget which, but it is not to the purpose), he walked through three miles and a half of these young ladies all dressed out with parasols and silk stockings. But as I am not aware that any worse consequence ensued, than a sudden looking-up of all the parasols and silk stockings in the market; and perhaps the bankruptcy of some speculative New Englander who bought them all up at any price, in expectation of a demand that never came; I set no great store by the circumstance.

In this brief account of Lowell, and inadequate expression of the gratification it yielded me, and cannot fail to afford to any foreigner to whom the condition of such people at home is a subject of interest and anxious speculation, I have carefully abstained from drawing a comparison between these factories and those of our own land. Many of the circumstances whose strong influence has been at work for years in our manufacturing towns have not arisen here; and there is no manufacturing population in Lowell, so to speak: for these girls (often the daughters of small farmers) come from other States, remain a few years in the mills, and then go home for good.

The contrast would be a strong one, for it would be between the Good and Evil, the living light and deepest shadow. I abstain from it, because I deem it just to do so. But I only the more earnestly adjure all those whose eyes may rest on these pages, to pause and reflect upon the difference between this town and those great haunts of desperate misery : to call to mind, if they can in the midst of party strife and squabble, the efforts that must be made to purge them of their suffering and danger : and last, and foremost, to remember how the precious Time is rushing by.

I returned at night by the same railroad and in the same kind of car. One of the passengers being exceedingly anxious to expound at great length to my companion (not to me, of course) the true principles on which books of travel in America should be written by Englishmen, I feigned to fall asleep. But glancing all the way out at window from the corners of my eyes, I found abundance of entertainment for the rest of the ride in watching the effects of the wood fire, which had been invisible in the morning but were now brought out in full relief by the darkness : for we were travelling in a whirlwind of bright sparks, which showered about us like a storm of fiery snow.

CHAPTER V

WORCESTER.   THE CONNECTICUT RIVER.   HARTFORD.
NEW HAVEN.   TO NEW YORK

LEAVING Boston on the afternoon of Saturday the fifth of
February, we proceeded by another railroad to Worcester:
a pretty New England town, where we had arranged to
remain under the hospitable roof of the Governor of the
State, until Monday morning.

These towns and cities of New England (many of which
would be villages in Old England), are as favourable
specimens of rural America, as their people are of rural
Americans. The well-trimmed lawns and green meadows of
home are not there; and the grass, compared with our
ornamental plots and pastures, is rank, and rough, and wild:
but delicate slopes of land, gently-swelling hills, wooded
valleys, and slender streams, abound. Every little colony of
houses has its church and school-house peeping from among
the white roofs and shady trees; every house is the whitest
of the white; every Venetian blind the greenest of the green;
every fine day's sky the bluest of the blue. A sharp dry
wind and a slight frost had so hardened the roads when we
alighted at Worcester, that their furrowed tracks were like
ridges of granite. There was the usual aspect of newness on
every object, of course. All the buildings looked as if they
had been built and painted that morning, and could be taken
down on Monday with very little trouble. In the keen
evening air, every sharp outline looked a hundred times
sharper than ever. The clean cardboard colonnades had no
more perspective than a Chinese bridge on a teacup, and
appeared equally well calculated for use. The razor-like
edges of the detached cottages seemed to cut the very wind
as it whistled against them, and to send it smarting on its
way with a shriller cry than before. Those slightly-built
wooden dwellings behind which the sun was setting with a

brilliant lustre, could be so looked through and through, that
the idea of any inhabitant being able to hide himself from
the public gaze, or to have any secrets from the public eye,
was not entertainable for a moment. Even where a blazing
fire shone through the uncurtained windows of some distant
house, it had the air of being newly lighted, and of lacking
warmth; and instead of awakening thoughts of a snug
chamber, bright with faces that first saw the light round that
same hearth, and ruddy with warm hangings, it came upon
one suggestive of the smell of new mortar and damp walls.

So I thought, at least, that evening. Next morning when
the sun was shining brightly, and the clear church bells were
ringing, and sedate people in their best clothes enlivened the
pathway near at hand and dotted the distant thread of road,
there was a pleasant Sabbath peacefulness on everything,
which it was good to feel. It would have been the better
for an old church; better still for some old graves; but as it
was, a wholesome repose and tranquillity pervaded the scene,
which after the restless ocean and the hurried city, had a
doubly grateful influence on the spirits.

We went on next morning, still by railroad, to Springfield.
From that place to Hartford, whither we were bound, is a
distance of only five-and-twenty miles, but at that time of
the year the roads were so bad that the journey would
probably have occupied ten or twelve hours. Fortunately,
however, the winter having been unusually mild, the Connecticut River was "open," or, in other words, not frozen.
The captain of a small steamboat was going to make his
first trip for the season that day (the second February trip,
I believe, within the memory of man), and only waited for
us to go on board. Accordingly, we went on board, with as
little delay as might be. He was as good as his word, and
started directly.

It certainly was not called a small steamboat without
reason. I omitted to ask the question, but I should think it
must have been of about half a pony power. Mr. Paap, the
celebrated Dwarf, might have lived and died happily in the
cabin, which was fitted with common sash-windows like an
ordinary dwelling-house. These windows had bright-red
curtains, too, hung on slack strings across the lower panes;
so that it looked like the parlour of a Liliputian public-
house, which had got afloat in a flood or some other water
accident, and was drifting nobody knew where. But even

in this chamber there was a rocking-chair. It would be impossible to get on anywhere, in America, without a rocking-chair.

I am afraid to tell how many feet short this vessel was, or how many feet narrow: to apply the words length and width to such measurement would be a contradiction in terms. But I may state that we all kept the middle of the deck, lest the boat should unexpectedly tip over; and that the machinery, by some surprising process of condensation, worked between it and the keel: the whole forming a warm sandwich, about three feet thick.

It rained all day as I once thought it never did rain anywhere, but in the Highlands of Scotland. The river was full of floating blocks of ice, which were constantly crunching and cracking under us; and the depth of water, in the course we took to avoid the larger masses, carried down the middle of the river by the current, did not exceed a few inches. Nevertheless, we moved onward, dexterously; and being well wrapped up, bade defiance to the weather, and enjoyed the journey. The Connecticut River is a fine stream; and the banks in summer-time are, I have no doubt, beautiful: at all events, I was told so by a young lady in the cabin; and she should be a judge of beauty, if the possession of a quality include the appreciation of it, for a more beautiful creature I never looked upon.

After two hours and a half of this odd travelling (including a stoppage at a small town, where we were saluted by a gun considerably bigger than our own chimney), we reached Hartford, and straightway repaired to an extremely comfortable hotel: except, as usual, in the article of bedrooms, which, in almost every place we visited, were very conducive to early rising.

We tarried here, four days. The town is beautifully situated in a basin of green hills; the soil is rich, well-wooded, and carefully improved. It is the seat of the local legislature of Connecticut, which sage body enacted, in bygone times, the renowned code of "Blue Laws," in virtue whereof, among other enlightened provisions, any citizen who could be proved to have kissed his wife on Sunday, was punishable, I believe, with the stocks. Too much of the old Puritan spirit exists in these parts to the present hour; but its influence has not tended, that I know, to make the people less hard in their bargains, or more equal in their dealings.

As I never heard of its working that effect anywhere else, I infer that it never will, here. Indeed, I am accustomed, with reference to great professions and severe faces, to judge of the goods of the other world pretty much as I judge of the goods of this; and whenever I see a dealer in such commodities with too great a display of them in his window, I doubt the quality of the article within.

In Hartford stands the famous oak in which the charter of King Charles was hidden. It is now enclosed in a gentleman's garden. In the State House is the Charter itself. I found the courts of law here, just the same as at Boston; the public institutions almost as good. The Insane Asylum is admirably conducted, and so is the Institution for the Deaf and Dumb.

I very much questioned within myself, as I walked through the Insane Asylum, whether I should have known the attendants from the patients, but for the few words which passed between the former and the Doctor, in reference to the persons under their charge. Of course I limit this remark merely to their looks; for the conversation of the mad people was mad enough.

There was one little prim old lady, of very smiling and good-humoured appearance, who came sidling up to me from the end of a long passage, and with a curtsey of inexpressible condescension, propounded this unaccountable inquiry:

"Does Pontefract still flourish, Sir, upon the soil of England?"

"He does, ma'am," I rejoined.

"When you last saw him, Sir, he was—— "

"Well, ma'am," said I, "extremely well. He begged me to present his compliments. I never saw him looking better."

At this, the old lady was very much delighted. After glancing at me for a moment, as if to be quite sure that I was serious in my respectful air, she sidled back some paces; sidled forward again; made a sudden skip (at which I precipitately retreated a step or two); and said:

"*I* am an antediluvian, Sir."

I thought the best thing to say was, that I had suspected as much from the first. Therefore I said so.

"It is an extremely proud and pleasant thing, Sir, to be an antediluvian," said the old lady.

"I should think it was, ma'am," I rejoined.

The old lady kissed her hand, gave another skip, smirked and sidled down the gallery in a most extraordinary manner, and ambled gracefully into her own bedchamber.

In another part of the building, there was a male patient in bed; very much flushed and heated.

"Well," said he, starting up, and pulling off his night-cap: "It's all settled at last. I have arranged it with Queen Victoria."

"Arranged what?" asked the Doctor.

"Why, that business," passing his hand wearily across his forehead, "about the siege of New York."

"Oh!" said I, like a man suddenly enlightened. For he looked at me for an answer.

"Yes. Every house without a signal will be fired upon by the British troops. No harm will be done to the others. No harm at all. Those that want to be safe, must hoist flags. That's all they'll have to do. They must hoist flags."

Even while he was speaking he seemed, I thought, to have some faint idea that his talk was incoherent. Directly he had said these words, he lay down again; gave a kind of a groan; and covered his hot head with the blankets.

There was another: a young man, whose madness was love and music. After playing on the accordion a march he had composed, he was very anxious that I should walk into his chamber, which I immediately did.

By way of being very knowing, and humouring him to the top of his bent, I went to the window, which commanded a beautiful prospect, and remarked, with an address upon which I greatly plumed myself:

"What a delicious country you have about these lodgings of yours!"

"Poh!" said he, moving his fingers carelessly over the notes of his instrument: "*Well enough for such an Institution as this!*"

I don't think I was ever so taken aback in all my life.

"I come here just for a whim," he said coolly. "That's all."

"Oh! That's all!" said I.

"Yes. That's all. The Doctor's a smart man. He quite enters into it. It's a joke of mine. I like it for a time. You needn't mention it, but I think I shall go out next Tuesday!"

D

I assured him that I would consider our interview perfectly confidential; and rejoined the Doctor. As we were passing through a gallery on our way out, a well-dressed lady, of quiet and composed manners, came up, and proffering a slip of paper and a pen, begged that I would oblige her with an autograph. I complied, and we parted.

"I think I remember having had a few interviews like that, with ladies out of doors. I hope *she* is not mad?"

"Yes."

"On what subject? Autographs?"

"No. She hears voices in the air."

"Well!" thought I, "it would be well if we could shut up a few false prophets of these later times, who have professed to do the same; and I should like to try the experiment on a Mormonist or two to begin with."

In this place, there is the best Jail for untried offenders in the world. There is also a very well-ordered State prison, arranged upon the same plan as that at Boston, except that here, there is always a sentry on the wall with a loaded gun. It contained at that time about two hundred prisoners. A spot was shown me in the sleeping ward, where a watchman was murdered some years since in the dead of night, in a desperate attempt to escape, made by a prisoner who had broken from his cell. A woman, too, was pointed out to me, who, for the murder of her husband, had been a close prisoner for sixteen years.

"Do you think," I asked of my conductor, "that after so very long an imprisonment, she has any thought or hope of ever regaining her liberty?"

"Oh dear yes," he answered. "To be sure she has."

"She has no chance of obtaining it, I suppose?"

"Well, I don't know:" which, by-the-by, is a national answer. "Her friends mistrust her."

"What have *they* to do with it?" I naturally inquired.

"Well, they won't petition."

"But if they did, they couldn't get her out, I suppose?"

"Well, not the first time, perhaps, nor yet the second, but tiring and wearying for a few years might do it."

"Does that ever do it?"

"Why yes, that'll do it sometimes. Political friends 'll do it sometimes. It's pretty often done, one way or another."

I shall always entertain a very pleasant and grateful recollection of Hartford. It is a lovely place, and I had many friends there, whom I can never remember with indifference. We left it with no little regret on the evening of Friday the 11th, and travelled that night by railroad to New Haven. Upon the way, the guard and I were formally introduced to each other (as we usually were on such occasions), and exchanged a variety of small-talk. We reached New Haven at about eight o'clock, after a journey of three hours, and put up for the night at the best inn.

New Haven, known also as the City of Elms, is a fine town. Many of its streets (as its *alias* sufficiently imports) are planted with rows of grand old elm-trees ; and the same natural ornaments surround Yale College, an establishment of considerable eminence and reputation. The various departments of this Institution are erected in a kind of park or common in the middle of the town, where they are dimly visible among the shadowing trees. The effect is very like that of an old cathedral yard in England ; and when their branches are in full leaf, must be extremely picturesque. Even in the winter time, these groups of well-grown trees, clustering among the busy streets and houses of a thriving city, have a very quaint appearance : seeming to bring about a kind of compromise between town and country ; as if each had met the other half-way, and shaken hands upon it ; which is at once novel and pleasant.

After a night's rest, we rose early, and in good time went down to the wharf, and on board the packet "New York" *for* New York. This was the first American steamboat of any size that I had seen ; and certainly to an English eye it was infinitely less like a steamboat than a huge floating bath. I could hardly persuade myself, indeed, but that the bathing establishment off Westminster Bridge, which I left a baby, had suddenly grown to an enormous size ; run away from home ; and set up in foreign parts as a steamer. Being in America, too, which our vagabonds do so particularly favour, it seemed the more probable.

The great difference in appearance between these packets and ours, is, that there is so much of them out of the water : the main-deck being enclosed on all sides, and filled with casks and goods, like any second or third floor in a stack of warehouses ; and the promenade or hurricane-deck being a-top of that again. A part of the machinery is always above this deck ; where the connecting-rod, in a strong and lofty frame, is seen working away like an iron top-sawyer. There

is seldom any mast or tackle: nothing aloft but two tall
black chimneys. The man at the helm is shut up in a little
house in the fore part of the boat (the wheel being connected
with the rudder by iron chains, working the whole length of
the deck); and the passengers, unless the weather be very
fine indeed, usually congregate below. Directly you have
left the wharf, all the life, and stir, and bustle of a packet
cease. You wonder for a long time how she goes on, for
there seems to be nobody in charge of her; and when
another of these dull machines comes splashing by, you feel
quite indignant with it, as a sullen, cumbrous, ungraceful,
unshiplike leviathan: quite forgetting that the vessel you
are on board of, is its very counterpart.

There is always a clerk's office on the lower deck, where
you pay your fare; a ladies' cabin; baggage and stowage
rooms; engineer's room; and in short a great variety of
perplexities which render the discovery of the gentlemen's
cabin, a matter of some difficulty. It often occupies the
whole length of the boat (as it did in this case), and has
three or four tiers of berths on each side. When I first
descended into the cabin of the "New York," it looked, in my
unaccustomed eyes, about as long as the Burlington Arcade.

The Sound which has to be crossed on this passage, is not
always a very safe or pleasant navigation, and has been the
scene of some unfortunate accidents. It was a wet morning,
and very misty, and we soon lost sight of land. The day
was calm, however, and brightened towards noon. After
exhausting (with good help from a friend) the larder, and
the stock of bottled beer, I lay down to sleep: being very
much tired with the fatigues of yesterday. But I woke
from my nap in time to hurry up, and see Hell Gate, the
Hog's Back, the Frying Pan, and other notorious localities,
attractive to all readers of famous Diedrich Knickerbocker's
History. We were now in a narrow channel, with sloping
banks on either side, besprinkled with pleasant villas, and
made refreshing to the sight by turf and trees. Soon we
shot in quick succession, past a lighthouse; a madhouse.
(how the lunatics flung up their caps and roared in sympathy
with the headlong engine and the driving tide!); a jail; and
other buildings: and so emerged into a noble bay, whose
waters sparkled in the now cloudless sunshine like Nature's
eyes turned up to Heaven.

Then there lay stretched out before us, to the right, con-

fused heaps of buildings, with here and there a spire or
steeple, looking down upon the herd below; and here and
there, again, a cloud of lazy smoke; and in the foreground
a forest of ships' masts, cheery with flapping sails and waving
flags.   Crossing from among them to the opposite shore,
were steam ferry-boats laden with people, coaches, horses,
waggons, baskets, boxes: crossed and recrossed by other
ferry-boats: all travelling to and fro: and never idle.
Stately among these restless Insects, were two or three
large ships, moving with slow majestic pace, as creatures of
a prouder kind, disdainful of their puny journeys, and
making for the broad sea.   Beyond, were shining heights,
and islands in the glancing river, and a distance scarcely
less blue and bright than the sky it seemed to meet.   The
city's hum and buzz, the clinking of capstans, the ringing of
bells, the barking of dogs, the clattering of wheels, tingled
in the listening ear.   All of which life and stir, coming
across the stirring water, caught new life and animation
from its free companionship; and, sympathising with its
buoyant spirits, glistened as it seemed in sport upon its
surface, and hemmed the vessel round, and plashed the
water high about her sides, and, floating her gallantly into
the dock, flew off again to welcome other comers, and speed
before them to the busy port.

CHAPTER VI

NEW YORK

THE beautiful metropolis of America is by no means so clean a city as Boston, but many of its streets have the same characteristics; except that the houses are not quite so fresh-coloured, the sign-boards are not quite so gaudy, the gilded letters not quite so golden, the bricks not quite so red, the stone not quite so white, the blinds and area railings not quite so green, the knobs and plates upon the street doors not quite so bright and twinkling. There are many by-streets, almost as neutral in clean colours, and positive in dirty ones, as by-streets in London; and there is one quarter, commonly called the Five Points, which, in respect of filth and wretchedness, may be safely backed against Seven Dials, or any other part of famed St. Giles's.

The great promenade and thoroughfare, as most people know, is Broadway; a wide and bustling street, which, from the Battery Gardens to its opposite termination in a country road, may be four miles long. Shall we sit down in an upper floor of the Carlton House Hotel (situated in the best part of this main artery of New York), and when we are tired of looking down upon the life below, sally forth arm-in-arm, and mingle with the stream?

Warm weather! The sun strikes upon our heads at this open window, as though its rays were concentrated through a burning-glass; but the day is in its zenith, and the season an unusual one. Was there ever such a sunny street as this Broadway? The pavement stones are polished with the tread of feet until they shine again; the red bricks of the houses might be yet in the dry, hot kilns; and the roofs of those omnibuses look as though, if water were poured on them, they would hiss and smoke, and smell like half-quenched fires. No stint of omnibuses here! Half-a-dozen have gone by within as many minutes. Plenty of hackney cabs and coaches too; gigs, phaetons, large-wheeled tilburies, and private carriages—rather of a clumsy make, and not very different from the public vehicles, but built for the heavy roads beyond the city pavement. Negro coachmen and white; in straw hats, black hats, white hats, glazed caps, fur caps; in coats of drab, black, brown, green, blue, nankeen, striped jean and linen; and there, in that one instance (look while it passes, or it will be too late), in suits of livery. Some southern republican that, who puts his blacks in uniform, and swells with Sultan pomp and power. Yonder, where that phaeton with the well-clipped pair of greys has stopped—standing at their heads now—is a Yorkshire groom, who has not been very long in these parts, and looks sorrowfully round for a companion pair of top-boots, which he may traverse the city half a year without meeting. Heaven save the ladies, how they dress! We have seen more colours in these ten minutes, than we should have seen elsewhere, in as many days. What various parasols! what rainbow silks and satins! what pinking of thin stockings, and pinching of thin shoes, and fluttering of ribbons and silk tassels, and display of rich cloaks with gaudy hoods and linings! The young gentlemen are fond, you see, of turning down their shirt-collars and cultivating their whiskers, especially under the chin; but they cannot approach the ladies in their dress or bearing, being, to say the truth, humanity of quite another sort. Byrons of the desk and counter, pass on, and let us see what kind of men those are behind ye: those two labourers in holiday clothes, of whom one carries in his hand a crumpled scrap of paper from which he tries to spell out a hard name, while the other looks about for it on all the doors and windows.

Irishmen both! You might know them, if they were masked, by their long-tailed blue coats and bright buttons, and their drab trousers, which they wear like men well used to working dresses, who are easy in no others. It would be hard to keep your model republics going, without the country-men and countrywomen of those two labourers. For who else would dig, and delve, and drudge, and do domestic work, and make canals and roads, and execute great lines of Internal Improvement! Irishmen both, and sorely puzzled too, to find out what they seek. Let us go down, and help them, for the love of home, and that spirit of liberty which admits of honest service to honest men, and honest work for honest bread, no matter what it be.

That's well! We have got at the right address at last, though it is written in strange characters truly, and might have been scrawled with the blunt handle of the spade the writer better knows the use of, than a pen. Their way lies yonder, but what business takes them there? They carry savings: to hoard up? No. They are brothers, those men. One crossed the sea alone, and working very hard for one half year, and living harder, saved funds enough to bring the other out. That done, they worked together side by side, contentedly sharing hard labour and hard living for another term, and then their sisters came, and then another brother, and lastly, their old mother. And what now? Why, the poor old crone is restless in a strange land, and yearns to lay her bones, she says, among her people in the old grave-yard at home: and so they go to pay her passage back: and God help her and them, and every simple heart, and all who turn to the Jerusalem of their younger days, and have an altar-fire upon the cold hearth of their fathers.

This narrow thoroughfare, baking and blistering in the sun, is Wall Street: the Stock Exchange and Lombard Street of New York. Many a rapid fortune has been made in this street, and many a no less rapid ruin. Some of these very merchants whom you see hanging about here now, have locked up money in their strong-boxes, like the man in the Arabian Nights, and opening them again, have found but withered leaves. Below, here by the water-side, where the bowsprits of ships stretch across the footway, and almost thrust themselves into the windows, lie the noble American vessels which have made their Packet Service the finest in the world. They have brought hither the foreigners who abound in all the streets: not, perhaps, that there are more here, than in other commercial cities; but elsewhere, they have particular haunts, and you must find them out; here, they pervade the town.

We must cross Broadway again; gaining some refresh-ment from the heat, in the sight of the great blocks of clean ice which are being carried into shops and bar-rooms; and the pine-apples and water-melons profusely displayed for sale. Fine streets of spacious houses here, you see!—Wall Street has furnished and dismantled many of them very often—and here a deep green leafy square. Be sure that is a hospitable house with inmates to be affectionately remembered always, where they have the open door and pretty show of plants within, and where the child with laughing eyes is peeping out of window at the little dog below. You wonder what may be the use of this tall flagstaff in the by-street, with something like Liberty's head-dress on its top: so do I. But there is a passion for tall flagstaffs hereabout, and you may see its twin brother in five minutes, if you have a mind.

Again across Broadway, and so—passing from the many-coloured crowd and glittering shops—into another long main street, the Bowery. A railroad yonder, see, where two stout horses trot along, drawing a score or two of people and a great wooden ark, with ease. The stores are poorer here; the passengers less gay. Clothes ready-made, and meat ready-cooked, are to be bought in these parts; and the lively whirl of carriages is exchanged for the deep rumble of carts and waggons. These signs which are so plentiful, in shape like river buoys, or small balloons, hoisted by cords to poles, and dangling there, announce, as you may see by looking up, "OYSTERS IN EVERY STYLE." They tempt the hungry most at night, for then dull candles glimmering inside, illuminate these dainty words, and make the mouths of idlers water, as they read and linger.

What is this dismal-fronted pile of bastard Egyptian, like an enchanter's palace in a melodrama!—a famous prison, called The Tombs. Shall we go in?

So. A long narrow lofty building, stove-heated as usual, with four galleries, one above the other, going round it, and communicating by stairs. Between the two sides of each gallery, and in its centre, a bridge, for the greater convenience of crossing. On each of these bridges sits a man: dozing or reading, or talking to an idle companion. On each tier, are two opposite rows of small iron doors. They look like furnace-doors, but are cold and black, as though the fires within had all gone out. Some two or three are open, and women, with drooping heads bent down, are talking to the inmates. The whole is lighted by a skylight, but it is fast closed; and from the roof there dangle, limp and drooping, two useless windsails.

A man with keys appears, to show us round. A good-looking fellow, and, in his way, civil and obliging.

"Are those black doors the cells?"

"Yes."

"Are they all full?"

"Well, they're pretty nigh full, and that's a fact, and no two ways about it."

"Those at the bottom are unwholesome, surely?"

"Why, we *do* only put coloured people in 'em. That's the truth."

"When do the prisoners take exercise?"

"Well, they do without it pretty much."

"Do they never walk in the yard?"

"Considerable seldom."

"Sometimes, I suppose?"

"Well, it's rare they do. They keep pretty bright without it."

"But suppose a man were here for a twelvemonth. I know this is only a prison for criminals who are charged with grave offences, while they are awaiting their trial, or under remand, but the law here, affords criminals many means of delay. What with motions for new trials, and in arrest of judgment, and what not, a prisoner might be here for twelve months, I take it, might he not?"

"Well, I guess he might."

"Do you mean to say that in all that time he would never come out at that little iron door, for exercise?"

"He might walk some, perhaps—not much."

"Will you open one of the doors?"

"All, if you like."

The fastenings jar and rattle, and one of the doors turns slowly on its hinges. Let us look in. A small bare cell, into which the light enters through a high chink in the wall. There is a rude means of washing, a table, and a bedstead. Upon the latter, sits a man of sixty; reading. He looks up for a moment; gives an impatient dogged shake; and fixes his eyes upon his book again. As we withdraw our heads, the door closes on him, and is fastened as before. This man has murdered his wife, and will probably be hanged.

"How long has he been here?"

"A month."

"When will he be tried?"

"Next term."

"When is that?"

"Next month."

"In England, if a man be under sentence of death, even he has air and exercise at certain periods of the day."

"Possible?"

With what stupendous and untranslatable coolness he says this, and how loungingly he leads on to the women's side: making, as he goes, a kind of iron castanet of the key and the stair-rail!

Each cell door on this side has a square aperture in it. Some of the women peep anxiously through it at the sound of footsteps; others shrink away in shame.—For what offence can that lonely child, of ten or twelve years old, be shut up here? Oh! that boy? He is the son of the prisoner we saw just now; is a witness against his father; and is detained here for safe keeping, until the trial; that's all.

But it is a dreadful place for the child to pass the long days and nights in. This is rather hard treatment for a young witness, is it not?—What says our conductor?

"Well, it an't a very rowdy life, and *that's* a fact!"

Again he clinks his metal castanet, and leads us leisurely away. I have a question to ask him as we go.

"Pray, why do they call this place The Tombs?"

"Well, it's the cant name."

"I know it is. Why?"

"Some suicides happened here, when it was first built. I expect it come about from that."

"I saw just now, that that man's clothes were scattered about the floor of his cell. Don't you oblige the prisoners to be orderly, and put such things away?"

"Where should they put 'em?"

"Not on the ground surely. What do you say to hanging them up?"

He stops and looks round to emphasise his answer:

"Why, I say that's just it. When they had hooks they *would* hang themselves, so they're taken out of every cell, and there's only the marks left where they used to be!"

The prison-yard in which he pauses now, has been the scene of terrible performances. Into this narrow, grave-like place, men are brought out to die. The wretched creature stands beneath the gibbet on the ground; the rope about his neck; and when the sign is given, a weight at its other end comes running down, and swings him up into the air—a corpse.

The law requires that there be present at this dismal spectacle, the judge, the jury, and citizens to the amount of twenty-five. From the community it is hidden. To the dissolute and bad, the thing remains a frightful mystery. Between the criminal and them, the prison-wall is interposed as a thick gloomy veil. It is the curtain to his bed of death, his winding-sheet, and grave. From him it shuts out life, and all the motives to unrepenting hardihood in that last hour, which its mere sight and presence is often all-sufficient to sustain. There are no bold eyes to make him bold ; no ruffians to uphold a ruffian's name before. All beyond the pitiless stone wall, is unknown space.

Let us go forth again into the cheerful streets.

Once more in Broadway ! Here are the same ladies in bright colours, walking to and fro, in pairs and singly ; yonder the very same light blue parasol which passed and repassed the hotel-window twenty times while we were sitting there. We are going to cross here. Take care of the pigs. Two portly sows are trotting up behind this carriage, and a select party of half-a-dozen gentlemen hogs have just now turned the corner.

Here is a solitary swine lounging homeward by himself. He has only one ear ; having parted with the other to vagrant-dogs in the course of his city rambles. But he gets on very well without it ; and leads a roving, gentlemanly, vagabond kind of life, somewhat answering to that of our club-men at home. He leaves his lodgings every morning at a certain hour, throws himself upon the town, gets through his day in some manner quite satisfactory to himself, and regularly appears at the door of his own house again at night, like the mysterious master of Gil Blas. He is a free-and-easy, careless, indifferent kind of pig, having a very large acquaintance among other pigs of the same character, whom he rather knows by sight than conversation, as he seldom troubles himself to stop and exchange civilities, but goes grunting down the kennel, turning up the news and small-talk of the city in the shape of cabbage-stalks and offal, and bearing no tails but his own : which is a very short one, for his old enemies, the dogs, have been at that too, and have left him hardly enough to swear by. He is in every respect a republican pig, going wherever he pleases, and mingling with the best society, on an equal, if not superior footing, for every one makes way when he appears, and the haughtiest give him the wall, if he prefer it. He is a great philosopher, and seldom moved, unless by the dogs before mentioned. Sometimes, indeed, you may see his small eye twinkling on a slaughtered friend, whose carcase garnishes a butcher's door-post, but he grunts out "Such is life: all flesh is pork!" buries his nose in the mire again, and waddles down the gutter: comforting himself with the reflection that there is one snout the less to anticipate stray cabbage-stalks, at any rate.

They are the city scavengers, these pigs. Ugly brutes they are; having, for the most part, scanty brown backs, like the lids of old horsehair trunks: spotted with unwholesome black blotches. They have long, gaunt legs, too, and such peaked snouts, that if one of them could be persuaded to sit for his profile, nobody would recognise it for a pig's likeness. They are never attended upon, or fed, or driven, or caught, but are thrown upon their own resources in early life, and become preternaturally knowing in consequence. Every pig knows where he lives, much better than anybody could tell him. At this hour, just as evening is closing in, you will see them roaming towards bed by scores, eating their way to the last. Occasionally, some youth among them who has over-eaten himself, or has been worried by dogs, trots shrinkingly homeward, like a prodigal son: but this is a rare case: perfect self-possession and self-reliance, and immovable composure, being their foremost attributes.

The streets and shops are lighted now; and as the eye travels down the long thoroughfare, dotted with bright jets of gas, it is reminded of Oxford Street, or Piccadilly. Here and there a flight of broad stone cellar-steps appears, and a painted lamp directs you to the Bowling Saloon, or Ten-Pin alley; Ten-Pins being a game of mingled chance and skill, invented when the legislature passed an act forbidding Nine-Pins. At other downward flights of steps, are other lamps, marking the whereabouts of oyster-cellars—pleasant retreats, say I: not only by reason of their wonderful cookery of oysters, pretty nigh as large as cheese-plates (or for thy dear sake, heartiest of Greek Professors!), but because of all kinds of eaters of fish, or flesh, or fowl, in these latitudes, the swallowers of oysters alone are not gregarious; but subduing themselves, as it were, to the nature of what they work in, and copying the coyness of the thing they eat, do sit apart in curtained boxes, and consort by twos, not by two hundreds.

But how quiet the streets are! Are there no itinerant bands; no wind or stringed instruments? No, not one. By day, are there no Punches, Fantoccini, Dancing-dogs, Jugglers, Conjurers, Orchestrinas, or even Barrel-organs? No, not one.

Yes, I remember one. One barrel-organ and a dancing-monkey—sportive by nature, but fast fading into a dull, lumpish monkey, of the Utilitarian school. Beyond that, nothing lively; no, not so much as a white mouse in a twirling cage.

Are there no amusements? Yes. There is a lecture-room across the way, from which that glare of light proceeds, and there may be evening service for the ladies thrice a week, or oftener. For the young gentlemen, there is the counting-house, the store, the bar-room: the latter, as you may see through these windows, pretty full. Hark! to the clinking sound of hammers breaking lumps of ice, and to the cool gurgling of the pounded bits, as, in the process of mixing, they are poured from glass to glass! No amusements? What are these suckers of cigars and swallowers of strong drinks, whose hats and legs we see in every possible variety of twist, doing, but amusing themselves? What are the fifty newspapers, which those precocious urchins are bawling down the street, and which are kept filed within, what are they but amusements? Not vapid waterish amusements, but good strong stuff; dealing in round abuse and blackguard names; pulling off the roofs of private houses, as the Halting Devil did in Spain; pimping and pandering for all degrees of vicious taste, and gorging with coined lies the most voracious maw; imputing to every man in public life the coarsest and the vilest motives; scaring away from the stabbed and prostrate body-politic, every Samaritan of clear conscience and good deeds; and setting on, with yell and whistle and the clapping of foul hands, the vilest vermin and worst birds of prey.—No amusements!

Let us go on again; and passing this wilderness of an hotel with stores about its base, like some Continental theatre, or the London Opera House shorn of its colonnade, plunge into the Five Points. But it is needful, first, that we take as our escort these two heads of the police, whom you would know for sharp and well-trained officers if you met them in the Great Desert. So true it is, that certain pursuits, wherever carried on, will stamp men with the same character. These two might have been begotten, born, and bred, in Bow Street.

We have seen no beggars in the streets by night or day; but of other kinds of strollers, plenty. Poverty, wretchedness, and vice, are rife enough where we are going now.

This is the place: these narrow ways, diverging to the right and left, and reeking everywhere with dirt and filth. Such lives as are led here. bear the same fruits here as elsewhere. The coarse and bloated faces at the doors, have counterparts at home, and all the wide world over. Debauchery has made the very houses prematurely old. See how the rotten beams are tumbling down, and how the patched and broken windows seem to scowl dimly, like eyes that have been hurt in drunken frays. Many of those pigs live here. Do they ever wonder why their masters walk upright in lieu of going on all-fours? and why they talk instead of grunting?

So far, nearly every house is a low tavern; and on the bar-room walls, are coloured prints of Washington, and Queen Victoria of England, and the American Eagle. Among the pigeon-holes that hold the bottles, are pieces of plate-glass and coloured paper, for there is, in some sort, a taste for decoration, even here. And as seamen frequent these haunts, there are maritime pictures by the dozen: of partings between sailors and their lady-loves, portraits of William, of the ballad, and his Black-Eyed Susan; of Will Watch, the Bold Smuggler; of Paul Jones the Pirate, and the like: on which the painted eyes of Queen Victoria, and of Washington to boot, rest in as strange companionship, as on most of the scenes that are enacted in their wondering presence.

What place is this, to which the squalid street conducts us? A kind of square of leprous houses, some of which are attainable only by crazy wooden stairs without. What lies beyond this tottering flight of steps, that creak beneath our tread?—a miserable room, lighted by one dim candle, and destitute of all comfort, save that which may be hidden in a wretched bed. Beside it, sits a man: his elbows on his knees: his forehead hidden in his hands. "What ails that man?" asks the foremost officer. "Fever," he sullenly replies, without looking up. Conceive the fancies of a feverish brain, in such a place as this!

Ascend these pitch-dark stairs, heedful of a false footing on the trembling boards, and grope your way with me into this wolfish den, where neither ray of light nor breath of air, appears to come. A negro lad, startled from his sleep by the officer's voice—he knows it well—but comforted by his assurance that he has not come on business, officiously bestirs himself to light a candle. The match flickers for a moment, and shows great mounds of dusty rags upon the ground; then dies away and leaves a denser darkness than before, if there can be degrees in such extremes. He stumbles down the stairs and presently comes back, shading a flaring taper with his hand. Then the mounds of rags are seen to be astir, and rise slowly up, and the floor is covered with heaps of negro women, waking from their sleep: their white teeth chattering, and their bright eyes glistening and winking on all sides with surprise and fear, like the countless repetition of one astonished African face in some strange mirror.

Mount up these other stairs with no less caution (there are traps and pitfalls here, for those who are not so well escorted as ourselves) into the housetop; where the bare beams and rafters meet overhead, and calm night looks down through the crevices in the roof.   Open the door of one of these cramped hutches full of sleeping negroes. Pah ! They have a charcoal fire within ; there is a smell of singeing clothes, or flesh, so close they gather round the brazier ; and vapours issue forth that blind and suffocate. From every corner, as you glance about you in these dark retreats, some figure crawls half-awakened, as if the judgment-hour were near at hand, and every obscene grave were giving up its dead. Where dogs would howl to lie, women, and men, and boys slink off to sleep, forcing the dislodged rats to move away in quest of better lodgings.

Here too are lanes and alleys, paved with mud knee-deep, underground chambers, where they dance and game ; the walls bedecked with rough designs of ships, and forts, and flags, and American eagles out of number: ruined houses, open to the street, whence, through wide gaps in the walls, other ruins loom upon the eye, as though the world of vice and misery had nothing else to show: hideous tenements which take their name from robbery and murder: all that is loathsome, drooping, and decayed is here.

Our leader has his hand upon the latch of " Almack's," and calls to us from the bottom of the steps ; for the assembly-room of the Five Point fashionables is approached by a descent. Shall we go in ? It is but a moment.

Heyday ! the landlady of Almack's thrives ! A buxom fat mulatto woman, with sparkling eyes, whose head is daintily ornamented with a handkerchief of many colours. Nor is the landlord much behind her in his finery, being attired in a smart blue jacket, like a ship's steward, with a thick gold ring upon his little finger, and round his neck a gleaming golden watch-guard. How glad he is to see us ! What will we please to call for? A dance? It shall be done directly, Sir: "a regular break-down."

The corpulent black fiddler, and his friend who plays the tambourine, stamp upon the boarding of the small raised orchestra in which they sit, and play a lively measure. Five or six couple come upon the floor, marshalled by a lively young negro, who is the wit of the assembly, and the greatest dancer known. He never leaves off making queer faces, and is the delight of all the rest, who grin from ear to ear incessantly. Among the dancers are two young mulatto girls, with large, black, drooping eyes, and head-gear after the fashion of the hostess, who are as shy, or feign to be, as though they never danced before, and so look down before the visitors, that their partners can see nothing but the long fringed lashes.

But the dance commences. Every gentleman sets as long as he likes to the opposite lady, and the opposite lady to him, and all are so long about it that the sport begins to languish, when suddenly the lively hero dashes in to the rescue. Instantly the fiddler grins, and goes at it tooth and nail; there is new energy in the tambourine; new laughter in the dancers; new smiles in the landlady; new confidence in the landlord; new brightness in the very candles. Single shuffle, double shuffle, cut and cross-cut; snapping his fingers, rolling his eyes, turning in his knees, presenting the backs of his legs in front, spinning about on his toes and heels like nothing but the man's fingers on the tambourine; dancing with two left legs, two right legs, two wooden legs, two wire legs, two spring legs—all sorts of legs and no legs—what is this to him? And in what walk of life, or dance of life, does man ever get such stimulating applause as thunders about him, when, having danced his partner off her feet, and himself too, he finishes by leaping gloriously on the bar-counter, and calling for something to drink, with the chuckle of a million of counterfeit Jim Crows, in one inimitable sound!

The air, even in these distempered parts, is fresh after the stifling atmosphere of the houses; and now, as we emerge into a broader street, it blows upon us with a purer breath, and the stars look bright again. Here are The Tombs once more. The city watch-house is a part of the building. It follows naturally on the sights we have just left. Let us see that, and then to bed.

What! do you thrust your common offenders against the police discipline of the town, into such holes as these? Do

men and women, against whom no crime is proved, lie here
all night in perfect darkness, surrounded by the noisome
vapours which encircle that flagging lamp you light us with,
and breathing this filthy and offensive stench! Why, such
indecent and disgusting dungeons as these cells, would bring
disgrace upon the most despotic empire in the world! Look
at them, man—you, who see them every night, and keep the
keys. Do you see what they are? Do you know how drains
are made below the streets, and wherein these human sewers
differ, except in being always stagnant?

Well, he don't know. He has had five-and-twenty young
women locked up in this very cell at one time, and you'd
hardly realise what handsome faces there were among 'em.

In God's name! shut the door upon the wretched creature
who is in it now, and put its screen before a place, quite unsurpassed in all the vice, neglect, and devilry, of the worst old
town in Europe.

Are people really left all night, untried, in those black
sties?—Every night. The watch is set at seven in the evening. The magistrate opens his court at five in the morning.
That is the earliest hour at which the first prisoner can be
released; and if an officer appear against him, he is not taken
out till nine o'clock or ten.—But if any one among them die
in the interval, as one man did, not long ago? Then he is
half-eaten by the rats in an hour's time; as that man was;
and there an end.

What is this intolerable tolling of great bells, and crashing
of wheels, and shouting in the distance? A fire. And what
that deep red light in the opposite direction? Another fire.
And what these charred and blackened walls we stand before?
A dwelling where a fire has been. It was more than hinted,
in an official report, not long ago, that some of these confla-
grations were not wholly accidental, and that speculation and
enterprise found a field of exertion, even in flames: but be
this as it may, there was a fire last night, there are two to-
night, and you may lay an even wager there will be at least
one, to-morrow. So, carrying that with us for our comfort
let us say, Good night, and climb upstairs to bed.

———

One day, during my stay in New York, I paid a visit to
the different public institutions on Long Island, or Rhode
Island: I forget which. One of them is a Lunatic Asylum.

The building is handsome ; and is remarkable for a spacious and elegant staircase. The whole structure is not yet finished, but it is already one of considerable size and extent, and is capable of accommodating a very large number of patients.

I cannot say that I derived much comfort from the inspection of this charity. The different wards might have been cleaner and better ordered ; I saw nothing of that salutary system which had impressed me so favourably elsewhere; and everything had a lounging, listless, madhouse air, which was very painful. The moping idiot, cowering down with long dishevelled hair ; the gibbering maniac, with his hideous laugh and pointed finger ; the vacant eye, the fierce wild face, the gloomy picking of the hands and lips, and munching of the nails : there they were all, without disguise, in naked ugliness and horror. In the dining-room, a bare, dull, dreary place, with nothing for the eye to rest on but the empty walls, a woman was locked up alone. She was bent, they told me, on committing suicide. If anything could have strengthened her in her resolution, it would certainly have been the insupportable monotony of such an existence.

The terrible crowd with which these halls and galleries were filled, so shocked me, that I abridged my stay within the shortest limits, and declined to see that portion of the building in which the refractory and violent were under closer restraint. I have no doubt that the gentleman who presided over this establishment at the time I write of, was competent to manage it, and had done all in his power to promote its usefulness : but will it be believed that the miserable strife of Party feeling is carried even into this sad refuge of afflicted and degraded humanity ? Will it be believed that the eyes which are to watch over and control the wanderings of minds on which the most dreadful visitation to which our nature is exposed has fallen, must wear the glasses of some wretched side in Politics ? Will it be believed that the governor of such a house as this, is appointed, and deposed, and changed perpetually, as Parties fluctuate and vary, and as their despicable weathercocks are blown this way or that ? A hundred times in every week, some new most paltry exhibition of that narrow-minded and injurious Party Spirit, which is the Simoom of America, sickening and blighting everything of wholesome life within its reach, was forced upon my notice ; but I never turned my back upon it with feelings of such deep disgust and measureless contempt, as when I crossed the threshold of this madhouse.

At a short distance from this building is another called the Alms House, that is to say, the workhouse of New York. This is a large Institution also : lodging, I believe, when I was there, nearly a thousand poor. It was badly ventilated, and badly lighted ; was not too clean ; and impressed me, on the whole, very uncomfortably. But it must be remembered that New York, as a great emporium of commerce, and as a place of general resort, not only from all parts of the States, but from most parts of the world, has always a large pauper population to provide for ; and labours, therefore, under peculiar difficulties in this respect. Nor must it be forgotten that New York is a large town, and that in all large towns a vast amount of good and evil is intermixed and jumbled up together.

In the same neighbourhood is the Farm, where young orphans are nursed and bred. I did not see it, but I believe it is well conducted ; and I can the more easily credit it, from knowing how mindful they usually are, in America, of that beautiful passage in the Litany which remembers all sick persons and young children.

I was taken to these Institutions by water, in a boat belonging to the Island Jail, and rowed by a crew of prisoners, who were dressed in a striped uniform of black and buff, in which they looked like faded tigers. They took me, by the same conveyance, to the Jail itself.

It is an old prison, and quite a pioneer establishment, on the plan I have already described. I was glad to hear this, for it is unquestionably a very indifferent one. The most is made, however, of the means it possesses, and it is as well regulated as such a place can be.

The women work in covered sheds, erected for that purpose. If I remember right, there are no shops for the men, but be that as it may, the greater part of them labour in certain stone-quarries near at hand. The day being very wet indeed, this labour was suspended, and the prisoners were in their cells. Imagine these cells, some two or three hundred in number, and in every one a man locked up ; this one at his door for air, with his hands thrust through the grate ; this one in bed (in the middle of the day, remember) ; and this one flung down in a heap upon the ground,

with his head against the bars, like a wild beast. Make the
rain pour down, outside, in torrents. Put the everlasting
stove in the midst; hot, and suffocating, and vaporous, as
a witch's cauldron. Add a collection of gentle odours, such
as would arise from a thousand mildewed umbrellas, wet
through, and a thousand buck-baskets, full of half-washed
linen—and there is the prison, as it was that day.

The prison for the State at Sing Sing, is, on the other
hand, a model jail. That, and Auburn, are, I believe, the
largest and best examples of the silent system.

In another part of the city, is the Refuge for the Destitute: an Institution whose object is to reclaim youthful offenders, male and female, black and white, without distinction; to teach them useful trades, apprentice them to respectable masters, and make them worthy members of society.
Its design, it will be seen, is similar to that at Boston ; and
it is a no less meritorious and admirable establishment. A
suspicion crossed my mind during my inspection of this
noble charity, whether the superintendent had quite sufficient knowledge of the world and worldly characters; and
whether he did not commit a great mistake in treating some
young girls, who were to all intents and purposes, by their
years and their past lives, women, as though they were little
children ; which certainly had a ludicrous effect in my eyes,
and, or I am much mistaken, in theirs also. As the Institution, however, is always under a vigilant examination of
a body of gentlemen of great intelligence and experience, it
cannot fail to be well conducted; and whether I am right or
wrong in this slight particular, is unimportant to its deserts
and character, which it would be difficult to estimate too highly.

In addition to these establishments, there are in New
York, excellent hospitals and schools, literary institutions
and libraries; an admirable fire department (as indeed it
should be, having constant practice), and charities of every
sort and kind. In the suburbs there is a spacious cemetery:
unfinished yet, but every day improving. The saddest tomb
I saw there was "The Strangers' Grave. Dedicated to the
different hotels in this city."

There are three principal theatres. Two of them, the Park
and the Bowery, are large, elegant, and handsome buildings,
and are, I grieve to write it, generally deserted. The third, the
Olympic, is a tiny show-box for vaudevilles and burlesques.
It is singularly well conducted by Mr. Mitchell, a comic

actor of great quiet humour and originality, who is well remembered and esteemed by London playgoers. I am happy to report of this deserving gentleman, that his benches are usually well filled, and that his theatre rings with merriment every night. I had almost forgotten a small summer theatre, called Niblo's, with gardens and open air amusements attached; but I believe it is not exempt from the general depression under which Theatrical Property, or what is humorously called by that name, unfortunately labours.

The country round New York is surpassingly and exquisitely picturesque. The climate, as I have already intimated, is somewhat of the warmest. What it would be, without the sea breezes which come from its beautiful Bay in the evening time, I will not throw myself or my readers into a fever by inquiring.

The tone of the best society in this city, is like that of Boston; here and there, it may be, with a greater infusion of the mercantile spirit, but generally polished and refined, and always most hospitable. The houses and tables are elegant; the hours later and more rakish; and there is, perhaps, a greater spirit of contention in reference to appearances, and the display of wealth and costly living. The ladies are singularly beautiful.

Before I left New York I made arrangements for securing a passage home in the George Washington packet ship, which was advertised to sail in June: that being the month in which I had determined, if prevented by no accident in the course of my ramblings, to leave America.

I never thought that going back to England, returning to all who are dear to me, and to pursuits that have insensibly grown to be a part of my nature, I could have felt so much sorrow as I endured, when I parted at last, on board this ship, with the friends who had accompanied me from this city. I never thought the name of any place, so far away and so lately known, could ever associate itself in my mind with the crowd of affectionate remembrances that now cluster about it. There are those in this city who would brighten, to me, the darkest winter-day that ever glimmered and went out in Lapland; and before whose presence even Home grew dim, when they and I exchanged that painful word which mingles with our every thought and deed; which haunts our cradle-heads in infancy, and closes up the vista of our lives in age.

CHAPTER VII

THE journey from New York to Philadelphia, is made by railroad, and two ferries; and usually occupies between five and six hours. It was a fine evening when we were passengers in the train: and watching the bright sunset from a little window near the door by which we sat, my attention was attracted to a remarkable appearance issuing from the windows of the gentleman's car immediately in front of us, which I supposed for some time was occasioned by a number of industrious persons inside, ripping open feather-beds, and giving the feathers to the wind. At length it occurred to me that they were only spitting, which was indeed the case; though how any number of passengers which it was possible for that car to contain, could have maintained such a playful and incessant shower of expectoration, I am still at a loss to understand: notwithstanding the experience in all salivatory phenomena which I afterwards acquired.

I made acquaintance, on this journey, with a mild and modest young quaker, who opened the discourse by informing me, in a grave whisper, that his grandfather was the inventor of cold-drawn castor oil. I mention the circumstance here, thinking it probable that this is the first occasion on which the valuable medicine in question was ever used as a conversational aperient.

We reached the city, late that night. Looking out of my chamber-window, before going to bed, I saw, on the opposite side of the way, a handsome building of white marble, which had a mournful ghost-like aspect, dreary to behold. I attributed this to the sombre influence of the night, and on rising in the morning looked out again, expecting to see its steps and portico thronged with groups of people passing in and out. The door was still tight shut, however; the same cold cheerless air prevailed; and the building looked as if the marble statue of Don Guzman could alone have any business to transact within its gloomy walls. I hastened to inquire its name and purpose, and then my surprise vanished. It was the Tomb of many fortunes; the Great Catacomb of investment; the memorable United States Bank.

The stoppage of this bank, with all its ruinous consequences, had cast (as I was told on every side) a gloom on Philadelphia, under the depressing effect of which it yet laboured. It certainly did seem rather dull and out of spirits.

It is a handsome city, but distractingly regular. After walking about it for an hour or two, I felt that I would have given the world for a crooked street. The collar of my coat appeared to stiffen, and the brim of my hat to expand, beneath its quakery influence. My hair shrunk into a sleek short crop, my hands folded themselves upon my breast of their own calm accord, and thoughts of taking lodgings in Mark Lane over against the Market Place, and of making a large fortune by speculations in corn, came over me involuntarily.

Philadelphia is most bountifully provided with fresh water, which is showered and jerked about, and turned on, and poured off, everywhere. The Waterworks, which are on a height near the city, are no less ornamental than useful, being tastefully laid out as a public garden, and kept in the best and neatest order. The river is dammed at this point, and forced by its own power into certain high tanks or reservoirs, whence the whole city, to the top stories of the houses, is supplied at a very trifling expense.

There are various public institutions. Among them a most excellent Hospital—a quaker establishment, but not sectarian in the great benefits it confers; a quiet, quaint old Library, named after Franklin; a handsome Exchange and Post Office; and so forth. In connexion with the quaker Hospital, there is a picture by West, which is exhibited for the benefit of the funds of the institution. The subject is, our Saviour healing the sick, and it is, perhaps, as favourable a specimen of the master as can be seen anywhere. Whether this be high or low praise, depends upon the reader's taste.

In the same room, there is a very characteristic and lifelike portrait by Mr. Sully, a distinguished American artist.

My stay in Philadelphia was very short, but what I saw of its society, I greatly liked. Treating of its general characteristics, I should be disposed to say that it is more provincial than Boston or New York, and that there is afloat in the fair city, an assumption of taste and criticism, savouring rather of those genteel discussions upon the same themes, in connexion with Shakspeare and the Musical Glasses, of which we read in the Vicar of Wakefield. Near the city, is a most splendid unfinished marble structure for the Girard College, founded by a deceased gentleman of that name and of enormous wealth, which, if completed according to the original design, will be perhaps the richest edifice of modern times. But the bequest is involved in legal disputes, and pending them the work has stopped; so that like many other great undertakings in America, even this is rather going to be done one of these days, than doing now.

In the outskirts, stands a great prison, called the Eastern Penitentiary; conducted on a plan peculiar to the state of Pennsylvania. The system here, is rigid, strict, and hopeless solitary confinement. I believe it, in its effects, to be cruel and wrong.

In its intention, I am well convinced that it is kind, humane, and meant for reformation; but I am persuaded that those who devised this system of Prison Discipline, and those benevolent gentlemen who carry it into execution, do not know what it is that they are doing. I believe that very few men are capable of estimating the immense amount of torture and agony which this dreadful punishment, prolonged for years, inflicts upon the sufferers; and in guessing at it myself, and in reasoning from what I have seen written upon their faces, and what to my certain knowledge they feel within, I am only the more convinced that there is a depth of terrible endurance in it which none but the sufferers themselves can fathom, and which no man has a right to inflict upon his fellow-creature. I hold this slow and daily tampering with the mysteries of the brain, to be immeasurably worse than any torture of the body: and because its ghastly signs and tokens are not so palpable to the eye and sense of touch as scars upon the flesh; because its wounds are not upon the surface, and it extorts few cries that human ears can hear; therefore I the more denounce it, as a secret punishment which slumbering humanity is not roused up to stay. I hesitated once, debating with myself, whether, if I had the power of saying "Yes" or "No," I would allow it to be tried in certain cases, where the terms of imprisonment

were short ; but now, I solemnly declare, that with no re-
wards or honours could I walk a happy man beneath the open
sky by day, or lie me down upon my bed at night, with the
consciousness that one human creature, for any length of
time, no matter what, lay suffering this unknown punishment
in his silent cell, and I the cause, or I consenting to it in
the least degree.

I was accompanied to this prison by two gentlemen offi-
cially connected with its management, and passed the day in
going from cell to cell, and talking with the inmates. Every
facility was afforded me, that the utmost courtesy could
suggest. Nothing was concealed or hidden from my view,
and every piece of information that I sought, was openly and
frankly given. The perfect order of the building cannot be
praised too highly, and of the excellent motives of all who
are immediately concerned in the administration of the system, there can be no kind of question.

Between the body of the prison and the outer wall, there
is a spacious garden. Entering it, by a wicket in the massive
gate, we pursued the path before us to its other termination,
and passed into a large chamber, from which seven long
passages radiate. On either side of each, is a long, long row
of low cell doors, with a certain number over every one.
Above, a gallery of cells like those below, except that they
have no narrow yard attached (as those in the ground tier
have), and are somewhat smaller. The possession of two of
these, is supposed to compensate for the absence of so much
air and exercise as can be had in the dull strip attached to
each of the others, in an hour's time every day ; and therefore
every prisoner in this upper story has two cells, adjoining and
communicating with, each other.

Standing at the central point, and looking down these
dreary passages, the dull repose and quiet that prevails, is
awful. Occasionally, there is a drowsy sound from some lone
weaver's shuttle, or shoemaker's last, but it is stifled by the
thick walls and heavy dungeon-door, and only serves to make
the general stillness more profound. Over the head and face
of every prisoner who comes into this melancholy house, a
black hood is drawn ; and in this dark shroud, an emblem of
the curtain dropped between him and the living world, he is
led to the cell from which he never again comes forth, until
his whole term of imprisonment has expired. He never hears
of wife and children ; home or friends ; the life or death of

any single creature. He sees the prison-officers, but with
that exception he never looks upon a human countenance, or
hears a human voice. He is a man buried alive ; to be dug
out in the slow round of years ; and in the meantime dead
to everything but torturing anxieties and horrible despair.

His name, and crime, and term of suffering, are unknown,
even to the officer who delivers him his daily food. There is
a number over his cell-door, and in a book of which the
governor of the prison has one copy, and the moral instructor
another : this is the index of his history. Beyond these pages
the prison has no record of his existence : and though he live
to be in the same cell ten weary years, he has no means of
knowing, down to the very last hour, in what part of the
building it is situated ; what kind of men there are about
him ; whether in the long winter nights there are living
people near, or he is in some lonely corner of the great jail,
with walls, and passages, and iron doors between him and the
nearest sharer in its solitary horrors.

Every cell has double doors : the outer one of sturdy oak,
the other of grated iron, wherein there is a trap through
which his food is handed. He has a Bible, and a slate and
pencil, and, under certain restrictions, has sometimes other
books, provided for the purpose, and pen and ink and paper.
His razor, plate, and can, and basin, hang upon the wall, or
shine upon the little shelf. Fresh water is laid on in every
cell, and he can draw it at his pleasure. During the day,
his bedstead turns up against the wall, and leaves more space
for him to work in. His loom, or bench, or wheel, is there ;
and there he labours, sleeps and wakes, and counts the
seasons as they change, and grows old.

The first man I saw, was seated at his loom, at work. He
had been there six years, and was to remain, I think, three
more. He had been convicted as a receiver of stolen goods,
but even after his long imprisonment, denied his guilt, and
said he had been hardly dealt by. It was his second offence.
He stopped his work when we went in, took off his spectacles, and answered freely to everything that was said to
him, but always with a strange kind of pause first, and in a
low, thoughtful voice. He wore a paper hat of his own
making, and was pleased to have it noticed and commended.
He had very ingeniously manufactured a sort of Dutch clock
from some disregarded odds and ends ; and his vinegar-
bottle served for the pendulum. Seeing me interested in this

contrivance, he looked up at it with a great deal of pride, and
said that he had been thinking of improving it, and that he
hoped the hammer and a little piece of broken glass beside
it " would play music before long." He had extracted some
colours from the yarn with which he worked, and painted a
few poor figures on the wall. One, of a female, over the
door, he called "The Lady of the Lake."

He smiled as I looked at these contrivances to while away
the time ; but when I looked from them to him, I saw that
his lip trembled, and could have counted the beating of his
heart. I forget how it came about, but some allusion was
made to his having a wife. He shook his head at the word,
turned aside, and covered his face with his hands.

" But you are resigned now ! " said one of the gentlemen
after a short pause, during which he had resumed his former
manner. He answered with a sigh that seemed quite reckless
in its hopelessness, "Oh yes, oh yes ! I am resigned to it."
" And are a better man, you think ? " " Well, I hope so :
I'm sure I hope I may be." " And time goes pretty quickly?"
" Time is very long, gentlemen, within these four walls ! "

He gazed about him—Heaven only knows how wearily !—
as he said these words ; and in the act of doing so, fell into
a strange stare as if he had forgotten something. A moment
afterwards he sighed heavily, put on his spectacles, and went
about his work again.

In another cell, there was a German, sentenced to five years'
imprisonment for larceny, two of which had just expired.
With colours procured in the same manner, he had painted
every inch of the walls and ceiling quite beautifully. He
had laid out the few feet of ground, behind, with exquisite
neatness, and had made a little bed in the centre, that looked
by-the-bye like a grave. The taste and ingenuity he had
displayed in everything were most extraordinary ; and yet a
more dejected, heart-broken, wretched creature, it would be
difficult to imagine. I never saw such a picture of forlorn
affliction and distress of mind. My heart bled for him ; and
when the tears ran down his cheeks, and he took one of the
visitors aside, to ask, with his trembling hands nervously
clutching at his coat to detain him, whether there was no
hope of his dismal sentence being commuted, the spectacle
was really too painful to witness. I never saw or heard of
any kind of misery that impressed me more than the wretchedness of this man.

In a third cell, was a tall strong black, a burglar, working at his proper trade of making screws and the like. His time was nearly out. He was not only a very dexterous thief, but was notorious for his boldness and hardihood, and for the number of his previous convictions. He entertained us with a long account of his achievements, which he narrated with such infinite relish, that he actually seemed to lick his lips as he told us racy anecdotes of stolen plate, and of old ladies whom he had watched as they sat at windows in silver spectacles (he had plainly had an eye to their metal even from the other side of the street) and had afterwards robbed. This fellow, upon the slightest encouragement, would have mingled with his professional recollections the most detestable cant ; but I am very much mistaken if he could have surpassed the unmitigated hypocrisy with which he declared that he blessed the day on which he came into that prison, and that he never would commit another robbery as long as he lived.

There was one man who was allowed, as an indulgence, to keep rabbits. His room having rather a close smell in consequence, they called to him at the door to come out into the passage. He complied of course, and stood shading his haggard face in the unwonted sunlight of the great window, looking as wan and unearthly as if he had been summoned from the grave. He had a white rabbit in his breast ; and when the little creature, getting down upon the ground, stole back into the cell, and he, being dismissed, crept timidly after it, I thought it would have been very hard to say in what respect the man was the nobler animal of the two.

There was an English thief, who had been there but a few days out of seven years : a villainous, low-browed, thin-lipped fellow, with a white face; who had as yet no relish for visitors, and who, but for the additional penalty, would have gladly stabbed me with his shoemaker's knife. There was another German who had entered the jail but yesterday, and who started from his bed when we looked in, and pleaded, in his broken English, very hard for work. There was a poet, who after doing two days' work in every four-and-twenty hours, one for himself and one for the prison, wrote verses about ships (he was by trade a mariner), and "the maddening wine-cup," and his friends at home. There were very many of them. Some reddened at the sight of visitors, and some turned very pale. Some two or three had prisoner nurses with them, for they were very sick; and one, a fat old negro whose leg had been taken off within the jail, had for his attendant a classical scholar and an accomplished surgeon, himself a prisoner likewise. Sitting upon the stairs, engaged in some slight work, was a pretty coloured boy. "Is there no refuge for young criminals in Philadelphia, then?" said I. "Yes, but only for white children." Noble aristocracy in crime!

There was a sailor who had been there upwards of eleven years, and who in a few months' time would be free. Eleven years of solitary confinement!

"I am very glad to hear your time is nearly out." What does he say? Nothing. Why does he stare at his hands, and pick the flesh upon his fingers, and raise his eyes for an instant, every now and then, to those bare walls which have seen his head turn grey? It is a way he has sometimes.

Does he never look men in the face, and does he always pluck at those hands of his, as though he were bent on parting skin and bone? It is his humour: nothing more.

It is his humour too, to say that he does not look forward to going out; that he is not glad the time is drawing near; that he did look forward to it once, but that was very long ago; that he has lost all care for everything. It is his humour to be a helpless, crushed, and broken man. And, Heaven be his witness that he has his humour thoroughly gratified!

There were three young women in adjoining cells, all convicted at the same time of a conspiracy to rob their prosecutor. In the silence and solitude of their lives they had grown to be quite beautiful. Their looks were very sad, and might have moved the sternest visitor to tears, but not to that kind of sorrow which the contemplation of the men awakens. One was a young girl; not twenty, as I recollect; whose snow-white room was hung with the work of some former prisoner, and upon whose downcast face the sun in all its splendour shone down through the high chink in the wall, where one narrow strip of bright blue sky was visible. She was very penitent and quiet; had come to be resigned, she said (and I believe her); and had a mind at peace. "In a word, you are happy here?" said one of my companions. She struggled—she did struggle very hard—to answer, Yes; but raising her eyes, and meeting that glimpse of freedom overhead, she burst into tears, and said, "She tried to be;

she uttered no complaint; but it was natural that she should sometimes long to go out of that one cell; she could not help *that*," she sobbed, poor thing!

I went from cell to cell that day; and every face I saw, or word I heard, or incident I noted, is present to my mind in all its painfulness. But let me pass them by, for one, more pleasant, glance of a prison on the same plan which I afterwards saw at Pittsburg.

When I had gone over that, in the same manner, I asked the governor if he had any person in his charge who was shortly going out. He had one, he said, whose time was up next day; but he had only been a prisoner two years.

Two years! I looked back through two years of my own life—out of jail, prosperous, happy, surrounded by blessings, comforts, good fortune—and thought how wide a gap it was, and how long those two years passed in solitary captivity would have been. I have the face of this man, who was going to be released next day, before me now. It is almost more memorable in its happiness than the other faces in their misery. How easy and how natural it was for him to say that the system was a good one; and that the time went "pretty quick—considering;" and that when a man once felt that he had offended the law, and must satisfy it, "he got along, somehow:" and so forth!

"What did he call you back to say to you, in that strange flutter?" I asked of my conductor, when he had locked the door and joined me in the passage.

"Oh! That he was afraid the soles of his boots were not fit for walking, as they were a good deal worn when he came in; and that he would thank me very much to have them mended, ready."

Those boots had been taken off his feet, and put away with the rest of his clothes, two years before!

I took that opportunity of inquiring how they conducted themselves immediately before going out; adding that I presumed they trembled very much.

"Well, it's not so much a trembling," was the answer—"though they do quiver—as a complete derangement of the nervous system. They can't sign their names to the book; sometimes can't even hold the pen; look about 'em without appearing to know why, or where they are; and sometimes get up and sit down again, twenty times in a minute. This is when they're in the office, where they are taken with the hood on, as they were brought in. When they get outside the gate, they stop, and look first one way and then the other; not knowing which to take. Sometimes they stagger as if they were drunk, and sometimes are forced to lean against the fence, they're so bad:—but they clear off in course of time."

As I walked among these solitary cells, and looked at the faces of the men within them, I tried to picture to myself the thoughts and feelings natural to their condition. I imagined the hood just taken off, and the scene of their captivity disclosed to them in all its dismal monotony.

At first, the man is stunned. His confinement is a hideous vision; and his old life a reality. He throws himself upon his bed, and lies there abandoned to despair. By degrees the insupportable solitude and barrenness of the place rouses him from this stupor, and when the trap in his grated door is opened, he humbly begs and prays for work. "Give me some work to do, or I shall go raving mad!"

He has it; and by fits and starts applies himself to labour; but every now and then there comes upon him a burning sense of the years that must be wasted in that stone coffin, and an agony so piercing in the recollection of those who are hidden from his view and knowledge, that he starts from his seat, and striding up and down the narrow room with both hands clasped on his uplifted head, hears spirits tempting him to beat his brains out on the wall.

Again he falls upon his bed, and lies there, moaning. Suddenly he starts up, wondering whether any other man is near; whether there is another cell like that on either side of him: and listens keenly.

There is no sound, but other prisoners may be near for all that. He remembers to have heard once, when he little thought of coming here himself, that the cells were so constructed that the prisoners could not hear each other, though the officers could hear them. Where is the nearest man— upon the right, or on the left? or is there one in both directions? Where is he sitting now—with his face to the light? or is he walking to and fro? How is he dressed? Has he been here long? Is he much worn away? Is he very white and spectre-like? Does *he* think of his neighbour too?

Scarcely venturing to breathe, and listening while he

The Solitary Prisoner

thinks, he conjures up a figure with his back towards him, and imagines it moving about in this next cell. He has no idea of the face, but he is certain of the dark form of a stooping man. In the cell upon the other side, he puts another figure, whose face is hidden from him also. Day after day, and often when he wakes up in the middle of the night, he thinks of these two men until he is almost distracted. He never changes them. There they are always as he first imagined them—an old man on the right; a younger man upon the left—whose hidden features torture him to death, and have a mystery that makes him tremble.

The weary days pass on with solemn pace, like mourners at a funeral; and slowly he begins to feel that the white walls of the cell have something dreadful in them : that their colour is horrible : that their smooth surface chills his blood : that there is one hateful corner which torments him. Every morning when he wakes, he hides his head beneath the coverlet, and shudders to see the ghastly ceiling looking down upon him. The blessed light of day itself peeps in, an ugly phantom face, through the unchangeable crevice which is his prison window.

By slow but sure degrees, the terrors of that hateful corner swell until they beset him at all times ; invade his rest, make his dreams hideous, and his nights dreadful. At first, he took a strange dislike to it ; feeling as though it gave birth in his brain to something of corresponding shape, which ought not to be there, and racked his head with pains. Then he began to fear it, then to dream of it, and of men whispering its name and pointing to it. Then he could not bear to look at it, nor yet to turn his back upon it. Now, it is every night the lurking-place of a ghost : a shadow :— a silent something, horrible to see, but whether bird, or beast, or muffled human shape, he cannot tell.

When he is in his cell by day, he fears the little yard without. When he is in the yard, he dreads to re-enter the cell. When night comes, there stands the phantom in the corner. If he have the courage to stand in its place, and drive it out (he had once : being desperate), it broods upon his bed. In the twilight, and always at the same hour, a voice calls to him by name ; as the darkness thickens. his Loom begins to live ; and even that, his comfort, is a hideous figure, watching him till daybreak.

Again, by slow degrees, these horrible fancies depart from

him one by one: returning sometimes, unexpectedly, but at longer intervals, and in less alarming shapes. He has talked upon religious matters with the gentleman who visits him, and has read his Bible, and has written a prayer upon his slate, and hung it up as a kind of protection, and an assurance of Heavenly companionship. He dreams now, sometimes, of his children or his wife, but is sure that they are dead, or have deserted him. He is easily moved to tears; is gentle, submissive, and broken-spirited. Occasionally, the old agony comes back: a very little thing will revive it; even a familiar sound, or the scent of summer flowers in the air; but it does not last long, now: for the world without, has come to be the vision, and this solitary life, the sad reality.

If his term of imprisonment be short—I mean comparatively, for short it cannot be—the last half year is almost worse than all; for then he thinks the prison will take fire and he be burnt in the ruins, or that he is doomed to die within the walls, or that he will be detained on some false charge and sentenced for another term: or that something, no matter what, must happen to prevent his going at large. And this is natural, and impossible to be reasoned against, because, after his long separation from human life, and his great suffering, any event will appear to him more probable in the contemplation, than the being restored to liberty and his fellow-creatures.

If his period of confinement has been very long, the prospect of release bewilders and confuses him. His broken heart may flutter for a moment, when he thinks of the world outside, and what it might have been to him in all those lonely years, but that is all. The cell-door has been closed too long on all its hopes and cares. Better to have hanged him in the beginning than bring him to this pass, and send him forth to mingle with his kind, who are his kind no more.

On the haggard face of every man among these prisoners, the same expression sat. I know not what to liken it to. It had something of that strained attention which we see upon the faces of the blind and deaf, mingled with a kind of horror, as though they had all been secretly terrified. In every little chamber that I entered, and at every grate through which I looked, I seemed to see the same appalling countenance. It lives in my memory, with the fascination of a remarkable picture. Parade before my eyes, a hundred men, with one among them newly released from this solitary suffering, and I would point him out.

The faces of the women, as I have said, it humanises and refines. Whether this be because of their better nature, which is elicited in solitude, or because of their being gentler creatures, of greater patience and longer suffering, I do not know ; but so it is. That the punishment is nevertheless, to my thinking, fully as cruel and as wrong in their case, as in that of the men, I need scarcely add.

My firm conviction is that, independent of the mental anguish it occasions—an anguish so acute and so tremendous, that all imagination of it must fall far short of the reality—it wears the mind into a morbid state, which renders it unfit for the rough contact and busy action of the world.   It is my fixed opinion that those who have undergone this punishment, MUST pass into society again morally unhealthy and diseased.   There are many instances on record, of men who have chosen, or have been condemned, to lives of perfect solitude, but I scarcely remember one, even among sages of strong and vigorous intellect, where its effect has not become apparent, in some disordered train of thought, or some gloomy hallucination.   What monstrous phantoms, bred of despondency and doubt, and born and reared in solitude, have stalked upon the earth, making creation ugly, and darkening the face of Heaven !

Suicides are rare among these prisoners : are almost, indeed, unknown.   But no argument in favour of the system, can reasonably be deduced from this circumstance, although it is very often urged.   All men who have made diseases of the mind their study, know perfectly well that such extreme depression and despair as will change the whole character, and beat down all its powers of elasticity and self-resistance, may be at work within a man, and yet stop short of self-destruction.   This is a common case.

That it makes the senses dull, and by degrees impairs the bodily faculties, I am quite sure.   I remarked to those who were with me in this very establishment at Philadelphia, that the criminals who had been there long, were deaf. They, who were in the habit of seeing these men constantly, were perfectly amazed at the idea, which they regarded as groundless and fanciful.   And yet the very first prisoner to whom they appealed—one of their own selection—confirmed my impression (which was unknown to him) instantly, and said, with a genuine air it was impossible to doubt, that he couldn't think how it happened, but he *was* growing very dull of hearing.

That it is a singularly unequal punishment, and affects the worst man least, there is no doubt. In its superior efficiency as a means of reformation, compared with that other code of regulations which allows the prisoners to work in company without communicating together, I have not the smallest faith. All the instances of reformation that were mentioned to me, were of a kind that might have been—and I have no doubt whatever, in my own mind, would have been— equally well brought about by the Silent System. With regard to such men as the negro burglar and the English thief, even the most enthusiastic have scarcely any hope of their conversion.

It seems to me that the objection that nothing wholesome or good has ever had its growth in such unnatural solitude, and that even a dog or any of the more intelligent among beasts, would pine, and mope, and rust away, beneath its influence, would be in itself a sufficient argument against this system. But when we recollect, in addition, how very cruel and severe it is, and that a solitary life is always liable to peculiar and distinct objections of a most deplorable nature, which have arisen here, and call to mind, moreover, that the choice is not between this system, and a bad or ill-considered one, but between it and another which has worked well, and is, in its whole design and practice, excellent ; there is surely more than sufficient reason for abandoning a mode of punishment attended by so little hope or promise, and fraught, beyond dispute, with such a host of evils.

As a relief to its contemplation, I will close this chapter with a curious story arising out of the same theme, which was related to me, on the occasion of this visit, by some of the gentlemen concerned.

At one of the periodical meetings of the inspectors of this prison, a working man of Philadelphia presented himself before the Board, and earnestly requested to be placed in solitary confinement. On being asked what motive could possibly prompt him to make this strange demand, he answered that he had an irresistible propensity to get drunk ; that he was constantly indulging it, to his great misery and ruin ; that he had no power of resistance ; that he wished to be put beyond the reach of temptation ; and that he could think of no better way than this.   It was pointed out to him, in reply, that the prison was for criminals who had been tried and sentenced by the law, and could not be made available for any such fanciful purposes ; he was exhorted to abstain from intoxicating drinks, as he surely might if he would ; and received other very good advice, with which he retired, exceedingly dissatisfied with the result of his application.

He came again, and again, and again, and was so very earnest and importunate, that at last they took counsel to· gether, and said, "He will certainly qualify himself for admission, if we reject him any more.   Let us shut him up. He will soon be glad to go away, and then we shall get rid of him."   So they made him sign a statement which would prevent his ever sustaining an action for false imprison-ment, to the effect that his incarceration was voluntary, and of his own seeking ; they requested him to take notice that the officer in attendance had orders to release him at any hour of the day or night, when he might knock upon his door for that purpose ; but desired him to understand, that once going out, he would not be admitted any more.   These con-ditions agreed upon, and he still remaining in the same mind, he was conducted to the prison, and shut up in one of the cells.

In this cell, the man, who had not the firmness to leave a glass of liquor standing untasted on a table before him—in this cell, in solitary confinement, and working every day at his trade of shoemaking, this man remained nearly two years. His health beginning to fail at the expiration of that time, the surgeon recommended that he should work occasionally in the garden ; and as he liked the notion very much, he went about this new occupation with great cheerfulness.

He was digging here, one summer day, very industriously, when the wicket in the outer gate chanced to be left open : showing, beyond, the well-remembered dusty road and sun·burnt fields.   The way was as free to him as to any man living, but he no sooner raised his head and caught sight of it, all shining in the light, than, with the involuntary instinct of a prisoner, he cast away his spade, scampered off as fast as his legs would carry him, and never once looked back.

CHAPTER VIII

WE left Philadelphia by steamboat, at six o'clock one very
cold morning, and turned our faces towards Washington.

In the course of this day's journey, as on subsequent occasions, we encountered some Englishmen (small farmers,
perhaps, or country publicans at home) who were settled in
America, and were travelling on their own affairs. Of all
grades and kinds of men that jostle one in the public con-
veyances of the States, these are often the most intolerable and
the most insufferable companions. United to every disagreeable characteristic that the worst kind of American travellers
possess, these countrymen of ours display an amount of
insolent conceit and cool assumption of superiority, quite
monstrous to behold. In the coarse familiarity of their approach, and the effrontery of their inquisitiveness (which
they are in great haste to assert, as if they panted to revenge
themselves upon the decent old restraints of home), they
surpass any native specimens that came within my range
of observation : and I often grew so patriotic when I saw
and heard them, that I would cheerfully have submitted to
a reasonable fine, if I could have given any other country
in the whole world, the honour of claiming them for its
children.

As Washington may be called the head-quarters of tobacco-
tinctured saliva, the time is come when I must confess,
without any disguise, that the prevalence of those two odious
practices of chewing and expectorating began about this time
to be anything but agreeable, and soon became most offensive
and sickening. In all the public places of America, this filthy
custom is recognised. In the courts of law, the judge has
his spittoon, the crier his, the witness his, and the prisoner
his ; while the jurymen and spectators are provided for, as

so many men who in the course of nature must desire to spit incessantly. In the hospitals, the students of medicine are requested, by notices upon the wall, to eject their tobacco juice into the boxes provided for that purpose, and not to discolour the stairs. In public buildings, visitors are implored, through the same agency, to squirt the essence of their quids, or "plugs," as I have heard them called by gentlemen learned in this kind of sweetmeat, into the national spittoons, and not about the bases of the marble columns. But in some parts, this custom is inseparably mixed up with every meal and morning call, and with all the transactions of social life. The stranger, who follows in the track I took myself, will find it in its full bloom and glory, luxuriant in all its alarming recklessness, at Washington. And let him not persuade himself (as I once did, to my shame) that previous tourists have exaggerated its extent. The thing itself is an exaggeration of nastiness, which cannot be outdone.

On board this steamboat, there were two young gentlemen, with shirt-collars reversed as usual, and armed with very big walking-sticks; who planted two seats in the middle of the deck, at a distance of some four paces apart; took out their tobacco-boxes; and sat down opposite each other, to chew. In less than a quarter of an hour's time, these hopeful youths had shed about them on the clean boards, a copious shower of yellow rain; clearing, by that means, a kind of magic circle, within whose limits no intruders dared to come, and which they never failed to refresh and re-refresh before a spot was dry. This being before breakfast, rather disposed me, I confess, to nausea; but looking attentively at one of the expectorators, I plainly saw that he was young in chewing, and felt inwardly uneasy, himself. A glow of delight came over me at this discovery; and as I marked his face turn paler and paler, and saw the ball of tobacco in his left cheek, quiver with his suppressed agony, while yet he spat, and chewed, and spat again, in emulation of his older friend, I could have fallen on his neck and implored him to go on for hours.

We all sat down to a comfortable breakfast in the cabin below, where there was no more hurry or confusion than at such a meal in England, and where there was certainly greater politeness exhibited than at most of our stage-coach banquets. At about nine o'clock we arrived at the railroad station, and went on by the cars. At noon we turned out again, to cross a wide river in another steamboat; landed at a continuation of the railroad on the opposite shore; and went on by other cars; in which, in the course of the next hour or so, we crossed by wooden bridges, each a mile in length, two creeks, called respectively Great and Little Gunpowder. The water in both was blackened with flights of canvas-backed ducks, which are most delicious eating, and abound hereabouts at that season of the year.

These bridges are of wood, have no parapet, and are only just wide enough for the passage of the trains; which, in the event of the smallest accident, would inevitably be plunged into the river. They are startling contrivances, and are most agreeable when passed.

We stopped to dine at Baltimore, and being now in Maryland, were waited on, for the first time, by slaves. The sensation of exacting any service from human creatures who are bought and sold, and being, for the time, a party as it were to their condition, is not an enviable one. The institution exists, perhaps, in its least repulsive and most mitigated form in such a town as this; but it *is* slavery; and though I was, with respect to it, an innocent man, its presence filled me with a sense of shame and self-reproach.

After dinner, we went down to the railroad again, and took our seats in the cars for Washington. Being rather early, those men and boys who happened to have nothing particular to do, and were curious in foreigners, came (according to custom) round the carriage in which I sat; let down all the windows; thrust in their heads and shoulders; hooked themselves on conveniently, by their elbows; and fell to comparing notes on the subject of my personal appearance, with as much indifference as if I were a stuffed figure. I never gained so much uncompromising information with reference to my own nose and eyes, and various impressions wrought by my mouth and chin on different minds, and how my head looks when it is viewed from behind, as on these occasions. Some gentlemen were only satisfied by exercising their sense of touch; and the boys (who are surprisingly precocious in America) were seldom satisfied, even by that, but would return to the charge over and over again. Many a budding president has walked into my room with his cap on his head and his hands in his pockets, and stared at me for two whole hours: occasionally refreshing himself with a tweak of his nose, or a draught from the water-jug; or by walking to the windows and inviting other boys in the street below, to come up and do likewise: crying, "Here he is!" "Come on!" "Bring all your brothers!" with other hospitable entreaties of that nature.

We reached Washington at about half-past six that evening. and had upon the way a beautiful view of the Capitol, which is a fine building of the Corinthian order, placed upon a noble and commanding eminence. Arrived at the hotel; I saw no more of the place that night; being very tired, and glad to get to bed.

Breakfast over next morning, I walk about the streets for an hour or two, and, coming home, throw up the window in the front and back, and look out. Here is Washington, fresh in my mind and under my eye.

Take the worst parts of the City Road and Pentonville. or the straggling outskirts of Paris, where the houses are smallest, preserving all their oddities, but especially the small shops and dwellings, occupied in Pentonville (but not in Washington) by furniture-brokers, keepers of poor eating-houses, and fanciers of birds. Burn the whole down; build it up again in wood and plaster; widen it a little; throw in part of St. John's Wood; put green blinds outside all the private houses, with a red curtain and a white one in every window; plough up all the roads; plant a great deal of coarse turf in every place where it ought *not* to be; erect three handsome buildings in stone and marble, anywhere, but the more entirely out of everybody's way the better; call one the Post Office, one the Patent Office, and one the Treasury; make it scorching hot in the morning, and freezing cold in the afternoon, with an occasional tornado of wind and dust; leave a brick-field without the bricks, in all central places where a street may naturally be expected; and that's Washington.

The hotel in which we live, is a long row of small houses fronting on the street, and opening at the back upon a common yard, in which hangs a great triangle. Whenever a servant is wanted, somebody beats on this triangle from one stroke up to seven, according to the number of the house in which his presence is required; and as all the servants are always being wanted, and none of them ever come, this enlivening engine is in full performance the whole day through. Clothes are drying in the same yard; female slaves, with cotton handkerchiefs twisted round their heads, are running to and fro on the hotel business; black waiters cross and recross with dishes in their hands; two great dogs are playing upon a mound of loose bricks in the centre of the little square; a pig is turning up his stomach to the sun, and grunting "that's comfortable!" and neither the men, nor the women, nor the dogs, nor the pig, nor any created creature, takes the smallest notice of the triangle, which is tingling madly all the time.

I walk to the front window, and look across the road upon a long, straggling row of houses, one story high, terminating, nearly opposite, but a little to the left, in a melancholy piece of waste ground with frowzy grass, which looks like a small piece of country that has taken to drinking, and has quite lost itself. Standing anyhow and all wrong, upon this open space, like something meteoric that has fallen down from the moon, is an odd, lop-sided, one-eyed kind of wooden building, that looks like a church, with a flag-staff as long as itself sticking out of a steeple something larger than a tea-chest. Under the window, is a small stand of coaches, whose slave-drivers are sunning themselves on the steps of our door, and talking idly together. The three most obtrusive houses near at hand, are the three meanest. On one—a shop, which never has anything in the window, and never has the door open—is painted in large characters, "THE CITY LUNCH." At another, which looks like a backway to somewhere else, but is an independent building in itself, oysters are procurable in every style. At the third, which is a very, very little tailor's shop, pants are fixed to order; or in other words, pantaloons are made to measure. And that is our street in Washington.

It is sometimes called the City of Magnificent Distances, but it might with greater propriety be termed the City of Magnificent Intentions; for it is only on taking a bird's-eye view of it from the top of the Capitol, that one can at all comprehend the vast designs of its projector, an aspiring Frenchman. Spacious avenues, that begin in nothing, and lead nowhere; streets, mile-long, that only want houses, roads and inhabitants; public buildings that need but a public to be complete; and ornaments of great thoroughfares, which only lack great thoroughfares to ornament—are its leading features. One might fancy the season over, and most of the houses gone out of town for ever with their

masters. To the admirers of cities it is a Barmecide Feast:
a pleasant field for the imagination to rove in; a monument
raised to a deceased project, with not even a legible inscription
to record its departed greatness.

Such as it is, it is likely to remain. It was originally
chosen for the seat of Government, as a means of averting
the conflicting jealousies and interests of the different States;
and very probably, too, as being remote from mobs; a consideration not to be slighted, even in America. It has no
trade or commerce of its own: having little or no population
beyond the President and his establishment; the members
of the legislature who reside there during the session; the
Government clerks and officers employed in the various
departments; the keepers of the hotels and boarding-houses;
and the tradesmen who supply their tables. It is very
unhealthy. Few people would live in Washington, I take it,
who were not obliged to reside there; and the tides of
emigration and speculation, those rapid and regardless
currents, are little likely to flow at any time towards such
dull and sluggish water.

The principal features of the Capitol, are, of course, the
two houses of Assembly. But there is, besides, in the
centre of the building, a fine rotunda, ninety-six feet in
diameter, and ninety-six high, whose circular wall is divided
into compartments, ornamented by historical pictures. Four
of these have for their subjects prominent events in the
revolutionary struggle. They were painted by Colonel Trum-
bull, himself a member of Washington's staff at the time of
their occurrence; from which circumstance they derive a
peculiar interest of their own. In this same hall Mr.
Greenough's large statue of Washington has been lately
placed. It has great merits of course, but it struck me as
being rather strained and violent for its subject. I could
wish, however, to have seen it in a better light than it can
ever be viewed in, where it stands.

There is a very pleasant and commodious library in the
Capitol; and from a balcony in front, the bird's-eye view, of
which I have just spoken, may be had, together with a
beautiful prospect of the adjacent country. In one of the
ornamented portions of the building, there is a figure of
Justice; whereunto the Guide Book says, "the artist at first
contemplated giving more of nudity, but he was warned that
the public sentiment of this country would not admit of it,

and in his caution he has gone, perhaps, into the opposite extreme." Poor Justice! she has been made to wear much stranger garments in America than those she pines in, in the Capitol. Let us hope that she has changed her dressmaker since they were fashioned, and that the public sentiment of the country did not cut out the clothes she hides her lovely figure in, just now.

The House of Representatives is a beautiful and spacious hall, of semicircular shape, supported by handsome pillars. One part of the gallery is appropriated to the ladies, and there they sit in front rows, and come in, and go out, as at a play or concert. The chair is canopied, and raised considerably above the floor of the House; and every member has an easy chair and a writing-desk to himself: which is denounced by some people out of doors as a most unfortunate and injudicious arrangement, tending to long sittings and prosaic speeches. It is an elegant chamber to look at, but a singularly bad one for all purposes of hearing. The Senate, which is smaller, is free from this objection, and is exceedingly well adapted to the uses for which it is designed. The sittings, I need hardly add, take place in the day; and the parliamentary forms are modelled on those of the old country.

I was sometimes asked, in my progress through other places, whether I had not been very much impressed by the *heads* of the law-makers at Washington; meaning not their chiefs and leaders, but literally their individual and personal heads, whereon their hair grew, and whereby the phrenological character of each legislator was expressed: and I almost as often struck my questioner dumb with indignant consternation by answering "No, that I didn't remember being at all overcome." As I must, at whatever hazard, repeat the avowal here, I will follow it up by relating my impressions on this subject in as few words as possible.

In the first place—it may be from some imperfect development of my organ of veneration—I do not remember having ever fainted away, or having even been moved to tears of joyful pride, at sight of any legislative body. I have borne the House of Commons like a man, and have yielded to no weakness, but slumber, in the House of Lords. I have seen elections for borough and county, and have never been impelled (no matter which party won) to damage my hat by throwing it up into the air in triumph, or to crack my

voice by shouting forth any reference to our Glorious Con-
stitution, to the noble purity of our independent voters, or,
the unimpeachable integrity of our independent members.
Having withstood such strong attacks upon my fortitude, it
is possible that I may be of a cold and insensible temperament, amounting to iciness, in such matters ; and therefore
my impressions of the live pillars of the Capitol at Washington must be received with such grains of allowance as this
free confession may seem to demand.

Did I see in this public body an assemblage of men, bound
together in the sacred names of Liberty and Freedom, and
so asserting the chaste dignity of those twin goddesses, in all
their discussions, as to exalt at once the Eternal Principles
to which their names are given, and their own character and
the character of their countrymen, in the admiring eyes of
the whole world ?

It was but a week, since an aged, grey-haired man, a
lasting honour to the land that gave him birth, who has
done good service to his country, as his forefathers did, and
who will be remembered scores upon scores of years after
the worms bred in its corruption, are but so many grains of
dust—it was but a week, since this old man had stood for
days upon his trial before this very body, charged with
having dared to assert the infamy of that traffic, which has
for its accursed merchandise men and women, and their
unborn children. Yes. And publicly exhibited in the same
city all the while ; gilded, framed and glazed ; hung up for
general admiration ; shown to strangers not with shame, but
pride ; its face not turned towards the wall, itself not taken
down and burned ; is the Unanimous Declaration of the
Thirteen United States of America, which solemnly declares
that All Men are created Equal ; and are endowed by their
Creator with the Inalienable Rights of Life, Liberty, and the
Pursuit of Happiness !

It was not a month, since this same body had sat calmly
by, and heard a man, one of themselves, with oaths which
beggars in their drink reject, threaten to cut another's throat
from ear to ear.   There he sat, among them ; not crushed
by the general feeling of the assembly, but as good a man
as any.

There was but a week to come, and another of that body,
for doing his duty to those who sent him there ; for claiming
in a Republic the Liberty and Freedom of expressing their

sentiments, and making known their prayer; would be tried, found guilty, and have strong censure passed upon him by the rest.   His was a grave offence indeed; for years before, he had risen up and said, "A gang of male and female slaves for sale, warranted to breed like cattle, linked to each other by iron fetters, are passing now along the open street beneath the windows of your Temple of Equality!   Look!"   But there are many kinds of hunters engaged in the Pursuit of Happiness, and they go variously armed.   It is the Inalienable Right of some among them, to take the field after *their* Happiness equipped with cat and cartwhip, stocks, and iron collar, and to shout their view halloa! (always in praise of Liberty) to the music of clanking chains and bloody stripes.

Where sat the many legislators of coarse threats; of words and blows such as coalheavers deal upon each other, when they forget their breeding?   On every side.   Every session had its anecdotes of that kind, and the actors were all there.

Did I recognise in this assembly, a body of men, who, applying themselves in a new world to correct some of the falsehoods and vices of the old, purified the avenues to Public Life, paved the dirty ways to Place and Power, debated and made laws for the Common Good, and had no party but their Country?

I saw in them, the wheels that move the meanest perversion of virtuous Political Machinery that the worst tools ever wrought.   Despicable trickery at elections; under-handed tamperings with public officers; cowardly attacks upon opponents, with scurrilous newspapers for shields, and hired pens for daggers; shameful trucklings to mercenary knaves, whose claim to be considered, is, that every day and week they sow new crops of ruin with their venal types, which are the dragon's teeth of yore, in everything but sharpness; aidings and abettings of every bad inclination in the popular mind, and artful suppressions of all its good influences: such things as these, and in a word, Dishonest Faction in its most depraved and most unblushing form, stared out from every corner of the crowded hall.

Did I see among them, the intelligence and refinement: the true, honest, patriotic heart of America?   Here and there, were drops of its blood and life, but they scarcely coloured the stream of desperate adventurers which sets that way for profit and for pay.   It is the game of these men, and

of their profligate organs, to make the strife of politics so
fierce and brutal, and so destructive of all self-respect in
worthy men, that sensitive and delicate-minded persons shall
be kept aloof, and they, and such as they, be left to battle
out their selfish views unchecked.   And thus this lowest of
all scrambling fights goes on, and they who in other countries
would, from their intelligence and station, most aspire to make
the laws, do here recoil the farthest from that degradation.

That there are, among the representatives of the people
in both Houses, and among all parties, some men of high
character and great abilities, I need not say.   The foremost
among those politicians who are known in Europe, have been
already described, and I see no reason to depart from the
rule I have laid down for my guidance, of abstaining from
all mention of individuals.   It will be sufficient to add, that
to the most favourable accounts that have been written of
them, I more than fully and most heartily subscribe ; and
that personal intercourse and free communication have bred
within me, not the result predicted in the very doubtful
proverb, but increased admiration and respect.   They are
striking men to look at, hard to deceive, prompt to act, lions
in energy, Crichtons in varied accomplishments, Indians in
fire of eye and gesture, Americans in strong and generous
impulse ; and they as well represent the honour and wisdom
of their country at home, as the distinguished gentleman who
is now its Minister at the British Court sustains its highest
character abroad.

I visited both houses nearly every day, during my stay
in Washington.   On my initiatory visit to the House of
Representatives, they divided against a decision of the chair ;
but the chair won.   The second time I went, the member
who was speaking, being interrupted by a laugh, mimicked
it, as one child would in quarrelling with another, and
added, "that he would make honourable gentlemen opposite,
sing out a little more on the other side of their mouths
presently."   But interruptions are rare ; the speaker being
usually heard in silence.   There are more quarrels than
with us, and more threatenings than gentlemen are accustomed to exchange in any civilised society of which we have
record : but farm-yard imitations have not as yet been imported from the Parliament of the United Kingdom.   The
feature in oratory which appears to be the most practised,
and most relished, is the constant repetition of the same

idea or shadow of an idea in fresh words; and the inquiry out of doors is not, "What did he say?" but, "How long did he speak?" These, however, are but enlargements of a principle which prevails elsewhere.

The Senate is a dignified and decorous body, and its proceedings are conducted with much gravity and order. Both houses are handsomely carpeted; but the state to which these carpets are reduced by the universal disregard of the spittoon with which every honourable member is accommodated, and the extraordinary improvements on the pattern which are squirted and dabbled upon it in every direction, do not admit of being described. I will merely observe, that I strongly recommend all strangers not to look at the floor; and if they happen to drop anything, though it be their purse, not to pick it up with an ungloved hand on any account.

It is somewhat remarkable too, at first, to say the least, to see so many honourable members with swelled faces; and it is scarcely less remarkable to discover that this appearance is caused by the quantity of tobacco they contrive to stow within the hollow of the cheek. It is strange enough too, to see an honourable gentleman leaning back in his tilted chair with his legs on the desk before him, shaping a convenient "plug" with his penknife, and when it is quite ready for use, shooting the old one from his mouth, as from a pop-gun, and clapping the new one in its place.

I was surprised to observe that even steady old chewers of great experience, are not always good marksmen, which has rather inclined me to doubt that general proficiency with the rifle, of which we have heard so much in England. Several gentlemen called upon me who, in the course of conversation, frequently missed the spittoon at five paces; and one (but he was certainly short-sighted) mistook the closed sash for the open window, at three. On another occasion, when I dined out, and was sitting with two ladies and some gentlemen round a fire before dinner, one of the company fell short of the fireplace, six distinct times. I am disposed to think, however, that this was occasioned by his not aiming at that object; as there was a white marble hearth before the fender, which was more convenient, and may have suited his purpose better.

The Patent Office at Washington, furnishes an extraordinary example of American enterprise and ingenuity; for

the immense number of models it contains, are the accumu-
lated inventions of only five years; the whole of the
previous collection having been destroyed by fire. The
elegant structure in which they are arranged, is one of
design rather than execution, for there is but one side erected
out of four, though the works are stopped. The Post Office
is a very compact and very beautiful building. In one of
the departments, among a collection of rare and curious
articles, are deposited the presents which have been made
from time to time to the American ambassadors at foreign
courts by the various potentates to whom they were the
accredited agents of the Republic; gifts which by the law
they are not permitted to retain. I confess that I looked
upon this as a very painful exhibition, and one by no means
flattering to the national standard of honesty and honour.
That can scarcely be a high state of moral feeling which
imagines a gentleman of repute and station, likely to be
corrupted, in the discharge of his duty, by the present of
a snuff-box, or a richly-mounted sword, or an Eastern shawl;
and surely the Nation who reposes confidence in her appointed servants, is likely to be better served, than she
who makes them the subject of such very mean and paltry
suspicions.

At George Town, in the suburbs, there is a Jesuit College;
delightfully situated, and, so far as I had an opportunity of
seeing, well managed. Many persons who are not members
of the Romish Church, avail themselves, I believe, of these
institutions, and of the advantageous opportunities they
afford for the education of their children. The heights of
this neighbourhood, above the Potomac River, are very
picturesque: and are free, I should conceive, from some of
the insalubrities of Washington. The air, at that elevation,
was quite cool and refreshing, when in the city it was
burning hot.

The President's mansion is more like an English club-
house, both within and without, than any other kind of
establishment with which I can compare it. The ornamental
ground about it has been laid out in garden walks; they are
pretty, and agreeable to the eye; though they have that
uncomfortable air of having been made yesterday, which is
far from favourable to the display of such beauties.

My first visit to this house was on the morning after my
arrival, when I was carried thither by an official gentleman,

who was so kind as to charge himself with my presentation to the President.

We entered a large hall, and having twice or thrice rung a bell which nobody answered, walked without further ceremony through the rooms on the ground floor, as divers other gentlemen (mostly with their hats on, and their hands in their pockets) were doing very leisurely. Some of these had ladies with them, to whom they were showing the premises; others were lounging on the chairs and sofas; others, in a perfect state of exhaustion from listlessness, were yawning drearily. The greater portion of this assemblage were rather asserting their supremacy than doing anything else, as they had no particular business there, that anybody knew of. A few were closely eyeing the movables, as if to make quite sure that the President (who was far from popular) had not made away with any of the furniture, or sold the fixtures for his private benefit.

After glancing at these loungers; who were scattered over a pretty drawing-room, opening upon a terrace which commanded a beautiful prospect of the river and the adjacent country; and who were sauntering, too, about a larger state-room called the Eastern Drawing-room; we went upstairs into another chamber, where were certain visitors, waiting for audiences. At sight of my conductor, a black in plain clothes and yellow slippers who was gliding noiselessly about, and whispering messages in the ears of the more impatient, made a sign of recognition, and glided off to announce him.

We had previously looked into another chamber fitted all round with a great bare wooden desk or counter, whereon lay files of newspapers, to which sundry gentlemen were referring. But there were no such means of beguiling the time in this apartment, which was as unpromising and tiresome as any waiting-room in one of our public establishments, or any physician's dining-room during his hours of consultation at home.

There were some fifteen or twenty persons in the room. One, a tall, wiry, muscular old man, from the west; sunburnt and swarthy; with a brown white hat on his knees, and a giant umbrella resting between his legs; who sat bolt upright in his chair, frowning steadily at the carpet, and twitching the hard lines about his mouth, as if he had made up his mind "to fix" the President on what he had to say, and wouldn't bate him a grain. Another, a Kentucky farmer, six-feet-six in height, with his hat on, and his hands under his coat-tails, who leaned against the wall and kicked the floor with his heel, as though he had Time's head under his shoe, and were literally "killing" him. A third, an oval-faced, bilious-looking man, with sleek black hair cropped close, and whiskers and beard shaved down to blue dots, who sucked the head of a thick stick, and from time to time took it out of his mouth, to see how it was getting on. A fourth did nothing but whistle. A fifth did nothing but spit. And indeed all these gentlemen were so very persevering and energetic in this latter particular, and bestowed their favours so abundantly upon the carpet, that I take it for granted the Presidential housemaids have high wages, or, to speak more genteelly, an ample amount of "compensation:" which is the American word for salary, in the case of all public servants.

We had not waited in this room many minutes, before the black messenger returned, and conducted us into another of smaller dimensions, where, at a business-like table covered with papers, sat the President himself. He looked somewhat worn and anxious, and well he might; being at war with everybody—but the expression of his face was mild and pleasant, and his manner was remarkably unaffected, gentlemanly, and agreeable. I thought that in his whole carriage and demeanour, he became his station singularly well.

Being advised that the sensible etiquette of the republican court, admitted of a traveller, like myself, declining, without any impropriety, an invitation to dinner, which did not reach me until I had concluded my arrangements for leaving Washington some days before that to which it referred, I only returned to this house once. It was on the occasion of one of those general assemblies which are held on certain nights, between the hours of nine and twelve o'clock, and are called, rather oddly, Levees.

I went, with my wife, at about ten. There was a pretty dense crowd of carriages and people in the court-yard, and so far as I could make out, there were no very clear regulations for the taking up or setting down of company. There were certainly no policemen to soothe startled horses, either by sawing at their bridles or flourishing truncheons in their eyes; and I am ready to make oath that no inoffensive persons were knocked violently on the head, or poked acutely in their backs or stomachs; or brought to a stand-still by any such gentle means, and then taken into custody for not moving on. But there was no confusion or disorder. Our carriage reached the porch in its turn, without any blustering, swearing, shouting, backing, or other disturbance : and we dismounted with as much ease and comfort as though we had been escorted by the whole Metropolitan Force from A to Z inclusive.

The suite of rooms on the ground-floor, were lighted up ; and a military band was playing in the hall. In the smaller drawing-room, the centre of a circle of company, were the President and his daughter-in-law, who acted as the lady of the mansion ; and a very interesting, graceful, and accomplished lady too. One gentleman who stood among this group, appeared to take upon himself the functions of a master of the ceremonies. I saw no other officers or attendants, and none were needed.

The great drawing-room, which I have already mentioned, and the other chambers on the ground-floor, were crowded to excess. The company was not, in our sense of the term, select, for it comprehended persons of very many grades and classes ; nor was there any great display of costly attire : indeed, some of the costumes may have been, for aught I know, grotesque enough. But the decorum and propriety of behaviour which prevailed, were unbroken by any rude or disagreeable incident ; and every man, even among the miscellaneous crowd in the hall who were admitted without any orders or tickets to look on, appeared to feel that he was a part of the Institution, and was responsible for its preserving a becoming character, and appearing to the best advantage.

That these visitors, too, whatever their station, were not without some refinement of taste and appreciation of intellectual gifts, and gratitude to those men who, by the peaceful exercise of great abilities, shed new charms and associations upon the homes of their countrymen, and elevate their character in other lands, was most earnestly testified by their reception of Washington Irving, my dear friend, who had recently been appointed Minister at the court of Spain, and who was among them that night, in his new character, for the first and last time before going abroad. I sincerely believe that in all the madness of American politics, few public men would have been so earnestly, devotedly, and affectionately caressed, as this most charming writer : and I have seldom respected a public assembly more, than I did this eager throng, when I saw them turning with one mind from noisy orators

and officers of state, and flocking with a generous and honest
impulse round the man of quiet pursuits : proud in his pro-
motion as reflecting back upon their country : and grateful to
him with their whole hearts for the store of graceful fancies
he had poured out among them. Long may he dispense such
treasures with unsparing hand ; and long may they remember him as worthily !

The term we had assigned for the duration of our stay in
Washington, was now at an end, and we were to begin to
travel ; for the railroad distances we had traversed yet, in
journeying among these older towns, are on that great
continent looked upon as nothing.

I had at first intended going South—to Charleston. But
when I came to consider the length of time which this journey
would occupy, and the premature heat of the season, which
even at Washington had been often very trying ; and weighed
moreover, in my own mind, the pain of living in the constant
contemplation of slavery, against the more than doubtful
chances of my ever seeing it, in the time I had to spare,
stripped of the disguises in which it would certainly be
dressed, and so adding any item to the host of facts already
heaped together on the subject ; I began to listen to old
whisperings which had often been present to me at home in
England, when I little thought of ever being here ; and to
dream again of cities growing up, like palaces in fairy tales,
among the wilds and forests of the west.

The advice I received in most quarters when I began to yield
to my desire of travelling towards that point of the compass
was, according to custom, sufficiently cheerless : my companion
being threatened with more perils, dangers, and discomforts,
than I can remember or would catalogue if I could ; but of
which it will be sufficient to remark that blowings-up in
steamboats and breakings-down in coaches were among the
least. But, having a western route sketched out for me by
the best and kindest authority to which I could have resorted,
and putting no great faith in these discouragements, I soon
determined on my plan of action.

This was to travel south, only to Richmond in Virginia ;
and then to turn, and shape our course for the Far West ;
whither I beseech the reader's company, in a new chapter.

CHAPTER IX

A NIGHT STEAMER ON THE POTOMAC RIVER. VIRGINIA
ROAD, AND A BLACK DRIVER. RICHMOND. BALTIMORE.
THE HARRISBURG MAIL, AND A GLIMPSE OF THE CITY.
A CANAL BOAT

WE were to proceed in the first instance by steamboat; and
as it is usual to sleep on board, in consequence of the starting-
hour being four o'clock in the morning, we went down to
where she lay, at that very uncomfortable time for such
expeditions when slippers are most valuable, and a familiar
bed, in the perspective of an hour or two, looks uncommonly
pleasant.

It is ten o'clock at night: say half-past ten: moonlight,
warm, and dull enough. The steamer (not unlike a child's
Noah's ark in form, with the machinery on the top of the
roof) is riding lazily up and down, and bumping clumsily
against the wooden pier, as the ripple of the river trifles with
its unwieldy carcase. The wharf is some distance from the
city. There is nobody down here; and one or two dull lamps
upon the steamer's decks are the only signs of life remaining,
when our coach has driven away. As soon as our footsteps
are heard upon the planks, a fat negress, particularly favoured
by nature in respect of bustle, emerges from some dark stairs,
and marshals my wife towards the ladies' cabin, to which
retreat she goes, followed by a mighty bale of cloaks and
great-coats. I valiantly resolve not to go to bed at all, but to
walk up and down the pier till morning.

I begin my promenade—thinking of all kinds of distant
things and persons, and of nothing near—and pace up and
down for half-an-hour. Then I go on board again; and getting into the light of one of the lamps, look at my watch and
think it must have stopped; and wonder what has become of
the faithful secretary whom I brought along with me from
Boston. He is supping with our late landlord (a Field Mar-

shal, at least, no doubt) in honour of our departure, and may
be two hours longer. I walk again, but it gets duller and
duller : the moon goes down : next June seems farther off in
the dark, and the echoes of my footsteps make me nervous.
It has turned cold too ; and walking up and down without my
companion in such lonely circumstances, is but poor amusement. So I break my staunch resolution, and think it may
be, perhaps, as well to go to bed.

I go on board again ; open the door of the gentlemen's
cabin ; and walk in. Somehow or other—from its being so
quiet, I suppose—I have taken it into my head that there
is nobody there. To my horror and amazement it is full of
sleepers in every stage, shape, attitude, and variety of slumber :
in the berths, on the chairs, on the floors, on the tables, and
particularly round the stove, my detested enemy. I take
another step forward, and slip on the shining face of a black
steward, who lies rolled in a blanket on the floor. He jumps
up, grins, half in pain and half in hospitality ; whispers my
own name in my ear ; and groping among the sleepers, leads
me to my berth. Standing beside it, I count these slumbering passengers, and get past forty. There is no use in going
further, so I begin to undress. As the chairs are all occupied,
and there is nothing else to put my clothes on, I deposit
them upon the ground : not without soiling my hands, for it
is in the same condition as the carpets in the Capitol, and
from the same cause. Having but partially undressed, I
clamber on my shelf, and hold the curtain open for a few
minutes while I look round on all my fellow-travellers again.
That done, I let it fall on them, and on the world : turn
round : and go to sleep.

I wake, of course, when we get under weigh, for there is a
good deal of noise. The day is then just breaking. Everybody wakes at the same time. Some are self-possessed directly,
and some are much perplexed to make out where they are
until they have rubbed their eyes, and leaning on one elbow,
looked about them. Some yawn, some groan, nearly all spit,
and a few get up. I am among the risers : for it is easy to
feel, without going into the fresh air, that the atmosphere of
the cabin is vile in the last degree. I huddle on my clothes,
go down into the fore-cabin, get shaved by the barber, and
wash myself. The washing and dressing apparatus for the
passengers generally, consists of two jack-towels, three small
wooden basins, a keg of water and a ladle to serve it out

with, six square inches of looking-glass, two ditto ditto of yellow soap, a comb and brush for the head, and nothing for the teeth. Everybody uses the comb and brush, except myself. Everybody stares to see me using my own ; and two or three gentlemen are strongly disposed to banter me on my prejudices, but don't. When I have made my toilet, I go upon the hurricane-deck, and set in for two hours of hard walking up and down. The sun is rising brilliantly ; we are passing Mount Vernon, where Washington lies buried ; the river is wide and rapid ; and its banks are beautiful. All the glory and splendour of the day are coming on, and growing brighter every minute.

At eight o'clock, we breakfast in the cabin where I passed the night, but the windows and doors are all thrown open, and now it is fresh enough. There is no hurry or greediness apparent in the dispatch of the meal. It is longer than a travelling breakfast with us ; more orderly, and more polite.

Soon after nine o'clock we come to Potomac Creek, where we are to land ; and then comes the oddest part of the journey. Seven stage-coaches are preparing to carry us on. Some of them are ready, some of them are not ready. Some of the drivers are blacks, some whites. There are four horses to each coach, and all the horses, harnessed or unharnessed, are there. The passengers are getting out of the steamboat, and into the coaches ; the luggage is being transferred in noisy wheelbarrows ; the horses are frightened, and impatient to start ; the black drivers are chattering to them like so many monkeys ; and the white ones whooping like so many drovers : for the main thing to be done in all kinds of hostlering here, is to make as much noise as possible. The coaches are something like the French coaches, but not nearly so good. In lieu of springs, they are hung on bands of the strongest leather. There is very little choice or difference between them ; and they may be likened to the car portion of the swings at an English fair, roofed, put upon axle-trees and wheels, and curtained with painted canvas. They are covered with mud from the roof to the wheel-tire, and have never been cleaned since they were first built.

The tickets we have received on board the steamboat are marked No. 1, so we belong to coach No. 1. I throw my coat on the box, and hoist my wife and her maid into the inside. It has only one step, and that being about a yard from the ground, is usually approached by a chair: when there is no chair, ladies trust in Providence. The coach holds nine inside, having a seat across from door to door, where we in England put our legs: so that there is only one feat more difficult in the performance than getting in, and that is, getting out again. There is only one outside passenger, and he sits upon the box. As I am that one, I climb up; and while they are strapping the luggage on the roof, and heaping it into a kind of tray behind, have a good opportunity of looking at the driver.

He is a negro—very black indeed. He is dressed in a coarse pepper-and-salt suit excessively patched and darned (particularly at the knees), grey stockings, enormous un-blacked high-low shoes, and very short trousers. He has two odd gloves: one of parti-coloured worsted, and one of leather. He has a very short whip, broken in the middle and ban-daged up with string. And yet he wears a low-crowned, broad-brimmed, black hat: faintly shadowing forth a kind of insane imitation of an English coachman! But somebody in authority cries "Go ahead!" as I am making these observa-tions. The mail takes the lead in a four-horse waggon, and all the coaches follow in procession: headed by No. i.

By-the-way, whenever an Englishman would cry "All right!" an American cries "Go ahead!" which is somewhat expressive of the national character of the two countries.

The first half-mile of the road is over bridges made of loose planks laid across two parallel poles, which tilt up as the wheels roll over them; and in the river. The river has a clayey bottom and is full of holes, so that half a horse is constantly disappearing unexpectedly, and can't be found again for some time.

But we get past even this, and come to the road itself, which is a series of alternate swamps and gravel-pits. A tremendous place is close before us, the black driver rolls his eyes, screws his mouth up very round, and looks straight between the two leaders, as if he were saying to himself, "We have done this often before, but *now* I think we shall have a crash." He takes a rein in each hand; jerks and pulls at both; and dances on the splashboard with both feet (keeping his seat, of course) like the late lamented Ducrow on two of his fiery coursers. We come to the spot, sink down in the mire nearly to the coach windows, tilt on one side at an angle of forty-five degrees, and stick there. The insides scream dismally; the coach stops; the horses flounder;

all the other six coaches stop; and their four-and-twenty
horses flounder likewise : but merely for company, and in
sympathy with ours. Then the following circumstances occur.

BLACK DRIVER (to the horses).   " Hi ! "

Nothing happens.   Insides scream again.

BLACK DRIVER (to the horses).   " Ho ! "

Horses plunge, and splash the black driver.

GENTLEMAN INSIDE (looking out).   "Why, what on airth—"

Gentleman receives a variety of splashes and draws his
head in again, without finishing his question or waiting for
an answer.

BLACK DRIVER (still to the horses).   " Jiddy ! Jiddy ! "

Horses pull violently, drag the coach out of the hole, and
draw it up a bank ; so steep, that the black driver's legs fly
up into the air, and he goes back among the luggage on the
roof.   But he immediately recovers himself, and cries (still
to the horses),

" Pill ! "

No effect.   On the contrary, the coach begins to roll back
upon No. 2, which rolls back upon No. 3, which rolls back
upon No. 4, and so on, until No. 7 is heard to curse and
swear, nearly a quarter of a mile behind.

BLACK DRIVER (louder than before).   " Pill ! "

Horses make another struggle to get up the bank, and
again the coach rolls backward.

BLACK DRIVER (louder than before).   " Pe-e-e-ill ! "

Horses make a desperate struggle.

BLACK DRIVER (recovering spirits).   " Hi, Jiddy, Jiddy,
Pill ! "

Horses make another effort.

BLACK DRIVER (with great vigour).   " Ally Loo ! Hi.
Jiddy, Jiddy.   Pill.   Ally Loo ! "

Horses almost do it.

BLACK DRIVER (with his eyes starting out of his head).
" Lee, den.   Lee, dere.   Hi.   Jiddy, Jiddy.   Pill.   Ally Loo.
Lee-e-e-e-e ! "

They run up the bank, and go down again on the other
side at a fearful pace.   It is impossible to stop them, and at
the bottom there is a deep hollow, full of water.   The coach
rolls frightfully.   The insides scream.   The mud and water
fly about us.   The black driver dances like a madman.
Suddenly we are all right by some extraordinary means, and
stop to breathe.

A black friend of the black driver is sitting on a fence. The black driver recognises him by twirling his head round and round like a harlequin, rolling his eyes, shrugging his shoulders, and grinning from ear to ear. He stops short, turns to me, and says:

"We shall get you through sa, like a fiddle, and hope a please you when we get you through sa. Old 'ooman at home sa:" chuckling very much. "Outside gentleman sa, he often remember old 'ooman at home sa," grinning again.

"Ay ay, we'll take care of the old woman. Don't be afraid."

The black driver grins again, but there is another hole, and beyond that, another bank, close before us. So he stops short: cries (to the horses again) "Easy. Easy den. Ease. Steady. Hi. Jiddy. Pill. Ally. Loo," but never "Lee!" until we are reduced to the very last extremity, and are in the midst of difficulties, extrication from which appears to be all but impossible.

And so we do the ten miles or thereabouts in two hours and a half; breaking no bones, though bruising a great many; and in short getting through the distance, "like a fiddle."

This singular kind of coaching terminates at Fredericksburgh, whence there is a railway to Richmond. The tract of country through which it takes its course was once productive; but the soil has been exhausted by the system of employing a great amount of slave labour in forcing crops, without strengthening the land: and it is now little better than a sandy desert overgrown with trees. Dreary and uninteresting as its aspect is, I was glad to the heart to find anything on which one of the curses of this horrible institution has fallen; and had greater pleasure in contemplating the withered ground, than the richest and most thriving cultivation in the same place could possibly have afforded me.

In this district, as in all others where slavery sits brooding, (I have frequently heard this admitted, even by those who are its warmest advocates:) there is an air of ruin and decay abroad, which is inseparable from the system. The barns and outhouses are mouldering away; the sheds are patched and half roofless; the log cabins (built in Virginia with external chimneys made of clay or wood) are squalid in the last degree. There is no look of decent comfort anywhere. The miserable stations by the railway side; the great wild wood-yards, whence the engine is supplied with fuel; the negro children rolling on the ground before the cabin doors, with dogs and pigs; the biped beasts of burden slinking past: gloom and dejection are upon them all.

In the negro car belonging to the train in which we made this journey, were a mother and her children who had just been purchased; the husband and father being left behind with their old owner. The children cried the whole way, and the mother was misery's picture. The champion of Life, Liberty, and the Pursuit of Happiness, who had bought them, rode in the same train; and, every time we stopped, got down to see that they were safe. The black in Sinbad's Travels with one eye in the middle of his forehead which shone like a burning coal, was nature's aristocrat compared with this white gentleman.

It was between six and seven o'clock in the evening, when we drove to the hotel: in front of which, and on the top of the broad flight of steps leading to the door, two or three citizens were balancing themselves on rocking-chairs, and smoking cigars. We found it a very large and elegant establishment, and were as well entertained as travellers need desire to be. The climate being a thirsty one, there was never, at any hour of the day, a scarcity of loungers in the spacious bar, or a cessation of the mixing of cool liquors: but they were a merrier people here, and had musical instruments playing to them o' nights, which it was a treat to hear again.

The next day, and the next, we rode and walked about the town, which is delightfully situated on eight hills, overhanging James River; a sparkling stream, studded here and there with bright islands, or brawling over broken rocks. Although it was yet but the middle of March, the weather in this southern temperature was extremely warm; the peach-trees and magnolias were in full bloom; and the trees were green. In a low ground among the hills, is a valley known as "Bloody Run," from a terrible conflict with the Indians which once occurred there. It is a good place for such a struggle, and, like every other spot I saw associated with any legend of that wild people now so rapidly fading from the earth, interested me very much.

The city is the seat of the local parliament of Virginia; and in its shady legislative halls, some orators were drowsily holding forth to the hot noon day. By dint of constant

Black and White

repetition, however, these constitutional sights had very little
more interest for me than so many parochial vestries ; and I
was glad to exchange this one for a lounge in a well-arranged
public library of some ten thousand volumes, and a visit to
a tobacco manufactory, where the workmen are all slaves.

I saw in this place the whole process of picking, rolling,
pressing, drying, packing in casks, and branding. All the
tobacco thus dealt with, was in course of manufacture for
chewing ; and one would have supposed there was enough in
that one storehouse to have filled even the comprehensive
jaws of America. In this form, the weed looks like the oil-
cake on which we fatten cattle ; and even without reference
to its consequences, is sufficiently uninviting.

Many of the workmen appeared to be strong men, and it
is hardly necessary to add that they were all labouring
quietly, then. After two o'clock in the day, they are allowed
to sing, a certain number at a time. The hour striking
while I was there, some twenty sang a hymn in parts, and
sang it by no means ill ; pursuing their work meanwhile. A
bell rang as I was about to leave, and they all poured forth
into a building on the opposite side of the street to dinner.
I said several times that I should like to see them at their
meal ; but as the gentleman to whom I mentioned this desire
appeared to be suddenly taken rather deaf, I did not pursue
the request. Of their appearance I shall have something to
say, presently.

On the following day, I visited a plantation or farm, of
about twelve hundred acres, on the opposite bank of the
river. Here again, although I went down with the owner of
the estate, to " the quarter," as that part of it in which the
slaves live is called, I was not invited to enter into any of
their huts. All I saw of them, was, that they were very
crazy, wretched cabins, near to which groups of half-naked
children basked in the sun, or wallowed on the dusty ground.
But I believe that this gentleman is a considerate and
excellent master, who inherited his fifty slaves, and is neither
a buyer nor a seller of human stock ; and I am sure, from
my own observation and conviction, that he is a kind-hearted,
worthy man.

The planter's house was an airy rustic dwelling, that
brought Defoe's description of such places strongly to my
recollection. The day was very warm, but the blinds being
all closed, and the windows and doors set wide open, a shady

F

coolness rustled through the rooms, which was exquisitely refreshing after the glare and heat without. Before the windows was an open piazza, where, in what they call the hot weather —whatever that may be—they sling hammocks, and drink and doze luxuriously. I do not know how their cool refections may taste within the hammocks, but, having experience, I can report that, out of them, the mounds of ices and the bowls of mint-julep and sherry-cobbler they make in these latitudes, are refreshments never to be thought of afterwards, in summer, by those who would preserve contented minds.

There are two bridges across the river: one belongs to the railroad, and the other, which is a very crazy affair, is the private property of some old lady in the neighbourhood, who levies tolls upon the townspeople. Crossing this bridge, on my way back, I saw a notice painted on the gate, cautioning all persons to drive slowly: under a penalty, if the offender were a white man, of five dollars; if a negro, fifteen stripes.

The same decay and gloom that overhang the way by which it is approached, hover above the town of Richmond. There are pretty villas and cheerful houses in its streets, and Nature smiles upon the country round ; but jostling its handsome residences, like slavery itself going hand in hand with many lofty virtues, are deplorable tenements, fences unrepaired, walls crumbling into ruinous heaps. Hinting gloomily at things below the surface, these, and many other tokens of the same description, force themselves upon the notice, and are remembered with depressing influence, when livelier features are forgotten.

To those who are happily unaccustomed to them, the countenances in the streets and labouring-places, too, are shocking. All men who know that there are laws against instructing slaves, of which the pains and penalties greatly exceed in their amount the fines imposed on those who maim and torture them, must be prepared to find their faces very low in the scale of intellectual expression. But the darkness —not of skin, but mind—which meets the stranger's eye at every turn; the brutalizing and blotting out of all fairer characters traced by Nature's hand ; immeasurably outdo his worst belief. That travelled creation of the great satirist's brain, who fresh from living among horses, peered from a high casement down upon his own kind with trembling horror, was scarcely more repelled and daunted by the sight, than those who look upon some of these faces for the first time must surely be.

I left the last of them behind me in the person of a wretched drudge, who, after running to and fro all day till midnight, and moping in his stealthy winks of sleep upon the stairs betweenwhiles, was washing the dark passages at four o'clock in the morning; and went upon my way with a grateful heart that I was not doomed to live where slavery was, and had never had my senses blunted to its wrongs and horrors in a slave-rocked cradle.

It had been my intention to proceed by James River and Chesapeake Bay to Baltimore; but one of the steamboats being absent from her station through some accident, and the means of conveyance being consequently rendered uncertain, we returned to Washington by the way we had come (there were two constables on board the steamboat, in pursuit of runaway slaves), and halting there again for one night, went on to Baltimore next afternoon.

The most comfortable of all the hotels of which I had any experience in the United States, and they were not a few, is Barnum's, in that city: where the English traveller will find curtains to his bed, for the first and probably the last time in America (this is a disinterested remark, for I never use them); and where he will be likely to have enough water for washing himself, which is not at all a common case.

This capital of the state of Maryland is a bustling busy town, with a great deal of traffic of various kinds, and in particular of water commerce. That portion of the town which it most favours is none of the cleanest, it is true; but the upper part is of a very different character, and has many agreeable streets and public buildings. The Washington Monument, which is a handsome pillar with a statue on its summit; the Medical College; and the Battle Monument in memory of an engagement with the British at North Point; are the most conspicuous among them.

There is a very good prison in this city, and the State Penitentiary is also among its institutions. In this latter establishment there were two curious cases.

One, was that of a young man, who had been tried for the murder of his father. The evidence was entirely circumstantial, and was very conflicting and doubtful; nor was it

possible to assign any motive which could have tempted him
to the commission of so tremendous a crime. He had been
tried twice ; and on the second occasion the jury felt so much
hesitation in convicting him, that they found a verdict of
manslaughter, or murder in the second degree; which it could
not possibly be, as there had, beyond all doubt, been no
quarrel or provocation, and if he were guilty at all, he was
unquestionably guilty of murder in its broadest and worst
signification.

The remarkable feature in the case was, that if the unfortunate deceased were not really murdered by this own son of
his, he must have been murdered by his own brother.   The
evidence lay in a most remarkable manner, between those
two.   On all the suspicious points, the dead man's brother
was the witness : all the explanations for the prisoner (some
of them extremely plausible) went, by construction and
inference, to inculcate him as plotting to fix the guilt upon
his nephew.   It must have been one of them : and the jury
had to decide between two sets of suspicions, almost equally
unnatural, unaccountable, and strange.

The other case, was that of a man who once went to a
certain distiller's and stole a copper measure containing a
quantity of liquor.   He was pursued and taken with the
property in his possession, and was sentenced to two years'
imprisonment.   On coming out of the gaol, at the expiration
of that term, he went back to the same distiller's, and stole
the same copper measure containing the same quantity of
liquor.   There was not the slightest reason to suppose that
the man wished to return to prison : indeed everything, but
the commission of the offence, made directly against that
assumption.   There are only two ways of accounting for this
extraordinary proceeding.   One is, that after undergoing so
much for this copper measure he conceived he had established
a sort of claim and right to it.   The other that, by dint of
long thinking about, it had become a monomania with him,
and had acquired a fascination which he found it impossible
to resist ; swelling from an Earthly Copper Gallon into an
Ethereal Golden Vat.

After remaining here a couple of days I bound myself to a
rigid adherence to the plan I had laid down so recently, and
resolved to set forward on our western journey without any
more delay.   Accordingly, having reduced the luggage within
the smallest possible compass (by sending back to New York,

to be afterwards forwarded to us in Canada, so much of it as was not absolutely wanted) ; and having procured the necessary credentials to banking-houses on the way ; and having moreover looked for two evenings at the setting sun, with as well-defined an idea of the country before us as if we had been going to travel into the very centre of that planet ; we left Baltimore by another railway at half-past eight in the morning, and reached the town of York, some sixty miles off, by the early dinner-time of the Hotel which was the starting-place of the four-horse coach, wherein we were to proceed to Harrisburg.

This conveyance, the box of which I was fortunate enough to secure, had come down to meet us at the railroad station, and was as muddy and cumbersome as usual.   As more passengers were waiting for us at the inn-door, the coachman observed under his breath, in the usual self-communicative voice, looking the while at his mouldy harness as if it were to that he was addressing himself,

" I expect we shall want *the big* coach."

I could not help wondering within myself what the size of this big coach might be, and how many persons it might be designed to hold ; for the vehicle which was too small for our purpose was something larger than two English heavy night coaches, and might have been the twin-brother of a French Diligence.   My speculations were speedily set at rest, however, for as soon as we had dined, there came rumbling up the street, shaking its sides like a corpulent giant, a kind of barge on wheels.   After much blundering and backing, it stopped at the door : rolling heavily from side to side when its other motion had ceased, as if it had taken cold in its damp stable, and between that, and the having been required in its dropsical old age to move at any faster pace than a walk, were distressed by shortness of wind.

" If here ain't the Harrisburg mail at last, and dreadful bright and smart to look at too," cried an elderly gentleman in some excitement, " darn my mother ! "

I don't know what the sensation of being darned may be, or whether a man's mother has a keener relish or disrelish of the process than anybody else ; but if the endurance of this mysterious ceremony by the old lady in question had depended on the accuracy of her son's vision in respect to the abstract brightness and smartness of the Harrisburg mail, she would certainly have undergone its infliction.   However, they booked twelve people inside ; and the luggage (including such trifles as a large rocking-chair, and a good-sized dining-table) being at length made fast upon the roof, we started off in great state.

At the door of another hotel, there was another passenger to be taken up.

"Any room, Sir ? " cries the new passenger to the coachman.

"Well there's room enough," replies the coachman, without getting down, or even looking at him.

"There an't no room at all, Sir," bawls a gentleman inside. Which another gentleman (also inside) confirms, by predicting that the attempt to introduce any more passengers "won't fit nohow."

The new passenger, without any expression of anxiety, looks into the coach, and then looks up at the coachman: "Now, how do you mean to fix it ? " says he, after a pause: "for I *must* go."

The coachman employs himself in twisting the lash of his whip into a knot, and takes no more notice of the question : clearly signifying that it is anybody's business but his, and that the passengers would do well to fix it, among themselves. In this state of things, matters seem to be approximating to a fix of another kind, when another inside passenger in a corner, who is nearly suffocated, cries faintly, "I'll get out."

This is no matter of relief or self-congratulation to the driver, for his immovable philosophy is perfectly undisturbed by anything that happens in the coach. Of all things in the world, the coach would seem to be the very last upon his mind. The exchange is made, however, and then the passenger who has given up his seat makes a third upon the box, seating himself in what he calls the middle ; that is, with half his person on my legs, and the other half on the driver's.

"Go ahead, cap'en," cries the colonel, who directs.

"Gŏ-lăng ! " cries the cap'en to his company, the horses, and away we go.

We took up at a rural bar-room, after we had gone a few miles, an intoxicated gentleman who climbed upon the roof among the luggage, and subsequently slipping off without hurting himself, was seen in the distant perspective reeling back to the grog-shop where we had found him. We also parted with more of our freight at different times, so that when we came to change horses, I was again alone outside.

The coachmen always change with the horses, and are usually as dirty as the coach. The first was dressed like a very shabby English baker; the second like a Russian peasant: for he wore a loose purple camlet robe, with a fur collar, tied round his waist with a parti-coloured worsted sash; grey trousers; light blue gloves: and a cap of bear-skin. It had by this time come on to rain very heavily, and there was a cold damp mist besides, which penetrated to the skin. I was glad to take advantage of a stoppage and get down to stretch my legs, shake the water off my great-coat, and swallow the usual anti-temperance recipe for keeping out the cold.

When I mounted to my seat again, I observed a new parcel lying on the coach roof, which I took to be a rather large fiddle in a brown bag. In the course of a few miles, however, I discovered that it had a glazed cap at one end and a pair of muddy shoes at the other; and further observation demonstrated it to be a small boy in a snuff-coloured coat, with his arms quite pinioned to his sides, by deep forcing into his pockets. He was, I presume, a relative or friend of the coachman's, as he lay a-top of the luggage with his face towards the rain; and except when a change of position brought his shoes in contact with my hat, he appeared to be asleep. At last, on some occasion of our stopping, this thing slowly upreared itself to the height of three feet six, and fixing its eyes on me, observed in piping accents, with a complaisant yawn, half quenched in an obliging air of friendly patronage, "Well now, stranger, I guess you find this a'most like an English arternoon, hey?"

The scenery which had been tame enough at first, was, for the last ten or twelve miles, beautiful. Our road wound through the pleasant valley of the Susquehanna; the river, dotted with innumerable green islands, lay upon our right; and on the left, a steep ascent, craggy with broken rock, and dark with pine trees. The mist, wreathing itself into a hundred fantastic shapes, moved solemnly upon the water; and the gloom of evening gave to all an air of mystery and silence which greatly enhanced its natural interest.

We crossed this river by a wooden bridge, roofed and covered in on all sides, and nearly a mile in length. It was profoundly dark; perplexed, with great beams, crossing and

recrossing it at every possible angle ; and through the broad
chinks and crevices in the floor, the rapid river gleamed, far
down below, like a legion of eyes. We had no lamps ; and
as the horses stumbled and floundered through this place,
towards the distant speck of dying light, it seemed interminable. I really could not at first persuade myself as we
rumbled heavily on, filling the bridge with hollow noises,
and I held down my head to save it from the rafters above,
but that I was in a painful dream ; for I have often dreamed
of toiling through such places, and as often argued, even at
the time, "this cannot be reality."

At length, however, we emerged upon the streets of Harrisburg, whose feeble lights, reflected dismally from the wet
ground, did not shine out upon a very cheerful city. We
were soon established in a snug hotel, which though smaller
and far less splendid than many we put up at, is raised above
them all in my remembrance, by having for its landlord the
most obliging, considerate, and gentlemanly person I ever
had to deal with.

As we were not to proceed upon our journey until the
afternoon, I walked out, after breakfast the next morning, to
look about me ; and was duly shown a model prison on the
solitary system, just erected, and as yet without an inmate ;
the trunk of an old tree to which Harris, the first settler
here (afterwards buried under it), was tied by hostile Indians,
with his funeral pile about him, when he was saved by the
timely appearance of a friendly party on the opposite shore
of the river ; the local legislature (for there was another of
those bodies here again, in full debate) ; and the other
curiosities of the town.

I was very much interested in looking over a number of
treaties made from time to time with the poor Indians,
signed by the different chiefs at the period of their ratifica-
tion, and preserved in the office of the Secretary to the
Commonwealth. These signatures, traced of course by their
own hands, are rough drawings of the creatures or weapons
they were called after. Thus, the Great Turtle makes a
crooked pen-and-ink outline of a great turtle ; the Buffalo
sketches a buffalo ; the War Hatchet sets a rough image of
that weapon for his mark. So with the Arrow, the Fish,
the Scalp, the Big Canoe, and all of them.

I could not but think—as I looked at these feeble and
tremulous productions of hands which could draw the longest

arrow to the head in a stout elk-horn bow, or split a bead
or feather with a rifle-ball—of Crabbe's musings over the
Parish Register, and the irregular scratches made with a pen,
by men who would plough a lengthy furrow straight from
end to end. Nor could I help bestowing many sorrowful
thoughts upon the simple warriors whose hands and hearts
were set there, in all truth and honesty; and who only
learned in course of time from white men how to break their
faith, and quibble out of forms and bonds. I wonder, too,
how many times the credulous Big Turtle, or trusting Little
Hatchet, had put his mark to treaties which were falsely
read to him ; and had signed away, he knew not what, until
it went and cast him loose upon the new possessors of the
land, a savage indeed.

Our host announced, before our early dinner, that some
members of the legislative body proposed to do us the honour
of calling. He had kindly yielded up to us his wife's own
little parlour, and when I begged that he would show them
in, I saw him look with painful apprehension at its pretty
carpet; though, being otherwise occupied at the time, the
cause of his uneasiness did not occur to me.

It certainly would have been more pleasant to all parties
concerned, and would not, I think, have compromised their
independence in any material degree, if some of these gentlemen had not only yielded to the prejudice in favour of
spittoons, but had abandoned themselves, for the moment,
even to the conventional absurdity of pocket-handkerchiefs.

It still continued to rain heavily, and when we went down
to the canal boat (for that was the mode of conveyance by
which we were to proceed) after dinner, the weather was as
unpromising and obstinately wet as one would desire to see.
Nor was the sight of this canal boat, in which we were to
spend three or four days, by any means a cheerful one ; as it
involved some uneasy speculations concerning the disposal of
the passengers at night, and opened a wide field of inquiry
.touching the other domestic arrangements of the establishment, which was sufficiently disconcerting.

However, there it was—a barge with a little house in it,
viewed from the outside ; and a caravan at a fair, viewed
from within: the gentlemen being accommodated, as the
spectators usually are, in one of those locomotive museums
of penny wonders ; and the ladies being partitioned off by a
red curtain, after the manner of the dwarfs and giants in

the same establishments, whose private lives are passed in rather close exclusiveness.

We sat here, looking silently at the row of little tables, which extended down both sides of the cabin, and listening to the rain as it dripped and pattered on the boat, and plashed with a dismal merriment in the water, until the arrival of the railway train, for whose final contribution to our stock of passengers, our departure was alone deferred. It brought a great many boxes, which were bumped and tossed upon the roof, almost as painfully as if they had been deposited on one's own head, without the intervention of a porter's knot ; and several damp gentlemen, whose clothes, on their drawing round the stove, began to steam again. No doubt it would have been a thought more comfortable if the driving rain, which now poured down more soakingly than ever, had admitted of a window being opened, or if our number had been something less than thirty ; but there was scarcely time to think as much, when a train of three horses was attached to the tow-rope, the boy upon the leader smacked his whip, the rudder creaked and groaned complainingly, and we had begun our journey.

CHAPTER X

As it continued to rain most perseveringly, we all remained
below: the damp gentlemen round the stove, gradually becoming mildewed by the action of the fire; and the dry
gentlemen lying at full length upon the seats, or slumbering
uneasily with their faces on the tables, or walking up and
down the cabin, which it was barely possible for a man of
the middle height to do, without making bald places on his
head by scraping it against the roof. At about six o'clock,
all the small tables were put together to form one long table,
and everybody sat down to tea, coffee, bread, butter, salmon,
shad, liver, steaks, potatoes, pickles, ham, chops, black-
puddings, and sausages.

"Will you try," said my opposite neighbour, handing me
a dish of potatoes, broken up in milk and butter, "will you
try some of these fixings?"

There are few words which perform such various duties
as this word "fix." It is the Caleb Quotem of the American
vocabulary. You call upon a gentleman in a country town,
and his help informs you that he is "fixing himself" just
now, but will be down directly: by which you are to understand that he is dressing. You inquire, on board a steamboat, of a fellow-passenger, whether breakfast will be ready
soon, and he tells you he should think so, for when he was
last below, they were "fixing the tables:" in other words,
laying the cloth. You beg a porter to collect your luggage,
and he entreats you not to be uneasy, for he'll "fix it
presently:" and if you complain of indisposition, you are
advised to have recourse to Doctor So-and-so, who will "fix
you" in no time.

One night, I ordered a bottle of mulled wine at an hotel where I was staying, and waited a long time for it; at length it was put upon the table with an apology from the landlord that he feared it wasn't "fixed properly." And I recollect once, at a stage-coach dinner, overhearing a very stern gentleman demand of a waiter who presented him with a plate of underdone roast-beef, "whether he called *that*, fixing God A'mighty's vittles?"

There is no doubt that the meal, at which the invitation was tendered to me which has occasioned this digression, was disposed of somewhat ravenously; and that the gentlemen thrust the broad-bladed knives and the two-pronged forks further down their throats than I ever saw the same weapons go before, except in the hands of a skilful juggler: but no man sat down until the ladies were seated; or omitted any little act of politeness which could contribute to their comfort. Nor did I ever once, on any occasion, anywhere, during my rambles in America, see a woman exposed to the slightest act of rudeness, incivility, or even inattention.

By the time the meal was over, the rain, which seemed to have worn itself out by coming down so fast, was nearly over too; and it became feasible to go on deck: which was a great relief, notwithstanding its being a very small deck, and being rendered still smaller by the luggage, which was heaped together in the middle under a tarpaulin covering; leaving, on either side, a path so narrow, that it became a science to walk to and fro without tumbling overboard into the canal. It was somewhat embarrassing at first, too, to have to duck nimbly every five minutes whenever the man at the helm cried "Bridge!" and sometimes, when the cry was "Low Bridge," to lie down nearly flat. But custom familiarises one to anything, and there were so many bridges that it took a very short time to get used to this.

As night came on, and we drew in sight of the first range of hills, which are the outposts of the Alleghany Mountains, the scenery, which had been uninteresting hitherto, became more bold and striking. The wet ground reeked and smoked, after the heavy fall of rain; and the croaking of the frogs (whose noise in these parts is almost incredible) sounded as though a million of fairy teams with bells, were travelling through the air, and keeping pace with us. The night was cloudy yet, but moonlight too: and when we crossed the Susquehanna river—over which there is an extraordinary wooden bridge with two galleries, one above the other, so that even there, two boat teams meeting, may pass without confusion—it was wild and grand.

I have mentioned my having been in some uncertainty and doubt, at first, relative to the sleeping arrangements on board this boat. I remained in the same vague state of mind until ten o'clock or thereabouts, when going below, I found suspended on either side of the cabin, three long tiers of hanging book-shelves, designed apparently for volumes of the small octavo size. Looking with greater attention at these contrivances (wondering to find such literary preparations in such a place), I descried on each shelf a sort of microscopic sheet and blanket; then I began dimly to comprehend that the passengers were the library, and that they were to be arranged, edge-wise, on these shelves, till morning.

I was assisted to this conclusion by seeing some of them gathered round the master of the boat, at one of the tables, drawing lots with all the anxieties and passions of gamesters depicted in their countenances; while others, with small pieces of cardboard in their hands, were groping among the shelves in search of numbers corresponding with those they had drawn. As soon as any gentleman found his number, he took possession of it by immediately undressing himself and crawling into bed. The rapidity with which an agitated gambler subsided into a snoring slumberer, was one of the most singular effects I have ever witnessed. As to the ladies, they were already abed, behind the red curtain, which was carefully drawn and pinned up the centre; though as every cough, or sneeze, or whisper, behind this curtain, was perfectly audible before it, we had still a lively consciousness of their society.

The politeness of the person in authority had secured to me a shelf in a nook near this red curtain, in some degree removed from the great body of sleepers: to which place I retired, with many acknowledgments to him for his attention. I found it, on after-measurement, just the width of an ordinary sheet of Bath post letter-paper; and I was at first in some uncertainty as to the best means of getting into it. But the shelf being a bottom one, I finally determined on lying upon the floor, rolling gently in, stopping immediately I touched the mattress, and remaining for the night with that side uppermost, whatever it might be. Luckily,

I came upon my back at exactly the right moment. I was much alarmed on looking upward, to see, by the shape of his half-yard of sacking (which his weight had bent into an exceedingly tight bag), that there was a very heavy gentleman above me, whom the slender cords seemed quite incapable of holding; and I could not help reflecting upon the grief of my wife and family in the event of his coming down in the night. But as I could not have got up again without a severe bodily struggle, which might have alarmed the ladies; and as I had nowhere to go to, even if I had; I shut my eyes upon the danger, and remained there.

One of two remarkable circumstances is indisputably a fact, with reference to that class of society who travel in these boats. Either they carry their restlessness to such a pitch that they never sleep at all; or they expectorate in dreams, which would be a remarkable mingling of the real and ideal. All night long, and every night, on this canal, there was a perfect storm and tempest of spitting; and once my coat, being in the very centre of the hurricane sustained by five gentlemen (which moved vertically, strictly carrying out Reid's Theory of the Law of Storms), I was fain the next morning to lay it on the deck, and rub it down with fair water before it was in a condition to be worn again.

Between five and six o'clock in the morning we got up, and some of us went on deck, to give them an opportunity of taking the shelves down; while others, the morning being very cold, crowded round the rusty stove, cherishing the newly kindled fire, and filling the grate with those voluntary contributions of which they had been so liberal all night. The washing accommodations were primitive. There was a tin ladle chained to the deck, with which every gentleman who thought it necessary to cleanse himself (many were superior to this weakness), fished the dirty water out of the canal, and poured it into a tin basin, secured in like manner. There was also a jack-towel. And, hanging up before a little looking-glass in the bar, in the immediate vicinity of the bread and cheese and biscuits, were a public comb and hair-brush.

At eight o'clock, the shelves being taken down and put away and the tables joined together, everybody sat down to the tea, coffee, bread, butter, salmon, shad, liver, steak, potatoes, pickles, ham, chops, black-puddings, and sausages, all over again. Some were fond of compounding this variety, and having it all on their plates at once. As each gentleman got through his own personal amount of tea, coffee, bread, butter, salmon, shad, liver, steak, potatoes, pickles, ham, chops, black-puddings, and sausages, he rose up and walked off. When everybody had done with everything, the fragments were cleared away : and one of the waiters appearing anew in the character of a barber, shaved such of the company as desired to be shaved; while the remainder looked on, or yawned over their newspapers. Dinner was breakfast again, without the tea and coffee; and supper and breakfast were identical.

There was a man on board this boat, with a light fresh-coloured face, and a pepper-and-salt suit of clothes, who was the most inquisitive fellow that can possibly be imagined. He never spoke otherwise than interrogatively. He was an embodied inquiry. Sitting down or standing up, still or moving, walking the deck or taking his meals, there he was, with a great note of interrogation in each eye, two in his cocked ears, two more in his turned-up nose and chin, at least half-a-dozen more about the corners of his mouth, and the largest one of all in his hair, which was brushed pertly off his forehead in a flaxen clump. Every button in his clothes said, "Eh? What's that? Did you speak? Say that again, will you?" He was always wide awake, like the enchanted bride who drove her husband frantic; always restless; always thirsting for answers; perpetually seeking and never finding. There never was such a curious man.

I wore a fur great-coat at that time, and before we were well clear of the wharf, he questioned me concerning it, and its price, and where I bought it, and when, and what fur it was, and what it weighed, and what it cost. Then he took notice of my watch, and asked me what *that* cost, and whether it was a French watch, and where I got it, and how I got it, and whether I bought it or had it given me, and how it went, and where the key-hole was, and when I wound it, every night or every morning, and whether I ever forgot to wind it at all, and if I did, what then? Where had I been to last, and where was I going next, and where was I going after that, and had I seen the President, and what did he say, and what did I say, and what did he say when I had said that? Eh? Lor now! do tell!

Finding that nothing would satisfy him. I evaded his questions after the first score or two, and in particular

pleaded ignorance respecting the name of the fur whereof the
coat was made. I am unable to say whether this was the
reason, but that coat fascinated him afterwards ; he usually
kept close behind me as I walked, and moved as I moved,
that he might look at it the better ; and he frequently dived
into narrow places after me at the risk of his life, that he
might have the satisfaction of passing his hand up the back,
and rubbing it the wrong way.

We had another odd specimen on board, of a different
kind. This was a thin-faced, spare-figured man of middle
age and stature, dressed in a dusty drabbish-coloured suit,
such as I never saw before. He was perfectly quiet during
the first part of the journey : indeed I don't remember having
so much as seen him until he was brought out by circumstances, as great men often are. The conjunction of events
which made him famous, happened, briefly, thus.

The canal extends to the foot of the mountain, and there,
of course, it stops ; the passengers being conveyed across it
by land carriage, and taken on afterwards by another canal
boat, the counterpart of the first, which awaits them on the
other side. There are two canal lines of passage-boats ; one
is called The Express, and one (a cheaper one) The Pioneer.
The Pioneer gets first to the mountain, and waits for the
Express people to come up ; both sets of passengers being
conveyed across it at the same time. We were the Express
company ; but when we had crossed the mountain, and had
come to the second boat, the proprietors took it into their
heads to draft all the Pioneers into it likewise, so that we
were five-and-forty at least, and the accession of passengers
was not at all of that kind which improved the prospect of
sleeping at night. Our people grumbled at this, as people
do in such cases ; but suffered the boat to be towed off with
the whole freight aboard nevertheless ; and away we went
down the canal. At home, I should have protested lustily,
but being a foreigner here, I held my peace. Not so this
passenger. He cleft a path among the people on deck (we
were nearly all on deck), and without addressing anybody
whomsoever, soliloquised as follows:

"This may suit *you*, this may, but it don't suit *me*. This
may be all very well with Down Easters, and men of Boston
raising, but it won't suit my figure nohow ; and no two
ways about *that;* and so I tell you. Now! I'm from the
brown forests of the Mississippi, *I* am, and when the sun

shines on me, it does shine—a little. It don't glimmer where
I live, the sun don't. No. I'm a brown forester, I am. I
an't a Johnny Cake. There are no smooth skins where I
live. We're rough men there. Rather. If Down Easters
and men of Boston raising like this, I'm glad of it, but I'm
none of that raising nor of that breed. No. This company
wants a little fixing, *it* does. I'm the wrong sort of man
for 'em, *I* am. They won't like me, *they* won't. This is
piling of it up, a little too moŭntaïnoŭs, this is." At the
end of every one of these short sentences he turned upon his
heel, and walked the other way; checking himself abruptly
when he had finished another short sentence, and turning
back again.

It is impossible for me to say what terrific meaning was
hidden in the words of this brown forester, but I know that
the other passengers looked on in a sort of admiring horror,
and that presently the boat was put back to the wharf, and
as many of the Pioneers as could be coaxed or bullied into
going away, were got rid of.

When we started again, some of the boldest spirits on
board, made bold to say to the obvious occasion of this
improvement in our prospects, "Much obliged to you, Sir;"
whereunto the brown forester (waving his hand, and still
walking up and down as before), replied, "No you an't.
You're none o' my raising. You may act for yourselves, *you*
may. I have pinted out the way. Down Easters and Johnny
Cakes can follow if they please. I an't a Johnny Cake, *I*
an't. I am from the brown forests of the Mississippi, *I* am "
—and so on, as before. He was unanimously voted one of
the tables for his bed at night—there is a great contest for
the tables—in consideration for his public services: and he
had the warmest corner by the stove throughout the rest of
the journey. But I never could find out that he did anything except sit there; nor did I hear him speak again until,
in the midst of the bustle and turmoil of getting the luggage
ashore in the dark at Pittsburg, I stumbled over him as he
sat smoking a cigar on the cabin steps, and heard him
muttering to himself, with a short laugh of defiance, "I an't
a Johnny Cake, *I* an't. I'm from the brown forests of the
Mississippi, *I* am, damme!" I am inclined to argue from
this, that he had never left off saying so; but I could not
make an affidavit of that part of the story, if required to do
so by my Queen and Country.

As we have not reached Pittsburg yet, however, in the
order of our narrative, I may go on to remark that breakfast
was perhaps the least desirable meal of the day, as in addition
to the many savoury odours arising from the eatables already
mentioned, there were whiffs of gin, whiskey, brandy, and
rum, from the little bar hard by, and a decided seasoning
of stale tobacco. Many of the gentlemen passengers were
far from particular in respect of their linen, which was in
some cases as yellow as the little rivulets that had trickled
from the corners of their mouths in chewing, and dried there.
Nor was the atmosphere quite free from zephyr whisperings
of the thirty beds which had just been cleared away, and of
which we were further and more pressingly reminded by the
occasional appearance on the table-cloth of a kind of Game,
not mentioned in the Bill of Fare.

And yet despite these oddities—and even they had, for me
at least, a humour of their own—there was much in this
mode of travelling which I heartily enjoyed at the time, and
look back upon with great pleasure. Even the running up,
bare-necked, at five o'clock in the morning, from the tainted
cabin to the dirty deck; scooping up the icy water, plunging
one's head into it, and drawing it out, all fresh and glowing
with the cold; was a good thing. The fast, brisk walk upon
the towing-path, between that time and breakfast, when every
vein and artery seemed to tingle with health; the exquisite
beauty of the opening day, when light came gleaming off
from everything; the lazy motion of the boat, when one lay
idly on the deck, looking through, rather than at, the deep
blue sky; the gliding on at night, so noiselessly, past frowning hills, sullen with dark trees, and sometimes angry in one
red burning spot high up, where unseen men lay crouching
round a fire; the shining out of the bright stars undisturbed
by noise of wheels or steam, or any other sound than the
limpid rippling of the water as the boat went on: all these
were pure delights.

Then there were new settlements and detached log-cabins
and frame-houses, full of interest for strangers from an old
country: cabins with simple ovens, outside, made of clay;
and lodgings for the pigs nearly as good as many of the
human quarters; broken windows, patched with worn-out
hats, old clothes, old boards, fragments of blankets and
paper; and home-made dressers standing in the open air
without the door, whereon was ranged the household store,

not hard to count, of earthen jars and pots. The eye was pained to see the stumps of great trees thickly strewn in every field of wheat, and seldom to lose the eternal swamp and dull morass, with hundreds of rotten trunks and twisted branches steeped in its unwholesome water. It was quite sad and oppressive, to come upon great tracts where settlers had been burning down the trees, and where their wounded bodies lay about, like those of murdered creatures, while here and there some charred and blackened giant reared aloft two withered arms, and seemed to call down curses on his foes. Sometimes, at night, the way wound through some lonely gorge, like a mountain pass in Scotland, shining and coldly glittering in the light of the moon, and so closed in by high steep hills all round, that there seemed to be no egress save through the narrower path by which we had come, until one rugged hill-side seemed to open, and shutting out the moonlight as we passed into its gloomy throat, wrapped our new course in shade and darkness.

We had left Harrisburg on Friday. On Sunday morning we arrived at the foot of the mountain, which is crossed by railroad. There are ten inclined planes; five ascending, and five descending; the carriages are dragged up the former, and let slowly down the latter, by means of stationary engines; the comparatively level spaces between, being traversed, sometimes by horse, and sometimes by engine power, as the case demands. Occasionally the rails are laid upon the extreme verge of a giddy precipice; and looking from the carriage window, the traveller gazes sheer down, without a stone or scrap of fence between, into the mountain depths below. The journey is very carefully made, however; only two carriages travelling together; and while proper precautions are taken, is not to be dreaded for its dangers.

It was very pretty travelling thus, at a rapid pace along the heights of the mountain in a keen wind, to look down into a valley full of light and softness; catching glimpses, through the tree-tops, of scattered cabins; children running to the doors; dogs bursting out to bark, whom we could see without hearing; terrified pigs scampering homewards; families sitting out in their rude gardens; cows gazing upward with a stupid indifference; men in their shirt-sleeves looking on at their unfinished houses, planning out to-morrow's work; and we riding onward, high above them, like a whirlwind. It was amusing, too, when we had dined, and rattled down a steep pass, having no other moving power than the weight of the carriages themselves, to see the engine released, long after us, come buzzing down alone, like a great insect, its back of green and gold so shining in the sun, that if it had spread a pair of wings and soared away, no one would have had occasion, as I fancied, for the least surprise. But it stopped short of us in a very business-like manner when we reached the canal: and, before we left the wharf, went panting up this hill again, with the passengers who had waited our arrival for the means of traversing the road by which we had come.

On the Monday evening, furnace fires and clanking hammers on the banks of the canal, warned us that we approached the termination of this part of our journey. After going through another dreamy place—a long aqueduct across the Alleghany River, which was stranger than the bridge at Harrisburg, being a vast low wooden chamber full of water—we emerged upon that ugly confusion of backs of buildings and crazy galleries and stairs, which always abuts on water, whether it be river, sea, canal, or ditch: and were at Pittsburg.

Pittsburg is like Birmingham in England; at least its townspeople say so. Setting aside the streets, the shops, the houses, waggons, factories, public buildings, and population, perhaps it may be. It certainly has a great quantity of smoke hanging about it, and is famous for its iron-works. Besides the prison to which I have already referred, this town contains a pretty arsenal and other institutions. It is very beautifully situated on the Alleghany River, over which there are two bridges; and the villas of the wealthier citizens sprinkled about the high grounds in the neighbourhood, are pretty enough. We lodged at a most excellent hotel, and were admirably served. As usual it was full of boarders, was very large, and had a broad colonnade to every story of the house.

We tarried here, three days. Our next point was Cincinnati: and as this was a steamboat journey, and western steamboats usually blow up one or two a week in the season, it was advisable to collect opinions in reference to the comparative safety of the vessels bound that way, then lying in the river. One called "The Messenger" was the best recommended. She had been advertised to start positively, every day for a fortnight or so, and had not gone yet, nor did her captain seem to have any very fixed intention on the subject. But this is the custom: for if the law were to bind down a free and independent citizen to keep his word with the public, what would become of the liberty of the subject? Besides, it is in the way of trade. And if passengers be decoyed in the way of trade, and people be inconvenienced in the way of trade, what man, who is a sharp tradesman himself, shall say, "We must put a stop to this?"

Impressed by the deep solemnity of the public announcement, I (being then ignorant of these usages) was for hurrying on board in a breathless state, immediately; but receiving private and confidential information that the boat would certainly not start until Friday, April the First, we made ourselves very comfortable in the meanwhile, and went on board at noon that day.

CHAPTER XI

"The Messenger," was one among a crowd of high-pressure steamboats, clustered together by a wharf-side, which, looked down upon from the rising ground that forms the landing-place, and backed by the lofty bank on the opposite side of the river, appeared no larger than so many floating models. She had some forty passengers on board, exclusive of the poorer persons on the lower deck; and in half an hour, or less, proceeded on her way.

We had, for ourselves, a tiny state-room with two berths in it, opening out of the ladies' cabin.   There was, undoubtedly, something satisfactory in this "location," inasmuch as it was in the stern, and we had been a great many times very gravely recommended to keep as far aft as possible, "because the steamboats generally blew up forward."   Nor was this an unnecessary caution, as the occurrence and circumstances of more than one such fatality during our stay sufficiently testified.   Apart from this source of self-congratulation, it was an unspeakable relief to have any place, no matter how confined, where one could be alone: and as the row of little chambers of which this was one, had each a second glass door besides that in the ladies' cabin, which opened on a narrow gallery outside the vessel, where the other passengers seldom came, and where one could sit in peace and gaze upon the shifting prospect, we took possession of our new quarters with much pleasure.

If the native packets I have already described be unlike anything we are in the habit of seeing on water, these western vessels are still more foreign to all the ideas we are accustomed to entertain of boats.   I hardly know what to liken them to, or how to describe them.

In the first place, they have no mast, cordage, tackle,

rigging, or other such boat-like gear ; nor have they anything in their shape at all calculated to remind one of a boat's head, stern, sides, or keel. Except that they are in the water, and display a couple of paddle-boxes, they might be intended, for anything that appears to the contrary, to perform some unknown service, high and dry, upon a mountain top. There is no visible deck, even: nothing but a long, black, ugly roof, covered with burn-out feathery sparks; above which tower two iron chimneys, and a hoarse escape valve, and a glass steerage-house. Then, in order as the eye descends towards the water, are the sides, and doors, and windows of the state-rooms, jumbled as oddly together as though they formed a small street, built by the varying tastes of a dozen men : the whole is supported on beams and pillars resting on a dirty barge, but a few inches above the water's edge : and in the narrow space between this upper structure and this barge's deck, are the furnace fires and machinery, open at the sides to every wind that blows, and every storm of rain it drives along its path.

Passing one of these boats at night, and seeing the great body of fire, exposed as I have just described, that rages and roars beneath the frail pile of painted wood: the machinery, not warded off or guarded in any way, but doing its work in the midst of the crowd of idlers and emigrants and children, who throng the lower deck: under the management, too, of reckless men whose acquaintance with its mysteries may have been of six months' standing: one feels directly that the wonder is, not that there should be so many fatal accidents, but that any journey should be safely made.

Within, there is one long narrow cabin, the whole length of the boat ; from which the state-rooms open, on both sides. A small portion of it at the stern is partitioned off for the ladies ; and the bar is at the opposite extreme. There is a long table down the centre, and at either end a stove. The washing apparatus is forward, on the deck. It is a little better than on board the canal boat, but not much. In all modes of travelling, the American customs, with reference to the means of personal cleanliness and wholesome ablution, are extremely negligent and filthy ; and I strongly incline to the belief that a considerable amount of illness is referable to this cause.

We are to be on board "The Messenger" three days: arriving at Cincinnati (barring accidents) on Monday morning. There are three meals a day. Breakfast at seven, dinner at half-past twelve, supper about six. At each, there are a great many small dishes and plates upon the table, with very little in them; so that although there is every appearance of a mighty "spread," there is seldom really more than a joint: except for those who fancy slices of beet-root, shreds of dried beef, complicated entanglements of yellow pickle; maize, Indian corn, apple-sauce, and pumpkin.

Some people fancy all these little dainties together (and sweet preserves beside), by way of relish to their roast pig. They are generally those dyspeptic ladies and gentlemen who eat unheard-of quantities of hot corn bread (almost as good for the digestion as a kneaded pin-cushion), for breakfast, and for supper. Those who do not observe this custom, and who help themselves several times instead, usually suck their knives and forks meditatively, until they have decided what to take next: then pull them out of their mouths: put them in the dish; help themselves; and fall to work again. At dinner, there is nothing to drink upon the table, but great jugs full of cold water. Nobody says anything, at any meal, to anybody. All the passengers are very dismal, and seem to have tremendous secrets weighing on their minds. There is no conversation, no laughter, no cheerfulness, no sociality, except in spitting; and that is done in silent fellowship round the stove, when the meal is over. Every man sits down, dull and languid; swallows his fare as if breakfasts, dinners, and suppers, were necessities of nature never to be coupled with recreation or enjoyment; and having bolted his food in a gloomy silence, bolts himself, in the same state. But for these animal observances, you might suppose the whole male portion of the company to be the melancholy ghosts of departed book-keepers, who had fallen dead at the desk: such is their weary air of business and calculation. Undertakers on duty would be sprightly beside them; and a collation of funeral baked-meats, in comparison with these meals, would be a sparkling festivity.

The people are all alike, too. There is no diversity of character. They travel about on the same errands, say and do the same things in exactly the same manner, and follow in the same dull cheerless round. All down the long table, there is scarcely a man who is in anything different from his neighbour. It is quite a relief to have, sitting opposite, that little girl of fifteen with the loquacious chin: who, to do her justice, acts up to it, and fully identifies nature's handwriting, for of all the small chatterboxes that ever invaded the repose of drowsy ladies' cabin, she is the first and foremost. The beautiful girl, who sits a little beyond her—farther down the table there—married the young man with the dark whiskers, who sits beyond *her*, only last month. They are going to settle in the very Far West, where he has lived four years, but where she has never been. They were both overturned in a stage-coach the other day (a bad omen anywhere else, where overturns are not so common), and his head, which bears the marks of a recent wound, is bound up still. She was hurt too, at the same time, and lay insensible for some days; bright as her eyes are, now.

Further down still, sits a man who is going some miles beyond their place of destination, to "improve" a newly-discovered copper mine. He carries the village—that is to be—with him: a few frame-cottages, and an apparatus for smelting the copper. He carries its people too. They are partly American and partly Irish, and herd together on the lower deck; where they amused themselves last evening till the night was pretty far advanced, by alternately firing off pistols and singing hymns.

They, and the very few who have been left at table twenty minutes, rise, and go away. We do so too; and passing through our little state-room, resume our seats in the quiet gallery without.

A fine broad river always, but in some parts much wider than in others: and then there is usually a green island, covered with trees, dividing it into two streams. Occasionally, we stop for a few minutes, maybe to take in wood, maybe for passengers, at some small town or village (I ought to say city, every place is a city here); but the banks are for the most part deep solitudes, overgrown with trees, which, hereabouts, are already in leaf and very green. For miles, and miles, and miles, these solitudes are unbroken by any sign of human life or trace of human footstep; nor is anything seen to move about them but the blue jay, whose colour is so bright, and yet so delicate, that it looks like a flying flower. At lengthened intervals a log cabin, with its little space of cleared land about it, nestles under a rising ground, and sends its thread of blue smoke curling up into the sky. It stands in the corner of the poor field of wheat, which is full of great unsightly stumps, like earthy butchers'-blocks. Sometimes the ground is only just now cleared : the felled trees lying yet upon the soil : and the log-house only this morning begun. As we pass this clearing, the settler leans upon his axe or hammer, and looks wistfully at the people from the world. The children creep out of the temporary hut, which is like a gipsy tent upon the ground, and clap their hands and shout. The dog only glances round at us, and then looks up into his master's face again, as if he were rendered uneasy by any suspension of the common business, and had nothing more to do with pleasurers. And still there is the same, eternal foreground. The river has washed away its banks, and stately trees have fallen down into the stream. Some have been there so long, that they are mere dry grizzly skeletons. Some have just toppled over, and having earth yet about their roots, are bathing their green heads in the river, and putting forth new shoots and branches. Some are almost sliding down, as you look at them. And some were drowned so long ago, that their bleached arms start out from the middle of the current, and seem to try to grasp the boat, and drag it under water.

Through such a scene as this, the unwieldy machine takes its hoarse sullen way : venting, at every revolution of the paddles, a loud high-pressure blast ; enough, one would think, to waken up the host of Indians who lie buried in a great mound yonder : so old, that mighty oaks and other forest trees have struck their roots into its earth ; and so high, that it is a hill, even among the hills that Nature planted round it. The very river, as though it shared one's feelings of compassion for the extinct tribes who lived so pleasantly here, in their blessed ignorance of white existence, hundreds of years ago, steals out of its way to ripple near this mound : and there are few places where the Ohio sparkles more brightly than in the Big Grave Creek.

All this I see as I sit in the little stern-gallery mentioned just now. Evening slowly steals upon the landscape and changes it before me, when we stop to set some emigrants ashore.

Five men, as many women, and a little girl. All their worldly goods are a bag, a large chest and an old chair: one old, high-backed, rush-bottomed chair: a solitary settler in itself. They are rowed ashore in the boat, while the vessel stands a little off awaiting its return, the water being shallow. They are landed at the foot of a high bank, on the summit of which are a few log cabins, attainable only by a long winding path. It is growing dusk; but the sun is very red, and shines in the water and on some of the tree-tops, like fire.

The men get out of the boat first; help out the women; take out the bag, the chest, the chair; bid the rowers "good-bye;" and shove the boat off for them. At the first plash of the oars in the water, the oldest woman of the party sits down in the old chair, close to the water's edge, without speaking a word. None of the others sit down, though the chest is large enough for many seats. They all stand where they landed, as if stricken into stone; and look after the boat. So they remain, quite still and silent: the old woman and her old chair, in the centre; the bag and chest upon the shore, without anybody heeding them: all eyes fixed upon the boat. It comes alongside, is made fast, the men jump on board, the engine is put in motion, and we go hoarsely on again. There they stand yet, without the motion of a hand. I can see them through my glass, when, in the distance and increasing darkness, they are mere specks to the eye: lingering there still: the old woman in the old chair, and all the rest about her: not stirring in the least degree. And thus I slowly lose them.

The night is dark, and we proceed within the shadow of the wooded bank, which makes it darker. After gliding past the sombre maze of boughs for a long time, we come upon an open space where the tall trees are burning. The shape of every branch and twig is expressed in a deep red glow, and as the light wind stirs and ruffles it, they seem to vegetate in fire. It is such a sight as we read of in legends of enchanted forests: saving that it is sad to see these noble works wasting away so awfully, alone; and to think how many years must come and go before the magic that created them will rear their like upon this ground again. But the time will come; and when, in their changed ashes, the growth of centuries unborn has struck its roots, the restless men of distant ages will repair to these again unpeopled solitudes; and their fellows, in cities far away, that slumber now, perhaps, beneath the rolling sea, will read in language strange to any ears in being now, but very old to them, of primeval forests where the axe was never heard, and where the jungled ground was never trodden by a human foot.

Midnight and sleep blot out these scenes and thoughts: and when the morning shines again, it gilds the house-tops of a lively city, before whose broad paved wharf the boat is moored;

with other boats, and flags, and moving wheels, and hum of men around it; as though there were not a solitary or silent rood of ground within the compass of a thousand miles.

Cincinnati is a beautiful city; cheerful, thriving, and animated. I have not often seen a place that commends itself so favourably and pleasantly to a stranger at the first glance as this does: with its clean houses of red and white, its well-paved roads, and foot-ways of bright tile. Nor does it become less prepossessing on a closer acquaintance. The streets are broad and airy, the shops extremely good, the private residences remarkable for their elegance and neatness. There is something of invention and fancy in the varying styles of these latter erections, which, after the dull company of the steamboat, is perfectly delightful, as conveying an assurance that there are such qualities still in existence. The disposition to ornament these pretty villas and render them attractive, leads to the culture of trees and flowers, and the laying out of well-kept gardens, the sight of which, to those who walk along the streets, is inexpressibly refreshing and agreeable. I was quite charmed with the appearance of the town, and its adjoining suburb of Mount Auburn: from which the city, lying in an amphitheatre of hills, forms a picture of remarkable beauty, and is seen to great advantage.

There happened to be a great Temperance Convention held here on the day after our arrival; and as the order of march brought the procession under the windows of the hotel in which we lodged, when they started in the morning, I had a good opportunity of seeing it. It comprised several thousand men; the members of various "Washington Auxiliary Temperance Societies;" and was marshalled by officers on horseback, who cantered briskly up and down the line, with scarves and ribbons of bright colours fluttering out behind them gaily. There were bands of music too, and banners out of number: and it was a fresh, holiday-looking concourse altogether.

I was particularly pleased to see the Irishmen, who formed a distinct society among themselves, and mustered very strong with their green scarves; carrying their national Harp and their Portrait of Father Mathew, high above the people's heads. They looked as jolly and good-humoured as ever; and, working (here) the hardest for their living and doing any kind of sturdy labour that came in their way, were the most independent fellows there, I thought.

The banners were very well painted, and flaunted down the

street famously. There was the smiting of the rock, and the gushing forth of the waters ; and there was a temperate man with "considerable of a hatchet" (as the standard-bearer would probably have said), aiming a deadly blow at a serpent which was apparently about to spring upon him from the top of a barrel of spirits. But the chief feature of this part of the show was a huge allegorical device, borne among the ship-carpenters, on one side whereof the steamboat Alcohol was represented bursting her boiler and exploding with a great crash, while upon the other, the good ship Temperance sailed away with a fair wind, to the heart's content of the captain, crew, and passengers.

After going round the town, the procession repaired to a certain appointed place, where, as the printed programme set forth, it would be received by the children of the different free schools, "singing Temperance Songs." I was prevented from getting there, in time to hear these Little Warblers, or to report upon this novel kind of vocal entertainment : novel, at least, to me ; but I found in a large open space, each society gathered round its own banners, and listening in silent atten-tion to its own orator.   The speeches, judging from the little I could hear of them, were certainly adapted to the occasion, as having that degree of relationship to cold water which wet blankets may claim : but the main thing was the conduct and appearance of the audience throughout the day ; and that was admirable and full of promise.

Cincinnati is honourably famous for its free schools, of which it has so many that no person's child among its population can, by possibility, want the means of education, which are extended, upon an average, to four thousand pupils, annually. I was only present in one of these establishments during the hours of instruction.   In the boys' department, which was full of little urchins (varying in their ages, I should say, from six years old to ten or twelve), the master offered to institute an extemporary examination of the pupils in algebra ; a pro-posal, which, as I was by no means confident of my ability to detect mistakes in that science, I declined with some alarm. In the girls' school, reading was proposed ; and as I felt tolerably equal to that art, I expressed my willingness to hear a class.   Books were distributed accordingly, and some half-dozen girls relieved each other in reading paragraphs from English history.   But it seemed to be a dry compilation, infinitely above their powers ; and when they had blundered through three or four dreary passages concerning the Treaty of Amiens, and other thrilling topics of the same nature (obviously without comprehending ten words), I expressed myself quite satisfied. It is very possible that they only mounted to this exalted stave in the Ladder of Learning for the astonishment of a visitor ; and that at other times they keep upon its lower rounds ; but I should have been much better pleased and satisfied if I had heard them exercised in simpler lessons, which they understood.

As in every other place I visited, the Judges here were gentlemen of high character and attainments. I was in one of the courts for a few minutes, and found it like those to which I have already referred. A nuisance cause was trying ; there were not many spectators ; and the witnesses, counsel, and jury, formed a sort of family circle, sufficiently jocose and snug.

The society with which I mingled, was intelligent, courteous, and agreeable. The inhabitants of Cincinnati are proud of their city as one of the most interesting in America : and with good reason : for beautiful and thriving as it is now, and containing, as it does, a population of fifty thousand souls, but two-and-fifty years have passed away since the ground on which it stands (bought at that time for a few dollars) was a wild wood, and its citizens were but a handful of dwellers in scattered log huts upon the river's shore.

CHAPTER XII

LEAVING Cincinnati at eleven o'clock in the forenoon, we
embarked for Louisville in "The Pike" steamboat, which, carrying the mails, was a packet of a much better class than
that in which we had come from Pittsburg.   As this passage
does not occupy more than twelve or thirteen hours, we
arranged to go ashore that night: not coveting the distinction
of sleeping in a state-room, when it was possible to sleep
anywhere else.

There chanced to be on board this boat, in addition to the
usual dreary crowd of passengers, one Pitchlynn, a chief of
the Choctaw tribe of Indians, who *sent in his card* to me, and
with whom I had the pleasure of a long conversation.

He spoke English perfectly well, though he had not begun
to learn the language, he told me, until he was a young man
grown.   He had read many books; and Scott's poetry
appeared to have left a strong impression on his mind:
especially the opening of the Lady of the Lake, and the great
battle scene in Marmion, in which, no doubt from the
congeniality of the subjects to his own pursuits and tastes,
he had great interest and delight.   He appeared to understand correctly all he had read; and whatever fiction had
enlisted his sympathy in its belief, had done so keenly and
earnestly.   I might almost say fiercely.   He was dressed in
our ordinary every-day costume, which hung about his fine
figure loosely, and with indifferent grace.   On my telling
him that I regretted not to see him in his own attire, he
threw up his right arm, for a moment, as though he were
brandishing some heavy weapon, and answered, as he let it
fall again, that his race were losing many things besides

their dress, and would soon be seen upon the earth no more: but he wore it at home, he added proudly.

He told me that he had been away from his home, west of the Mississippi, seventeen months: and was now returning. He had been chiefly at Washington on some negotiations pending between his Tribe and the Government: which were not settled yet (he said in a melancholy way), and he feared never would be: for what could a few poor Indians do, against such well-skilled men of business as the whites? He had no love for Washington; tired of towns and cities very soon; and longed for the Forest and the Prairie.

I asked him what he thought of Congress? He answered, with a smile, that it wanted dignity, in an Indian's eyes.

He would very much like, he said, to see England before he died; and spoke with much interest about the great things to be seen there. When I told him of that chamber in the British Museum wherein are preserved household memorials of a race that ceased to be, thousands of years ago, he was very attentive, and it was not hard to see that he had a reference in his mind to the gradual fading away of his own people.

This led us to speak of Mr. Catlin's gallery, which he praised highly: observing that his own portrait was among the collection, and that all the likenesses were "elegant." Mr. Cooper, he said, had painted the Red Man well; and so would I, he knew, if I would go home with him and hunt buffaloes, which he was quite anxious I should do. When I told him that supposing I went, I should not be very likely to damage the buffaloes much, he took it as a great joke and laughed heartily.

He was a remarkably handsome man; some years past forty, I should judge; with long black hair, an aquiline nose, broad cheek-bones, a sunburnt complexion, and a very bright, keen, dark, and piercing eye. There were but twenty thousand of the Choctaws left, he said, and their number was decreasing every day. A few of his brother chiefs had been obliged to become civilised, and to make themselves acquainted with what the whites knew, for it was their only chance of existence. But they were not many; and the rest were as they always had been. He dwelt on this: and said several times that unless they tried to assimilate themselves to their conquerors, they must be swept away before the strides of civilised society.

When we shook hands at parting, I told him he must come to England, as he longed to see the land so much : that I should hope to see him there, one day : and that I could promise him he would be well received and kindly treated. He was evidently pleased by this assurance, though he rejoined with a good-humoured smile and an arch shake of his head, that the English used to be very fond of the Red Men when they wanted their help, but had not cared much for them, since.

He took his leave ; as stately and complete a gentleman of Nature's making, as ever I beheld ; and moved among the people in the boat, another kind of being. He sent me a lithographed portrait of himself soon afterwards ; very like, though scarcely handsome enough ; which I have carefully preserved in memory of our brief acquaintance.

There was nothing very interesting in the scenery of this day's journey, which brought us at midnight to Louisville. We slept at the Galt House ; a splendid hotel ; and were as handsomely lodged as though we had been in Paris, rather than hundreds of miles beyond the Alleghanies.

The city presenting no objects of sufficient interest to detain us on our way, we resolved to proceed next day by another steamboat, "The Fulton," and to join it, about noon, at a suburb called Portland, where it would be delayed some time in passing through a canal.

The interval, after breakfast, we devoted to riding through the town, which is regular and cheerful : the streets being laid out at right angles, and planted with young trees. The buildings are smoky and blackened, from the use of bituminous coal, but an Englishman is well used to that appearance, and indisposed to quarrel with it. There did not appear to be much business stirring ; and some unfinished buildings and improvements seemed to intimate that the city had been overbuilt in the ardour of "going-ahead," and was suffering under the reaction consequent upon such feverish forcing of its powers.

On our way to Portland, we passed a "Magistrate's office," which amused me, as looking far more like a dame school than any police establishment : for this awful Institution was nothing but a little lazy, good-for-nothing front parlour, open to the street ; wherein two or three figures (I presume the magistrate and his myrmidons) were basking in the sun-shine, the very effigies of languor and repose. It was a

G

perfect picture of Justice retired from business for want of customers; her sword and scales sold off; napping comfortably with her legs upon the table.

Here, as elsewhere in these parts, the road was perfectly alive with pigs of all ages; lying about in every direction, fast asleep; or grunting along in quest of hidden dainties. I had always a sneaking kindness for these odd animals, and found a constant source of amusement, when all others failed, in watching their proceedings. As we were riding along this morning, I observed a little incident between two youthful pigs, which was so very human as to be inexpressibly comical and grotesque at the time, though I dare say, in telling, it is tame enough.

One young gentleman (a very delicate porker with several straws sticking about his nose, betokening recent investigations in a dunghill) was walking deliberately on, profoundly thinking, when suddenly his brother, who was lying in a miry hole unseen by him, rose up immediately before his startled eyes, ghostly with damp mud. Never was pig's whole mass of blood so turned. He started back at least three feet, gazed for a moment, and then shot off as hard as he could go: his excessively little tail vibrating with speed and terror like a distracted pendulum. But before he had gone very far, he began to reason with himself as to the nature of this frightful appearance; and as he reasoned, he relaxed his speed by gradual degrees; until at last he stopped, and faced about. There was his brother, with the mud upon him glazing in the sun, yet staring out of the very same hole, perfectly amazed at his proceedings! He was no sooner assured of this; and he assured himself so carefully that one may almost say he shaded his eyes with his hand to see the better; than he came back at a round trot, pounced upon him, and summarily took off a piece of his tail; as a caution to him to be careful what he was about for the future, and never to play tricks with his family any more.

We found the steamboat in the canal, waiting for the slow process of getting through the lock, and went on board, where we shortly afterwards had a new kind of visitor in the person of a certain Kentucky Giant whose name is Porter, and who is of the moderate height of seven feet eight inches, in his stockings.

There never was a race of people who so completely gave the lie to history as these giants, or whom all the chroniclers have so cruelly libelled. Instead of roaring and ravaging about the world, constantly catering for their cannibal larders, and perpetually going to market in an unlawful manner, they are the meekest people in any man's acquaintance : rather inclining to milk and vegetable diet, and bearing anything for a quiet life. So decidedly are amiability and mildness their characteristics, that I confess I look upon that youth who distinguished himself by the slaughter of these inoffensive persons, as a false-hearted brigand, who, pretending to philanthropic motives, was secretly influenced only by the wealth stored up within their castles, and the hope of plunder. And I lean the more to this opinion from finding that even the historian of those exploits, with all his partiality for his hero, is fain to admit that the slaughtered monsters in question were of a very innocent and simple turn ; extremely guileless and ready of belief; lending a credulous ear to the most improbable tales; suffering themselves to be easily entrapped into pits; and even (as in the case of the Welsh Giant) with an excess of the hospitable politeness of a landlord, ripping themselves open, rather than hint at the possibility of their guests being versed in the vagabond arts of sleight-of-hand and hocus-pocus.

The Kentucky Giant was but another illustration of the truth of this position. He had a weakness in the region of the knees, and a trustfulness in his long face, which appealed even to five-feet nine for encouragement and support. He was only twenty-five years old, he said, and had grown recently, for it had been found necessary to make an addition to the legs of his inexpressibles. At fifteen he was a short boy, and in those days his English father and his Irish mother had rather snubbed him, as being too small of stature to sustain the credit of the family. He added that his health had not been good, though it was better now; but short people are not wanting who whisper that he drinks too hard.

I understand he drives a hackney-coach, though how he does it, unless he stands on the footboard behind, and lies along the roof upon his chest, with his chin in the box, it would be difficult to comprehend. He brought his gun with him, as a curiosity. Christened "The Little Rifle," and displayed outside a shop-window, it would make the fortune of any retail business in Holborn. When he had shown himself and talked a little while, he withdrew with his pocket-instrument, and went bobbing down the cabin, among men of six feet high and upwards, like a lighthouse walking among lamp-posts.

Within a few minutes afterwards, we were out of the canal, and in the Ohio river again.

The arrangements of the boat were like those of "The Messenger," and the passengers were of the same order of people. We fed at the same times, on the same kind of viands, in the same dull manner, and with the same observances. The company appeared to be oppressed by the same tremendous concealments, and had as little capacity of enjoyment or light-heartedness. I never in my life did see such listless, heavy dulness as brooded over these meals: the very recollection of it weighs me down, and makes me, for the moment, wretched. Reading and writing on my knee, in our little cabin, I really dreaded the coming of the hour that summoned us to table; and was as glad to escape from it again, as if it had been a penance or a punishment. Healthy cheerfulness and good spirits forming a part of the banquet, I could soak my crusts in the fountain with Le Sage's strolling player, and revel in their glad enjoyment: but sitting down with so many fellow-animals to ward off thirst and hunger as a business; to empty, each creature, his Yahoo's trough as quickly as he can, and then slink sullenly away; to have these social sacraments stripped of everything but the mere greedy satisfaction of the natural cravings; goes so against the grain with me, that I seriously believe the recollection of these funeral feasts will be a waking nightmare to me all my life.

There was some relief in this boat, too, which there had not been in the other, for the captain (a blunt good-natured fellow) had his handsome wife with him, who was disposed to be lively and agreeable, as were a few other lady-passengers who had their seats about us at the same end of the table. But nothing could have made head against the depressing influence of the general body. There was a magnetism of dulness in them which would have beaten down the most facetious companion that the earth ever knew. A jest would have been a crime, and a smile would have faded into a grinning horror. Such deadly leaden people; such systematic plodding weary insupportable heaviness; such a mass of animated indigestion in respect of all that was genial, jovial, frank, social, or hearty; never, sure, was brought together elsewhere since the world began.

Nor was the scenery, as we approached the junction of the Ohio and Mississippi rivers, at all inspiriting in its influence. The trees were stunted in their growth ; the banks were low and flat ; the settlements and log cabins fewer in number : their inhabitants more wan and wretched than any we had encountered yet. No songs of birds were in the air, no pleasant scents, no moving lights and shadows from swift passing clouds. Hour after hour, the changeless glare of the hot, unwinking sky, shone upon the same monotonous objects. Hour after hour, the river rolled along, as wearily and slowly as the time itself.

At length, upon the morning of the third day, we arrived at a spot so much more desolate than any we had yet beheld, that the forlornest places we had passed, were, in comparison with it, full of interest. At the junction of the two rivers, on ground so flat and low and marshy, that at certain seasons of the year it is inundated to the house-tops, lies a breeding-place of fever, ague, and death ; vaunted in England as a mine of Golden Hope, and speculated in, on the faith of monstrous representations, to many people's ruin. A dismal swamp, on which the half-built houses rot away : cleared here and there for the space of a few yards ; and teeming, then, with rank unwholesome vegetation, in whose baleful shade the wretched wanderers who are tempted hither, droop, and die, and lay their bones ; the hateful Mississippi circling and eddying before it, and turning off upon its southern course a slimy monster hideous to behold ; a hotbed of disease, an ugly sepulchre, a grave uncheered by any gleam of promise : a place without one single quality, in earth or air or water, to commend it : such is this dismal Cairo.

But what words shall describe the Mississippi, great father of rivers, who (praise be to Heaven) has no young children like him ! An enormous ditch, sometimes two or three miles wide, running liquid mud, six miles an hour : its strong and frothy current choked and obstructed everywhere by huge logs and whole forest trees : now twining themselves together in great rafts, from the interstices of which a sedgy lazy foam works up, to float upon the water's top ; now rolling past like monstrous bodies, their tangled roots showing like matted hair ; now glancing singly by like giant leeches ; and now writhing round and round in the vortex of some small whirlpool, like wounded snakes. The banks low, the trees dwarfish, the marshes swarming with frogs, the wretched cabins few and far apart, their inmates hollow-cheeked and pale, the weather very hot, mosquitoes penetrating into every crack and crevice of the boat, mud and slime on everything: nothing pleasant in its aspect, but the harmless lightning which flickers every night upon the dark horizon.

For two days we toiled up this foul stream, striking constantly against the floating timber, or stopping to avoid those more dangerous obstacles, the snags, or sawyers, which are the hidden trunks of trees that have their roots below the tide. When the nights are very dark, the look-out stationed in the head of the boat, knows by the ripple of the water if any great impediment be near at hand, and rings a bell beside him, which is the signal for the engine to be stopped: but always in the night this bell has work to do, and after every ring, there comes a blow which renders it no easy matter to remain in bed.

The decline of day here was very gorgeous; tingeing the firmament deeply with red and gold, up to the very keystone of the arch above us. As the sun went down behind the bank, the slightest blades of grass upon it seemed to become as distinctly visible as the arteries in the skeleton of a leaf; and when, as it slowly sank, the red and golden bars upon the water grew dimmer, and dimmer yet, as if they were sinking too; and all the glowing colours of departing day paled, inch by inch, before the sombre night; the scene became a thousand times more lonesome and more dreary than before, and all its influences darkened with the sky.

We drank the muddy water of this river while we were upon it. It is considered wholesome by the natives, and is something more opaque than gruel. I have seen water like it at the Filter-shops, but nowhere else.

On the fourth night after leaving Louisville, we reached St. Louis, and here I witnessed the conclusion of an incident, trifling enough in itself, but very pleasant to see, which had interested me during the whole journey.

There was a little woman on board, with a little baby; and both little woman and little child were cheerful, good-looking, bright-eyed, and fair to see. The little woman had been passing a long time with her sick mother in New York, and had left her home in St. Louis, in that condition in which ladies who truly love their lords desire to be. The baby was born in her mother's house; and she had not seen her husband (to whom she was now returning), for twelve months: having left him a month or two after their marriage.

Well, to be sure, there never was a little woman so full of hope, and tenderness, and love, and anxiety, as this little woman was: and all day long she wondered whether "He" would be at the wharf; and whether "He" had got her letter; and whether, if she sent the baby ashore by somebody else, "He" would know it, meeting it in the street: which, seeing that he had never set eyes upon it in his life, was not very likely in the abstract, but was probable enough, to the young mother. She was such an artless little creature; and was in such a sunny, beaming, hopeful state; and let out all this matter clinging close about her heart, so freely; that all the other lady passengers entered into the spirit of it as much as she; and the captain (who heard all about it from his wife) was wondrous sly, I promise you: inquiring, every time we met at table, as in forgetfulness, whether she expected anybody to meet her at St. Louis, and whether she would want to go ashore the night we reached it (but he supposed she wouldn't), and cutting many other dry jokes of that nature. There was one little weazen, dried-apple-faced old woman, who took occasion to doubt the constancy of husbands in such circumstances of bereavement; and there was another lady (with a lap-dog) old enough to moralize on the lightness of human affections, and yet not so old that she could help nursing the baby, now and then, or laughing with the rest, when the little woman called it by its father's name, and asked it all manner of fantastic questions concerning him in the joy of her heart.

It was something of a blow to the little woman, that when we were within twenty miles of our destination, it became clearly necessary to put this baby to bed. But she got over it with the same good humour; tied a handkerchief round her head; and came out into the little gallery with the rest. Then, such an oracle as she became in reference to the localities! and such facetiousness as was displayed by the married ladies! and such sympathy as was shown by the single ones! and such peals of laughter as the little woman herself (who would just as soon have cried) greeted every jest with!

At last, there were the lights of St. Louis, and here was the wharf, and those were the steps: and the little woman covering her face with her hands, and laughing (or seeming to laugh) more than ever, ran into her own cabin, and shut herself up. I have no doubt that in the charming incon- sistency of such excitement, she stopped her ears, lest she should hear "Him" asking for her: but I did not see her do it.

Then, a great crowd of people rushed on board, though the boat was not yet made fast, but was wandering about, among the other boats, to find a landing-place: and every- body looked for the husband: and nobody saw him: when, in the midst of us all—Heaven knows how she ever got there —there was the little woman clinging with both arms tight round the neck of a fine, good-looking, sturdy young fellow! and in a moment afterwards, there she was again, actually clapping her little hands for joy, as she dragged him through the small door of her small cabin, to look at the baby as he lay asleep!

We went to a large hotel, called the Planter's House: built like an English hospital, with long passages and bare walls, and skylights above the room-doors for the free circu- lation of air. There were a great many boarders in it; and as many lights sparkled and glistened from the windows down into the street below, when we drove up, as if it had been illuminated on some occasion of rejoicing. It is an excellent house, and the proprietors have most bountiful notions of providing the creature comforts. Dining alone with my wife in our own room, one day, I counted fourteen dishes on the table at once.

In the old French portion of the town, the thoroughfares are narrow and crooked, and some of the houses are very quaint and picturesque: being built of wood, with tumble- down galleries before the windows, approachable by stairs or rather ladders from the street. There are queer little barbers' shops and drinking-houses too, in this quarter; and abun- dance of crazy old tenements with blinking casements, such as may be seen in Flanders. Some of these ancient habita- tions, with high garret gable-windows perking into the roofs, have a kind of French shrug about them; and being lop- sided with age, appear to hold their heads askew, besides, as if they were grimacing in astonishment at the American Improvements.

It is hardly necessary to say, that these consist of wharfs and warehouses, and new buildings in all directions; and of a great many vast plans which are still "progressing."

The Little Wife

Already, however, some very good houses, broad streets, and marble-fronted shops, have gone so far ahead as to be in a state of completion ; and the town bids fair in a few years to improve considerably : though it is not likely ever to vie, in point of elegance or beauty, with Cincinnati.

The Roman Catholic religion, introduced here by the early French settlers, prevails extensively. Among the public institutions are a Jesuit college ; a convent for " the Ladies of the Sacred Heart ; " and a large chapel attached to the college, which was in course of erection at the time of my visit, and was intended to be consecrated on the second of December in the next year. The architect of this building, is one of the reverend fathers of the school, and the works proceed under his sole direction. The organ will be sent from Belgium.

In addition to these establishments, there is a Roman Catholic cathedral, dedicated to Saint Francis Xavier ; and a hospital, founded by the munificence of a deceased resident, who was a member of that church. It also sends missionaries from hence among the Indian tribes.

The Unitarian church is represented, in this remote place, as in most other parts of America, by a gentleman of great worth and excellence. The poor have good reason to remember and bless it ; for it befriends them, and aids the cause of rational education, without any sectarian or selfish views. It is liberal in all its actions ; of kind construction ; and of wide benevolence.

There are three free-schools already erected, and in full operation in this city. A fourth is building, and will soon be opened.

No man ever admits the unhealthiness of the place he dwells in (unless he is going away from it), and I shall there-fore, I have no doubt, be at issue with the inhabitants of St. Louis, in questioning the perfect salubrity of its climate, and in hinting that I think it must rather dispose to fever, in the summer and autumnal seasons. Just adding, that it is very hot, lies among great rivers, and has vast tracks of undrained swampy land around it, I leave the reader to form his own opinion.

As I had a great desire to see a Prairie before turning back from the furthest point of my wanderings ; and as some gentlemen of the town had, in their hospitable con-sideration, an equal desire to gratify me ; a day was fixed, before my departure, for an expedition to the Looking-Glass Prairie, which is within thirty miles of the town. Deeming it possible that my readers may not object to know what kind of thing such a gipsy party may be at that distance from home, and among what sort of objects it moves, I will describe the jaunt in another chapter.

CHAPTER XIII

A JAUNT TO THE LOOKING-GLASS PRAIRIE AND BACK

I MAY premise that the word Prairie is variously pronounced *paraaer, parearer*, and *paroarer*. The latter mode of pronunciation is perhaps the most in favour.

We were fourteen in all, and all young men: indeed it is a singular though very natural feature in the society of these distant settlements, that it is mainly composed of adventurous persons in the prime of life, and has very few grey heads among it. There were no ladies: the trip being a fatiguing one: and we were to start at five o'clock in the morning punctually.

I was called at four, that I might be certain of keeping nobody waiting; and having got some bread and milk for breakfast, threw up the window and looked down into the street, expecting to see the whole party busily astir, and great preparations going on below. But as everything was very quiet, and the street presented that hopeless aspect with which five o'clock in the morning is familiar elsewhere, I deemed it as well to go to bed again, and went accordingly.

I woke again at seven o'clock, and by that time the party had assembled, and were gathered round, one light carriage, with a very stout axletree; one something on wheels like an amateur carrier's cart; one double phaeton of great antiquity and unearthly construction; one gig with a great hole in its back and a broken head; and one rider on horseback who was to go on before. I got into the first coach with three companions; the rest bestowed themselves in the other vehicles; two large baskets were made fast to the lightest; two large stone jars in wicker cases, technically known as demi-johns, were consigned to the "least rowdy" of the party for safe-keeping; and the procession moved off to the ferry-boat, in which it was to cross the river bodily, men, horses, carriages, and all, as the manner in these parts is.

We got over the river in due course, and mustered again before a little wooden box on wheels, hove down all aslant in a morass, with "MERCHANT TAILOR" painted in very large letters over the door. Having settled the order of proceeding, and the road to be taken, we started off once more and began to make our way through an ill-favoured Black Hollow, called, less expressively, the American Bottom.

The previous day had been—not to say hot, for the term is weak and lukewarm in its power of conveying an idea of the temperature. The town had been on fire; in a blaze. But at night it had come on to rain in torrents, and all night long it had rained without cessation. We had a pair of very strong horses, but travelled at the rate of little more than a couple of miles an hour, through one unbroken slough of black mud and water. It had no variety but in depth. Now it was only half over the wheels, now it hid the axle-tree, and now the coach sank down in it almost to the windows. The air resounded in all directions with the loud chirping of the frogs, who, with the pigs (a coarse, ugly breed, as unwholesome-looking as though they were the spontaneous growth of the country), had the whole scene to themselves. Here and there we passed a log hut : but the wretched cabins were wide apart and thinly scattered, for though the soil is very rich in this place, few people can exist in such a deadly atmosphere. On either side of the track, if it deserve the name, was the thick "bush;" and everywhere was stagnant, slimy, rotten, filthy water.

As it is the custom in these parts to give a horse a gallon or so of cold water whenever he is in a foam with heat, we halted for that purpose, at a log inn in the wood, far removed from any other residence. It consisted of one room, bare-roofed and bare-walled of course, with a loft above. The ministering priest was a swarthy young savage, in a shirt of cotton print like bed-furniture, and a pair of ragged trousers. There were a couple of young boys, too, nearly naked, lying idle by the well ; and they, and he, and *the* traveller at the inn, turned out to look at us.

The traveller was an old man with a grey grizzly beard two inches long, a shaggy moustache of the same hue, and enormous eyebrows ; which almost obscured his lazy, semi-drunken glance, as he stood regarding us with folded arms : poising himself alternately upon his toes and heels. On being addressed by one of the party, he drew nearer, and said,

rubbing his chin (which scraped under his horny hand like
fresh gravel beneath a nailed shoe), that he was from Dela-
ware, and had lately bought a farm "down there," pointing
into one of the marshes where the stunted trees were thickest.
He was "going," he added, to St. Louis, to fetch his family,
whom he had left behind ; but he seemed in no great hurry
to bring on these incumbrances, for when we moved away,
he loitered back into the cabin, and was plainly bent on
stopping there so long as his money lasted. He was a great
politician of course, and explained his opinions at some
length to one of our company ; but I only remember that
he concluded with two sentiments, one of which was, Somebody for ever ; and the other, Blast everybody else ! which
is by no means a bad abstract of the general creed in these
matters.

When the horses were swollen out to about twice their
natural dimensions (there seems to be an idea here, that this
kind of inflation improves their going), we went forward
again, through mud and mire, and damp, and festering heat,
and brake and bush, attended always by the music of the
frogs and pigs, until nearly noon, when we halted at a place
called Belleville.

Belleville was a small collection of wooden houses, huddled
together in the very heart of the bush and swamp. Many
of them had singularly bright doors of red and yellow ; for
the place had been lately visited by a travelling painter,
"who got along," as I was told, "by eating his way." The
criminal court was sitting, and was at that moment trying
some criminals for horse-stealing : with whom it would most
likely go hard : for live stock of all kinds being necessarily
very much exposed in the woods, is held by the community
in rather higher value than human life ; and for this reason,
juries generally make a point of finding all men indicted for
cattle-stealing, guilty, whether or no.

The horses belonging to the bar, the judge, and witnesses,
were tied to temporary racks set up roughly in the road ; by
which is to be understood, a forest path, nearly knee-deep in
mud and slime.

There was an hotel in this place, which, like all hotels in
America, had its large dining-room for the public table. It
was an odd, shambling, low-roofed out-house, half-cowshed
and half-kitchen, with a coarse brown canvas table-cloth, and
tin sconces stuck against the walls, to hold candles at supper-

time. The horseman had gone forward to have coffee and some eatables prepared, and they were by this time nearly ready. He had ordered "wheat-bread and chicken fixings," in preference to "corn-bread and common doings." The latter kind of refection includes only pork and bacon. The former comprehends broiled ham, sausages, veal cutlets, steaks, and such other viands of that nature as may be supposed, by a tolerably wide poetical construction, "to fix" a chicken comfortably in the digestive organs of any lady or gentleman.

On one of the door-posts at this inn, was a tin plate, whereon was inscribed in characters of gold, "Doctor Crocus;" and on a sheet of paper, pasted up by the side of this plate, was a written announcement that Dr. Crocus would that evening deliver a lecture on Phrenology for the benefit of the Belleville public; at a charge, for admission, of so much a head.

Straying upstairs, during the preparation of the chicken fixings, I happened to pass the doctor's chamber; and as the door stood wide open, and the room was empty, I made bold to peep in.

It was a bare, unfurnished, comfortless room, with an unframed portrait hanging up at the head of the bed; a likeness, I take it, of the Doctor, for the forehead was fully displayed, and great stress was laid by the artist upon its phrenological developments. The bed itself was covered with an old patch-work counterpane. The room was destitute of carpet or of curtain. There was a damp fireplace without any stove, full of wood ashes; a chair, and a very small table; and on the last-named piece of furniture was displayed, in grand array, the doctor's library, consisting of some half-dozen greasy old books.

Now, it certainly looked about the last apartment on the whole earth out of which any man would be likely to get anything to do him good. But the door, as I have said, stood coaxingly open, and plainly said in conjunction with the chair, the portrait, the table, and the books, "Walk in, gentlemen, walk in! Don't be ill, gentlemen, when you may be well in no time. Doctor Crocus is here, gentlemen, the celebrated Dr. Crocus! Doctor Crocus has come all this way to cure you, gentlemen. If you haven't heard of Dr. Crocus, it's your fault, gentlemen, who live a little way out of the world here: not Dr. Crocus's. Walk in, gentlemen, walk in!"

In the passage below, when I went downstairs again, was Dr. Crocus himself. A crowd had flocked in from the Court House, and a voice from among them called out to the landlord, "Colonel! introduce Dr. Crocus."

"Mr. Dickens," says the colonel, "Doctor Crocus."

Upon which Doctor Crocus, who is a tall, fine-looking Scotchman, but rather fierce and warlike in appearance for a professor of the peaceful art of healing, bursts out of the concourse with his right arm extended, and his chest thrown out as far as it will possibly come, and says:

"Your countryman, Sir!"

Whereupon Doctor Crocus and I shake hands; and Doctor Crocus looks as if I didn't by any means realise his expectations, which, in a linen blouse, and a great straw hat, with a green ribbon, and no gloves, and my face and nose profusely ornamented with the stings of mosquitoes and the bites of bugs, it is very likely I did not.

"Long in these parts, Sir?" says I.

"Three or four months, Sir," says the Doctor.

"Do you think of soon returning to the old country?" says I.

Doctor Crocus makes no verbal answer, but gives me an imploring look, which says so plainly "Will you ask me that again, a little louder, if you please?" that I repeat the question.

"Think of soon returning to the old country, Sir?" repeats the Doctor.

"To the old country, Sir," I rejoin.

Doctor Crocus looks round upon the crowd to observe the effect he produces, rubs his hands, and says, in a very loud voice:

"Not yet awhile, Sir, not yet. You won't catch me at that just yet, Sir. I am a little too fond of freedom for *that*, Sir. Ha, ha! It's not so easy for a man to tear himself from a free country such as this is, Sir. Ha, ha! No, no! Ha, ha! None of that till one's obliged to do it, Sir. No, no!"

As Doctor Crocus says these latter words, he shakes his head, knowingly, and laughs again. Many of the bystanders shake their heads in concert with the doctor, and laugh too, and look at each other as much as to say, "A pretty bright and first-rate sort of chap is Crocus!" and unless I am very much mistaken, a good many people went to the lecture that night, who never thought about phrenology, or about Doctor Crocus either, in all their lives before.

From Belleville, we went on, through the same desolate kind of waste, and constantly attended, without the interval of a moment, by the same music; until, at three o'clock in the afternoon, we halted once more at a village called Lebanon to inflate the horses again, and give them some corn besides: of which they stood much in need. Pending this ceremony, I walked into the village, where I met a full-sized dwelling-house coming down-hill at a round trot, drawn by a score or more of oxen.

The public-house was so very clean and good a one, that the managers of the jaunt resolved to return to it and put up there for the night, if possible. This course decided on, and the horses being well refreshed, we again pushed forward, and came upon the Prairie at sunset.

It would be difficult to say why, or how—though it was possibly from having heard and read so much about it—but the effect on me was disappointment. Looking towards the setting sun, there lay, stretched out before my view, a vast expanse of level ground; unbroken, save by one thin line of trees, which scarcely amounted to a scratch upon the great blank; until it met the glowing sky, wherein it seemed to dip: mingling with its rich colours, and mellowing in its distant blue. There it lay, a tranquil sea or lake without water, if such a simile be admissible, with the day going down upon it: a few birds wheeling here and there: and solitude and silence reigning paramount around. But the grass was not yet high; there were bare black patches on the ground; and the few wild flowers that the eye could see, were poor and scanty. Great as the picture was, its very flatness and extent, which left nothing to the imagination, tamed it down and cramped its interest. I felt little of that sense of freedom and exhilaration which a Scottish heath inspires, or even our English downs awaken. It was lonely and wild, but oppressive in its barren monotony. I felt that in traversing the Prairies, I could never abandon myself to the scene, forgetful of all else; as I should do instinctively, were the heather underneath my feet, or an iron-bound coast beyond; but should often glance towards the distant and frequently-receding line of the horizon, and wish it gained and passed. It is not a scene to be forgotten, but it is scarcely one, I think (at all events, as I saw it), to remember with much pleasure, or to covet the looking-on again, in after-life.

We encamped near a solitary log-house, for the sake of its water, and dined upon the plain. The baskets contained roast fowls, buffalo's tongue (an exquisite dainty, by-the-way), ham, bread, cheese, and butter; biscuits, champagne, sherry; lemons and sugar for punch; and abundance of rough ice. The meal was delicious, and the entertainers were the soul of kindness and good humour. I have often recalled that cheerful party to my pleasant recollection since, and shall not easily forget, in junketings nearer home with friends of older date, my boon companions on the Prairie.

Returning to Lebanon that night, we lay at the little inn at which we had halted in the afternoon. In point of cleanliness and comfort it would have suffered by no comparison with any English alehouse, of a homely kind, in England.

Rising at five o'clock next morning, I took a walk about the village: none of the houses were strolling about to-day, but it was early for them yet, perhaps: and then amused myself by lounging in a kind of farm-yard behind the tavern, of which the leading features were, a strange jumble of rough sheds for stables; a rude colonnade, built as a cool place of summer resort; a deep well; a great earthen mound for keeping vegetables in, in winter time; and a pigeon-house, whose little apertures looked, as they do in all pigeon-houses, very much too small for the admission of the plump and swelling-breasted birds who were strutting about it, though they tried to get in never so hard. That interest exhausted, I took a survey of the inn's two parlours, which were decorated with coloured prints of Washington, and President Madison, and of a white-faced young lady (much speckled by the flies), who held up her gold neck-chain for the admiration of the spectator, and informed all admiring comers that she was "Just Seventeen:" although I should have thought her older. In the best room were two oil portraits of the kit-cat size, representing the landlord and his infant son; both looking as bold as lions, and staring out of the canvas with an intensity that would have been cheap at any price. They were painted, I think, by the artist who had touched up the Belleville doors with red and gold; for I seemed to recognise his style immediately.

After breakfast, we started to return by a different way from that which we had taken yesterday, and coming up at ten o'clock with an encampment of German emigrants carrying their goods in carts, who had made a rousing fire which they were just quitting, stopped there to refresh. And very pleasant the fire was ; for, hot though it had been yesterday, it was quite cold to-day, and the wind blew keenly. Looming in the distance, as we rode along, was another of the ancient Indian burial-places, called The Monks' Mound ; in memory of a body of fanatics of the order of La Trappe, who founded a desolate convent there, many years ago, when there were no settlers within a thousand miles, and were all swept off by the pernicious climate : in which lamentable fatality, few rational people will suppose, perhaps, that society experienced any very severe deprivation.

The track of to-day had the same features as the track of yesterday. There was the swamp, the bush, and the perpetual chorus of frogs, the rank unseemly growth, the unwholesome steaming earth. Here and there, and frequently too, we encountered a solitary broken-down waggon, full of some new settler's goods. It was a pitiful sight to see one of these vehicles deep in the mire ; the axletree broken ; the wheel lying idly by its side ; the man gone miles away, to look for assistance ; the woman seated among their wandering household gods with a baby at her breast, a picture of forlorn, dejected patience ; the team of oxen crouching down mournfully in the mud, and breathing forth such clouds of vapour from their mouths and nostrils, that all the damp mist and fog around seemed to have come direct from them.

In due time we mustered once again before the merchant tailor's, and having done so, crossed over to the city in the ferry-boat : passing, on the way, a spot called Bloody Island, the duelling-ground of St. Louis, and so designated in honour of the last fatal combat fought there, which was with pistols, breast to breast. Both combatants fell dead upon the ground ; and possibly some rational people may think of them, as of the gloomy madmen on the Monks' Mound, that they were no great loss to the community.

CHAPTER XIV

As I had a desire to travel through the interior of the state
of Ohio, and to "strike the lakes," as the phrase is, at a
small town called Sandusky, to which that route would
conduct us on our way to Niagara, we had to return from
St. Louis by the way we had come, and to retrace our former
track as far as Cincinnati.

The day on which we were to take leave of St. Louis
being very fine; and the steamboat, which was to have
started I don't know how early in the morning, postponing,
for the third or fourth time, her departure until the afternoon; we rode forward to an old French village on the
river, called properly Carondelet, and nicknamed Vide Poche,
and arranged that the packet should call for us there.

The place consisted of a few poor cottages, and two or
three public-houses; the state of whose larders certainly
seemed to justify the second designation of the village, for
there was nothing to eat in any of them. At length, however, by going back some half a mile or so, we found a
solitary house where ham and coffee were procurable; and
there we tarried to await the advent of the boat, which
would come in sight from the green before the door, a long
way off.

It was a neat, unpretending village tavern, and we took
our repast in a quaint little room with a bed in it, decorated
with some old oil paintings, which in their time had probably
done duty in a Catholic chapel or monastery. The fare was
very good, and served with great cleanliness. The house was
kept by a characteristic old couple, with whom we had a long
talk, and who were perhaps a very good sample of that kind
of people in the West.

The landlord was a dry, tough, hard-faced old fellow (not so very old either, for he was but just turned sixty, I should think), who had been out with the militia in the last war with England, and had seen all kinds of service,—except a battle; and he had been very near seeing that, he added: very near. He had all his life been restless and locomotive, with an irresistible desire for change; and was still the son of his old self: for if he had nothing to keep him at home, he said (slightly jerking his hat and his thumb towards the window of the room in which the old lady sat, as we stood talking in front of the house), he would clean up his musket, and be off to Texas to-morrow morning. He was one of the very many descendants of Cain proper to this continent, who seem destined from their birth to serve as pioneers in the great human army: who gladly go on from year to year extending its outposts, and leaving home after home behind them; and die at last, utterly regardless of their graves being left thousands of miles behind, by the wandering generation who succeed.

His wife was a domesticated kind-hearted old soul, who had come with him, "from the queen city of the world," which, it seemed, was Philadelphia; but had no love for this Western country, and indeed had little reason to bear it any; having seen her children, one by one, die here of fever, in the full prime and beauty of their youth. Her heart was sore, she said, to think of them; and to talk on this theme, even to strangers, in that blighted place, so far from her old home, eased it somewhat, and became a melancholy pleasure.

The boat appearing towards evening, we bade adieu to the poor old lady and her vagrant spouse, and making for the nearest landing-place, were soon on board "The Messenger" again, in our old cabin, and steaming down the Mississippi.

If the coming up this river, slowly making head against the stream, be an irksome journey, the shooting down it with the turbid current is almost worse; for then the boat, proceeding at the rate of twelve or fifteen miles an hour, has to force its passage through a labyrinth of floating logs, which, in the dark, it is often impossible to see beforehand or avoid. All that night, the bell was never silent for five minutes at a time; and after every ring the vessel reeled again, sometimes beneath a single blow, sometimes beneath a dozen dealt in quick succession, the lightest of which seemed more than enough to beat in her frail keel, as though it had been pie-crust. Looking down upon the filthy river after dark, it seemed to be alive with monsters, as these black masses rolled upon the surface, or came starting up again, head first, when the boat, in ploughing her way among a shoal of such obstructions, drove a few among them for the moment under water. Sometimes the engine stopped during a long interval, and then before her and behind, and gathering close about her on all sides, were so many of these ill-favoured obstacles that she was fairly hemmed in ; the centre of a floating island ; and was constrained to pause until they parted, somewhere, as dark clouds will do before the wind, and opened by degrees a channel out.

In good time next morning, however, we came again in sight of the detestable morass called Cairo ; and stopping there to take in wood, lay alongside a barge, whose starting timbers scarcely held together. It was moored to the bank, and on its side was painted "Coffee House ; " that being, I suppose, the floating paradise to which the people fly for shelter when they lose their houses for a month or two beneath the hideous waters of the Mississippi. But looking southward from this point, we had the satisfaction of seeing that intolerable river dragging its slimy length and ugly freight abruptly off towards New Orleans ; and passing a yellow line which stretched across the current, were again upon the clear Ohio, never, I trust, to see the Mississippi more, saving in troubled dreams and nightmares. Leaving it for the company of its sparkling neighbour, was like the transition from pain to ease, or the awakening from a horrible vision to cheerful realities.

We arrived at Louisville on the fourth night, and gladly availed ourselves of its excellent hotel. Next day we went on in the "Ben Franklin," a beautiful mail steamboat, and reached Cincinnati shortly after midnight. Being by this time nearly tired of sleeping upon shelves, we had remained awake to go ashore straightway ; and groping a passage across the dark decks of other boats, and among labyrinths of engine-machinery and leaking casks of molasses, we reached the streets, knocked up the porter at the hotel where we had stayed before, and were, to our great joy, safely housed soon afterwards.

We rested but one day at Cincinnati, and then resumed our journey to Sandusky. As it comprised two varieties of stage-coach travelling, which, with those I have already

glanced at, comprehend the main characteristics of this mode
of transit in America, I will take the reader as our fellow-
passenger, and pledge myself to perform the distance with all
possible dispatch.

Our place of destination in the first instance is Columbus.
It is distant about a hundred and twenty miles from Cincinnati, but there is a macadamised road (rare blessing!) the
whole way, and the rate of travelling upon it is six miles an
hour.

We start at eight o'clock in the morning, in a great mail-
coach, whose huge cheeks are so very ruddy and plethoric,
that it appears to be troubled with a tendency of blood to
the head.   Dropsical it certainly is, for it will hold a dozen
passengers inside.   But, wonderful to add, it is very clean
and bright, being nearly new;   and rattles through the
streets of Cincinnati gaily.

Our way lies through a beautiful country, richly cultivated,
and luxuriant in its promise of an abundant harvest.   Sometimes we pass a field where the strong bristling stalks of
Indian corn look like a crop of walking-sticks, and sometimes
an enclosure where the green wheat is springing up among
a labyrinth of stumps;   the primitive worm-fence is universal,
and an ugly thing it is;   but the farms are neatly kept, and,
save for these differences, one might be travelling just now
in Kent.

We often stop to water at a roadside inn, which is always
dull and silent.   The coachman dismounts and fills his
bucket, and holds it to the horses' heads.   There is scarcely
ever any one to help him;   there are seldom any loungers
standing round;   and never any stable-company with jokes
to crack.   Sometimes, when we have changed our team,
there is a difficulty in starting again, arising out of the
prevalent mode of breaking a young horse: which is to
catch him, harness him against his will, and put him in
a stage-coach without further notice: but we get on somehow or other, after a great many kicks and a violent struggle;
and jog on as before again.

Occasionally, when we stop to change, some two or three
half-drunken loafers will come loitering out with their hands
in their pockets, or will be seen kicking their heels in
rocking-chairs, or lounging on the window-sill, or sitting on
a rail within the colonnade: they have not often anything to
say though, either to us or to each other, but sit there idly

staring at the coach and horses. The landlord of the inn is usually among them, and seems, of all the party, to be the least connected with the business of the house. Indeed he is with reference to the tavern, what the driver is in relation to the coach and passengers : whatever happens in his sphere of action, he is quite indifferent, and perfectly easy in his mind.

The frequent change of coachmen works no change or variety in the coachman's character. He is always dirty, sullen, and taciturn. If he be capable of smartness of any kind, moral or physical, he has a faculty of concealing it which is truly marvellous. He never speaks to you as you sit beside him on the box, and if you speak to him, he answers (if at all) in monosyllables. He points out nothing on the road, and seldom looks at anything: being, to all appearance, thoroughly weary of it and of existence generally. As to doing the honours of his coach, his business, as I have said, is with the horses. The coach follows because it is attached to them and goes on wheels: not because you are in it. Sometimes, towards the end of a long stage, he suddenly breaks out into a discordant fragment of an election song, but his face never sings along with him: it is only his voice, and not often that.

He always chews and always spits, and never encumbers himself with a pocket-handkerchief. The consequences to the box passenger, especially when the wind blows towards him, are not agreeable.

Whenever the coach stops, and you can hear the voices of the inside passengers ; or whenever any bystander addresses them, or any one among them ; or they address each other ; you will hear one phrase repeated over and over and over again to the most extraordinary extent. It is an ordinary and unpromising phrase enough, being neither more nor less than "Yes, Sir ; " but it is adapted to every variety of circumstance, and fills up every pause in the conversation. Thus :—

The time is one o'clock at noon. The scene, a place where we are to stay and dine, on this journey. The coach drives up to the door of an inn. The day is warm, and there are several idlers lingering about the tavern, and waiting for the public dinner. Among them, is a stout gentleman in a brown hat, swinging himself to and fro in a rocking-chair on the pavement.

As the coach stops, a gentleman in a straw hat looks out of the window :

STRAW HAT. (To the stout gentleman in the rocking-chair.) I reckon that's Judge Jefferson, an't it ?

BROWN HAT. (Still swinging ; speaking very slowly ; and without any emotion whatever.) Yes, Sir.

STRAW HAT. Warm weather, Judge.

BROWN HAT. Yes, Sir.

STRAW HAT. There was a snap of cold, last week.

BROWN HAT. Yes, Sir.

STRAW HAT. Yes, Sir.

A pause. They look at each other, very seriously.

STRAW HAT. I calculate you'll have got through that case of the corporation, Judge, by this time, now ?

BROWN HAT. Yes, Sir.

STRAW HAT. How did the verdict go, Sir ?

BROWN HAT. For the defendant, Sir.

STRAW HAT. (Interrogatively.) Yes, Sir ?

BROWN HAT. (Affirmatively.) Yes, Sir.

BOTH. (Musingly, as each gazes down the street.) Yes, Sir.

Another pause. They look at each other again, still more seriously than before.

BROWN HAT. This coach is rather behind its time to-day, I guess.

STRAW HAT. (Doubtingly.) Yes, Sir.

BROWN HAT. (Looking at his watch.) Yes, Sir ; nigh upon two hours.

STRAW HAT. (Raising his eyebrows in very great surprise.) Yes, Sir !

BROWN HAT. (Decisively, as he puts up his watch.) Yes, Sir.

ALL THE OTHER INSIDE PASSENGERS. (Among themselves.) Yes, Sir.

COACHMAN. (In a very surly tone.) No it an't.

STRAW HAT. (To the coachman.) Well. I don't know, Sir. We were a pretty tall time coming that last fifteen mile. That's a fact.

The coachman making no reply, and plainly declining to enter into any controversy on a subject so far removed from his sympathies and feelings, another passenger says, "Yes, Sir ; " and the gentleman in the straw hat in acknowledgment of his courtesy, says "Yes, Sir," to him, in return.

The straw hat then inquires of the brown hat, whether that coach in which he (the straw hat) then sits, is not a new one? To which the brown hat again makes answer, "Yes, Sir."

STRAW HAT. I thought so. Pretty loud smell of varnish, Sir?

BROWN HAT. Yes, Sir.

ALL THE OTHER INSIDE PASSENGERS. Yes, Sir.

BROWN HAT. (To the company in general.) Yes, Sir.

The conversational powers of the company having been by this time pretty heavily taxed, the straw hat opens the door and gets out; and all the rest alight also. We dine soon afterwards with the boarders in the house, and have nothing to drink but tea and coffee. As they are both very bad and the water is worse, I ask for brandy; but it is a Temperance Hotel, and spirits are not to be had for love or money. This preposterous forcing of unpleasant drinks down the reluctant throats of travellers is not at all uncommon in America, but I never discovered that the scruples of such wincing landlords induced them to preserve any unusually nice balance between the quality of their fare, and their scale of charges: on the contrary, I rather suspected them of diminishing the one and exalting the other, by way of recompence for the loss of their profit on the sale of spirituous liquors. After all, perhaps, the plainest course for persons of such tender consciences, would be, a total abstinence from tavern-keeping.

Dinner over, we get into another vehicle which is ready at the door (for the coach has been changed in the interval), and resume our journey; which continues through the same kind of country until evening, when we come to the town where we are to stop for tea and supper; and having delivered the mail bags at the Post-office, ride through the usual wide street, lined with the usual stores and houses (the drapers always having hung up at their door, by way of sign, a piece of bright red cloth), to the hotel where this meal is prepared. There being many boarders here, we sit down, a large party, and a very melancholy one as usual. But there is a buxom hostess at the head of the table, and opposite, a simple Welsh schoolmaster with his wife and child; who came here, on a speculation of greater promise than performance, to teach the classics: and they are sufficient subjects of interest until the meal is over, and another coach is ready. In it we go on once more, lighted by a bright moon, until midnight; when we stop to change the coach again, and remain for half an hour or so in a miserable room, with a blurred lithograph of Washington over the smoky fireplace, and a mighty jug of cold water on the table: to which refreshment the moody passengers do so apply themselves that they would seem to be, one and all, keen patients of Dr. Sangrado.   Among them is a very little boy, who chews tobacco like a very big one ; and a droning gentleman, who talks arithmetically and statistically on all subjects, from poetry downwards ; and who always speaks in the same key, with exactly the same emphasis, and with very grave deliberation.   He came outside just now, and told me how that the uncle of a certain young lady who had been spirited away and married by a certain captain, lived in these parts ; and how this uncle was so valiant and ferocious that he shouldn't wonder if he were to follow the said captain to England, ''and shoot him down in the street wherever he found him ;'' in the feasibility of which strong measure I, being for the moment rather prone to contradiction, from feeling half asleep and very tired, declined to acquiesce : assuring him that if the uncle did resort to it, or gratified any other little whim of the like nature, he would find himself one morning prematurely throttled at the Old Bailey: and that he would do well to make his will before he went, as he would certainly want it before he had been in Britain very long.

On we go, all night, and by-and-by the day begins to break, and presently the first cheerful rays of the warm sun come slanting on us brightly.   It sheds its light upon a miserable waste of sodden grass, and dull trees, and squalid huts, whose aspect is forlorn and grievous in the last degree. A very desert in the wood, whose growth of green is dank and noxious like that upon the top of standing water : where poisonous fungus grows in the rare footprint on the oozy ground, and sprouts like witches' coral, from the crevices in the cabin wall and floor ; it is a hideous thing to lie upon the very threshold of a city.   But it was purchased years ago, and as the owner cannot be discovered, the State has been unable to reclaim it.   So there it remains, in the midst of cultivation and improvement, like ground accursed, and made obscene and rank by some great crime.

We reached Columbus shortly before seven o'clock, and stayed there, to refresh, that day and night : having excellent apartments in a very large unfinished hotel called the Neill

House, which were richly fitted with the polished wood of the black walnut, and opened on a handsome portico and stone verandah, like rooms in some Italian mansion. The town is clean and pretty, and of course is "going to be" much larger. It is the seat of the State legislature of Ohio, and lays claim, in consequence, to some consideration and importance.

There being no stage-coach next day, upon the road we wished to take, I hired "an extra," at a reasonable charge, to carry us to Tiffin; a small town from whence there is a railroad to Sandusky. This extra was an ordinary four-horse stage-coach, such as I have described, changing horses and drivers, as the stage-coach would, but was exclusively our own for the journey. To ensure our having horses at the proper stations, and being incommoded by no strangers, the proprietors sent an agent on the box, who was to accompany us the whole way through; and thus attended, and bearing with us, besides, a hamper full of savoury cold meats, and fruit, and wine, we started off again in high spirits, at half-past six o'clock next morning, very much delighted to be by ourselves, and disposed to enjoy even the roughest journey.

It was well for us, that we were in this humour, for the road we went over that day, was certainly enough to have shaken tempers that were not resolutely at Set Fair, down to some inches below Stormy. At one time we were all flung together in a heap at the bottom of the coach, and at another we were crushing our heads against the roof. Now, one side was down deep in the mire, and we were holding on to the other. Now, the coach was lying on the tails of the two wheelers; and now it was rearing up in the air, in a frantic state, with all four horses standing on the top of an insur-mountable eminence, looking coolly back at it, as though they would say "Unharness us. It can't be done." The drivers on these roads, who certainly get over the ground in a manner which is quite miraculous, so twist and turn the team about in forcing a passage, corkscrew fashion, through the bogs and swamps, that it was quite a common circum-stance on looking out of the window, to see the coachman with the ends of a pair of reins in his hands, apparently driving nothing, or playing at horses, and the leaders staring at one unexpectedly from the back of the coach, as if they had some idea of getting up behind. A great portion of the way was over what is called a corduroy road, which is made by throwing trunks of trees into a marsh, and leaving them to settle there. The very slightest of the jolts with which the ponderous carriage fell from log to log, was enough, it seemed, to have dislocated all the bones in the human body. It would be impossible to experience a similar set of sensations, in any other circumstances, unless perhaps in attempting to go up to the top of St. Paul's in an omnibus. Never, never once, that day, was the coach in any position, attitude, or kind of motion to which we are accustomed in coaches. Never did it make the smallest approach to one's experience of the proceedings of any sort of vehicle that goes on wheels.

Still, it was a fine day, and the temperature was delicious, and though we had left Summer behind us in the west, and were fast leaving Spring, we were moving towards Niagara and home. We alighted in a pleasant wood towards the middle of the day, dined on a fallen tree, and leaving our best fragments with a cottager, and our worst with the pigs (who swarm in this part of the country like grains of sand on the sea-shore, to the great comfort of our commissariat in Canada), we went forward again, gaily.

As night came on, the track grew narrower and narrower, until at last it so lost itself among the trees, that the driver seemed to find his way by instinct. We had the comfort of knowing, at least, that there was no danger of his falling asleep, for every now and then a wheel would strike against an unseen stump with such a jerk, that he was fain to hold on pretty tight and pretty quick, to keep himself upon the box. Nor was there any reason to dread the least danger from furious driving, inasmuch as over that broken ground the horses had enough to do to walk; as to shying, there was no room for that; and a herd of wild elephants could not have run away in such a wood, with such a coach at their heels. So we stumbled along, quite satisfied.

These stumps of trees are a curious feature in American travelling. The varying illusions they present to the unaccustomed eye as it grows dark, are quite astonishing in their number and reality. Now, there is a Grecian urn erected in the centre of a lonely field; now there is a woman weeping at a tomb; now a very commonplace old gentleman in a white waistcoat, with a thumb thrust into each arm-hole of his coat; now a student poring on a book; now a crouching negro; now, a horse, a dog, a cannon, an armed man; a hunchback throwing off his cloak and stepping forth into the light. They were often as entertaining to me as so many glasses in a magic lantern, and never took their shapes at my bidding, but seemed to force themselves upon me, whether I would or no; and strange to say, I sometimes recognised in them counterparts of figures once familiar to me in pictures attached to childish books, forgotten long ago.

It soon became too dark, however, even for this amusement, and the trees were so close together that their dry branches rattled against the coach on either side, and obliged us all to keep our heads within. It lightened too, for three whole hours; each flash being very bright, and blue, and long; and as the vivid streaks came darting in among the crowded branches, and the thunder rolled gloomily above the tree tops, one could scarcely help thinking that there were better neighbourhoods at such a time than thick woods afforded.

At length, between ten and eleven o'clock at night, a few feeble lights appeared in the distance, and Upper Sandusky, an Indian village, where we were to stay till morning, lay before us.

They were gone to bed at the log Inn, which was the only house of entertainment in the place, but soon answered to our knocking, and got some tea for us in a sort of kitchen or common room, tapestried with old newspapers, pasted against the wall. The bedchamber to which my wife and I were shown, was a large, low, ghostly room; with a quantity of withered branches on the hearth, and two doors without any fastening, opposite to each other, both opening on the black night and wild country, and so contrived, that one of them always blew the other open: a novelty in domestic architecture, which I do not remember to have seen before, and which I was somewhat disconcerted to have forced on my attention after getting into bed, as I had a considerable sum in gold for our travelling expenses, in my dressing-case. Some of the luggage, however, piled against the panels, soon settled this difficulty, and my sleep would not have been very much affected that night, I believe, though it had failed to do so.

My Boston friend climbed up to bed, somewhere in the roof, where another guest was already snoring hugely. But being bitten beyond his power of endurance, he turned out again, and fled for shelter to the coach, which was airing itself in front of the house. This was not a very politic step, as it turned out; for the pigs scenting him, and looking upon the coach as a kind of pie with some manner of meat inside, grunted round it so hideously, that he was afraid to come out again, and lay there shivering, till morning. Nor was it possible to warm him, when he did come out, by means of a glass of brandy: for in Indian villages, the legislature, with a very good and wise intention, forbids the sale of spirits by tavern keepers. The precaution, however, is quite ineffi-cacious, for the Indians never fail to procure liquor of a worse kind, at a dearer price, from travelling pedlars.

It is a settlement of the Wyandot Indians who inhabit this place. Among the company at breakfast was a mild old gentleman, who had been for many years employed by the United States Government in conducting negotiations with the Indians, and who had just concluded a treaty with these people by which they bound themselves, in consideration of a certain annual sum, to remove next year to some land provided for them, west of the Mississippi, and a little way beyond St. Louis. He gave me a moving account of their strong attachment to the familiar scenes of their infancy, and in particular to the burial-places of their kindred; and of their great reluctance to leave them. He had witnessed many such removals, and always with pain, though he knew that they departed for their own good. The question whether this tribe should go or stay, had been discussed among them a day or two before, in a hut erected for the purpose, the logs of which still lay upon the ground before the inn. When the speaking was done, the ayes and noes were ranged on opposite sides, and every male adult voted in his turn. The moment the result was known, the minority (a large one) cheerfully yielded to the rest, and withdrew all kind of opposition.

We met some of these poor Indians afterwards, riding on shaggy ponies. They were so like the meaner sort of gipsies, that if I could have seen any of them in England, I should have concluded, as a matter of course, that they belonged to that wandering and restless people.

Leaving this town directly after breakfast, we pushed forward again, over a rather worse road than yesterday, if possible, and arrived about noon at Tiffin, where we parted with the extra. At two o'clock we took the railroad; the travelling on which was very slow, its construction being indifferent, and the ground wet and marshy; and arrived at Sandusky in time to dine that evening. We put up at a comfortable little hotel on the brink of Lake Erie, lay there that night, and had no choice but to wait there next day, until a steamboat bound for Buffalo appeared. The town, which was sluggish and uninteresting enough, was something like the back of an English watering-place, out of the season.

Our host, who was very attentive and anxious to make us comfortable, was a handsome middle-aged man, who had come to this town from New England, in which part of the country he was "raised." When I say that he constantly walked in and out of the room with his hat on ; and stopped to converse in the same free-and-easy state ; and lay down on our sofa, and pulled his newspaper out of his pocket, and read it at his ease ; I merely mention these traits as characteristic of the country ; not at all as being matter of complaint, or as having been disagreeable to me. I should undoubtedly be offended by such proceedings at home, because there they are not the custom, and where they are not, they would be impertinences; but in America, the only desire of a good-natured fellow of this kind, is to treat his guests hospitably and well; and I had no more right, and I can truly say no more disposition, to measure his conduct by our English rule and standard, than I had to quarrel with him for not being of the exact stature which would qualify him for admission into the Queen's Grenadier Guards. As little inclination had I to find fault with a funny old lady who was an upper domestic in this establishment, and who, when she came to wait upon us at any meal, sat herself down comfortably in the most convenient chair, and producing a large pin to pick her teeth with, remained performing that ceremony, and steadfastly regarding us meanwhile with much gravity and composure (now and then pressing us to eat a little more), until it was time to clear away. It was enough for us, that whatever we wished done was done with great civility and readiness, and a desire to oblige, not only here, but everywhere else ; and that all our wants were, in general, zealously anticipated.

We were taking an early dinner at this house, on the day after our arrival, which was Sunday, when a steamboat came in sight, and presently touched at the wharf. As she proved to be on her way to Buffalo, we hurried on board with all speed, and soon left Sandusky far behind us.

She was a large vessel of five hundred tons, and handsomely fitted up, though with high-pressure engines ; which always conveyed that kind of feeling to me, which I should be likely to experience, I think, if I had lodgings on the first-floor

H

of a powder-mill. She was laden with flour, some casks of
which commodity were stored upon the deck. The captain
coming up to have a little conversation, and to introduce
a friend, seated himself astride of one of these barrels, like
a Bacchus of private life; and pulling a great clasp-knife out
of his pocket, began to "whittle" it as he talked, by paring
thin slices off the edges. And he whittled with such industry
and hearty good will, that but for his being called away very
soon, it must have disappeared bodily, and left nothing in its
place but grist and shavings.

After calling at one or two flat places, with low dams
stretching out into the lake, whereon were stumpy lighthouses,
like windmills without sails, the whole looking like a Dutch
vignette, we came at midnight to Cleveland, where we lay
all night, and until nine o'clock next morning.

I entertained quite a curiosity in reference to this place,
from having seen at Sandusky a specimen of its literature in
the shape of a newspaper, which was very strong indeed upon
the subject of Lord Ashburton's recent arrival at Washington,
to adjust the points in dispute between the United States
Government and Great Britain: informing its readers that as
America had "whipped" England in her infancy, and whipped
her again in her youth, so it was clearly necessary that she
must whip her once again in her maturity; and pledging its
credit to all True Americans, that if Mr. Webster did his
duty in the approaching negotiations, and sent the English
Lord home again in double quick time, they should, within
two years, sing "Yankee Doodle in Hyde Park, and Hail
Columbia in the scarlet courts of Westminster!" I found it
a pretty town, and had the satisfaction of beholding the
outside of the office of the journal from which I have just
quoted. I did not enjoy the delight of seeing the wit who
indited the paragraph in question, but I have no doubt he
is a prodigious man in his way, and held in high repute by
a select circle.

There was a gentleman on board, to whom, as I unintentionally learned through the thin partition which divided our
state-room from the cabin in which he and his wife conversed
together, I was unwittingly the occasion of very great uneasiness. I don't know why or wherefore, but I appeared to run
in his mind perpetually, and to dissatisfy him very much.
First of all I heard him say: and the most ludicrous part of
the business was, that he said it in my very ear, and could

not have communicated more directly with me, if he had leaned upon my shoulder, and whispered me: "Boz is on board still, my dear." After a considerable pause, he added, complainingly, "Boz keeps himself very close;" which was true enough, for I was not very well, and was lying down, with a book. I thought he had done with me after this, but I was deceived; for a long interval having elapsed, during which I imagine him to have been turning restlessly from side to side, and trying to go to sleep; he broke out again, with "I suppose *that* Boz will be writing a book by-and-by, and putting all our names in it!" at which imaginary consequence of being on board a boat with Boz, he groaned, and became silent.

We called at the town of Erie, at eight o'clock that night, and lay there an hour. Between five and six next morning, we arrived at Buffalo, where we breakfasted; and being too near the Great Falls to wait patiently anywhere else, we set off by the train, the same morning at nine o'clock, to Niagara.

It was a miserable day; chilly and raw; a damp mist falling; and the trees in that northern region quite bare and wintry. Whenever the train halted, I listened for the roar; and was constantly straining my eyes in the direction where I knew the Falls must be, from seeing the river rolling on towards them; every moment expecting to behold the spray. Within a few minutes of our stopping, not before, I saw two great white clouds rising up slowly and majestically from the depths of the earth. That was all. At length we alighted: and then for the first time, I heard the mighty rush of water, and felt the ground tremble underneath my feet.

The bank is very steep, and was slippery with rain, and half-melted ice. I hardly know how I got down, but I was soon at the bottom, and climbing, with two English officers who were crossing and had joined me, over some broken rocks, deafened by the noise, half-blinded by the spray, and wet to the skin. We were at the foot of the American Fall. I could see an immense torrent of water tearing headlong down from some great height, but had no idea of shape, or situation, or anything but vague immensity.

When we were seated in the little ferry-boat, and were crossing the swollen river immediately before both cataracts, I began to feel what it was: but I was in a manner stunned, and unable to comprehend the vastness of the scene. It

was not until I came on Table Rock, and looked—Great
Heaven, on what a fall of bright-green water!—that it came
upon me in its full might and majesty.

Then, when I felt how near to my Creator I was standing,
the first effect, and the enduring one—instant and lasting
—of the tremendous spectacle, was Peace.   Peace of Mind,
tranquillity, calm recollections of the Dead, great thoughts
of Eternal Rest and Happiness; nothing of gloom or terror.
Niagara was at once stamped upon my heart, an Image of
Beauty; to remain there, changeless and indelible, until its
pulses cease to beat, for ever.

Oh, how the strife and trouble of daily life receded from
my view, and lessened in the distance, during the ten memorable days we passed on that Enchanted Ground!   What
voices spoke from out the thundering water; what faces,
faded from the earth, looked out upon me from its gleaming
depths; what Heavenly promise glistened in those angels'
tears, the drops of many hues, that showered around, and
twined themselves about the gorgeous arches which the
changing rainbows made!

I never stirred in all that time from the Canadian side,
whither I had gone at first.   I never crossed the river again;
for I knew there were people on the other shore, and in
such a place it is natural to shun strange company.   To
wander to and fro all day, and see the cataracts from all
points of view; to stand upon the edge of the great Horse-
Shoe Fall, marking the hurried water gathering strength as
it approached the verge, yet seeming, too, to pause before it
shot into the gulf below; to gaze from the river's level up
at the torrent as it came streaming down; to climb the
neighbouring heights and watch it through the trees, and
see the wreathing water in the rapids hurrying on to take
its fearful plunge; to linger in the shadow of the solemn
rocks three miles below; watching the river as, stirred by
no visible cause, it heaved and eddied and awoke the echoes,
being troubled yet, far down beneath the surface, by its giant
leap; to have Niagara before me, lighted by the sun and by
the moon, red in the day's decline, and grey as evening slowly
fell upon it; to look upon it every day, and wake up in the
night and hear its ceaseless voice: this was enough.

I think in every quiet season now, still do those waters
roll and leap, and roar and tumble, all day long; still are
the rainbows spanning them, a hundred feet below.   Still,

when the sun is on them, do they shine and glow like molten gold. Still, when the day is gloomy, do they fall like snow, or seem to crumble away like the front of a great chalk cliff, or roll down the rock like dense white smoke. But always does the mighty stream appear to die as it comes down, and always from its unfathomable grave arises that tremendous ghost of spray and mist which is never laid : which has haunted this place with the same dread solemnity since Darkness brooded on the deep, and that first flood before the Deluge—Light—came rushing on Creation at the word of God.

CHAPTER XV

IN CANADA; TORONTO; KINGSTON; MONTREAL; QUEBEC;
ST. JOHN'S. IN THE UNITED STATES AGAIN; LEBANON;
THE SHAKER VILLAGE; WEST POINT

I WISH to abstain from instituting any comparison, or drawing any parallel whatever, between the social features of the
United States and those of the British Possessions in Canada.
For this reason, I shall confine myself to a very brief account
of our journeyings in the latter territory.

But before I leave Niagara, I must advert to one disgusting
circumstance which can hardly have escaped the observation
of any decent traveller who has visited the Falls.

On Table Rock, there is a cottage belonging to a Guide,
where little relics of the place are sold, and where visitors
register their names in a book kept for the purpose. On the
wall of the room in which a great many of these volumes are
preserved, the following request is posted: "Visitors will
please not copy nor extract the remarks and poetical effusions
from the registers and albums kept here."

But for this intimation, I should have let them lie upon
the tables on which they were strewn with careful negligence,
like books in a drawing-room: being quite satisfied with the
stupendous silliness of certain stanzas with an anti-climax
at the end of each, which were framed and hung up on the
wall. Curious, however, after reading this announcement,
to see what kind of morsels were so carefully preserved, I
turned a few leaves, and found them scrawled all over with
the vilest and the filthiest ribaldry that ever human hogs
delighted in.

It is humiliating enough to know that there are among
men, brutes so obscene and worthless, that they can delight
in laying their miserable profanations upon the very steps
of Nature's greatest altar. But that these should be hoarded
up for the delight of their fellow-swine, and kept in a

public place where any eyes may see them, is a disgrace
to the English language in which they are written (though
I hope few of these entries have been made by Englishmen), and a reproach to the English side, on which they are
preserved.

The quarters of our soldiers at Niagara, are finely and
airily situated. Some of them are large detached houses on
the plain above the Falls, which were originally designed
for hotels; and in the evening time, when the women and
children were leaning over the balconies watching the men
as they played at ball and other games upon the grass before
the door, they often presented a little picture of cheerfulness and animation which made it quite a pleasure to pass
that way.

At any garrisoned point where the line of demarcation
between one country and another is so very narrow as at
Niagara, desertion from the ranks can scarcely fail to be of
frequent occurrence: and it may be reasonably supposed
that when the soldiers entertain the wildest and maddest
hopes of the fortune and independence that await them on
the other side, the impulse to play traitor, which such a
place suggests to dishonest minds, is not weakened. But it
very rarely happens that the men who do desert, are happy
or contented afterwards; and many instances have been known
in which they have confessed their grievous disappointment,
and their earnest desire to return to their old service if they
could but be assured of pardon, or lenient treatment. Many
of their comrades, notwithstanding, do the like, from time
to time; and instances of loss of life in the effort to cross
the river with this object, are far from being uncommon.
Several men were drowned in the attempt to swim across,
not long ago; and one, who had the madness to trust
himself upon a table as a raft, was swept down to the
whirlpool, where his mangled body eddied round and round
some days.

I am inclined to think that the noise of the Falls is very
much exaggerated; and this will appear the more probable
when the depth of the great basin in which the water is
received, is taken into account. At no time during our stay
there, was the wind at all high or boisterous, but we never
heard them, three miles off, even at the very quiet time of
sunset, though we often tried.

Queenston, at which place the steamboats start for Toronto

(or I should rather say at which place they call, for their wharf is at Lewiston, on the opposite shore), is situated in a delicious valley, through which the Niagara river, in colour a very deep green, pursues its course. It is approached by a road that takes its winding way among the heights by which the town is sheltered ; and seen from this point is extremely beautiful and picturesque. On the most conspicuous of these heights stood a monument erected by the Provincial Legislature in memory of General Brock, who was slain in a battle with the American forces, after having won the victory. Some vagabond, supposed to be a fellow of the name of Lett, who is now, or who lately was, in prison as a felon, blew up this monument two years ago, and it is now a melancholy ruin, with a long fragment of iron railing hanging dejectedly from its top, and waving to and fro like a wild ivy branch or broken vine stem. It is of much higher importance than it may seem, that this statue should be repaired at the public cost, as it ought to have been long ago. Firstly, because it is beneath the dignity of England to allow a memorial raised in honour of one of her defenders, to remain in this condition, on the very spot where he died. Secondly, because the sight of it in its present state, and the recollection of the unpunished outrage which brought it to this pass, is not very likely to soothe down border feelings among English subjects here, or compose their border quarrels and dislikes.

I was standing on the wharf at this place, watching the passengers embarking in a steamboat which preceded that whose coming we awaited, and participating in the anxiety with which a sergeant's wife was collecting her few goods together—keeping one distracted eye hard upon the porters, who were hurrying them on board, and the other on a hoopless washing-tub for which, as being the most utterly worthless of all her movables, she seemed to entertain particular affection—when three or four soldiers with a recruit came up and went on board.

The recruit was a likely young fellow enough, strongly built and well made, but by no means sober : indeed he had all the air of a man who had been more or less drunk for some days. He carried a small bundle over his shoulder, slung at the end of a walking-stick, and had a short pipe in his mouth. He was as dusty and dirty as recruits usually are, and his shoes betokened that he had travelled on foot some distance, but he was in a very jocose state, and shook hands with this soldier, and clapped that one on the back, and talked and laughed continually, like a roaring idle dog as he was.

The soldiers rather laughed at this blade than with him: seeming to say, as they stood straightening their canes in their hands, and looking coolly at him over their glazed stocks, "Go on, my boy, while you may! you'll know better by-and-by:" when suddenly the novice, who had been backing towards the gangway in his noisy merriment, fell overboard before their eyes, and splashed heavily down into the river between the vessel and the dock.

I never saw such a good thing as the change that came over these soldiers in an instant. Almost before the man was down, their professional manner, their stiffness and constraint, were gone, and they were filled with the most violent energy. In less time than is required to tell it, they had him out again, feet first, with the tails of his coat flapping over his eyes, everything about him hanging the wrong way, and the water streaming off at every thread in his threadbare dress. But the moment they set him upright and found that he was none the worse, they were soldiers again, looking over their glazed stocks more composedly than ever.

The half-sobered recruit glanced round for a moment, as if his first impulse were to express some gratitude for his preservation, but seeing them with this air of total unconcern, and having his wet pipe presented to him with an oath by the soldier who had been by far the most anxious of the party, he stuck it in his mouth, thrust his hands into his moist pockets, and without even shaking the water off his clothes, walked on board whistling; not to say as if nothing had happened, but as if he had meant to do it, and it had been a perfect success.

Our steamboat came up directly this had left the wharf, and soon bore us to the mouth of the Niagara; where the stars and stripes of America flutter on one side and the Union Jack of England on the other: and so narrow is the space between them that the sentinels in either fort can often hear the watchword of the other country given. Thence we emerged on Lake Ontario, an inland sea; and by half-past six o'clock were at Toronto.

The country round this town being very flat, is bare of scenic interest; but the town itself is full of life and motion,

bustle, business, and improvement.   The streets are well
paved, and lighted with gas ; the houses are large and good ;
the shops excellent.   Many of them have a display of goods in
their windows, such as may be seen in thriving county towns
in England ; and there are some which would do no discredit
to the metropolis itself.   There is a good stone prison here ;
and there are, besides, a handsome church, a court-house,
public offices, many commodious private residences, and a
government observatory for noting and recording the mag-
netic variations.   In the College of Upper Canada, which is
one of the public establishments of the city, a sound education in every department of polite learning can be had, at a
very moderate expense : the annual charge for the instruction
of each pupil, not exceeding nine pounds sterling.   It has
pretty good endowments in the way of land, and is a valuable
and useful institution.

The first stone of a new college had been laid but a few
days before, by the Governor-General.   It will be a handsome, spacious edifice, approached by a long avenue, which is
already planted and made available as a public walk.   The
town is well adapted for wholesome exercise at all seasons,
for the footways in the thoroughfares which lie beyond the
principal street, are planked like floors, and kept in very
good and clean repair.

It is a matter of deep regret that political differences
should have run high in this place, and led to most discreditable and disgraceful results.   It is not long since guns were
discharged from a window in this town at the successful
candidates in an election, and the coachman of one of them
was actually shot in the body, though not dangerously
wounded.   But one man was killed on the same occasion ;
and from the very window whence he received his death, the
very flag which shielded his murderer (not only in the commission of his crime, but from its consequences), was displayed
again on the occasion of the public ceremony performed by
the Governor-General, to which I have just adverted.   Of all
the colours in the rainbow, there is but one which could be
so employed : I need not say that flag was orange.

The time of leaving Toronto for Kingston is noon.   By
eight o'clock next morning, the traveller is at the end of his
journey, which is performed by steamboat upon Lake
Ontario, calling at Port Hope and Coburg, the latter a
cheerful thriving little town.   Vast quantities of flour form

the chief item in the freight of these vessels. We had no fewer than one thousand and eighty barrels on board, between Coburg and Kingston.

The latter place, which is now the seat of government in Canada, is a very poor town, rendered still poorer in the appearance of its market-place by the ravages of a recent fire. Indeed, it may be said of Kingston, that one half of it appears to be burnt down, and the other half not to be built up. The Government House is neither elegant nor commodious, yet it is almost the only house of any importance in the neighbourhood.

There is an admirable jail here, well and wisely governed, and excellently regulated, in every respect. The men were employed as shoemakers, ropemakers, blacksmiths, tailors, carpenters, and stonecutters; and in building a new prison, which was pretty far advanced towards completion. The female prisoners were occupied in needlework. Among them was a beautiful girl of twenty, who had been there nearly three years. She acted as bearer of secret dispatches for the self-styled Patriots on Navy Island, during the Canadian Insurrection: sometimes dressing as a girl, and carrying them in her stays; sometimes attiring herself as a boy, and secreting them in the lining of her hat. In the latter character she always rode as a boy would, which was nothing to her, for she could govern any horse that any man could ride, and could drive four-in-hand with the best whip in those parts. Setting forth on one of her patriotic missions, she appropriated to herself the first horse she could lay her hands on; and this offence had brought her where I saw her. She had quite a lovely face, though, as the reader may suppose from this sketch of her history, there was a lurking devil in her bright eye, which looked out pretty sharply from between her prison bars.

There is a bomb-proof fort here of great strength, which occupies a bold position, and is capable, doubtless, of doing good service; though the town is much too close upon the frontier to be long held, I should imagine, for its present purpose in troubled times. There is also a small navy-yard, where a couple of Government steamboats were building, and getting on vigorously.

We left Kingston for Montreal on the tenth of May, at half-past nine in the morning, and proceeded in a steamboat down the St. Lawrence river. The beauty of this noble stream at almost any point, but especially in the commencement of this journey when it winds its way among the thousand Islands, can hardly be imagined. The number and constant successions of these islands, all green and richly wooded; their fluctuating sizes, some so large that for half an hour together one among them will appear as the opposite bank of the river, and some so small that they are mere dimples on its broad bosom; their infinite variety of shapes; and the numberless combinations of beautiful forms which the trees growing on them present: all form a picture fraught with uncommon interest and pleasure.

In the afternoon we shot down some rapids where the river boiled and bubbled strangely, and where the force and headlong violence of the current were tremendous. At seven o'clock we reached Dickenson's Landing, whence travellers proceed for two or three hours by stage-coach: the navigation of the river being rendered so dangerous and difficult in the interval, by rapids, that steamboats do not make the passage. The number and length of those *portages*, over which the roads are bad, and the travelling slow, render the way between the towns of Montreal and Kingston, somewhat tedious.

Our course lay over a wide, uninclosed tract of country at a little distance from the river-side, whence the bright warning lights on the dangerous parts of the St. Lawrence shone vividly. The night was dark and raw, and the way dreary enough. It was nearly ten o'clock when we reached the wharf where the next steamboat lay; and went on board, and to bed.

She lay there all night, and started as soon as it was day. The morning was ushered in by a violent thunderstorm, and was very wet, but gradually improved and brightened up. Going on deck after breakfast, I was amazed to see floating down with the stream, a most gigantic raft, with some thirty or forty wooden houses upon it, and at least as many flagmasts, so that it looked like a nautical street. I saw many of these rafts afterwards, but never one so large. All the timber, or "lumber," as it is called in America, which is brought down the St. Lawrence, is floated down in this manner. When the raft reaches its place of destination, it is broken up; the materials are sold; and the boatmen return for more.

At eight we landed again, and travelled by a stage-coach

for four hours through a pleasant and well-cultivated country, perfectly French in every respect: in the appearance of
the cottages; the air, language, and dress of the peasantry;
the sign-boards on the shops and taverns: and the Virgin's
shrines, and crosses, by the wayside. Nearly every common
labourer and boy, though he had no shoes to his feet, wore
round his waist a sash of some bright colour: generally red:
and the women, who were working in the fields and gardens,
and doing all kinds of husbandry, wore, one and all, great
flat straw hats with most capacious brims. There were
Catholic Priests and Sisters of Charity in the village streets;
and images of the Saviour at the corners of cross-roads, and
in other public places.

At noon we went on board another steamboat, and reached
the village of Lachine, nine miles from Montreal, by three
o'clock. There, we left the river, and went on by land.

Montreal is pleasantly situated on the margin of the St.
Lawrence, and is backed by some bold heights, about which
there are charming rides and drives. The streets are generally narrow and irregular, as in most French towns of any
age; but in the more modern parts of the city, they are wide
and airy. They display a great variety of very good shops;
and both in the town and suburbs there are many excellent
private dwellings. The granite quays are remarkable for
their beauty, solidity, and extent.

There is a very large Catholic cathedral here, recently
erected; with two tall spires, of which one is yet unfinished.
In the open space in front of this edifice, stands a solitary,
grim-looking, square brick tower, which has a quaint and
remarkable appearance, and which the wiseacres of the place
have consequently determined to pull down immediately.
The Government House is very superior to that at Kingston,
and the town is full of life and bustle. In one of the suburbs is a plank road—not footpath—five or six miles long,
and a famous road it is too. All the rides in the vicinity
were made doubly interesting by the bursting out of spring,
which is here so rapid, that it is but a day's leap from barren
winter, to the blooming youth of summer.

The steamboats to Quebec, perform the journey in the
night; that is to say, they leave Montreal at six in the
evening, and arrive at Quebec at six next morning. We made
this excursion during our stay in Montreal (which exceeded
a fortnight), and were charmed by its interest and beauty.

The impression made upon the visitor by this Gibraltar of America : its giddy heights ; its citadel suspended, as it were, in the air ; its picturesque steep streets and frowning gateways ; and the splendid views which burst upon the eye at every turn : is at once unique and lasting.

It is a place not to be forgotten or mixed up in the mind with other places, or altered for a moment in the crowd of scenes a traveller can recall. Apart from the realities of this most picturesque city, there are associations clustering about it which would make a desert rich in interest. The dangerous precipice along whose rocky front, Wolfe and his brave companions climbed to glory ; the Plains of Abraham, where he received his mortal wound ; the fortress so chivalrously defended by Montcalm ; and his soldier's grave, dug for him while yet alive, by the bursting of a shell ; are not the least among them, or among the gallant incidents of history. That is a noble Monument too, and worthy of two great nations, which perpetuates the memory of both brave generals, and on which their names are jointly written.

The city is rich in public institutions and in Catholic churches and charities, but it is mainly in the prospect from the site of the Old Government House, and from the Citadel, that its surpassing beauty lies. The exquisite expanse of country, rich in field and forest, mountain-height and water, which lies stretched out before the view, with miles of Canadian villages, glancing in long white streaks, like veins along the landscape ; the motley crowd of gables, roofs, and chimney-tops in the old hilly town immediately at hand ; the beautiful St. Lawrence sparkling and flashing in the sunlight; and the tiny ships below the rock from which you gaze, whose distant rigging looks like spiders' webs against the light, while casks and barrels on their decks dwindle into toys, and busy mariners become so many puppets ; all this, framed by a sunken window in the fortress and looked at from the shadowed room within, forms one of the brightest and most enchanting pictures that the eye can rest upon.

In the spring of the year, vast numbers of emigrants who have newly arrived from England or from Ireland, pass between Quebec and Montreal on their way to the backwoods and new settlements of Canada. If it be an entertaining lounge (as I very often found it) to take a morning stroll upon the quay at Montreal, and see them grouped in hundreds on the public wharfs about their chests and boxes, it is matter of deep interest to be their fellow-passenger on one of these steamboats, and mingling with the concourse, see and hear them unobserved.

The vessel in which we returned from Quebec to Montreal was crowded with them, and at night they spread their beds between decks (those who had beds, at least) and slept so close and thick about our cabin door, that the passage to and fro was quite blocked up. They were nearly all English; from Gloucestershire the greater part; and had had a long winter-passage out; but it was wonderful to see how clean the children had been kept, and how untiring in their love and self-denial all the poor parents were.

Cant as we may, and as we shall to the end of all things, it is very much harder for the poor to be virtuous than it is for the rich; and the good that is in them, shines the brighter for it. In many a noble mansion lives a man, the best of husbands and of fathers, whose private worth in both capacities is justly lauded to the skies. But bring him here, upon this crowded deck. Strip from his fair young wife her silken dress and jewels, unbind her braided hair, stamp early wrinkles on her brow, pinch her pale cheek with care and much privation, array her faded form in coarsely patched attire, let there be nothing but his love to set her forth or deck her out, and you shall put it to the proof indeed. So change his station in the world, that he shall see in those young things who climb about his knee: not records of his wealth and name: but little wrestlers with him for his daily bread; so many poachers on his scanty meal; so many units to divide his every sum of comfort, and farther to reduce its small amount. In lieu of the endearments of childhood in its sweetest aspect, heap upon him all its pains and wants, its sicknesses and ills, its fretfulness, caprice, and querulous endurance: let its prattle be, not of engaging infant fancies, but of cold, and thirst, and hunger: and if his fatherly affection outlive all this, and he be patient, watchful, tender; careful of his children's lives, and mindful always of their joys and sorrows; then send him back to Parliament, and Pulpit, and to Quarter Sessions, and when he hears fine talk of the depravity of those who live from hand to mouth, and labour hard to do it, let him speak up, as one who knows, and tell those holders forth that they, by parallel with such a class, should be High Angels in their daily lives, and lay but humble siege to Heaven at last.

Which of us shall say what he would be, if such realities, with small relief or change all through his days, were his! Looking round upon these people: far from home, houseless, indigent, wandering, weary with travel and hard living: and seeing how patiently they nursed and tended their young children: how they consulted ever their wants first, then half supplied their own; what gentle ministers of hope and faith the women were; how the men profited by their example; and how very, very seldom even a moment's petulance or harsh complaint broke out among them: I felt a stronger love and honour of my kind come glowing on my heart, and wished to God there had been many Atheists in the better part of human nature there, to read this simple lesson in the book of Life.

We left Montreal for New York again, on the thirtieth of May; crossing to La Prairie, on the opposite shore of the St. Lawrence, in a steamboat; we then took the railroad to St. John's, which is on the brink of Lake Champlain. Our last greeting in Canada was from the English officers in the pleasant barracks at that place (a class of gentlemen who had made every hour of our visit memorable by their hospitality and friendship); and with "Rule Britannia" sounding in our ears, soon left it far behind.

But Canada has held, and always will retain, a foremost place in my remembrance. Few Englishmen are prepared to find it what it is. Advancing quietly; old differences settling down, and being fast forgotten; public feeling and private enterprise alike in a sound and wholesome state; nothing of flush or fever in its system, but health and vigour throbbing in its steady pulse: it is full of hope and promise. To me—who had been accustomed to think of it as something left behind in the strides of advancing society, as something neglected and forgotten, slumbering and wasting in its sleep—the demand for labour and the rates of wages; the busy quays of Montreal; the vessels taking in their cargoes, and discharging them; the amount of shipping in the different ports; the commerce, roads, and public works, all made *to last*; the respectability and character of the public journals; and the amount of rational comfort and happiness which honest industry may earn: were very great surprises. The steamboats on the lakes, in their conveniences, cleanliness, and safety; in the gentlemanly character and bearing of their captains; and in the politeness and perfect comfort of their social regulations; are unsurpassed even by the famous Scotch vessels, deservedly so much esteemed at home. The inns are usually bad; because the custom of boarding at hotels is not so general here as in the States, and the British officers, who form a large portion of the society of every town, live chiefly at the regimental messes: but in every other respect, the traveller in Canada will find as good provision for his comfort as in any place I know.

There is one American boat—the vessel which carried us on Lake Champlain, from St. John's to Whitehall—which I praise very highly, but no more than it deserves, when I say that it is superior even to that in which we went from Queenston to Toronto, or to that in which we travelled from the latter place to Kingston, or I have no doubt I may add to any other in the world. This steamboat, which is called "The Burlington," is a perfectly exquisite achievement of neatness, elegance, and order. The decks are drawing-rooms; the cabins are boudoirs, choicely furnished and adorned with prints, pictures, and musical instruments; every nook and corner in the vessel is a perfect curiosity of graceful comfort and beautiful contrivance. Captain Sherman, her commander, to whose ingenuity and excellent taste these results are solely attributable, has bravely and worthily distinguished himself on more than one trying occasion: not least among them, in having the moral courage to carry British troops, at a time (during the Canadian rebellion) when no other conveyance was open to them. He and his vessel are held in universal respect, both by his own countrymen and ours; and no man ever enjoyed the popular esteem, who, in his sphere of action, won and wore it better than this gentleman.

By means of this floating palace we were soon in the United States again, and called that evening at Burlington; a pretty town, where we lay an hour or so. We reached Whitehall, where we were to disembark, at six next morning; and might have done so earlier, but that these steamboats lie by for some hours in the night, in consequence of the lake becoming very narrow at that part of the journey, and difficult of navigation in the dark. Its width is so contracted at one point, indeed, that they are obliged to warp round by means of a rope.

After breakfasting at Whitehall, we took the stage-coach for Albany: a large and busy town, where we arrived between

five and six o'clock that afternoon; after a very hot day's
journey, for we were now in the height of summer again.
At seven we started for New York on board a great North
River steamboat, which was so crowded with passengers that
the upper deck was like the box lobby of a theatre between
the pieces, and the lower one like Tottenham Court Road on
a Saturday night. But we slept soundly, notwithstanding,
and soon after five o'clock next morning reached New York.

Tarrying here, only that day and night, to recruit after
our late fatigues, we started off once more upon our last
journey in America. We had yet five days to spare before
embarking for England, and I had a great desire to see " the
Shaker Village," which is peopled by a religious sect from
whom it takes its name.

To this end, we went up the North River again, as far as
the town of Hudson, and there hired an extra to carry us to
Lebanon, thirty miles distant: and of course another and a
different Lebanon from that village where I slept on the
night of the Prairie trip.

The country through which the road meandered, was rich
and beautiful; the weather very fine; and for many miles the
Kaatskill mountains, where Rip Van Winkle and the ghastly
Dutchmen played at ninepins one memorable gusty afternoon,
towered in the blue distance, like stately clouds. At one
point, as we ascended a steep hill, athwart whose base a
railroad, yet constructing, took its course, we came upon an
Irish colony. With means at hand of building decent cabins,
it was wonderful to see how clumsy, rough, and wretched,
its hovels were. The best were poor protection from the
weather ; the worst let in the wind and rain through wide
breaches in the roofs of sodden grass, and in the walls of
mud ; some had neither door nor window ; some had nearly
fallen down, and were imperfectly propped up by stakes and
poles; all were ruinous and filthy. Hideously ugly old women
and very buxom young ones, pigs, dogs, men, children, babies,
pots, kettles, dunghills, vile refuse, rank straw, and standing
water, all wallowing together in an inseparable heap, composed
the furniture of every dark and dirty hut.

Between nine and ten o'clock at night, we arrived at
Lebanon : which is renowned for its warm baths, and for a
great hotel, well adapted, I have no doubt, to the gregarious
taste of those seekers after health or pleasure who repair here,
but inexpressibly comfortless to me. We were shown into

an immense apartment, lighted by two dim candles, called the drawing-room : from which there was a descent by a flight of steps, to another vast desert, called the dining-room : our bedchambers were among certain long rows of little whitewashed cells, which opened from either side of a dreary passage ; and were so like rooms in a prison that I half expected to be locked up when I went to bed, and listened involuntarily for the turning of the key on the outside. There need be baths somewhere in the neighbourhood, for the other washing arrangements were on as limited a scale as I ever saw, even in America : indeed, these bedrooms were so very bare of even such common luxuries as chairs, that I should say they were not provided with enough of anything, but that I bethink myself of our having been most bountifully bitten all night.

The house is very pleasantly situated, however, and we had a good breakfast. That done, we went to visit our place of destination, which was some two miles off, and the way to which was soon indicated by a finger-post, whereon was painted, "To the Shaker Village."

As we rode along, we passed a party of Shakers, who were at work upon the road ; who wore the broadest of all broad-brimmed hats ; and were in all visible respects such very wooden men, that I felt about as much sympathy for them, and as much interest in them, as if they had been so many figure-heads of ships. Presently we came to the beginning of the village, and alighting at the door of a house where the Shaker manufactures are sold, and which is the head-quarters of the elders, requested permission to see the Shaker worship.

Pending the conveyance of this request to some person in authority, we walked into a grim room, where several grim hats were hanging on grim pegs, and the time was grimly told by a grim clock which uttered every tick with a kind of struggle, as if it broke the grim silence reluctantly, and under protest. Ranged against the wall were six or eight stiff high-backed chairs, and they partook so strongly of the general grimness that one would much rather have sat on the floor than incurred the smallest obligation to any of them.

Presently, there stalked into this apartment, a grim old Shaker, with eyes as hard, and dull, and cold, as the great round metal buttons on his coat and waistcoat ; a sort of calm goblin. Being informed of our desire, he produced a newspaper wherein the body of elders, whereof he was a member, had advertised but a few days before, that in consequence of certain unseemly interruptions which their worship had received from strangers, their chapel was closed to the public for the space of one year.

As nothing was to be urged in opposition to this reasonable arrangement, we requested leave to make some trifling purchases of Shaker goods; which was grimly conceded. We accordingly repaired to a store in the same house and on the opposite side of the passage, where the stock was presided over by something alive in a russet case, which the elder said was a woman; and which I suppose *was* a woman, though I should not have suspected it.

On the opposite side of the road was their place of worship: a cool, clean edifice of wood, with large windows and green blinds: like a spacious summer-house. As there was no getting into this place, and nothing was to be done but walk up and down, and look at it and the other buildings in the village (which were chiefly of wood, painted a dark red like English barns, and composed of many stories like English factories), I have nothing to communicate to the reader, beyond the scanty results I gleaned the while our purchases were making.

These people are called Shakers from their peculiar form of adoration, which consists of a dance, performed by the men and women of all ages, who arrange themselves for that purpose in opposite parties: the men first divesting themselves of their hats and coats, which they gravely hang against the wall before they begin; and tying a ribbon round their shirt-sleeves, as though they were going to be bled. They accompany themselves with a droning, humming noise, and dance until they are quite exhausted, alternately advancing and retiring in a preposterous sort of trot. The effect is said to be unspeakably absurd: and if I may judge from a print of this ceremony which I have in my possession; and which I am informed by those who have visited the chapel, is perfectly accurate; it must be infinitely grotesque.

They are governed by a woman, and her rule is understood to be absolute, though she has the assistance of a council of elders. She lives, it is said, in strict seclusion, in certain rooms above the chapel, and is never shown to profane eyes.

If she at all resemble the lady who presided over the store, it is a great charity to keep her as close as possible, and I cannot too strongly express my perfect concurrence in this benevolent proceeding.

All the possessions and revenues of the settlement are thrown into a common stock, which is managed by the elders. As they have made converts among people who were well to do in the world, and are frugal and thrifty, it is understood that this fund prospers : the more especially as they have made large purchases of land. Nor is this at Lebanon the only Shaker settlement: there are, I think, at least, three others.

They are good farmers, and all their produce is eagerly purchased and highly esteemed. "Shaker seeds," "Shaker herbs," and "Shaker distilled waters," are commonly announced for sale in the shops of towns and cities. They are good breeders of cattle, and are kind and merciful to the brute creation. Consequently, Shaker beasts seldom fail to find a ready market.

They eat and drink together, after the Spartan model, at a great public table. There is no union of the sexes, and every Shaker, male and female, is devoted to a life of celibacy. Rumour has been busy upon this theme, but here again I must refer to the lady of the store, and say, that if many of the sister Shakers resemble her, I treat all such slander as bearing on its face the strongest marks of wild improbability. But that they take as proselytes, persons so young that they cannot know their own minds, and cannot possess much strength of resolution in this or any other respect, I can assert from my own observation of the extreme juvenility of certain youthful Shakers whom I saw at work among the party on the road.

They are said to be good drivers of bargains, but to be honest and just in their transactions, and even in horse-dealing to resist those thievish tendencies which would seem, for some undiscovered reason, to be almost inseparable from that branch of traffic. In all matters they hold their own course quietly, live in their gloomy silent commonwealth, and show little desire to interfere with other people.

This is well enough, but nevertheless I cannot, I confess, incline towards the Shakers ; view them with much favour, or extend towards them any very lenient construction. I so abhor, and from my soul detest that bad spirit, no matter by what class or sect it may be entertained, which would strip life of its healthful graces, rob youth of its innocent pleasures, pluck from maturity and age their pleasant ornaments, and make existence but a narrow path towards the grave: that odious spirit which, if it could have had full scope and sway upon the earth, must have blasted and made barren the imaginations of the greatest men, and left them, in their power of raising up enduring images before their fellow-creatures yet unborn, no better than the beasts: that, in these very broad-brimmed hats and very sombre coats—in stiff-necked solemn-visaged piety, in short, no matter what its garb, whether it have cropped hair as in a Shaker village, or long nails as in a Hindoo temple—I recognise the worst among the enemies of Heaven and Earth, who turn the water at the marriage-feasts of this poor world, not into wine, but gall. And if there must be people vowed to crush the harmless fancies and the love of innocent delights and gaieties, which are a part of human nature: as much a part of it as any other love or hope that is our common portion: let them, for me, stand openly revealed among the ribald and licentious; the very idiots know that *they* are not on the Immortal road, and will despise them, and avoid them readily.

Leaving the Shaker village with a hearty dislike of the old Shakers, and a hearty pity for the young ones: tempered by the strong probability of their running away as they grow older and wiser, which they not uncommonly do: we returned to Lebanon, and so to Hudson, by the way we had come upon the previous day. There, we took the steamboat down the North River towards New York, but stopped, some four hours' journey short of it, at West Point, where we remained that night, and all next day, and next night too.

In this beautiful place: the fairest among the fair and lovely Highlands of the North River: shut in by deep green heights and ruined forts, and looking down upon the distant town of Newburgh, along a glittering path of sunlit water, with here and there a skiff, whose white sail often bends on some new tack as sudden flaws of wind come down upon her from the gullies in the hills: hemmed in, besides, all round with memories of Washington, and events of the revolutionary war: is the Military School of America.

It could not stand on more appropriate ground, and any ground more beautiful can hardly be. The course of education is severe, but well devised, and manly. Through June, July, and August, the young men encamp upon the spacious plain whereon the college stands; and all the year their military exercises are performed there, daily. The term of study at this institution, which the State requires from all cadets, is four years; but, whether it be from the rigid nature of the discipline, or the national impatience of restraint, or both causes combined, not more than half the number who begin their studies here, ever remain to finish them.

The number of cadets being about equal to that of the members of Congress, one is sent here from every Congressional district: its member influencing the selection. Commissions in the service are distributed on the same principle. The dwellings of the various Professors are beautifully situated; and there is a most excellent hotel for strangers, though it has the two drawbacks of being a total abstinence house (wines and spirits being forbidden to the students), and of serving the public meals at rather uncomfortable hours: to wit, breakfast at seven, dinner at one, and supper at sunset.

The beauty and freshness of this calm retreat, in the very dawn and greenness of summer—it was then the beginning of June—were exquisite indeed. Leaving it upon the sixth, and returning to New York, to embark for England on the succeeding day, I was glad to think that among the last memorable beauties which had glided past us, and softened in the bright perspective, were those whose pictures, traced by no common hand, are fresh in most men's minds; not easily to grow old, or fade beneath the dust of Time: the Kaatskill Mountains, Sleepy Hollow, and the Tappaan Zee.

CHAPTER XVI

THE PASSAGE HOME

I NEVER had so much interest before, and very likely I shall never have so much interest again, in the state of the wind, as on the long-looked-for morning of Tuesday the Seventh of June. Some nautical authority had told me a day or two previous, "anything with west in it, will do;" so when I darted out of bed at daylight, and throwing up the window, was saluted by a lively breeze from the north-west which had sprung up in the night, it came upon me so freshly, rustling with so many happy associations, that I conceived upon the spot a special regard for all airs blowing from that quarter of the compass, which I shall cherish, I dare say, until my own wind has breathed its last frail puff, and withdrawn itself for ever from the mortal calendar.

The pilot had not been slow to take advantage of this favourable weather, and the ship which yesterday had been in such a crowded dock that she might have retired from trade for good and all, for any chance she seemed to have of going to sea, was now full sixteen miles away. A gallant sight she was, when we, fast gaining on her in a steamboat, saw her in the distance riding at anchor: her tall masts pointing up in graceful lines against the sky, and every rope and spar expressed in delicate and thread-like outline: gallant, too, when, we being all aboard, the anchor came up to the sturdy chorus "Cheerily men, oh cheerily!" and she followed proudly in the towing steamboat's wake: but bravest and most gallant of all, when the tow-rope being cast adrift, the canvas fluttered from her masts, and spreading her white wings she soared away upon her free and solitary course.

In the after-cabin we were only fifteen passengers in all, and the greater part were from Canada, where some of us had known each other. The night was rough and squally, so were the next two days, but they flew by quickly, and we were soon as cheerful and snug a party, with an honest, manly-hearted captain at our head, as ever came to the resolution of being mutually agreeable, on land or water.

We breakfasted at eight, lunched at twelve, dined at three, and took our tea at half-past seven. We had abundance of amusements, and dinner was not the least among them : firstly, for its own sake; secondly, because of its extraordinary length : its duration, inclusive of all the long pauses between the courses, being seldom less than two hours and a half; which was a subject of never-failing entertainment. By way of beguiling the tediousness of these banquets, a select association was formed at the lower end of the table, below the mast, to whose distinguished president modesty forbids me to make any further allusion, which, being a very hilarious and jovial institution, was (prejudice apart) in high favour with the rest of the community, and particularly with a black steward, who lived for three weeks in a broad grin at the marvellous humour of these incorporated worthies.

Then, we had chess for those who played it, whist, cribbage, books, backgammon, and shovelboard. In all weathers, fair or foul, calm or windy, we were every one on deck, walking up and down in pairs, lying in the boats, leaning over the side, or chatting in a lazy group together. We had no lack of music, for one played the accordion, another the violin, and another (who usually began at six o'clock A.M.) the key-bugle : the combined effect of which instruments, when they all played different tunes in different parts of the ship, at the same time, and within hearing of each other, as they sometimes did (everybody being intensely satisfied with his own performance), was sublimely hideous.

When all these means of entertainment failed, a sail would heave in sight : looming, perhaps, the very spirit of a ship, in the misty distance, or passing us so close that through our glasses we could see the people on her decks, and easily make out her name, and whither she was bound. For hours together we could watch the dolphins and porpoises as they rolled and leaped and dived around the vessel ; or those small creatures ever on the wing, the Mother Carey's chickens, which had borne us company from New York bay, and for a whole fortnight fluttered about the vessel's stern. For some days we had a dead calm, or very light winds, during which the crew amused themselves with fishing, and hooked an unlucky dolphin, who expired, in all his rainbow colours, on the deck: an event of such importance in our barren calendar, that afterwards we dated from the dolphin, and made the day on which he died, an era.

Besides all this, when we were five or six days out, there began to be much talk of icebergs, of which wandering islands an unusual number had been seen by the vessels that had come into New York a day or two before we left that port, and of whose dangerous neighbourhood we were warned by the sudden coldness of the weather, and the sinking of the mercury in the barometer. While these tokens lasted, a double look-out was kept, and many dismal tales were whispered after dark, of ships that had struck upon the ice and gone down in the night; but the wind obliging us to hold a southward course, we saw none of them, and the weather soon grew bright and warm again.

The observation every day at noon, and the subsequent working of the vessel's course, was, as may be supposed, a feature in our lives of paramount importance; nor were there wanting (as there never are) sagacious doubters of the captain's calculations, who, so soon as his back was turned, would, in the absence of compasses, measure the chart with bits of string, and ends of pocket-handkerchiefs, and points of snuffers, and clearly prove him to be wrong by an odd thousand miles or so. It was very edifying to see these unbelievers shake their heads and frown, and hear them hold forth strongly upon navigation: not that they knew anything about it, but that they always mistrusted the captain in calm weather, or when the wind was adverse. Indeed, the mercury itself is not so variable as this class of passengers, whom you will see, when the ship is going nobly through the water, quite pale with admiration, swearing that the captain beats all captains ever known, and even hinting at subscriptions for a piece of plate; and who, next morning, when the breeze has lulled, and all the sails hang useless in the idle air, shake their despondent heads again, and say, with screwed-up lips, they hope that captain is a sailor—but they shrewdly doubt him.

It even became an occupation in the calm, to wonder when the wind *would* spring up in the favourable quarter, where, it was clearly shown by all the rules and precedents, it ought to have sprung up long ago. The first mate, who whistled for it zealously, was much respected for his perseverance, and was regarded even by the unbelievers as a first-rate sailor.

Many gloomy looks would be cast upward through the cabin skylights at the flapping sails while dinner was in progress; and some, growing bold in ruefulness, predicted that we should land about the middle of July. There are always on board ship, a Sanguine One, and a Despondent One. The latter character carried it hollow at this period of the voyage, and triumphed over the Sanguine One at every meal, by inquiring where he supposed the Great Western (which left New York a week after us) was *now*: and where he supposed the 'Cunard' steam-packet was *now*: and what he thought of sailing vessels, as compared with steamships *now*: and so beset his life with pestilent attacks of that kind, that he too was obliged to affect despondency, for very peace and quietude.

These were additions to the list of entertaining incidents, but there was still another source of interest. We carried in the steerage nearly a hundred passengers: a little world of poverty: and as we came to know individuals among them by sight, from looking down upon the deck where they took the air in the daytime, and cooked their food, and very often ate it too, we became curious to know their histories, and with what expectations they had gone out to America, and on what errands they were going home, and what their circumstances were. The information we got on these heads from the carpenter, who had charge of these people, was often of the strangest kind. Some of them had been in America but three days, some but three months, and some had gone out in the last voyage of that very ship in which they were now returning home. Others had sold their clothes to raise the passage-money, and had hardly rags to cover them; others had no food, and lived upon the charity of the rest: and one man, it was discovered nearly at the end of the voyage, not before—for he kept his secret close, and did not court compassion—had had no sustenance whatever but the bones and scraps of fat he took from the plates used in the after-cabin dinner, when they were put out to be washed.

The whole system of shipping and conveying these unfortunate persons, is one that stands in need of thorough revision. If any class deserve to be protected and assisted by the Government, it is that class who are banished from their native land in search of the bare means of subsistence. All that could be done for these poor people by the great compassion and humanity of the captain and officers was done, but they require much more. The law is bound, at least upon the English side, to see that too many of them are not put on board one ship : and that their accommoda- tions are decent ; not demoralising and profligate. It is bound, too, in common humanity, to declare that no man shall be taken on board without his stock of provisions being previously inspected by some proper officer, and pronounced moderately sufficient for his support upon the voyage. It is bound to provide, or to require that there be provided, a medical attendant ; whereas in these ships there are none, though sickness of adults, and deaths of children, on the passage, are matters of the very commonest occurrence. Above all it is the duty of any Government, be it monarchy or republic, to interpose and put an end to that system by which a firm of traders in emigrants purchase of the owners the whole 'tween-decks of a ship, and send on board as many wretched people as they can lay hold of, on any terms they can get, without the smallest reference to the conveniences of the steerage, the number of berths, the slightest separation of the sexes, or anything but their own immediate profit. Nor is even this the worst of the vicious system : for, certain crimping agents of these houses, who have a percentage on all the passengers they inveigle, are constantly travelling about those districts where poverty and discontent are rife, and tempting the credulous into more misery, by holding out monstrous inducements to emigration which can never be realised.

The history of every family we had on board was pretty much the same. After hoarding up, and borrowing, and begging, and selling everything to pay the passage, they had gone out to New York, expecting to find its streets paved with gold ; and had found them paved with very hard and very real stones. Enterprise was dull ; labourers were not wanted ; jobs of work were to be got, but the payment was not. They were coming back, even poorer than they went. One of them was carrying an open letter from a young Eng- lish artisan, who had been in New York a fortnight, to a friend near Manchester, whom he strongly urged to follow him. One of the officers brought it to me as a curiosity. " This is the country, Jem," said the writer. " I like America. There is no despotism here ; that's the great thing. Employ- ment of all sorts is going a-begging, and wages are capital.

You have only to choose a trade, Jem, and be it. I haven't made choice of one yet, but I shall soon. *At present I haven't quite made up my mind whether to be a carpenter—or a tailor.*"

There was yet another kind of passenger, and but one more, who, in the calm and the light winds, was a constant theme of conversation and observation among us. This was an English sailor, a smart, thorough-built, English man-of-war's-man from his hat to his shoes, who was serving in the American navy, and having got leave of absence was on his way home to see his friends. When he presented himself to take and pay for his passage, it had been suggested to him that being an able seaman he might as well work it and save the money, but this piece of advice he very indignantly rejected: saying, "He'd be damned but for once he'd go aboard ship, as a gentleman." Accordingly, they took his money, but he no sooner came aboard, than he stowed his kit in the forecastle, arranged to mess with the crew, and the very first time the hands were turned up, went aloft like a cat, before anybody. And all through the passage there he was, first at the braces, outermost on the yards, perpetually lending a hand everywhere, but always with a sober dignity in his manner, and a sober grin on his face, which plainly said, "I do it as a gentleman. For my own pleasure, mind you!"

At length and at last, the promised wind came up in right good earnest, and away we went before it, with every stitch of canvas set, slashing through the water nobly. There was a grandeur in the motion of the splendid ship, as over-shadowed by her mass of sails, she rode at a furious pace upon the waves, which filled one with an indescribable sense of pride and exultation. As she plunged into a foaming valley, how I loved to see the green waves, bordered deep with white, come rushing on astern, to buoy her upward at their pleasure, and curl about her as she stooped again, but always own her for their haughty mistress still! On, on we flew, with changing lights upon the water, being now in the blessed region of fleecy skies ; a bright sun lighting us by day, and a bright moon by night ; the vane pointing directly homeward, alike the truthful index to the favouring wind and to our cheerful hearts ; until at sunrise, one fair Monday morning—the twenty-seventh of June, I shall not easily forget the day—there lay before us, old Cape Clear, God bless it, showing, in the mist of early morning, like a cloud :

the brightest and most welcome cloud, to us, that ever hid the face of Heaven's fallen sister—Home.

Dim speck as it was in the wide prospect, it made the sunrise a more cheerful sight, and gave to it that sort of human interest which it seems to want at sea. There, as elsewhere, the return of day is inseparable from some sense of renewed hope and gladness; but the light shining on the dreary waste of water, and showing it in all its vast extent of loneliness, presents a solemn spectacle, which even night, veiling it in darkness and uncertainty, does not surpass. The rising of the moon is more in keeping with the solitary ocean; and has an air of melancholy grandeur, which in its soft and gentle influence, seems to comfort while it saddens. I recollect when I was a very young child having a fancy that the reflection of the moon in water was a path to Heaven, trodden by the spirits of good people on their way to God; and this old feeling often came over me again, when I watched it on a tranquil night at sea.

The wind was very light on this same Monday morning, but it was still in the right quarter, and so, by slow degrees, we left Cape Clear behind, and sailed along within sight of the coast of Ireland. And how merry we all were, and how loyal to the George Washington, and how full of mutual congratulations, and how venturesome in predicting the exact hour at which we should arrive at Liverpool, may be easily imagined and readily understood. Also, how heartily we drank the captain's health that day at dinner; and how restless we became about packing up: and how two or three of the most sanguine spirits rejected the idea of going to bed at all that night as something it was not worth while to do, so near the shore, but went nevertheless, and slept soundly; and how to be so near our journey's end, was like a pleasant dream, from which one feared to wake.

The friendly breeze freshened again next day, and on we went once more before it gallantly: descrying now and then an English ship going homeward under shortened sail, while we with every inch of canvas crowded on, dashed gaily past, and left her far behind. Toward evening, the weather turned hazy, with a drizzling rain; and soon became so thick, that we sailed, as it were, in a cloud. Still we swept onward like a phantom ship, and many an eager eye glanced up to where the Look-out on the mast kept watch for Holyhead.

At length his long-expected cry was heard, and at the

same moment there shone out from the haze and mist ahead, a gleaming light, which presently was gone, and soon returned, and soon was gone again. Whenever it came back, the eyes of all on board, brightened and sparkled like itself: and there we all stood, watching this revolving light upon the rock at Holyhead, and praising it for its brightness and its friendly warning, and lauding it, in short, above all other signal lights that ever were displayed, until it once more glimmered faintly in the distance, far behind us.

Then, it was time to fire a gun, for a pilot; and almost before its smoke had cleared away, a little boat with a light at her mast-head came bearing down upon us, through the darkness, swiftly. And presently, our sails being backed, she ran alongside; and the hoarse pilot, wrapped and muffled in pea-coats and shawls to the very bridge of his weather-ploughed-up nose, stood bodily among us on the deck. And I think if that pilot had wanted to borrow fifty pounds for an indefinite period on no security, we should have engaged to lend it to him, among us, before his boat had dropped astern, or (which is the same thing) before every scrap of news in the paper he brought with him had become the common property of all on board.

We turned in pretty late that night, and turned out pretty early next morning. By six o'clock we clustered on the deck, prepared to go ashore; and looked upon the spires, and roofs, and smoke, of Liverpool. By eight we all sat down in one of its Hotels, to eat and drink together for the last time. And by nine we had shaken hands all round, and broken up our social company for ever.

The country, by the railroad, seemed, as we rattled through it, like a luxuriant garden. The beauty of the fields (so small they looked!), the hedge-rows, and the trees; the pretty cottages, the beds of flowers, the old churchyards, the antique houses, and every well-known object; the exquisite delights of that one journey, crowding in the short compass of a summer's day, the joy of many years, with the winding up with Home and all that makes it dear; no tongue can tell, or pen of mine describe.

CHAPTER XVII

SLAVERY

THE upholders of slavery in America—of the atrocities of which system, I shall not write one word for which I have not had ample proof and warrant—may be divided into three great classes.

The first, are those more moderate and rational owners of human cattle, who have come into the possession of them as so many coins in their trading capital, but who admit the frightful nature of the Institution in the abstract, and perceive the dangers to society with which it is fraught: dangers which however distant they may be, or howsoever tardy in their coming on, are as certain to fall upon its guilty head, as is the Day of Judgment.

The second, consists of all those owners, breeders, users, buyers and sellers of slaves, who will, until the bloody chapter has a bloody end, own, breed, use, buy, and sell them at all hazards ; who doggedly deny the horrors of the system in the teeth of such a mass of evidence as never was brought to bear on any other subject, and to which the experience of every day contributes its immense amount ; who would at this or any other moment, gladly involve America in a war, civil or foreign, provided that it had for its sole end and object the assertion of their right to perpetuate slavery, and to whip and work and torture slaves, unquestioned by any human authority, and unassailed by any human power ; who, when they speak of Freedom, mean the Freedom to oppress their kind, and to be savage, merciless, and cruel ; and of whom every man on his own ground, in republican America, is a more exacting, and a sterner, and a less responsible despot than the Caliph Haroun Alraschid in his angry robe of scarlet.

The third, and not the least numerous or influential, is composed of all that delicate gentility which cannot bear a superior, and cannot brook an equal ; of that class whose Republicanism means, " I will not tolerate a man above me: and of those below, none must approach too near ; " whose pride, in a land where voluntary servitude is shunned as a disgrace, must be ministered to by slaves ; and whose inalienable rights can only have their growth in negro wrongs.

It has been sometimes urged that, in the unavailing efforts which have been made to advance the cause of Human Freedom in the republic of America (strange cause for history to treat of !), sufficient regard has not been had to the existence of the first class of persons ; and it has been contended that they are hardly used, in being confounded with the second. This is, no doubt, the case ; noble instances of pecuniary and personal sacrifice have already had their growth among them ; and it is much to be regretted that the gulf between them and the advocates of emancipation should have been widened and deepened by any means: the rather, as there are, beyond dispute, among these slave-owners, many kind masters who are tender in the exercise of their unnatural power. Still, it is to be feared that this injustice is inseparable from the state of things with which humanity and truth are called upon to deal. Slavery is not a whit the more endurable because some hearts are to be found which can partially resist its hardening influences ; nor can the indignant tide of honest wrath stand still, because in its onward course it overwhelms a few who are comparatively innocent, among a host of guilty.

The ground most commonly taken by these better men among the advocates of slavery, is this: " It is a bad system ; and for myself I would willingly get rid of it, if I could ; most willingly. But it is not so bad, as you in England take it to be. You are deceived by the representations of the emancipationists. The greater part of my slaves are much attached to me. You will say that I do not allow them to be severely treated ; but I will put it to you whether you believe that it can be a general practice to treat them inhumanly, when it would impair their value, and would be obviously against the interests of their masters."

Is it the interest of any man to steal, to game, to waste his health and mental faculties by drunkenness, to lie, forswear himself, indulge hatred, seek desperate revenge, or do murder ? No. All these are roads to ruin. And why, then, do men tread them ? Because such inclinations are among

I

the vicious qualities of mankind. Blot out, ye friends of slavery, from the catalogue of human passions, brutal lust, cruelty, and the abuse of irresponsible power (of all earthly temptations the most difficult to be resisted), and when ye have done so, and not before, we will inquire whether it be the interest of a master to lash and maim the slaves, over whose lives and limbs he has an absolute control!

But again: this class, together with that last one I have named, the miserable aristocracy spawned of a false republic, lift up their voices and exclaim "Public opinion is all-sufficient to prevent such cruelty as you denounce." Public opinion! Why, public opinion in the slave States *is* slavery, is it not? Public opinion, in the slave States, has delivered the slaves over, to the gentle mercies of their masters. Public opinion has made the laws, and denied the slaves legislative protection. Public opinion has knotted the lash, heated the branding-iron, loaded the rifle, and shielded the murderer. Public opinion threatens the abolitionist with death, if he venture to the South; and drags him with a rope about his middle, in broad unblushing noon, through the first city in the East. Public opinion has, within a few years, burned a slave alive at a slow fire in the city of St. Louis; and public opinion has to this day maintained upon the bench that estimable Judge who charged the Jury, im-panelled there to try his murderers, that their most horrid deed was an act of public opinion, and being so, must not be punished by the laws the public sentiment had made. Public opinion hailed this doctrine with a howl of wild applause, and set the prisoners free, to walk the city, men of mark, and influence, and station, as they had been before.

Public opinion! what class of men have an immense pre-ponderance over the rest of the community, in their power of representing public opinion in the legislature? the slave-owners. They send from their twelve States one hundred members, while the fourteen free States, with a free popula-tion nearly double, return but a hundred and forty-two. Before whom do the presidential candidates bow down the most humbly, on whom do they fawn the most fondly, and for whose tastes do they cater the most assiduously in their servile protestations? The slave-owners always.

Public opinion! hear the public opinion of the free South, as expressed by its own members in the House of Repre-sentatives at Washington. "I have a great respect for the chair," quoth North Carolina, "I have a great respect for the chair as an officer of the house, and a great respect for him personally; nothing but that respect prevents me from rushing to the table and tearing that petition which has just been presented for the abolition of slavery in the district of Columbia, to pieces."—"I warn the abolitionists," says South Carolina, "ignorant, infuriated barbarians as they are, that if chance shall throw any of them into our hands, he may expect a felon's death."—"Let an abolitionist come within the borders of South Carolina," cries a third; mild Carolina's colleague; "and if we can catch him, we will try him, and notwithstanding the interference of all the governments on earth, including the Federal government, we will HANG him."

Public opinion has made this law.—It has declared that in Washington, in that city which takes its name from the father of American liberty, any justice of the peace may bind with fetters any negro passing down the street and thrust him into jail: no offence on the black man's part is necessary. The justice says, "I choose to think this man a runaway:" and locks him up. Public opinion empowers the man of law when this is done, to advertise the negro in the newspapers, warning his owner to come and claim him, or he will be sold to pay the jail fees. But supposing he is a free black, and has no owner, it may naturally be presumed that he is set at liberty. No: HE IS SOLD TO RECOMPENSE HIS JAILER. This has been done again, and again, and again. He has no means of proving his freedom; has no adviser, messenger, or assistance of any sort or kind; no investigation into his case is made, or inquiry instituted. He, a free man, who may have served for years, and bought his liberty, is thrown into jail on no process, for no crime, and on no pretence of crime: and is sold to pay the jail fees. This seems incredible, even of America, but it is the law.

Public opinion is deferred to, in such cases as the following: which is headed in the newspapers:—

"Interesting Law-Case.

"An interesting case is now on trial in the Supreme Court, arising out of the following facts. A gentleman residing in Maryland had allowed an aged pair of his slaves, substantial though not legal freedom for several years. While thus living, a daughter was born to them, who grew up in the same liberty, until she married a free negro, and went with him to reside in Pennsylvania. They had several children, and lived unmolested until the original owner died, when his heir attempted to regain them ; but the magistrate before whom they were brought, decided that he had no jurisdiction in the case. *The owner seized the woman and her children in the night, and carried them to Maryland.*"

" Cash for negroes," " cash for negroes," " cash for negroes," is the heading of advertisements in great capitals down the long columns of the crowded journals. Woodcuts of a runaway negro with manacled hands, crouching beneath a bluff pursuer in top boots, who, having caught him, grasps him by the throat, agreeably diversify the pleasant text. The leading article protests against "that abominable and hellish doctrine of abolition, which is repugnant alike to every law of God and nature." The delicate mamma, who smiles her acquiescence in this sprightly writing as she reads the paper in her cool piazza, quiets her youngest child who clings about her skirts, by promising the boy "a whip to beat the little niggers with."—But the negroes, little and big, are protected by public opinion.

Let us try this public opinion by another test, which is important in three points of view: first, as showing how desperately timid of the public opinion slave-owners are, in their delicate descriptions of fugitive slaves in widely circulated newspapers ; secondly, as showing how perfectly contented the slaves are, and how very seldom they run away ; thirdly, as exhibiting their entire freedom from scar, or blemish, or any mark of cruel infliction, as their pictures are drawn, not by lying abolitionists, but by their own truthful masters.

The following are a few specimens of the advertisements in the public papers. It is only four years since the oldest among them appeared ; and others of the same nature continue to be published every day, in shoals.

" Ran away, Negress Caroline. Had on a collar with one prong turned down."

" Ran away, a black woman, Betsy. Had an iron bar on her right leg."

" Ran away, the negro Manuel. Much marked with irons."

" Ran away, the negress Fanny. Had on an iron band about her neck."

"Ran away, a negro boy about twelve years old. Had round his neck a chain dog-collar with 'De Lampert' engraved on it."

"Ran away, the negro Hown. Has a ring of iron on his left foot. Also, Grise, *his wife*, having a ring and chain on the left leg."

"Ran away, a negro boy named James. Said boy was ironed when he left me."

"Committed to jail, a man who calls his name John. He has a clog of iron on his right foot which will weigh four or five pounds."

"Detained at the police jail, the negro wench, Myra. Has several marks of LASHING, and has irons on her feet."

"Ran away, a negro woman and two children. A few days before she went off, I burnt her with a hot iron, on the left side of her face. I tried to make the letter M."

"Ran away, a negro man named Henry; his left eye out, some scars from a dirk on and under his left arm, and much scarred with the whip."

"One hundred dollars reward, for a negro fellow, Pompey, 40 years old. He is branded on the left jaw."

"Committed to jail, a negro man. Has no toes on the left foot."

"Ran away, a negro woman named Rachel. Has lost all her toes except the large one."

"Ran away, Sam. He was shot a short time since through the hand, and has several shots in his left arm and side."

"Ran away, my negro man Dennis. Said negro has been shot in the left arm between the shoulder and elbow, which has paralysed the left hand."

"Ran away, my negro man named Simon. He has been shot badly, in his back and right arm."

"Ran away, a negro named Arthur. Has a considerable scar across his breast and each arm, made by a knife; loves to talk much of the goodness of God."

"Twenty-five dollars reward for my man Isaac. He has a scar on his forehead, caused by a blow; and one on his back, made by a shot from a pistol."

"Ran away, a negro girl called Mary. Has a small scar over her eye, a good many teeth missing, the letter A is branded on her cheek and forehead."

"Ran away, negro Ben. Has a scar on his right hand:

his thumb and forefinger being injured by being shot last fall. A part of the bone came out. He has also one or two large scars on his back and hips."

"Detained at the jail, a mulatto, named Tom. Has a scar on the right cheek, and appears to have been burned with powder on the face."

"Ran away, a negro man named Ned. Three of his fingers are drawn into the palm of his hand by a cut. Has a scar on the back of his neck, nearly half round, done by a knife."

"Was committed to jail, a negro man. Says his name is Josiah. His back very much scarred by the whip; and branded on the thigh and hips in three or four places, thus (J M). The rim of his right ear has been bit or cut off."

"Fifty dollars reward, for my fellow Edward. He has a scar on the corner of his mouth, two cuts on and under his arm, and the letter E on his arm."

"Ran away, negro boy Ellie. Has a scar on one of his arms from the bite of a dog."

"Ran away, from the plantation of James Surgette, the following negroes : Randal, has one ear cropped ; Bob, has lost one eye ; Kentucky Tom, has one jaw broken."

"Ran away, Anthony. One of his ears cut off, and his left hand cut with an axe."

"Fifty dollars reward for the negro Jim Blake. Has a piece cut out of each ear, and the middle finger of the left hand cut off to the second joint."

"Ran away, a negro woman named Maria. Has a scar on one side of her cheek, by a cut. Some scars on her back."

"Ran away, the Mulatto wench Mary. Has a cut on the left arm, a scar on the left shoulder, and two upper teeth missing."

I should say, perhaps, in explanation of this latter piece of description, that among the other blessings which public opinion secures to the negroes, is the common practice of violently punching out their teeth. To make them wear iron collars by day and night, and to worry them with dogs, are practices almost too ordinary to deserve mention.

"Ran away, my man Fountain. Has holes in his ears, a scar on the right side of his forehead, has been shot in the hind parts of his legs, and is marked on the back with the whip."

"Two hundred and fifty dollars reward for my negro man

Jim. He is much marked with shot in his right thigh. The shot entered on the outside, halfway between the hip and knee joints."

"Brought to jail, John. Left ear cropt."

"Taken up, a negro man. Is very much scarred about the face and body, and has the left ear bit off."

"Ran away, a black girl, named Mary. Has a scar on her cheek, and the end of one of her toes cut off."

"Ran away, my Mulatto woman, Judy. She has had her right arm broke."

"Ran away, my negro man, Levi. His left hand has been burnt, and I think the end of his forefinger is off."

"Ran away, a negro man, NAMED WASHINGTON. Has lost a part of his middle finger, and the end of his little finger."

"Twenty-five dollars reward for my man John. The tip of his nose is bit off."

"Twenty-five dollars reward for the negro slave, Sally. Walks *as though* crippled in the back."

"Ran away, Joe Dennis. Has a small notch in one of his ears."

"Ran away, negro boy, Jack. Has a small crop out of his left ear."

"Ran away, a negro man, named Ivory. Has a small piece cut out of the top of each ear."

While upon the subject of ears, I may observe that a distinguished abolitionist in New York once received a negro's ear, which had been cut off close to the head, in a general post letter. It was forwarded by the free and independent gentleman who had caused it to be amputated, with a polite request that he would place the specimen in his "collection."

I could enlarge this catalogue with broken arms, and broken legs, and gashed flesh, and missing teeth, and lacerated backs, and bites of dogs, and brands of red-hot irons innumerable: but as my readers will be sufficiently sickened and repelled already, I will turn to another branch of the subject.

These advertisements, of which a similar collection might be made for every year, and month, and week, and day ; and which are coolly read in families as things of course, and as a part of the current news and small-talk ; will serve to show how very much the slaves profit by public opinion, and

how tender it is in their behalf. But it may be worth
while to inquire how the slave-owners, and the class of
society to which great numbers of them belong, defer to
public opinion in their conduct, not to their slaves but to
each other ; how they are accustomed to restrain their
passions ; what their bearing is among themselves ; whether
they are fierce or gentle ; whether their social customs be
brutal, sanguinary, and violent, or bear the impress of
civilisation and refinement.

That we may have no partial evidence from abolitionists
in this inquiry, either, I will once more turn to their own
newspapers, and I will confine myself, this time, to a
selection from paragraphs which appeared from day to day,
during my visit to America, and which refer to occurrences
happening while I was there. The italics in these extracts,
as in the foregoing, are my own.

These cases did not ALL occur, it will be seen, in territory
actually belonging to legalised Slave States, though most, and
those the very worst among them did, as their counterparts
constantly do ; but the position of the scenes of action in
reference to places immediately at hand, where slavery is
the law ; and the strong resemblance between that class of
outrages and the rest ; lead to the just presumption that the
character of the parties concerned was formed in slave districts, and brutalised by slave customs.

" Horrible Tragedy.

" By a slip from *The Southport Telegraph*, Wisconsin, we
learn that the Hon. Charles C. P. Arndt, Member of the
Council for Brown county, was shot dead *on the floor of the
Council chamber*, by James R. Vinyard, Member from Grant
county. *The affair* grew out of a nomination for Sheriff of
Grant county. Mr. E. S. Baker was nominated and supported by Mr. Arndt. This nomination was opposed by
Vinyard, who wanted the appointment to vest in his own
brother. In the course of debate, the deceased made some
statements which Vinyard pronounced false, and made use of
violent and insulting language, dealing largely in personali-
ties, to which Mr. A. made no reply. After the adjournment,
Mr. A. stepped up to Vinyard, and requested him to retract,
which he refused to do, repeating the offensive words. Mr.
Arndt then made a blow at Vinyard, who stepped back a
pace, drew a pistol, and shot him dead.

"The issue appears to have been provoked on the part of Vinyard, who was determined at all hazards to defeat the appointment of Baker, and who, himself defeated, turned his ire and revenge upon the unfortunate Arndt."

"*The Wisconsin Tragedy.*

"Public indignation runs high in the territory of Wisconsin, in relation to the murder of C. C. P. Arndt, in the Legislative Hall of the Territory. Meetings have been held in different counties of Wisconsin, denouncing *the practice of secretly bearing arms in the Legislative chambers of the country.* We have seen the account of the expulsion of James R. Vinyard, the perpetrator of the bloody deed, and are amazed to hear, that, after this expulsion by those who saw Vinyard kill Mr. Arndt in the presence of his aged father, who was on a visit to see his son, little dreaming that he was to witness his murder, *Judge Dunn has discharged Vinyard on bail.* The Miners' Free Press speaks *in terms of merited rebuke* at the outrage upon the feelings of the people of Wisconsin. Vinyard was within arm's length of Mr. Arndt, when he took such deadly aim at him, that he never spoke. Vinyard might at pleasure, being so near, have only wounded him, but he chose to kill him."

"*Murder.*

"By a letter in a St. Louis paper of the 14th, we notice a terrible outrage at Burlington, Iowa. A Mr. Bridgman having had a difficulty with a citizen of the place, Mr. Ross; a brother-in-law of the latter provided himself with one of Colt's revolving pistols, met Mr. B. in the street, *and discharged the contents of five of the barrels at him: each shot taking effect.* Mr. B., though horribly wounded, and dying, returned the fire, and killed Ross on the spot."

"*Terrible Death of Robert Potter.*

"From the 'Caddo Gazette,' of the 12th inst., we learn the frightful death of Colonel Robert Potter. . . . He was beset in his house by an enemy, named Rose. He sprang from his couch, seized his gun, and, in his night-clothes, rushed from the house. For about two hundred yards his speed seemed to defy his pursuers; but, getting entangled in a thicket, he was captured. Rose told him *that he intended to act a generous part,* and give him a chance for his life. He then told Potter he might run, and he should not be interrupted till he reached a certain distance. Potter started at the word of command, and before a gun was fired he had reached the lake. His first impulse was to jump in the water and dive for it, which he did. Rose was close behind him, and formed his men on the bank ready to shoot him as he rose. In a few seconds he came up to breathe; and scarce had his head reached the surface of the water when it was completely riddled with the shot of their guns, and he sunk, to rise no more!"

" *Murder in Arkansas.*

" We understand *that a severe rencontre came off* a few days since in the Seneca Nation, between Mr. Loose, the sub-agent of the mixed band of the Senecas, Quapaw, and Shawnees, and Mr. James Gillespie, of the mercantile firm of Thomas G. Allison and Co., of Maysville, Benton County, Ark., in which the latter was slain with a bowie-knife. Some difficulty had for some time existed between the parties. It is said that Major Gillespie brought on the attack with a cane. A severe conflict ensued, during which two pistols were fired by Gillespie and one by Loose. Loose then stabbed Gillespie with one of those never-failing weapons, a bowie-knife. The death of Major G. is much regretted, as he was a liberal-minded and energetic man. Since the above was in type, we have learned that Major Allison has stated to some of our citizens in town that Mr. Loose gave the first blow. We forbear to give any particulars, as *the matter will be the subject of judicial investigation.*"

" *Foul Deed.*

' The steamer "Thames," just from Missouri river, brought us a handbill, offering a reward of 500 dollars, for the person who assassinated Lilburn W. Baggs, late Governor of this State, at Independence, on the night of the 6th inst. Governor Baggs, it is stated in a written memorandum, was not dead, but mortally wounded.

"Since the above was written, we received a note from the clerk of the "Thames," giving the following particulars. Gov. Baggs was shot by some villain on Friday, 6th inst., in the evening, while sitting in a room in his own house in Independence. His son, a boy, hearing a report, ran into the room, and found the Governor sitting in his chair, with his jaw fallen down, and his head leaning back; on discovering the injury done to his father, he gave the alarm. Foot tracks were found in the garden below the window, and a pistol picked up supposed to have been overloaded, and thrown from the hand of the scoundrel who fired it. Three buck shots of a heavy load, took effect; one going through his mouth, one into the brain, and another probably in or near the brain; all going into the back part of the neck and head. The Governor was still alive on the morning of the 7th; but no hopes for his recovery by his friends, and but slight hopes from his physicians.

"A man was suspected, and the Sheriff most probably has possession of him by this time.

"The pistol was one of a pair stolen some days previous from a baker in Independence, and the legal authorities have the description of the other."

"Rencontre.

"An unfortunate *affair* took place on Friday evening in Chatres Street, in which one of our most respectable citizens received a dangerous wound, from a poignard, in the abdomen. From "The Bee" (New Orleans) of yesterday, we learn the following particulars. It appears that an article was published in the French side of the paper on Monday last, containing some strictures on the Artillery Battalion for firing their guns on Sunday morning, in answer to those from the "Ontario" and "Woodbury," and thereby much alarm was caused to the families of those persons who were out all night preserving the peace of the city. Major C. Gally, Commander of the battalion, resenting this, called at the office and demanded the author's name; that of Mr. P. Arpin was given to him, who was absent at the time. Some angry words then passed with one of the proprietors, and a challenge followed; the friends of both parties tried to arrange the affair, but failed to do so. On Friday evening, about seven o'clock, Major Gally met Mr. P. Arpin in Chatres Street, and accosted him. 'Are you Mr. Arpin?'

" 'Yes, Sir.'

" 'Then I have to tell you that you are a—— ' (applying an appropriate epithet).

" 'I shall remind you of your words, Sir.'

" 'But I have said I would break my cane on your shoulders.'

" 'I know it, but I have not yet received the blow.'

"At these words, Major Gally, having a cane in his hands, struck Mr. Arpin across the face, and the latter drew a poignard from his pocket and stabbed Major Gally in the abdomen.

"Fears are entertained that the wound will be mortal. *We understand that Mr. Arpin has given security for his appearance at the Criminal Court to answer the charge.*"

"*Affray in Mississippi.*

"On the 27th ult., in an affray near Carthage, Leake county, Mississippi, between James Cottingham and John Wilburn, the latter was shot by the former, and so horribly wounded, that there was no hope of his recovery.   On the 2nd instant, there was an affray at Carthage between A. C. Sharkey and George Goff, in which the latter was shot, and thought mortally wounded.   Sharkey delivered himself up to the authorities, *but changed his mind and escaped!*"

"*Personal Encounter.*

"An encounter took place in Sparta, a few days since, between the barkeeper of an hotel, and a man named Bury. It appears that Bury had become somewhat noisy, *and that the barkeeper, determined to preserve order, had threatened to shoot Bury,* whereupon Bury drew a pistol and shot the barkeeper down.   He was not dead at the last accounts, but slight hopes were entertained of his recovery."

"*Duel.*

"The clerk of the steamboat "Tribune" informs us that another duel was fought on Tuesday last, by Mr. Robbins, a bank officer in Vicksburg, and Mr. Fall, the editor of the Vicksburg Sentinel.   According to the arrangement, the parties had six pistols each, which, after the word 'Fire!' *they were to discharge as fast as they pleased.*   Fall fired two pistols without effect.   Mr. Robbins' first shot took effect in Fall's thigh, who fell, and was unable to continue the combat."

"*Affray in Clarke County.*

"An *unfortunate affray* occurred in Clarke county (Mo.), near Waterloo, on Tuesday the 9th ult., which originated in settling the partnership concerns of Messrs. M'Kane and M'Allister, who had been engaged in the business of distilling,

and resulted in the death of the latter, who was shot down by Mr. M'Kane, because of his attempting to take possession of seven barrels of whiskey, the property of M'Kane, which had been knocked off to M'Allister at a sheriff's sale at one dollar per barrel. M'Kane immediately fled *and at the latest dates had not been taken.*

"*This unfortunate affray* caused considerable excitement in the neighbourhood, as both the parties were men with large families depending upon them and stood well in the community."

I will quote but one more paragraph, which, by reason of its monstrous absurdity, may be a relief to these atrocious deeds.

"*Affair of Honour.*

"We have just heard the particulars of a meeting which took place on Six Mile Island, on Tuesday, between two young bloods of our city : Samuel Thurston, *aged fifteen*, and William Hine, *aged thirteen* years. They were attended by young gentlemen of the same age. The weapons used on the occasion, were a couple of Dickson's best rifles ; the distance, thirty yards. They took one fire, without any damage being sustained by either party, except the ball of Thurston's gun passing through the crown of Hine's hat. *Through the intercession of the Board of Honour*, the challenge was withdrawn, and the difference amicably adjusted."

If the reader will picture to himself the kind of Board of Honour which amicably adjusted the difference between these two little boys, who in any other part of the world would have been amicably adjusted on two porters' backs and soundly flogged with birchen rods, he will be possessed, no doubt, with as strong a sense of its ludicrous character, as that which sets me laughing whenever its image rises up before me.

Now, I appeal to every human mind, imbued with the commonest of common sense, and the commonest of common humanity ; to all dispassionate, reasoning creatures, of any shade of opinion ; and ask, with these revolting evidences of the state of society which exists in and about the slave districts of America before them, can they have a doubt of the real condition of the slave, or can they for a moment make a

compromise between the institution or any of its flagrant fear
ful features, and their own just consciences? Will they say
of any tale of cruelty and horror, however aggravated in
degree, that it is improbable, when they can turn to the
public prints, and, running, read such signs as these, laid
before them by the men who rule the slaves: in their own
acts and under their own hands?

Do we not know that the worst deformity and ugliness of
slavery are at once the cause and the effect of the reckless
licence taken by these freeborn outlaws? Do we not know
that the man who has been born and bred among its wrongs;
who has seen in his childhood husbands obliged at the word
of command to flog their wives; women, indecently compelled
to hold up their own garments that men might lay the heavier
stripes upon their legs, driven and harried by brutal overseers
in their time of travail, and becoming mothers on the field
of toil, under the very lash itself; who has read in youth,
and seen his virgin sisters read, descriptions of runaway men
and women, and their disfigured persons, which could not be
published elsewhere, of so much stock upon a farm, or at a
show of beasts:—do we not know that that man, whenever
his wrath is kindled up, will be a brutal savage? Do we
not know that as he is a coward in his domestic life, stalking
among his shrinking men and women slaves armed with his
heavy whip, so he will be a coward out of doors, and carrying
cowards' weapons hidden in his breast, will shoot men down
and stab them when he quarrels? And if our reason did
not teach us this and much beyond; if we were such idiots
as to close our eyes to that fine mode of training which rears
up such men; should we not know that they who among
their equals stab and pistol in the legislative halls, and in the
counting-house, and on the market-place, and in all the elsewhere peaceful pursuits of life, must be to their dependants,
even though they were free servants, so many merciless and
unrelenting tyrants?

What! shall we declaim against the ignorant peasantry of
Ireland, and mince the matter when these American task-
masters are in question? Shall we cry shame on the brutality
of those who ham-string cattle: and spare the lights of
Freedom upon earth who notch the ears of men and women,
cut pleasant posies in the shrinking flesh, learn to write with
pens of red-hot iron on the human face, rack their poetic
fancies for liveries of mutilation which their slaves shall wear

for life and carry to the grave, breaking living limbs as did the soldiery who mocked and slew the Saviour of the world, and set defenceless creatures up for targets! Shall we whimper over legends of the tortures practised on each other by the Pagan Indians, and smile upon the cruelties of Christian men! Shall we, so long as these things last, exult above the scattered remnants of that race, and triumph in the white enjoyment of their possessions? Rather, for me, restore the forest and the Indian village; in lieu of stars and stripes, let some poor feather flutter in the breeze; replace the streets and squares by wigwams; and though the death-song of a hundred haughty warriors fill the air, it will be music to the shriek of one unhappy slave.

On one theme, which is commonly before our eyes, and in respect of which our national character is changing fast, let the plain Truth be spoken, and let us not, like dastards, beat about the bush by hinting at the Spaniard and the fierce Italian. When knives are drawn by Englishmen in conflict let it be said and known: "We owe this change to Republican Slavery. These are the weapons of Freedom. With sharp points and edges such as these, Liberty in America hews and hacks her slaves; or, failing that pursuit, her sons devote them to a better use, and turn them on each other."

CHAPTER XVIII

CONCLUDING REMARKS

THERE are many passages in this book, where I have been at some pains to resist the temptation of troubling my readers with my own deductions and conclusions : preferring that they should judge for themselves, from such premises as I have laid before them. My only object in the outset, was, to carry them with me faithfully wheresoever I went: and that task I have discharged.

But I may be pardoned, if on such a theme as the general character of the American people, and the general character of their social system, as presented to a stranger's eyes, I desire to express my own opinions in a few words, before I bring these volumes to a close.

They are, by nature, frank, brave, cordial, hospitable, and affectionate. Cultivation and refinement seem but to enhance their warmth of heart and ardent enthusiasm ; and it is the possession of these latter qualities in a most remarkable degree, which renders an educated American one of the most endearing and most generous of friends. I never was so won upon, as by this class ; never yielded up my full confidence and esteem so readily and pleasurably, as to them ; never can make again, in half a year, so many friends for whom I seem to entertain the regard of half a life.

These qualities are natural, I implicitly believe, to the whole people. That they are, however, sadly sapped and blighted in their growth among the mass ; and that there are influences at work which endanger them still more, and give but little present promise of their healthy restoration ; is a truth that ought to be told.

It is an essential part of every national character to pique itself mightily upon its faults, and to deduce tokens of its virtue or its wisdom from their very exaggeration. One great blemish in the popular mind of America, and the prolific parent of an innumerable brood of evils, is Universal Distrust. Yet the American citizen plumes himself upon this spirit, even when he is sufficiently dispassionate to perceive the ruin it works; and will often adduce it, in spite of his own reason, as an instance of the great sagacity and acuteness of the people, and their superior shrewdness and independence.

"You carry," says the stranger, "this jealousy and distrust into every transaction of public life. By repelling worthy men from your legislative assemblies, it has bred up a class of candidates for the suffrage, who, in their every act, disgrace your Institutions and your people's choice. It has rendered you so fickle, and so given to change, that your inconstancy has passed into a proverb; for you no sooner set up an idol firmly, than you are sure to pull it down and dash it into fragments: and this, because directly you reward a benefactor, or a public servant, you distrust him, merely because he *is* rewarded; and immediately apply yourselves to find out, either that you have been too bountiful in your acknowledgments, or he remiss in his deserts. Any man who attains a high place among you, from the President downwards, may date his downfall from that moment; for any printed lie that any notorious villain pens, although it militate directly against the character and conduct of a life, appeals at once to your distrust, and is believed. You will strain at a gnat in the way of trustfulness and confidence, however fairly won and well deserved; but you will swallow a whole caravan of camels, if they be laden with unworthy doubts and mean suspicions. Is this well, think you, or likely to elevate the character of the governors or the governed, among you?"

The answer is invariably the same: "There's freedom of opinion here, you know. Every man thinks for himself, and we are not to be easily overreached. That's how our people come to be suspicious."

Another prominent feature is the love of "smart" dealing: which gilds over many a swindle and gross breach of trust; many a defalcation, public and private; and enables many a knave to hold his head up with the best, who well deserves a halter; though it has not been without its retributive operation, for this smartness has done more in a few years to impair the public credit, and to cripple the public resources, than dull honesty, however rash, could have effected in a century. The merits of a broken speculation, or a bankruptcy, or of a successful scoundrel, are not gauged by its or his observance of the golden rule, "Do as you would be done by," but are considered with reference to their smartness. I recollect, on both occasions of our passing that ill-fated Cairo on the Mississippi, remarking on the bad effects such gross deceits must have when they exploded, in generating a want of confidence abroad, and discouraging foreign investment: but I was given to understand that this was a very smart scheme by which a deal of money had been made: and that its smartest feature was, that they forgot these things abroad, in a very short time, and speculated again, as freely as ever. The following dialogue I have held a hundred times: "Is it not a very disgraceful circumstance that such a man as So-and-so should be acquiring a large property by the most infamous and odious means, and notwithstanding all the crimes of which he has been guilty, should be tolerated and abetted by your Citizens? He is a public nuisance, is he not?" "Yes, Sir." "A convicted liar?" "Yes, Sir." "He has been kicked, and cuffed, and caned?" "Yes, Sir." "And he is utterly dishonourable, debased, and profligate?" "Yes, Sir." "In the name of wonder, then, what is his merit?" "Well, Sir, he is a smart man."

In like manner, all kinds of deficient and impolitic usages are referred to the national love of trade; though, oddly enough, it would be a weighty charge against a foreigner that he regarded the Americans as a trading people. The love of trade is assigned as a reason for that comfortless custom, so very prevalent in country towns, of married persons living in hotels, having no fireside of their own, and seldom meeting from early morning until late at night, but at the hasty public meals. The love of trade is a reason why the literature of America is to remain for ever unprotected: "For we are a trading people, and don't care for poetry:" though we *do*, by the way, profess to be very proud of our poets: while healthful amusements, cheerful means of recreation, and wholesome fancies, must fade before the stern utilitarian joys of trade.

These three characteristics are strongly presented at every turn, full in the stranger's view. But, the foul growth of America has a more tangled root than this; and it strikes its fibres, deep in its licentious Press.

Schools may be erected, East, West, North, and South; pupils be taught, and masters reared, by scores upon scores of thousands; colleges may thrive, churches may be crammed, temperance may be diffused, and advancing knowledge in all other forms walk through the land with giant strides: but while the newspaper press of America is in, or near, its present abject state, high moral improvement in that country is hopeless. Year by year, it must and will go back; year by year, the tone of public feeling must sink lower down; year by year, the Congress and the Senate must become of less account before all decent men; and year by year, the memory of the Great Fathers of the Revolution must be outraged more and more, in the bad life of their degenerate child.

Among the herd of journals which are published in the States, there are some, the reader scarcely need be told, of character and credit. From personal intercourse with accomplished gentlemen connected with publications of this class, I have derived both pleasure and profit. But the name of these is Few, and of the others Legion; and the influence of the good, is powerless to counteract the moral poison of the bad.

Among the gentry of America; among the well-informed and moderate : in the learned professions; at the bar and on the bench : there is, as there can be, but one opinion, in reference to the vicious character of these infamous journals. It is sometimes contended—I will not say strangely, for it is natural to seek excuses for such a disgrace—that their influence is not so great as a visitor would suppose. I must be pardoned for saying that there is no warrant for this plea, and that every fact and circumstance tends directly to the opposite conclusion.

When any man, of any grade of desert in intellect or character, can climb to any public distinction, no matter what, in America, without first grovelling down upon the earth, and bending the knee before this monster of depravity; when any private excellence is safe from its attacks; when any social confidence is left unbroken by it, or any tie of social decency and honour is held in the least regard; when any man in that free country has freedom of opinion, and presumes to think for himself, and speak for himself, without humble reference to a censorship which, for its rampant ignorance and base dishonesty, he utterly loathes and despises in his heart; when those who most acutely feel its infamy and the reproach it casts upon the nation, and who most denounce it to each other, dare to set their heels upon, and

crush it openly, in the sight of all men : then, I will believe
that its influence is lessening, and men are returning to their
manly senses. But while that Press has its evil eye in every
house, and its black hand in every appointment in the state,
from a president to a postman ; while, with ribald slander
for its only stock-in-trade, it is the standard literature of an
enormous class, who must find their reading in a newspaper,
or they will not read at all ; so long must its odium be upon
the country's head, and so long must the evil it works, be
plainly visible in the Republic.

To those who are accustomed to the leading English
journals, or to the respectable journals of the Continent of
Europe ; to those who are accustomed to anything else in
print and paper ; it would be impossible, without an amount
of extract for which I have neither space nor inclination, to
convey an adequate idea of this frightful engine in America.
But if any man desire confirmation of my statement on this
head, let him repair to any place in this city of London,
where scattered numbers of these publications are to be
found ; and there, let him form his own opinion[1].

It would be well, there can be no doubt, for the American
people as a whole, if they loved the Real less, and the Ideal
somewhat more. It would be well, if there were greater
encouragement to lightness of heart and gaiety, and a wider
cultivation of what is beautiful, without being eminently and
directly useful. But here, I think the general remonstrance,
"we are a new country," which is so often advanced as an
excuse for defects which are quite unjustifiable, as being, of
right, only the slow growth of an old one, may be very
reasonably urged : and I yet hope to hear of there being
some other national amusement in the United States, besides
newspaper politics.

They certainly are not a humorous people, and their
temperament always impressed me as being of a dull and
gloomy character. In shrewdness of remark, and a certain
cast-iron quaintness, the Yankees, or people of New England,

---

[1] NOTE TO THE ORIGINAL EDITION.—Or let him refer to an able, and
perfectly truthful article, in *The Foreign Quarterly Review*, published in
the present month of October [1842] ; to which my attention has been
attracted, since these sheets have been passing through the press.
He will find some specimens there, by no means remarkable to any
man who has been in America, but sufficiently striking to one who
has not.

unquestionably take the lead; as they do in most other evidences of intelligence. But in travelling about, out of the large cities—as I have remarked in former parts of these volumes—I was quite oppressed by the prevailing seriousness and melancholy air of business : which was so general and unvarying, that at every new town I came to, I seemed to meet the very same people whom I had left behind me, at the last. Such defects as are perceptible in the national manners, seem, to me, to be referable, in a great degree, to this cause: which has generated a dull, sullen persistence in coarse usages, and rejected the graces of life as undeserving of attention. There is no doubt that Washington, who was always most scrupulous and exact on points of ceremony, perceived the tendency towards this mistake, even in his time, and did his utmost to correct it.

I cannot hold with other writers on these subjects that the prevalence of various forms of dissent in America, is in any way attributable to the non-existence there of an established church : indeed, I think the temper of the people, if it admitted of such an Institution being founded amongst them, would lead them to desert it, as a matter of course, merely because it *was* established. But, supposing it to exist, I doubt its probable efficacy in summoning the wandering sheep to one great fold, simply because of the immense amount of dissent which prevails at home ; and because I do not find in America any one form of religion with which we in Europe, or even in England, are unacquainted. Dissenters resort thither in great numbers, as other people do, simply because it is a land of resort ; and great settlements of them are founded, because ground can be purchased, and towns and villages reared, where there were none of the human creation before. But even the Shakers emigrated from England ; our country is not unknown to Mr. Joseph Smith, the apostle of Mormonism, or to his benighted disciples ; I have beheld religious scenes myself in some of our populous towns which can hardly be surpassed by an American camp-meeting ; and I am not aware that any instance of superstitious imposture on the one hand, and superstitious credulity on the other, has had its origin in the United States, which we cannot more than parallel by the precedents of Mrs. Southcote, Mary Tofts the rabbit-breeder, or even Mr. Thom of Canterbury : which latter case arose, some time after the dark ages had passed away.

The Republican Institutions of America undoubtedly lead the people to assert their self-respect and their equality ; but a traveller is bound to bear those Institutions in his mind, and not hastily to resent the near approach of a class of strangers, who, at home, would keep aloof. This characteristic, when it was tinctured with no foolish pride, and stopped short of no honest service, never offended me ; and I very seldom, if ever, experienced its rude or unbecoming display. Once or twice it was comically developed, as in the following case ; but this was an amusing incident, and not the rule, or near it.

I wanted a pair of boots at a certain town, for I had none to travel in, but those with the memorable cork soles, which were much too hot for the fiery decks of a steamboat. I therefore sent a message to an artist in boots, importing, with my compliments, that I should be happy to see him, if he would do me the polite favour to call. He very kindly returned for answer, that he would " look round " at six o'clock that evening.

I was lying on the sofa, with a book and a wine-glass, at about that time, when the door opened, and a gentleman in a stiff cravat, within a year or two on either side of thirty, entered, in his hat and gloves ; walked up to the lookingglass ; arranged his hair ; took off his gloves ; slowly produced a measure from the uttermost depths of his coatpocket ; and requested me, in a languid tone, to " unfix " my straps. I complied, but looked with some curiosity at his hat, which was still upon his head. It might have been that, or it might have been the heat—but he took it off. Then, he sat himself down on a chair opposite to me ; rested an arm on each knee ; and, leaning forward very much, took from the ground, by a great effort, the specimen of metropolitan workmanship which I had just pulled off : whistling, pleasantly, as he did so. He turned it over and over ; surveyed it with a contempt no language can express ; and inquired if I wished him to fix me a boot like *that?* I courteously replied, that provided the boots were large enough, I would leave the rest to him ; that if convenient and practicable, I should not object to their bearing some resemblance to the model then before him ; but that I would be entirely guided by, and would beg to leave the whole subject to, his judgment and discretion. " You an't partickler, about this scoop in the heel, I suppose then ? " says he: "we don't foller that, here." I repeated my last observation. He looked at himself in the glass again; went closer to it to dash a grain or two of dust out of the corner of his eye; and settled his cravat. All this time, my leg and foot were in the air. "Nearly ready, Sir?" I inquired. "Well, pretty nigh," he said; "keep steady." I kept as steady as I could, both in foot and face; and having by this time got the dust out, and found his pencil-case, he measured me, and made the necessary notes. When he had finished, he fell into his old attitude, and taking up the boot again, mused for some time. "And this," he said, at last, "is an English boot, is it? This is a London boot, eh?" "That, Sir," I replied, "is a London boot." He mused over it again, after the manner of Hamlet with Yorick's skull; nodded his head, as who should say, "I pity the Institutions that led to the production of this boot;" rose; put up his pencil, notes, and paper—glancing at himself in the glass, all the time—put on his hat; drew on his gloves very slowly; and finally walked out. When he had been gone about a minute, the door reopened, and his hat and his head reappeared. He looked round the room, and at the boot again, which was still lying on the floor; appeared thoughtful for a minute; and then said "Well, good arternoon." "Good afternoon, Sir," said I: and that was the end of the interview.

There is but one other head on which I wish to offer a remark; and that has reference to the public health. In so vast a country, where there are thousands of millions of acres of land yet unsettled and uncleared, and on every rood of which, vegetable decomposition is annually taking place; where there are so many great rivers, and such opposite varieties of climate; there cannot fail to be a great amount of sickness at certain seasons. But I may venture to say, after conversing with many members of the medical profession in America, that I am not singular in the opinion that much of the disease which does prevail, might be avoided, if a few common precautions were observed. Greater means of personal cleanliness, are indispensable to this end; the custom of hastily swallowing large quantities of animal food, three times a-day, and rushing back to sedentary pursuits after each meal, must be changed; the gentler sex must go more wisely clad, and take more healthful exercise; and in the latter clause, the males must be included also. Above all, in public institutions, and throughout the whole of every town and city, the system of ventilation, and drainage, and removal of impurities requires to be thoroughly revised. There is no local Legislature in America which may not study Mr. Chadwick's excellent Report upon the Sanitary Condition of our Labouring Classes, with immense advantage.

———————

I HAVE now arrived at the close of this book. I have little reason to believe, from certain warnings I have had since I returned to England, that it will be tenderly or favourably received by the American people; and as I have written the Truth in relation to the mass of those who form their judgments and express their opinions, it will be seen that I have no desire to court, by any adventitious means, the popular applause.

It is enough for me, to know, that what I have set down in these pages, cannot cost me a single friend on the other side of the Atlantic, who is, in anything, deserving of the name. For the rest, I put my trust, implicitly, in the spirit in which they have been conceived and penned; and I can bide my time.

I have made no reference to my reception, nor have I suffered it to influence me in what I have written; for, in either case, I should have offered but a sorry acknowledgment, compared with that I bear within my breast, towards those partial readers of my former books, across the Water, who met me with an open hand, and not with one that closed upon an iron muzzle.

THE END

POSTSCRIPT

AT a Public Dinner given to me on Saturday the 18th of April, 1868, in the City of New York, by two hundred representatives of the Press of the United States of America, I made the following observations among others :

"So much of my voice has lately been heard in the land, that I might have been contented with troubling you no further from my present standing-point, were it not a duty with which I henceforth charge myself, not only here but on every suitable occasion, whatsoever and wheresoever, to express my high and grateful sense of my second reception in America, and to bear my honest testimony to the national generosity and magnanimity. Also, to declare how astounded I have been by the amazing changes I have seen around me on every side,—changes moral, changes physical, changes in the amount of land subdued and peopled, changes in the rise of vast new cities, changes in the growth of older cities almost out of recognition, changes in the graces and amenities of life, changes in the Press, without whose advancement no advancement can take place anywhere. Nor am I, believe me, so arrogant as to suppose that in five-and-twenty years there have been no changes in me, and that I had nothing to learn and no extreme impressions to correct when I was here first. And this brings me to a point on which I have, ever since I landed in the United States last November, observed a strict silence, though sometimes tempted to break it, but in reference to which I will, with your good leave, take you into my confidence now. Even the Press, being human, may be sometimes mistaken or misinformed, and I rather think that I have in one or two rare instances observed its information to be not strictly accurate with reference to myself. Indeed, I have, now and again, been more surprised by printed news that I have read of myself, than by any printed news that I have ever read in my present state of existence. Thus, the vigour and perseverance with which I have for some months past been collecting materials for, and hammering away at, a new book on America has much astonished me ; seeing that all that time my declaration has been perfectly well known to my publishers on both sides of the Atlantic, that no consideration on earth would induce me to write one. But what I have intended, what I have resolved upon (and this is the confidence I seek to place in you) is, on my return to England, in my own person, in my own Journal, to bear, for the behoof of my countrymen, such testimony to the gigantic changes in this country as I have hinted at to-night. Also, to record that wherever I have been, in the smallest places equally with the largest, I have been received with unsurpassable politeness, delicacy, sweet temper, hospitality, consideration, and with unsurpassable respect for the privacy daily enforced upon me by the nature of my avocation here and the state of my health. This testimony, so long as I live, and so long as my descendants have any legal right in my books, I shall cause to be republished, as an appendix to every copy of those two books of mine in which I have referred to America. And this I will do and cause to be done, not in mere love and thankfulness, but because I regard it as an act of plain justice and honour."

I said these words with the greatest earnestness that I could lay upon them, and I repeat them in print here with equal earnestness. So long as this book shall last, I hope that they will form a part of it, and will be fairly read as inseparable from my experiences and impressions of America.

CHARLES DICKENS.

May, 1868.

PICTURES FROM ITALY

The
Reader's Passport.

IF the readers of this volume will be so kind as to take their credentials for the different places which are the subject of its author's reminiscences, from the Author himself, perhaps they may visit them, in fancy, the more agreeably, and with a better understanding of what they are to expect.

Many books have been written upon Italy, affording many means of studying the history of that interesting country, and the innumerable associations entwined

The Villa d'Este at Tivoli from the Cypress Avenue.
A page from the first edition, 1846

CONTENTS

LIST OF ILLUSTRATIONS

THE READER'S PASSPORT

IF the readers of this volume will be so kind as to take their credentials for the different places which are the subject of its author's reminiscences, from the Author himself, perhaps they may visit them, in fancy, the more agreeably, and with a better understanding of what they are to expect.

Many books have been written upon Italy, affording many means of studying the history of that interesting country, and the innumerable associations entwined about it. I make but little reference to that stock of information; not at all regarding it as a necessary consequence of my having had recourse to the storehouse for my own benefit, that I should reproduce its easily accessible contents before the eyes of my readers.

Neither will there be found, in these pages, any grave examination into the government or misgovernment of any portion of the country. No visitor of that beautiful land can fail to have a strong conviction on the subject; but as I chose when residing there, a Foreigner, to abstain from the discussion of any such questions with any order of Italians, so I would rather not enter on the inquiry now. During my twelve months' occupation of a house at Genoa, I never found that authorities constitutionally jealous were distrustful of me; and I should be sorry to give them occasion to regret their free courtesy, either to myself or any of my countrymen.

There is, probably, not a famous Picture or Statue in all Italy, but could be easily buried under a mountain of printed paper devoted to dissertations on it. I do not, therefore, though an earnest admirer of Painting and Sculpture, expatiate at any length on famous Pictures and Statues.

K

This Book is a series of faint reflections—mere shadows in the water—of places to which the imaginations of most people are attracted in a greater or less degree, on which mine had dwelt for years, and which have some interest for all. The greater part of the descriptions were written on the spot, and sent home, from time to time, in private letters. I do not mention the circumstance as an excuse for any defects they may present, for it would be none; but as a guarantee to the Reader that they were at least penned in the fulness of the subject, and with the liveliest impressions of novelty and freshness.

If they have ever a fanciful and idle air, perhaps the reader will suppose them written in the shade of a Sunny Day, in the midst of the objects of which they treat, and will like them none the worse for having such influences of the country upon them.

I hope I am not likely to be misunderstood by Professors of the Roman Catholic faith, on account of anything contained in these pages. I have done my best, in one of my former productions, to do justice to them; and I trust, in this, they will do justice to me. When I mention any exhibition that impressed me as absurd or disagreeable, I do not seek to connect it, or recognise it as necessarily connected with, any essentials of their creed. When I treat of the ceremonies of the Holy Week, I merely treat of their effect, and do not challenge the good and learned Dr. Wiseman's interpretation of their meaning. When I hint a dislike of nunneries for young girls who abjure the world before they have ever proved or known it; or doubt the *ex officio* sanctity of all Priests and Friars; I do no more than many conscientious Catholics both abroad and at home.

I have likened these Pictures to shadows in the water, and would fain hope that I have, nowhere, stirred the water so roughly, as to mar the shadows. I could never desire to be on better terms with all my friends than now, when distant mountains rise, once more, in my path. For I need not hesitate to avow, that, bent on correcting a brief mistake I made, not long ago, in disturbing the old relations between myself and my readers, and departing for a moment from my old pursuits, I am about to resume them, joyfully, in Switzerland; where during another year of absence, I can at once work out the themes I have now in my mind, without interruption: and while I keep my English audience within speaking distance, extend my knowledge of a noble country, inexpressibly attractive to me [1].

This book is made as accessible as possible, because it would be a great pleasure to me if I could hope, through its means, to compare impressions with some among the multitudes who will hereafter visit the scenes described with interest and delight.

And I have only now, in passport wise, to sketch my reader's portrait, which I hope may be thus supposititiously traced for either sex:

Complexion	Fair.
Eyes	Very cheerful.
Nose	Not supercilious.
Mouth	Smiling.
Visage	Beaming.
General Expression . .	Extremely agreeable.

This was written in 1846.

GOING THROUGH FRANCE

On a fine Sunday morning in the Midsummer time and weather of eighteen hundred and forty-four, it was, my good friend, when—don't be alarmed; not when two travellers might have been observed slowly making their way over that picturesque and broken ground by which the first chapter of a Middle-Aged novel is usually attained—but when an English travelling-carriage of considerable proportions, fresh from the shady halls of the Pantechnicon near Belgrave Square, London, was observed (by a very small French soldier; for I saw him look at it) to issue from the gate of the Hôtel Meurice in the Rue Rivoli at Paris.

I am no more bound to explain why the English family travelling by this carriage, inside and out, should be starting for Italy on a Sunday morning, of all good days in the week, than I am to assign a reason for all the little men in France being soldiers, and all the big men postillions; which is the invariable rule. But, they had some sort of reason for what they did, I have no doubt; and their reason for being there at all, was, as you know, that they were going to live in fair Genoa for a year; and that the head of the family purposed, in that space of time, to stroll about, wherever his restless humour carried him.

And it would have been small comfort to me to have explained to the population of Paris generally, that I was that Head and Chief; and not the radiant embodiment of good humour who sat beside me in the person of a French Courier—best of servants and most beaming of men! Truth to say, he looked a great deal more patriarchal than I, who, in the shadow of his portly presence, dwindled down to no account at all.

There was, of course, very little in the aspect of Paris— as we rattled near the dismal Morgue and over the Pont Neuf—to reproach us for our Sunday travelling. The wine-shops (every second house) were driving a roaring trade; awnings were spreading, and chairs and tables arranging,

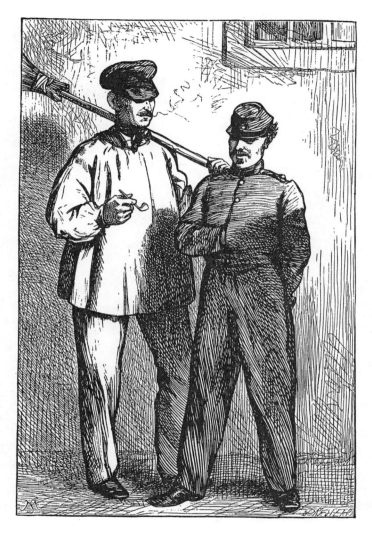

Civil and Military

outside the cafés, preparatory to the eating of ices, and drinking of cool liquids, later in the day; shoeblacks were busy on the bridges; shops were open; carts and waggons clattered to and fro; the narrow, up-hill, funnel-like streets across the River, were so many dense perspectives of crowd and bustle, parti-coloured nightcaps, tobacco-pipes, blouses, large boots, and shaggy heads of hair; nothing at that hour denoted a day of rest, unless it were the appearance, here and there, of a family pleasure-party, crammed into a bulky old lumbering cab; or of some contemplative holiday-maker in the freest and easiest dishabille, leaning out of a low garret window, watching the drying of his newly polished shoes on the little parapet outside (if a gentleman), or the airing of her stockings in the sun (if a lady), with calm anticipation.

Once clear of the never-to-be-forgotten-or-forgiven pavement which surrounds Paris, the first three days of travelling towards Marseilles are quiet and monotonous enough. To Sens. To Avallon. To Chalons. A sketch of one day's proceedings is a sketch of all three; and here it is.

We have four horses, and one postillion, who has a very long whip, and drives his team, something like the Courier of Saint Petersburg in the circle at Astley's or Franconi's: only he sits his own horse instead of standing on him. The immense jack-boots worn by these postillions, are sometimes a century or two old; and are so ludicrously disproportionate to the wearer's foot, that the spur, which is put where his own heel comes, is generally halfway up the leg of the boots. The man often comes out of the stable-yard, with his whip in his hand and his shoes on, and brings out, in both hands, one boot at a time, which he plants on the ground by the side of his horse, with great gravity, until everything is ready. When it is—and oh Heaven! the noise they make about it! —he gets into the boots, shoes and all, or is hoisted into them by a couple of friends; adjusts the rope harness, embossed by the labours of innumerable pigeons in the stables; makes all the horses kick and plunge; cracks his whip like a madman; shouts "En route—Hi!" and away we go. He is sure to have a contest with his horse before we have gone very far; and then he calls him a Thief, and a Brigand, and a Pig, and what not; and beats him about the head as if he were made of wood.

There is little more than one variety in the appearance of

the country, for the first two days.   From a dreary plain,
to an interminable avenue, and from an interminable avenue
to a dreary plain again.   Plenty of vines there are in the
open fields, but of a short low kind, and not trained in
festoons, but about straight sticks.   Beggars innumerable
there are, everywhere ; but an extraordinarily scanty population, and fewer children than I ever encountered.   I don't
believe we saw a hundred children between Paris and Chalons.
Queer old towns, drawbridged and walled : with odd little
towers at the angles, like grotesque faces, as if the wall had
put a mask on, and were staring down into the moat ; other
strange little towers, in gardens and fields, and down lanes,
and in farm-yards : all alone, and always round, with a
peaked roof, and never used for any purpose at all ; ruinous
buildings of all sorts ; sometimes an hôtel de ville, sometimes
a guard-house, sometimes a dwelling-house, sometimes a
château with a rank garden, prolific in dandelion, and watched
over by extinguisher-topped turrets, and blink-eyed little
casements ; are the standard objects, repeated over and over
again.   Sometimes we pass a village inn, with a crumbling
wall belonging to it, and a perfect town of out-houses ; and
painted over the gateway, " Stabling for Sixty Horses ; " as
indeed there might be stabling for sixty score, were there
any horses to be stabled there, or anybody resting there, or
anything stirring about the place but a dangling bush,
indicative of the wine inside : which flutters idly in the wind,
in lazy keeping with everything else, and certainly is never in
a green old age, though always so old as to be dropping to
pieces.   And all day long, strange little narrow waggons, in
strings of six or eight, bringing cheese from Switzerland, and
frequently in charge, the whole line, of one man, or even
boy—and he very often asleep in the foremost cart—come
jingling past : the horses drowsily ringing the bells upon their
harness, and looking as if they thought (no doubt they do)
their great blue woolly furniture, of immense weight and
thickness, with a pair of grotesque horns growing out of the
collar, very much too warm for the Midsummer weather.
  Then, there is the Diligence, twice or thrice a-day ; with
the dusty outsides in blue frocks, like butchers ; and the
insides in white nightcaps ; and its cabriolet head on the
roof, nodding and shaking, like an idiot's head ; and its
Young-France passengers staring out of window, with beards
down to their waists, and blue spectacles awfully shading

their warlike eyes, and very big sticks clenched in their National grasp. Also the Malle Poste, with only a couple of passengers, tearing along at a real good dare-devil pace, and out of sight in no time. Steady old Curés come jolting past, now and then, in such ramshackle, rusty, musty, clattering coaches as no Englishman would believe in; and bony women dawdle about in solitary places, holding cows by ropes while they feed, or digging and hoeing or doing field-work of a more laborious kind, or representing real shepherdesses with their flocks—to obtain an adequate idea of which pursuit and its followers, in any country, it is only necessary to take any pastoral poem, or picture, and imagine to yourself whatever is most exquisitely and widely unlike the descriptions therein contained.

You have been travelling along, stupidly enough, as you generally do in the last stage of the day; and the ninety-six bells upon the horses—twenty-four apiece—have been ringing sleepily in your ears for half an hour or so; and it has become a very jog-trot, monotonous, tiresome sort of business; and you have been thinking deeply about the dinner you will have at the next stage; when, down at the end of the long avenue of trees through which you are travelling, the first indication of a town appears, in the shape of some straggling cottages: and the carriage begins to rattle and roll over a horribly uneven pavement. As if the equipage were a great firework, and the mere sight of a smoking cottage chimney had lighted it, instantly it begins to crack and splutter, as if the very devil were in it. Crack, crack, crack, crack. Crack-crack-crack. Crick-crack. Crick-crack. Helo! Hola! Vite! Voleur! Brigand! Hi hi hi! En r-r-r-r-route! Whip, wheels, driver, stones, beggars, children, crack, crack, crack; helo! hola! charité pour l'amour de Dieu! crick-crack-crick-crack; crick, crick, crick; bump, jolt, crack, bump, crick-crack; round the corner, up the narrow street, down the paved hill on the other side; in the gutter; bump, bump; jolt, jog, crick, crick, crick; crack, crack, crack; into the shop-windows on the left-hand side of the street, preliminary to a sweeping turn into the wooden archway on the right; rumble, rumble, rumble; clatter, clatter, clatter; crick, crick, crick; and here we are in the yard of the Hôtel de l'Ecu d'Or; used up, gone out, smoking, spent, exhausted; but sometimes making a false start unexpectedly, with nothing coming of it—like a firework to the last!

The landlady of the Hôtel de l'Ecu d'Or is here; and the
landlord of the Hôtel de l'Ecu d'Or is here; and the femme
de chambre of the Hôtel de l'Ecu d'Or is here; and a gentleman in a glazed cap, with a red beard like a bosom friend,
who is staying at the Hôtel de l'Ecu d'Or, is here; and
Monsieur le Curé is walking up and down in a corner of the
yard by himself, with a shovel hat upon his head, and a black
gown on his back, and a book in one hand, and an umbrella
in the other; and everybody, except Monsieur le Curé, is
open-mouthed and open-eyed, for the opening of the carriage-
door. The landlord of the Hôtel de l'Ecu d'Or, dotes to
that extent upon the Courier, that he can hardly wait for
his coming down from the box, but embraces his very legs
and boot-heels as he descends. "My Courier! My brave
Courier! My friend! My brother!" The landlady loves
him, the femme de chambre blesses him, the garçon worships
him. The Courier asks if his letter has been received? It
has, it has. Are the rooms prepared? They are, they are.
The best rooms for my noble Courier. The rooms of state
for my gallant Courier; the whole house is at the service of
my best of friends! He keeps his hand upon the carriage-
door, and asks some other question to enhance the expectation. He carries a green leathern purse outside his coat,
suspended by a belt. The idlers look at it; one touches it.
It is full of five-franc pieces. Murmurs of admiration are
heard among the boys. The landlord falls upon the Courier's
neck, and folds him to his breast. He is so much fatter
than he was, he says! He looks so rosy and so well!

The door is opened. Breathless expectation. The lady
of the family gets out. Ah sweet lady! Beautiful lady!
The sister of the lady of the family gets out. Great Heaven,
Ma'amselle is charming! First little boy gets out. Ah,
what a beautiful little boy! First little girl gets out. Oh,
but this is an enchanting child! Second little girl gets out.
The landlady, yielding to the finest impulse of our common
nature, catches her up in her arms! Second little boy gets
out. Oh, the sweet boy! Oh, the tender little family!
The baby is handed out. Angelic baby! The baby has
topped everything. All the rapture is expended on the baby!
Then the two nurses tumble out; and the enthusiasm swelling
into madness, the whole family are swept upstairs as on a
cloud; while the idlers press about the carriage, and look
into it, and walk round it, and touch it. For it is something

to touch a carriage that has held so many people. It is a
legacy to leave one's children.

The rooms are on the first floor, except the nursery for
the night, which is a great rambling chamber, with four or
five beds in it: through a dark passage, up two steps, down
four, past a pump, across a balcony, and next door to the
stable. The other sleeping apartments are large and lofty;
each with two small bedsteads, tastefully hung, like the
windows, with red and white drapery. The sitting-room is
famous. Dinner is already laid in it for three; and the
napkins are folded in cocked-hat fashion. The floors are of
red tile. There are no carpets, and not much furniture to
speak of; but there is abundance of looking-glass, and there
are large vases under glass shades, filled with artificial flowers;
and there are plenty of clocks. The whole party are in
motion. The brave Courier, in particular, is everywhere:
looking after the beds, having wine poured down his throat
by his dear brother the landlord, and picking up green cucumbers—always cucumbers; Heaven knows where he gets them—
with which he walks about, one in each hand, like truncheons.

Dinner is announced. There is very thin soup; there are
very large loaves—one apiece; a fish; four dishes afterwards;
some poultry afterwards; a dessert afterwards; and no lack
of wine. There is not much in the dishes; but they are
very good, and always ready instantly. When it is nearly
dark, the brave Courier, having eaten the two cucumbers,
sliced up in the contents of a pretty large decanter of oil,
and another of vinegar, emerges from his retreat below, and
proposes a visit to the Cathedral, whose massive tower frowns
down upon the court-yard of the inn. Off we go; and very
solemn and grand it is, in the dim light: so dim at last, that
the polite, old, lantern-jawed Sacristan has a feeble little
bit of candle in his hand, to grope among the tombs with—
and looks among the grim columns, very like a lost ghost
who is searching for his own.

Underneath the balcony, when we return, the inferior
servants of the inn are supping in the open air, at a great
table; the dish, a stew of meat and vegetables, smoking hot,
and served in the iron cauldron it was boiled in. They
have a pitcher of thin wine, and are very merry; merrier
than the gentleman with the red beard, who is playing
billiards in the light room on the left of the yard, where
shadows, with cues in their hands, and cigars in their

mouths, cross and recross the window, constantly.   Still
the thin Curé walks up and down alone, with his book and
umbrella.   And there he walks, and there the billiard-balls
rattle, long after we are fast asleep.

We are astir at six next morning.   It is a delightful day,
shaming yesterday's mud upon the carriage, if anything
could shame a carriage, in a land where carriages are never
cleaned.   Everybody is brisk ; and as we finish breakfast,
the horses come jingling into the yard from the Post-house.
Everything taken out of the carriage is put back again.   The
brave Courier announces that all is ready, after walking into
every room, and looking all round it, to be certain that
nothing is left behind.   Everybody gets in.   Everybody
connected with the Hôtel de l'Ecu d'Or is again enchanted.
The brave Courier runs into the house for a parcel containing cold fowl, sliced ham, bread, and biscuits, for lunch ;
hands it into the coach ; and runs back again.

What has he got in his hand now ?   More cucumbers ?
No.   A long strip of paper.   It's the bill.

The brave Courier has two belts on, this morning : one
supporting the purse : another, a mighty good sort of leathern
bottle, filled to the throat with the best light Bordeaux wine
in the house.   He never pays the bill till this bottle is full.
Then he disputes it.

He disputes it now, violently.   He is still the landlord's
brother, but by another father or mother.   He is not so
nearly related to him as he was last night.   The landlord
scratches his head.   The brave Courier points to certain
figures in the bill, and intimates that if they remain there,
the Hôtel de l'Ecu d'Or is thenceforth and for ever an hôtel
de l'Ecu de cuivre.   The landlord goes into a little counting-
house.   The brave Courier follows, forces the bill and a pen
into his hand, and talks more rapidly than ever.   The landlord takes the pen.   The Courier smiles.   The landlord
makes an alteration.   The Courier cuts a joke.   The landlord is affectionate, but not weakly so.   He bears it like a
man.   He shakes hands with his brave brother ; but he don't
hug him.   Still, he loves his brother ; for he knows that he
will be returning that way, one of these fine days, with another
family, and he foresees that his heart will yearn towards
him again.   The brave Courier traverses all round the carriage once, looks at the drag, inspects the wheels, jumps up,
gives the word, and away we go !

It is market morning. The market is held in the little square outside in front of the cathedral. It is crowded with men and women, in blue, in red, in green, in white; with canvased stalls; and fluttering merchandise. The country people are grouped about, with their clean baskets before them. Here, the lace-sellers; there, the butter and egg-sellers; there, the fruit-sellers; there, the shoemakers. The whole place looks as if it were the stage of some great theatre, and the curtain had just run up, for a picturesque ballet. And there is the cathedral to boot: scene-like: all grim, and swarthy, and mouldering, and cold; just splashing the pavement in one place with faint purple drops, as the morning sun, entering by a little window on the eastern side, struggles through some stained glass panes, on the western.

In five minutes we have passed the iron cross, with a little ragged kneeling-place of turf before it, in the outskirts of the town; and are again upon the road.

LYONS, THE RHONE, AND THE GOBLIN
OF AVIGNON

CHALONS is a fair resting-place, in right of its good inn on the bank of the river, and the little steamboats, gay with green and red paint, that come and go upon it: which make up a pleasant and refreshing scene, after the dusty roads. But, unless you would like to dwell on an enormous plain, with jagged rows of irregular poplars on it, that look in the distance like so many combs with broken teeth: and unless you would like to pass your life without the possibility of going up-hill, or going up anything but stairs: you would hardly approve of Chalons as a place of residence.

You would probably like it better, however, than Lyons: which you may reach, if you will, in one of the before-mentioned steamboats, in eight hours.

What a city Lyons is! Talk about people feeling, at certain unlucky times, as if they had tumbled from the clouds! Here is a whole town that is tumbled, anyhow, out of the sky; having been first caught up, like other stones that tumble down from that region, out of fens and barren places, dismal to behold! The two great streets through which the two great rivers dash, and all the little streets whose name is Legion, were scorching, blistering, and sweltering. The houses, high and vast, dirty to excess, rotten as old cheeses, and as thickly peopled. All up the hills that hem the city in, these houses swarm; and the mites inside were lolling out of the windows, and drying their ragged clothes on poles, and crawling in and out at the doors, and coming out to pant and gasp upon the pavement, and creeping in and out among huge piles and bales of fusty, musty, stifling goods; and living, or rather not dying till their time should come, in an exhausted receiver. Every manufacturing town, melted into one, would hardly convey an impression of Lyons as it presented itself to me: for all the undrained, un-scavengered qualities of a foreign town, seemed grafted, there, upon the native miseries of a manufacturing one; and it bears such fruit as I would go some miles out of my way to avoid encountering again.

In the cool of the evening: or rather in the faded heat of the day: we went to see the Cathedral, where divers old women, and a few dogs, were engaged in contemplation. There was no difference, in point of cleanliness, between its stone pavement and that of the streets; and there was a wax saint, in a little box like a berth aboard ship, with a glass front to it, whom Madame Tussaud would have nothing to say to, on any terms, and which even Westminster Abbey might be ashamed of. If you would know all about the architecture of this church, or any other, its dates, dimensions, endowments, and history, is it not written in Mr. Murray's Guide-Book, and may you not read it there, with thanks to him, as I did?

For this reason, I should abstain from mentioning the curious clock in Lyons Cathedral, if it were not for a small mistake I made, in connexion with that piece of mechanism. The keeper of the church was very anxious it should be shown; partly for the honour of the establishment and the town; and partly, perhaps, because of his deriving a percentage from the additional consideration. However that may be, it was set in motion, and thereupon a host of little doors flew open, and innumerable little figures staggered out of them, and jerked themselves back again, with that special unsteadiness of purpose, and hitching in the gait, which usually attaches to figures that are moved by clockwork. Meanwhile, the Sacristan stood explaining these wonders, and pointing them out, severally, with a wand. There was a centre puppet of the Virgin Mary; and close to her, a small pigeon-hole, out of which another and a very ill-looking puppet made one of the most sudden plunges I ever saw accomplished: instantly flopping back again at sight of her, and banging his little door violently after him. Taking this to be emblematic of the victory over Sin and Death, and not at all unwilling to show that I perfectly understood the subject, in anticipation of the showman, I rashly said, "Aha! The Evil Spirit. To be sure. He is very soon disposed of." "Pardon, Monsieur," said the Sacristan, with a polite motion of his hand towards the little door, as if introducing somebody—"The Angel Gabriel!"

Soon after daybreak next morning, we were steaming down the Arrowy Rhone, at the rate of twenty miles an hour, in a very dirty vessel full of merchandise, and with only three or four other passengers for our companions: among whom, the most remarkable was a silly, old, meek-faced, garlic-eating, immeasurably polite Chevalier, with a dirty scrap of red ribbon hanging at his button-hole, as if he had tied it there to remind himself of something; as Tom Noddy, in the farce, ties knots in his pocket-handkerchief.

For the last two days, we had seen great sullen hills, the first indications of the Alps, lowering in the distance. Now, we were rushing on beside them: sometimes close beside them: sometimes with an intervening slope, covered with vineyards. Villages and small towns hanging in mid-air, with great woods of olives seen through the light open towers of their churches, and clouds moving slowly on, upon the steep acclivity behind them; ruined castles perched on every eminence; and scattered houses in the clefts and gullies of the hills; made it very beautiful. The great height of these, too, making the buildings look so tiny, that they had all the charm of elegant models; their excessive whiteness, as contrasted with the brown rocks, or the sombre, deep, dull, heavy green of the olive-tree; and the puny size, and little slow walk of the Liliputian men and women on the bank; made a charming picture. There were ferries out of number, too; bridges; the famous Pont d'Esprit, with I don't know how many arches; towns where memorable wines are made; Valence, where Napoleon studied; and the noble river, bringing at every winding turn, new beauties into view.

There lay before us, that same afternoon, the broken bridge of Avignon, and all the city baking in the sun; yet with an under-done-pie-crust, battlemented wall, that never will be brown, though it bake for centuries.

The grapes were hanging in clusters in the streets, and the brilliant Oleander was in full bloom everywhere. The streets are old and very narrow, but tolerably clean, and shaded by awnings stretched from house to house. Bright stuffs and handkerchiefs, curiosities, ancient frames of carved wood, old chairs, ghostly tables, saints, virgins, angels, and staring daubs of portraits, being exposed for sale beneath, it was very quaint and lively. All this was much set off, too, by the glimpses one caught, through a rusty gate standing ajar, of quiet sleepy court-yards, having stately old houses within, as silent as tombs. It was all very like one of the descriptions in the Arabian Nights. The three one-eyed

Calendars might have knocked at any one of those doors till the street rang again, and the porter who persisted in asking questions—the man who had the delicious purchases put into his basket in the morning—might have opened it quite naturally.

After breakfast next morning, we sallied forth to see the lions. Such a delicious breeze was blowing in, from the north, as made the walk delightful : though the pavement-stones, and stones of the walls and houses, were far too hot to have a hand laid on them comfortably.

We went, first of all, up a rocky height, to the cathedral : where Mass was performing to an auditory very like that of Lyons, namely, several old women, a baby, and a very self-possessed dog, who had marked out for himself a little course or platform for exercise, beginning at the altar-rails and ending at the door, up and down which constitutional walk he trotted, during the service, as methodically and calmly, as any old gentleman out of doors. It is a bare old church, and the paintings in the roof are sadly defaced by time and damp weather ; but the sun was shining in, splendidly, through the red curtains of the windows, and glittering on the altar furniture ; and it looked as bright and cheerful as need be.

Going apart, in this church, to see some painting which was being executed in fresco by a French artist and his pupil, I was led to observe more closely than I might otherwise have done, a great number of votive offerings with which the walls of the different chapels were profusely hung. I will not say decorated, for they were very roughly and comically got up ; most likely by poor sign-painters, who eke out their living in that way. They were all little pictures : each representing some sickness or calamity from which the person placing it there, had escaped, through the interposition of his or her patron saint, or of the Madonna ; and I may refer to them as good specimens of the class generally. They are abundant in Italy.

In a grotesque squareness of outline, an impossibility of perspective, they are not unlike the woodcuts in old books ; but they were oil-paintings, and the artist, like the painter of the Primrose family, had not been sparing of his colours. In one, a lady was having a toe amputated—an operation which a saintly personage had sailed into the room, upon a couch, to superintend. In another, a lady was lying in bed, tucked up very tight and prim, and staring with much composure at a tripod, with a slop-basin on it; the usual form of washing-stand, and the only piece of furniture, besides the bedstead, in her chamber. One would never have supposed her to be labouring under any complaint, beyond the inconvenience of being miraculously wide awake, if the painter had not hit upon the idea of putting all her family on their knees in one corner, with their legs sticking out behind them on the floor, like boot-trees. Above whom, the Virgin, on a kind of blue divan, promised to restore the patient. In another case, a lady was in the very act of being run over, immediately outside the city walls, by a sort of pianoforte van. But the Madonna was there again. Whether the supernatural appearance had startled the horse (a bay griffin), or whether it was invisible to him, I don't know; but he was galloping away, ding dong, without the smallest reverence or compunction. On every picture "Ex voto" was painted in yellow capitals in the sky.

Though votive offerings were not unknown in Pagan Temples, and are evidently among the many compromises made between the false religion and the true, when the true was in its infancy, I could wish that all the other compromises were as harmless. Gratitude and Devotion are Christian qualities; and a grateful, humble, Christian spirit may dictate the observance.

Hard by the cathedral stands the ancient Palace of the Popes, of which one portion is now a common jail, and another a noisy barrack: while gloomy suites of state apartments, shut up and deserted, mock their own old state and glory, like the embalmed bodies of kings. But we neither went there, to see state rooms, nor soldiers' quarters, nor a common jail, though we dropped some money into a prisoners' box outside, whilst the prisoners, themselves, looked through the iron bars, high up, and watched us eagerly. We went to see the ruins of the dreadful rooms in which the Inquisition used to sit.

A little, old, swarthy woman, with a pair of flashing black eyes,—proof that the world hadn't conjured down the devil within her, though it had had between sixty and seventy years to do it in,—came out of the Barrack Cabaret, of which she was the keeper, with some large keys in her hands, and marshalled us the way that we should go. How she told us, on the way, that she was a Government Officer (*concierge du palais apostolique*), and had been, for I don't know how many years; and how she had shown these dungeons to princes; and how she was the best of dungeon demonstrators; and how she had resided in the palace from an infant,—had been born there, if I recollect right,—I needn't relate. But such a fierce, little, rapid, sparkling, energetic she-devil I never beheld. She was alight and flaming, all the time. Her action was violent in the extreme. She never spoke, without stopping expressly for the purpose. She stamped her feet, clutched us by the arms, flung herself into attitudes, hammered against walls with her keys, for mere emphasis: now whispered as if the Inquisition were there still: now shrieked as if she were on the rack herself; and had a mysterious, hag-like way with her forefinger, when approaching the remains of some new horror—looking back and walking stealthily, and making horrible grimaces—that might alone have qualified her to walk up and down a sick man's counterpane, to the exclusion of all other figures, through a whole fever.

Passing through the court-yard, among groups of idle soldiers, we turned off by a gate, which this She-Goblin unlocked for our admission, and locked again behind us: and entered a narrow court, rendered narrower by fallen stones and heaps of rubbish; part of it choking up the mouth of a ruined subterranean passage, that once communicated (or is said to have done so) with another castle on the opposite bank of the river. Close to this court-yard is a dungeon— we stood within it, in another minute—in the dismal tower *des oubliettes*, where Rienzi was imprisoned, fastened by an iron chain to the very wall that stands there now, but shut out from the sky which now looks down into it. A few steps brought us to the Cachots, in which the prisoners of the Inquisition were confined for forty-eight hours after their capture, without food or drink, that their constancy might be shaken, even before they were confronted with their gloomy judges. The day has not got in there yet. They are still small cells, shut in by four unyielding, close, hard walls; still profoundly dark; still massively doored and fastened, as of old.

Goblin, looking back as I have described, went softly on, into a vaulted chamber, now used as a store-room: once the chapel of the Holy Office. The place where the tribunal sat, was plain. The platform might have been removed but yesterday. Conceive the parable of the Good Samaritan having been painted on the wall of one of these Inquisition chambers! But it was, and may be traced there yet.

High up in the jealous wall, are niches where the faltering replies of the accused were heard and noted down. Many of them had been brought out of the very cell we had just looked into, so awfully; along the same stone passage. We had trodden in their very footsteps.

I am gazing round me, with the horror that the place inspires, when Goblin clutches me by the wrist, and lays, not her skinny finger, but the handle of a key, upon her lip. She invites me, with a jerk, to follow her. I do so. She leads me out into a room adjoining—a rugged room, with a funnel-shaped, contracting roof, open at the top, to the bright day. I ask her what it is. She folds her arms, leers hideously, and stares. I ask again. She glances round, to see that all the little company are there; sits down upon a mound of stones; throws up her arms, and yells out, like a fiend, " La Salle de la Question ! "

The Chamber of Torture! And the roof was made of that shape to stifle the victim's cries! Oh Goblin, Goblin, let us think of this awhile, in silence. Peace, Goblin! Sit with your short arms crossed on your short legs, upon that heap of stones, for only five minutes, and then flame out again.

Minutes! Seconds are not marked upon the Palace clock, when, with her eyes flashing fire, Goblin is up, in the middle of the chamber, describing, with her sunburnt arms, a wheel of heavy blows. Thus it ran round! cries Goblin. Mash, mash, mash! An endless routine of heavy hammers. Mash, mash, mash! upon the sufferer's limbs. See the stone trough! ‹ ₋ys Goblin. For the water torture! Gurgle, swill, bloat, burst, for the Redeemer's honour! Suck the bloody rag, deep down into your unbelieving body, Heretic, at every breath you draw! And when the executioner plucks it out, reeking with the smaller mysteries of God's own Image, know us for His chosen servants, true believers in the Sermon on the Mount, elect disciples of Him who never did a miracle but to heal: who never struck a man with palsy, blindness, deafness, dumbness, madness, any one affliction of mankind; and never stretched His blessed hand out, but to give relief and ease!

See! cries Goblin. There the furnace was. There they made the irons red-hot. Those holes supported the sharp stake, on which the tortured persons hung poised: dangling with their whole weight from the roof. "But;" and Goblin whispers this; "Monsieur has heard of this tower? Yes? Let Monsieur look down, then!"

A cold air, laden with an earthy smell, falls upon the face of Monsieur; for she has opened, while speaking, a trap-door in the wall. Monsieur looks in. Downward to the bottom, upward to the top, of a steep, dark, lofty tower: very dismal, very dark, very cold. The Executioner of the Inquisition, says Goblin, edging in her head to look down also, flung those who were past all further torturing, down here. "But look! does Monsieur see the black stains on the wall?" A glance, over his shoulder, at Goblin's keen eye, shows Monsieur—and would without the aid of the directing-key— where they are. "What are they?" "Blood!"

In October, 1791, when the Revolution was at its height here, sixty persons: men and women ("and priests," says Goblin, "priests"): were murdered, and hurled, the dying and the dead, into this dreadful pit, where a quantity of quick-lime was tumbled down upon their bodies. Those ghastly tokens of the massacre were soon no more; but while one stone of the strong building in which the deed was done, remains upon another, there they will lie in the memories of men, as plain to see as the splashing of their blood upon the wall is now.

Was it a portion of the great scheme of Retribution, that the cruel deed should be committed in this place! That a part of the atrocities and monstrous institutions, which had been, for scores of years, at work, to change men's nature, should in its last service, tempt them with the ready means of gratifying their furious and beastly rage! Should enable them to show themselves, in the height of their frenzy, no worse than a great, solemn, legal establishment, in the height of its power! No worse! Much better. They used the Tower of the Forgotten, in the name of Liberty—their liberty; an earth-born creature, nursed in the black mud of the Bastille moats and dungeons, and necessarily betraying many evidences of its unwholesome bringing-up—but the Inquisition used it in the name of Heaven.

Goblin's finger is lifted; and she steals out again, into the Chapel of the Holy Office. She stops at a certain part of the flooring. Her great effect is at hand. She waits for the rest. She darts at the brave Courier, who is explaining something; hits him a sounding rap on the hat with the largest key; and bids him be silent. She assembles us all, round a little trap-door in the floor, as round a grave.

"Voilà!" she darts down at the ring, and flings the door open with a crash, in her goblin energy, though it is no light weight. "Voilà les oubliettes! Voilà les oubliettes! Subterranean! Frightful! Black! Terrible! Deadly! Les oubliettes de l'Inquisition!"

My blood ran cold, as I looked from Goblin, down into the vaults, where these forgotten creatures, with recollections of the world outside: of wives, friends, children, brothers: starved to death, and made the stones ring with their unavailing groans. But, the thrill I felt on seeing the accursed wall below, decayed and broken through, and the sun shining in through its gaping wounds, was like a sense of victory and triumph. I felt exalted with the proud delight of living in these degenerate times, to see it. As if I were the hero of some high achievement! The light in the doleful vaults was typical of the light that has streamed in, on all persecution in God's name, but which is not yet at its noon! It cannot look more lovely to a blind man newly restored to sight, than to a traveller who sees it, calmly and majestically, treading down the darkness of that Infernal Well.

GOBLIN, having shown *les oubliettes*, felt that her great *coup* was struck. She let the door fall with a crash, and stood upon it with her arms akimbo, sniffing prodigiously.

When we left the place, I accompanied her into her house, under the outer gateway of the fortress, to buy a little history of the building. Her cabaret, a dark low room, lighted by small windows, sunk in the thick wall—in the softened light, and with its forge-like chimney; its little counter by the door, with bottles, jars, and glasses on it; its household implements and scraps of dress against the wall; and a sober-looking woman (she must have a congenial life of it, with Goblin,) knitting at the door—looked exactly like a picture by OSTADE.

I walked round the building on the outside, in a sort of dream, and yet with the delightful sense of having awakened from it, of which the light, down in the vaults, had given me the assurance. The immense thickness and giddy height of the walls, the enormous strength of the massive towers, the great extent of the building, its gigantic proportions, frowning aspect, and barbarous irregularity, awaken awe and wonder. The recollection of its opposite old uses: an impregnable fortress, a luxurious palace, a horrible prison, a place of torture, the court of the Inquisition: at one and the same time, a house of feasting, fighting, religion, and blood: gives to every stone in its huge form a fearful interest, and imparts new meaning to its incongruities. I could think of little, however, then, or long afterwards, but the sun in the dungeons. The palace coming down to be the lounging-place of noisy soldiers, and being forced to echo their rough talk, and common oaths, and to have their garments fluttering from its dirty windows, was some reduction of its state, and something to rejoice at; but the day in its cells, and the sky for the roof of its chambers of cruelty—that was its desolation and defeat! If I had seen it in a blaze from ditch to rampart, I should have felt that not that light, nor all the

light in all the fire that burns, could waste it, like the sunbeams in its secret council-chamber, and its prisons.

Before I quit this Palace of the Popes, let me translate
from the little history I mentioned just now, a short anec-
dote, quite appropriate to itself, connected with its adven-
tures.

"An ancient tradition relates, that in 1441, a nephew of
Pierre de Lude, the Pope's legate, seriously insulted some
distinguished ladies of Avignon, whose relations, in revenge,
seized the young man, and horribly mutilated him. For
several years the legate kept *his* revenge within his own
breast, but he was not the less resolved upon its gratification at last. He even made, in the fulness of time, advances
towards a complete reconciliation ; and when their apparent
sincerity had prevailed, he invited to a splendid banquet, in
this palace, certain families, whole families, whom he sought
to exterminate. The utmost gaiety animated the repast ;
but the measures of the legate were well taken. When the
dessert was on the board, a Swiss presented himself, with
the announcement that a strange ambassador solicited an
extraordinary audience. The legate, excusing himself, for
the moment, to his guests, retired, followed by his officers.
Within a few minutes afterwards, five hundred persons were
reduced to ashes: the whole of that wing of the building
having been blown into the air with a terrible explosion ! "

After seeing the churches (I will not trouble you with
churches just now), we left Avignon that afternoon. The
heat being very great, the roads outside the walls were strewn
with people fast asleep in every little slip of shade, and with
lazy groups, half asleep and half awake, who were waiting
until the sun should be low enough to admit of their playing
bowls among the burnt-up trees, and on the dusty road.
The harvest here, was already gathered in, and mules and
horses were treading out the corn in the fields. We came,
at dusk, upon a wild and hilly country, once famous for
brigands ; and travelled slowly up a steep ascent. So we
went on, until eleven at night, when we halted at the town
of Aix (within two stages of Marseilles) to sleep.

The hotel, with all the blinds and shutters closed to keep
the light and heat out, was comfortable and airy next morning, and the town was very clean ; but so hot, and so intensely light, that when I walked out at noon it was like
coming suddenly from the darkened room into crisp blue

fire. The air was so very clear, that distant hills and rocky points appeared within an hour's walk; while the town immediately at hand—with a kind of blue wind between me and it—seemed to be white hot, and to be throwing off a fiery air from the surface.

We left this town towards evening, and took the road to Marseilles. A dusty road it was; the houses shut up close; and the vines powdered white. At nearly all the cottage doors, women were peeling and slicing onions into earthen bowls for supper. So they had been doing last night all the way from Avignon. We passed one or two shady dark châteaux, surrounded by trees, and embellished with cool basins of water: which were the more refreshing to behold, from the great scarcity of such residences on the road we had travelled. As we approached Marseilles, the road began to be covered with holiday people. Outside the public-houses were parties smoking, drinking, playing draughts and cards, and (once) dancing. But dust, dust, dust, everywhere. We went on, through a long, straggling, dirty suburb, thronged with people; having on our left a dreary slope of land, on which the country-houses of the Marseilles merchants, always staring white, are jumbled and heaped without the slightest order: backs, fronts, sides, and gables towards all points of the compass; until, at last, we entered the town.

I was there, twice or thrice afterwards, in fair weather and foul; and I am afraid there is no doubt that it is a dirty and disagreeable place. But the prospect, from the fortified heights, of the beautiful Mediterranean, with its lovely rocks and islands, is most delightful. These heights are a desirable retreat, for less picturesque reasons—as an escape from a compound of vile smells perpetually arising from a great harbour full of stagnant water, and befouled by the refuse of innumerable ships with all sorts of cargoes: which, in hot weather, is dreadful in the last degree.

There were foreign sailors, of all nations, in the streets; with red shirts, blue shirts, buff shirts, tawny shirts, and shirts of orange colour; with red caps, blue caps, green caps, great beards, and no beards; in Turkish turbans, glazed English hats, and Neapolitan head-dresses. There were the townspeople sitting in clusters on the pavement, or airing themselves on the tops of their houses, or walking up and down the closest and least airy of Boulevards; and there were crowds of fierce-looking people of the lower sort, blocking up the way, constantly. In the very heart of all this stir and uproar, was the common madhouse; a low, contracted, miserable building, looking straight upon the street, without the smallest screen or court-yard; where chattering madmen and madwomen were peeping out, through rusty bars, at the staring faces below, while the sun, darting fiercely aslant into their little cells, seemed to dry up their brains, and worry them, as if they were baited by a pack of dogs.

We were pretty well accommodated at the Hôtel du Paradis, situated in a narrow street of very high houses, with a hairdresser's shop opposite, exhibiting in one of its windows two full-length waxen ladies, twirling round and round: which so enchanted the hairdresser himself, that he and his family sat in arm-chairs, and in cool undresses, on the pavement outside, enjoying the gratification of the passers-by, with lazy dignity. The family had retired to rest when we went to bed, at midnight; but the hairdresser (a corpulent man, in drab slippers) was still sitting there, with his legs stretched out before him, and evidently couldn't bear to have the shutters put up.

Next day we went down to the harbour, where the sailors of all nations were discharging and taking in cargoes of all kinds: fruits, wines, oils, silks, stuffs, velvets, and every manner of merchandise. Taking one of a great number of lively little boats with gay-striped awnings, we rowed away, under the sterns of great ships, under tow-ropes and cables, against and among other boats, and very much too near the sides of vessels that were faint with oranges, to the " Marie Antoinette," a handsome steamer bound for Genoa, lying near the mouth of the harbour. By-and-by, the carriage, that unwieldy "trifle from the Pantechnicon," on a flat barge, bumping against everything, and giving occasion for a prodigious quantity of oaths and grimaces, came stupidly alongside; and by five o'clock we were steaming out in the open sea. The vessel was beautifully clean; the meals were served under an awning on deck; the night was calm and clear; the quiet beauty of the sea and sky unspeakable.

We were off Nice, early next morning, and coasted along, within a few miles of the Cornice road (of which more in its place) nearly all day. We could see Genoa before three; and watching it as it gradually developed its splendid amphitheatre, terrace rising above terrace, garden above garden, palace above palace, height upon height, was ample occupation for us, till we ran into the stately harbour. Having been duly astonished, here, by the sight of a few Cappuccini monks, who were watching the fair-weighing of some wood upon the wharf, we drove off to Albaro, two miles distant, where we had engaged a house.

The way lay through the main streets, but not through the Strada Nuova, or the Strada Balbi, which are the famous streets of palaces. I never in my life was so dismayed! The wonderful novelty of everything, the unusual smells, the unaccountable filth (though it is reckoned the cleanest of Italian towns), the disorderly jumbling of dirty houses, one upon the roof of another; the passages more squalid and more close than any in St. Giles's or old Paris; in and out of which, not vagabonds, but well-dressed women, with white veils and great fans, were passing and repassing; the perfect absence of resemblance in any dwelling-house, or shop, or wall, or post, or pillar, to anything one had ever seen before; and the disheartening dirt, discomfort, and decay; perfectly confounded me. I fell into a dismal reverie. I am conscious of a feverish and bewildered vision of saints' and virgins' shrines at the street corners—of great numbers of friars, monks, and soldiers—of vast red curtains, waving in the doorways of the churches—of always going up hill, and yet seeing every other street and passage going higher up—of fruit-stalls, with fresh lemons and oranges hanging in garlands made of vine-leaves—of a guard-house, and a drawbridge—and some gateways—and vendors of iced water, sitting with little trays upon the margin of the kennel—and this is all the consciousness I had, until I was set down in a rank, dull, weedy court-yard, attached to a kind of pink jail; and was told I lived there.

I little thought, that day, that I should ever come to have an attachment for the very stones in the streets of Genoa, and to look back upon the city with affection as connected with many hours of happiness and quiet! But these are my first impressions honestly set down; and how they changed, I will set down too. At present, let us breathe after this long-winded journey.

GENOA AND ITS NEIGHBOURHOOD

THE first impressions of such a place as ALBARO, the suburb of Genoa, where I am now, as my American friends would say, "located," can hardly fail, I should imagine, to be mournful and disappointing. It requires a little time and use to overcome the feeling of depression consequent, at first, on so much ruin and neglect. Novelty, pleasant to most people, is particularly delightful, I think, to me. I am not easily dispirited when I have the means of pursuing my own fancies and occupations; and I believe I have some natural aptitude for accommodating myself to circumstances. But, as yet, I stroll about here, in all the holes and corners of the neighbourhood, in a perpetual state of forlorn surprise; and returning to my villa: the Villa Bagnerello (it sounds romantic, but Signor Bagnerello is a butcher hard by): have sufficient occupation in pondering over my new experiences, and comparing them, very much to my own amusement, with my expectations, until I wander out again.

The Villa Bagnerello: or the Pink Jail, a far more expressive name for the mansion: is in one of the most splendid situations imaginable. The noble bay of Genoa, with the deep blue Mediterranean, lies stretched out near at hand; monstrous old desolate houses and palaces are dotted all about; lofty hills, with their tops often hidden in the clouds, and with strong forts perched high up on their craggy sides, are close upon the left; and in front, stretching from the walls of the house, down to a ruined chapel which stands upon the bold and picturesque rocks on the sea-shore, are green vineyards, where you may wander all day long in partial shade, through interminable vistas of grapes, trained on a rough trellis-work across the narrow paths.

This sequestered spot is approached by lanes so very narrow, that when we arrived at the Custom-house, we found the people here had *taken the measure* of the narrowest among them, and were waiting to apply it to the carriage; which ceremony was gravely performed in the street, while we all stood by in breathless suspense. It was found to be a very tight fit, but just a possibility, and no more—as I am reminded every day, by the sight of various large holes which it punched in the walls on either side as it came along. We are more fortunate, I am told, than an old lady, who took a house in these parts not long ago, and who stuck fast in *her* carriage in a lane; and as it was impossible to open one of the doors, she was obliged to submit to the indignity of being hauled through one of the little front windows, like a harlequin.

When you have got through these narrow lanes, you come to an archway, imperfectly stopped up by a rusty old gate— my gate. The rusty old gate has a bell to correspond, which you ring as long as you like, and which nobody answers, as it has no connexion whatever with the house. But there is a rusty old knocker, too—very loose, so that it slides round when you touch it—and if you learn the trick of it, and knock long enough, somebody comes. The brave Courier comes, and gives you admittance. You walk into a seedy little garden, all wild and weedy, from which the vineyard opens; cross it, enter a square hall like a cellar, walk up a cracked marble staircase, and pass into a most enormous room with a vaulted roof and whitewashed walls: not unlike a great Methodist chapel. This is the *sala*. It has five windows and five doors, and is decorated with pictures which would gladden the heart of one of those picture-cleaners in London who hang up, as a sign, a picture divided, like death and the lady, at the top of the old ballad: which always leaves you in a state of uncertainty whether the ingenious professor has cleaned one half, or dirtied the other. The furniture of this *sala* is a sort of red brocade. All the chairs are immovable, and the sofa weighs several tons.

On the same floor, and opening out of this same chamber, are dining-room, drawing-room, and divers bed-rooms: each with a multiplicity of doors and windows. Upstairs are divers other gaunt chambers, and a kitchen; and downstairs is another kitchen, which, with all sorts of strange contrivances for burning charcoal, looks like an alchemical laboratory. There are also some half-dozen small sitting-rooms, where the servants in this hot July, may escape from the heat of the fire, and where the brave Courier plays all sorts of musical instruments of his own manufacture, all the evening long. A mighty old, wandering, ghostly, echoing, grim, bare house it is, as ever I beheld or thought of.

There is a little vine-covered terrace, opening from the
drawing-room ; and under this terrace, and forming one side
of the little garden, is what used to be the stable. It is now
a cow-house, and has three cows in it, so that we get new
milk by the bucketful.   There is no pasturage near, and
they never go out, but are constantly lying down, and sur-
feiting themselves with vine-leaves—perfect Italian cows
enjoying the *dolce far' niente* all day long.   They are presided over, and slept with, by an old man named Antonio,
and his son ; two burnt-sienna natives with naked legs and
feet, who wear, each, a shirt, a pair of trousers, and a red
sash, with a relic, or some sacred charm like the bonbon off
a twelfth-cake, hanging round the neck.   The old man is
very anxious to convert me to the Catholic faith, and exhorts
me frequently.   We sit upon a stone by the door, sometimes in the evening, like Robinson Crusoe and Friday
reversed ; and he generally relates, towards my conversion,
an abridgment of the History of Saint Peter—chiefly, I
believe, from the unspeakable delight he has in his imitation
of the cock.

The view, as I have said, is charming ; but in the day you
must keep the lattice-blinds close shut, or the sun would drive
you mad ; and when the sun goes down you must shut up all
the windows, or the mosquitoes would tempt you to commit
suicide.   So at this time of the year, you don't see much of
the prospect within doors.   As for the flies, you don't mind
them.   Nor the fleas, whose size is prodigious, and whose
name is Legion, and who populate the coach-house to that
extent that I daily expect to see the carriage going off
bodily, drawn by myriads of industrious fleas in harness.
The rats are kept away, quite comfortable, by scores of lean
cats, who roam about the garden for that purpose.   The
lizards, of course, nobody cares for ; they play in the sun,
and don't bite.   The little scorpions are merely curious.   The
beetles are rather late, and have not appeared yet.   The
frogs are company.   There is a preserve of them in the
grounds of the next villa ; and after nightfall, one would
think that scores upon scores of women in pattens were
going up and down a wet stone pavement without a moment's
cessation.   That is exactly the noise they make.

The ruined chapel, on the picturesque and beautiful sea-
shore, was dedicated, once upon a time, to Saint John the
Baptist.   I believe there is a legend that Saint John's bones

were received there, with various solemnities, when they were first brought to Genoa; for Genoa possesses them to this day. When there is any uncommon tempest at sea, they are brought out and exhibited to the raging weather, which they never fail to calm. In consequence of this connexion of Saint John with the city, great numbers of the common people are christened Giovanni Baptista, which latter name is pronounced in the Genoese patois "Batcheetcha," like a sneeze. To hear everybody calling everybody else Batcheetcha, on a Sunday, or festa-day, when there are crowds in the streets, is not a little singular and amusing to a stranger.

The narrow lanes have great villas opening into them, whose walls (outside walls, I mean) are profusely painted with all sorts of subjects, grim and holy. But time and the sea-air have nearly obliterated them; and they look like the entrance to Vauxhall Gardens on a sunny day. The court-yards of these houses are overgrown with grass and weeds; all sorts of hideous patches cover the bases of the statues, as if they were afflicted with a cutaneous disorder; the outer gates are rusty; and the iron bars outside the lower windows are all tumbling down. Firewood is kept in halls where costly treasures might be heaped up, mountains high; water-falls are dry and choked; fountains, too dull to play, and too lazy to work, have just enough recollection of their identity, in their sleep, to make the neighbourhood damp; and the sirocco wind is often blowing over all these things for days together, like a gigantic oven out for a holiday.

Not long ago, there was a festa-day, in honour of the *Virgin's mother*, when the young men of the neighbourhood, having worn green wreaths of the vine in some procession or other, bathed in them, by scores. It looked very odd and pretty. Though I am bound to confess (not knowing of the festa at that time), that I thought, and was quite satisfied, they wore them as horses do—to keep the flies off.

Soon afterwards, there was another festa-day, in honour of St. Nazaro. One of the Albaro young men brought two large bouquets soon after breakfast, and coming upstairs into the great *sala*, presented them himself. This was a polite way of begging for a contribution towards the expenses of some music in the Saint's honour, so we gave him whatever it may have been, and his messenger departed: well satisfied. At six o'clock in the evening we went to the church—close

at hand—a very gaudy place, hung all over with festoons and
bright draperies, and filled, from the altar to the main door,
with women, all seated. They wear no bonnets here, simply
a long white veil—the " mezzero; " and it was the most gauzy,
ethereal-looking audience I ever saw. The young women are
not generally pretty, but they walk remarkably well, and in
their personal carriage and the management of their veils,
display much innate grace and elegance. There were some
men present: not very many: and a few of these were kneeling about the aisles, while everybody else tumbled over them.
Innumerable tapers were burning in the church; the bits of
silver and tin about the saints (especially in the Virgin's
necklace) sparkled brilliantly; the priests were seated about
the chief altar; the organ played away, lustily, and a full
band did the like; while a conductor, in a little gallery
opposite to the band, hammered away on the desk before
him, with a scroll; and a tenor, without any voice, sang.
The band played one way, the organ played another, the
singer went a third, and the unfortunate conductor banged
and banged, and flourished his scroll on some principle of
his own: apparently well satisfied with the whole performance. I never did hear such a discordant din. The heat
was intense all the time.

The men, in red caps, and with loose coats hanging on
their shoulders (they never put them on), were playing bowls,
and buying sweetmeats, immediately outside the church.
When half-a-dozen of them finished a game, they came into
the aisle, crossed themselves with the holy water, knelt on
one knee for an instant, and walked off again to play another
game at bowls. They are remarkably expert at this diversion,
and will play in the stony lanes and streets, and on the
most uneven and disastrous ground for such a purpose, with
as much nicety as on a billiard-table. But the most favourite
game is the national one of Mora, which they pursue with
surprising ardour, and at which they will stake everything
they possess. It is a destructive kind of gambling, requiring
no accessories but the ten fingers, which are always—I
intend no pun—at hand. Two men play together. One
calls a number—say the extreme one, ten. He marks what
portion of it he pleases by throwing out three, or four, or five
fingers; and his adversary has, in the same instant, at hazard,
and without seeing his hand, to throw out as many fingers,
as will make the exact balance. Their eyes and hands

become so used to this, and act with such astonishing rapidity, that an uninitiated bystander would find it very difficult, if not impossible, to follow the progress of the game. The initiated, however, of whom there is always an eager group looking on, devour it with the most intense avidity ; and as they are always ready to champion one side or the other in case of a dispute, and are frequently divided in their partisanship, it is often a very noisy proceeding. It is never the quietest game in the world ; for the numbers are always called in a loud sharp voice, and follow as close upon each other as they can be counted. On a holiday evening, standing at a window, or walking in a garden, or passing through the streets, or sauntering in any quiet place about the town, you will hear this game in progress in a score of wine-shops at once ; and looking over any vineyard walk, or turning almost any corner, will come upon a knot of players in full cry. It is observable that most men have a propensity to throw out some particular number oftener than another : and the vigilance with which two sharp-eyed players will mutually endeavour to detect this weakness, and adapt their game to it, is very curious and entertaining. The effect is greatly heightened by the universal suddenness and vehemence of gesture ; two men playing for half a farthing with an intensity as all-absorbing as if the stake were life.

Hard by here is a large Palazzo, formerly belonging to some member of the Brignole family, but just now hired by a school of Jesuits for their summer quarters. I walked into its dismantled precincts the other evening about sunset, and couldn't help pacing up and down for a little time drowsily taking in the aspect of the place : which is repeated hereabouts in all directions.

I loitered to and fro, under a colonnade, forming two sides of a weedy, grass-grown court-yard, whereof the house formed a third side, and a low terrace-walk, overlooking the garden and the neighbouring hills, the fourth. I don't believe there was an uncracked stone in the whole pavement. In the centre was a melancholy statue, so piebald in its decay, that it looked exactly as if it had been covered with sticking-plaster, and afterwards powdered. The stables, coach-houses, offices, were all empty, all ruinous, all utterly deserted.

Doors had lost their hinges, and were holding on by their latches ; windows were broken, painted plaster had peeled off, and was lying about in clods ; fowls and cats had so taken

L

possession of the out-buildings, that I couldn't help thinking
of the fairy tales, and eyeing them with suspicion, as trans-
formed retainers, waiting to be changed back again.   One
old Tom in particular : a scraggy brute, with a hungry green
eye (a poor relation, in reality, I am inclined to think) : came
prowling round and round me, as if he half believed, for the
moment, that I might be the hero come to marry the lady,
and set all to-rights ; but discovering his mistake, he suddenly
gave a grim snarl, and walked away with such a tremendous
tail, that he couldn't get into the little hole where he lived,
but was obliged to wait outside, until his indignation and his
tail had gone down together.

In a sort of summer-house, or whatever it may be, in this
colonnade, some Englishmen had been living, like grubs in
a nut ; but the Jesuits had given them notice to go, and
they had gone, and *that* was shut up too.   The house : a
wandering, echoing, thundering barrack of a place, with the
lower windows barred up, as usual, was wide open at the
door : and I have no doubt I might have gone in, and gone
to bed, and gone dead, and nobody a bit the wiser.   Only
one suite of rooms on an upper floor was tenanted ; and from
one of these, the voice of a young-lady vocalist, practising
bravura lustily, came flaunting out upon the silent evening.

I went down into the garden, intended to be prim and
quaint, with avenues, and terraces, and orange-trees, and
statues, and water in stone basins ; and everything was
green, gaunt, weedy, straggling, under-grown or over-grown,
mildewy, damp, redolent of all sorts of slabby, clammy,
creeping, and uncomfortable life.   There was nothing bright
in the whole scene but a firefly—one solitary firefly—showing
against the dark bushes like the last little speck of the
departed Glory of the house ; and even it went flitting up
and down at sudden angles, and leaving a place with a jerk,
and describing an irregular circle, and returning to the same
place with a twitch that startled one : as if it were looking
for the rest of the Glory, and wondering (Heaven knows it
might !) what had become of it.

In the course of two months, the flitting shapes and
shadows of my dismal entering reverie gradually resolved
themselves into familiar forms and substances ; and I already
began to think that when the time should come, a year
hence, for closing the long holiday and turning back to

England, I might part from Genoa with anything but a glad heart.

It is a place that "grows upon you" every day. There seems to be always something to find out in it. There are the most extraordinary alleys and by-ways to walk about in. You can lose your way (what a comfort that is, when you are idle !) twenty times a day, if you like ; and turn up again, under the most unexpected and surprising difficulties. It abounds in the strangest contrasts ; things that are picturesque, ugly, mean, magnificent, delightful, and offensive, break upon the view at every turn.

They who would know how beautiful the country immediately surrounding Genoa is, should climb (in clear weather) to the top of Monte Faccio, or, at least, ride round the city walls : a feat more easily performed. No prospect can be more diversified and lovely than the changing views of the harbour, and the valleys of the two rivers, the Polcevera and the Bizagno, from the heights along which the strongly fortified walls are carried, like the great wall of China in little. In not the least picturesque part of this ride, there is a fair specimen of a real Genoese tavern, where the visitor may derive good entertainment from real· Genoese dishes, such as Tagliarini ; Ravioli ; German sausages, strong of garlic, sliced and eaten with fresh green figs ; cocks' combs and sheep-kidneys, chopped up with mutton chops and liver ; small pieces of some unknown part of a calf, twisted into small shreds, fried, and served up in a great dish like whitebait ; and other curiosities of that kind. They often get wine at these suburban Trattorie, from France and Spain and Portugal, which is brought over by small captains in little trading-vessels. They buy it at so much a bottle, without asking what it is, or caring to remember if anybody tells them, and usually divide it into two heaps ; of which they label one Champagne, and the other Madeira. The various opposite flavours, qualities, countries, ages, and vintages that are comprised under these two general heads is quite extraordinary. The most limited range is probably from cool Gruel up to old Marsala, and down again to apple Tea.

The great majority of the streets are as narrow as any thoroughfare can well be, where people (even Italian people) are supposed to live and walk about ; being mere lanes, with here and there a kind of well, or breathing-place. The

houses are immensely high, painted in all sorts of colours,
and are in every stage and state of damage, dirt, and lack of
repair.   They are commonly let off in floors, or flats, like
the houses in the old town of Edinburgh, or many houses in
Paris.   There are few street doors ; the entrance halls are,
for the most part, looked upon as public property ; and any
moderately enterprising scavenger might make a fine fortune
by now and then clearing them out.   As it is impossible for
coaches to penetrate into these streets, there are sedan chairs,
gilded and otherwise, for hire in divers places.   A great
many private chairs are also kept among the nobility and
gentry ; and at night these are trotted to and fro in all
directions, preceded by bearers of great lanterns, made of
linen stretched upon a frame.   The sedans and lanterns are
the legitimate successors of the long strings of patient and
much-abused mules, that go jingling their little bells through
these confined streets all day long.   They follow them, as
regularly as the stars the sun.

When shall I forget the Streets of Palaces: the Strada
Nuova and the Strada Balbi ! or how the former looked one
summer day, when I first saw it underneath the brightest
and most intensely blue of summer skies : which its narrow
perspective of immense mansions reduced to a tapering and
most precious strip of brightness, looking down upon the
heavy shade below !   A brightness not too common, even in
July and August, to be well esteemed : for, if the Truth
must out, there were not eight blue skies in as many
midsummer weeks, saving, sometimes, early in the morning ;
when, looking out to sea, the water and the firmament were
one world of deep and brilliant blue.   At other times, there
were clouds and haze enough to make an Englishman
grumble in his own climate.

The endless details of these rich Palaces: the walls of
some of them, within, alive with masterpieces by Vandyke !
The great, heavy, stone balconies, one above another, and tier
over tier: with here and there, one larger than the rest,
towering high up—a huge marble platform ; the doorless
vestibules, massively barred lower windows, immense public
staircases, thick marble pillars, strong dungeon-like arches,
and dreary, dreaming, echoing vaulted chambers: among
which the eye wanders again, and again, and again, as every
palace is succeeded by another—the terrace gardens between
house and house, with green arches of the vine, and groves

of orange-trees, and blushing oleander in full bloom, twenty, thirty, forty feet above the street—the painted halls, mouldering, and blotting, and rotting in the damp corners, and still shining out in beautiful colours and voluptuous designs, where the walls are dry—the faded figures on the outsides of the houses, holding wreaths, and crowns, and flying upward, and downward, and standing in niches, and here and there looking fainter and more feeble than elsewhere, by contrast with some fresh little Cupids, who on a more recently decorated portion of the front, are stretching out what seems to be the semblance of a blanket, but is, indeed, a sun-dial—the steep, steep, up-hill streets of small palaces (but very large palaces for all that), with marble terraces looking down into close by-ways—the magnificent and innumerable Churches; and the rapid passage from a street of stately edifices, into a maze of the vilest squalor, steaming with unwholesome stenches, and swarming with half-naked children and whole worlds of dirty people—make up, altogether, such a scene of wonder: so lively, and yet so dead: so noisy, and yet so quiet: so obtrusive, and yet so shy and lowering: so wide awake, and yet so fast asleep : that it is a sort of intoxication to a stranger to walk on, and on, and on, and look about him. A bewildering phantasmagoria, with all the inconsistency of a dream, and all the pain and all the pleasure of an extravagant reality !

The different uses to which some of these Palaces are applied, all at once, is characteristic. For instance, the English Banker (my excellent and hospitable friend) has his office in a good-sized Palazzo in the Strada Nuova. In the hall (every inch of which is elaborately painted, but which is as dirty as a police-station in London), a hook-nosed Saracen's Head with an immense quantity of black hair (there is a man attached to it) sells walking-sticks. On the other side of the doorway, a lady with a showy handkerchief for head-dress (wife to the Saracen's Head, I believe) sells articles of her own knitting ; and sometimes flowers. A little further in, two or three blind men occasionally beg. Sometimes, they are visited by a man without legs, on a little go-cart, but who has such a fresh-coloured, lively face, and such a respectable, well-conditioned body, that he looks as if he had sunk into the ground up to his middle, or had come, but partially, up a flight of cellar-steps to speak to somebody. A little further in, a few men, perhaps, lie asleep in the middle of the day; or they may be chairmen waiting for their absent freight. If so, they have brought their chairs in with them, and there *they* stand also. On the left of the hall is a little room: a hatter's shop. On the first floor, is the English bank. On the first floor also, is a whole house, and a good large residence too. Heaven knows what there may be above that; but when you are there, you have only just begun to go upstairs. And yet, coming downstairs again, thinking of this; and passing out at a great crazy door in the back of the hall, instead of turning the other way, to get into the street again; it bangs behind you, making the dismallest and most lonesome echoes, and you stand in a yard (the yard of the same house) which seems to have been unvisited by human foot, for a hundred years. Not a sound disturbs its repose. Not a head, thrust out of any of the grim, dark, jealous windows, within sight, makes the weeds in the cracked pavement faint of heart, by suggesting the possibility of there being hands to grub them up. Opposite to you, is a giant figure carved in stone, reclining, with an urn, upon a lofty piece of artificial rockwork; and out of the urn, dangles the fag end of a leaden pipe, which, once upon a time, poured a small torrent down the rocks. But the eye-sockets of the giant are not drier than this channel is now. He seems to have given his urn, which is nearly upside down, a final tilt; and after crying, like a sepulchral child, "All gone!" to have lapsed into a stony silence.

In the streets of shops, the houses are much smaller, but of great size notwithstanding, and extremely high. They are very dirty: quite undrained, if my nose be at all reliable: and emit a peculiar fragrance, like the smell of very bad cheese, kept in very hot blankets. Notwithstanding the height of the houses, there would seem to have been a lack of room in the City, for new houses are thrust in everywhere. Wherever it has been possible to cram a tumble-down tenement into a crack or corner, in it has gone. If there be a nook or angle in the wall of a church, or a crevice in any other dead wall, of any sort, there you are sure to find some kind of habitation: looking as if it had grown there, like a fungus. Against the Government House, against the old Senate House, round about any large building, little shops stick so close, like parasite vermin to the great carcase. And for all this, look where you may: up steps, down steps, any-where, everywhere: there are irregular houses, receding,

starting forward, tumbling down, leaning against their neighbours, crippling themselves or their friends by some means or
other, until one, more irregular than the rest, chokes up the
way, and you can't see any further.

One of the rottenest-looking parts of the town, I think, is
down by the landing-wharf : though it may be, that its being
associated with a great deal of rottenness on the evening of
our arrival, has stamped it deeper in my mind. Here, again,
the houses are very high, and are of an infinite variety of
deformed shapes, and have (as most of the houses have) something hanging out of a great many windows, and wafting its
frowzy fragrance on the breeze. Sometimes, it is a curtain ;
sometimes, it is a carpet ; sometimes, it is a bed ; sometimes,
a whole lineful of clothes ; but there is almost always something. Before the basement of these houses, is an arcade
over the pavement : very massive, dark, and low, like an old
crypt. The stone, or plaster, of which it is made, has turned
quite black ; and against every one of these black piles, all
sorts of filth and garbage seem to accumulate spontaneously.
Beneath some of the arches, the sellers of maccaroni and
polenta establish their stalls, which are by no means inviting.
The offal of a fish-market, near at hand—that is to say, of a
back lane, where people sit upon the ground and on various
old bulkheads and sheds, and sell fish when they have any
to dispose of—and of a vegetable market, constructed on the
same principle—are contributed to the decoration of this
quarter ; and as all the mercantile business is transacted here,
and it is crowded all day, it has a very decided flavour about
it. The Porto Franco, or Free Port (where goods brought
in from foreign countries pay no duty until they are sold and
taken out, as in a bonded warehouse in England), is down
here also ; and two portentous officials, in cocked hats, stand
at the gate to search you if they choose, and to keep out
Monks and Ladies. For, Sanctity as well as Beauty has been
known to yield to the temptation of smuggling, and in the
same way : that is to say, by concealing the smuggled property beneath the loose folds of its dress. So Sanctity and
Beauty may, by no means, enter.

The streets of Genoa would be all the better for the im-
portation of a few Priests of prepossessing appearance. Every
fourth or fifth man in the streets is a Priest or a Monk ; and
there is pretty sure to be at least one itinerant ecclesiastic
inside or outside every hackney carriage on the neighbouring

roads.   I have no knowledge, elsewhere, of more repulsive
countenances than are to be found among these gentry.   If
Nature's handwriting be at all legible, greater varieties of'
sloth, deceit, and intellectual torpor, could hardly be observed
among any class of men in the world.

MR. PEPYS once heard a clergyman assert in his sermon,
in illustration of his respect for the Priestly office, that if he
could meet a Priest and angel together, he would salute the
Priest first.   I am rather of the opinion of PETRARCH, who,
when his pupil BOCCACCIO wrote to him in great tribulation,
that he had been visited and admonished for his writings by
a Carthusian Friar who claimed to be a messenger immediately commissioned by Heaven for that purpose, replied,
that for his own part, he would take the liberty of testing
the reality of the commission by personal observation of the
Messenger's face, eyes, forehead, behaviour, and discourse.   I
cannot but believe myself, from similar observation, that
many unaccredited celestial messengers may be seen skulking
through the streets of Genoa, or droning away their lives in
other Italian towns.

Perhaps the Cappuccini, though not a learned body, are,
as an order, the best friends of the people.   They seem to
mingle with them more immediately, as their counsellors and
comforters ; and to go among them more, when they are sick ;
and to pry less than some other orders, into the secrets of
families, for the purpose of establishing a baleful ascendency
over their weaker members ; and to be influenced by a less
fierce desire to make converts, and once made, to let them
go to ruin, soul and body.   They may be seen, in their coarse
dress, in all parts of the town at all times, and begging in
the markets early in the morning.   The Jesuits too, muster
strong in the streets, and go slinking noiselessly about, in
pairs, like black cats.

In some of the narrow passages, distinct trades congregate.
There is a street of jewellers, and there is a row of book-
sellers ; but even down in places where nobody ever can, or
ever could, penetrate in a carriage, there are mighty old
palaces shut in among the gloomiest and closest walls, and
almost shut out from the sun.   Very few of the tradesmen
have any idea of setting forth their goods, or disposing them
for show.   If you, a stranger, want to buy anything, you
usually look round the shop till you see it ; then clutch it,
if it be within reach, and inquire how much.   Everything is

sold at the most unlikely place. If you want coffee, you go to
a sweetmeat shop; and if you want meat, you will probably
find it behind an old checked curtain, down half-a-dozen
steps, in some sequestered nook as hard to find as if the
commodity were poison, and Genoa's law were death to any
that uttered it.

Most of the apothecaries' shops are great lounging-places.
Here, grave men with sticks, sit down in the shade for hours
together, passing a meagre Genoa paper from hand to hand,
and talking, drowsily and sparingly, about the News. Two
or three of these are poor physicians, ready to proclaim themselves on an emergency, and tear off with any messenger who
may arrive. You may know them by the way in which they
stretch their necks to listen, when you enter; and by the
sigh with which they fall back again into their dull corners,
on finding that you only want medicine. Few people lounge
in the barbers' shops; though they are very numerous, as
hardly any man shaves himself. But the apothecary's has
its group of loungers, who sit back among the bottles, with
their hands folded over the tops of their sticks. So still and
quiet, that either you don't see them in the darkened shop,
or mistake them—as I did one ghostly man in bottle-green,
one day, with a hat like a stopper—for Horse Medicine.

On a summer evening the Genoese are as fond of putting
themselves, as their ancestors were of putting houses, in every
available inch of space in and about the town. In all the
lanes and alleys, and up every little ascent, and on every
dwarf wall, and on every flight of steps, they cluster like
bees. Meanwhile (and especially on festa-days) the bells of
the churches ring incessantly; not in peals, or any known
form of sound, but in a horrible, irregular, jerking, dingle,
dingle, dingle: with a sudden stop at every fifteenth dingle
or so, which is maddening. This performance is usually
achieved by a boy up in the steeple, who takes hold of the
clapper, or a little rope attached to it, and tries to dingle
louder than every other boy similarly employed. The noise
is supposed to be particularly obnoxious to Evil Spirits; but
looking up into the steeples, and seeing (and hearing) these
young Christians thus engaged, one might very naturally
mistake them for the Enemy.

Festa-days, early in the autumn, are very numerous. All
the shops were shut up, twice within a week, for these holi-

days; and one night, all the houses in the neighbourhood of a particular church were illuminated, while the church itself was lighted, outside, with torches; and a grove of blazing links was erected, in an open space outside one of the city gates. This part of the ceremony is prettier and more singular a little way in the country, where you can trace the illuminated cottages all the way up a steep hill-side; and where you pass festoons of tapers, wasting away in the starlight night, before some lonely little house upon the road.

On these days, they always dress the church of the saint in whose honour the festa is holden, very gaily. Gold-embroidered festoons of different colours, hang from the arches; the altar furniture is set forth; and sometimes, even the lofty pillars are swathed from top to bottom in tight-fitting draperies. The cathedral is dedicated to St. Lorenzo. On St. Lorenzo's day, we went into it, just as the sun was setting. Although these decorations are usually in very indifferent taste, the effect, just then, was very superb indeed. For the whole building was dressed in red; and the sinking sun, streaming in, through a great red curtain in the chief doorway, made all the gorgeousness its own. When the sun went down, and it gradually grew quite dark inside, except for a few twinkling tapers on the principal altar, and some small dangling silver lamps, it was very mysterious and effective. But, sitting in any of the churches towards evening, is like a mild dose of opium.

With the money collected at a festa, they usually pay for the dressing of the church, and for the hiring of the band, and for the tapers. If there be any left (which seldom happens, I believe), the souls in Purgatory get the benefit of it. They are also supposed to have the benefit of the exertions of certain small boys, who shake money-boxes before some mysterious little buildings like rural turnpikes, which (usually shut up close) fly open on Red-letter days, and disclose an image and some flowers inside.

Just without the city gate, on the Albaro road, is a small house, with an altar in it, and a stationary money-box: also for the benefit of the souls in Purgatory. Still further to stimulate the charitable, there is a monstrous painting on the plaster, on either side of the grated door, representing a select party of souls, frying. One of them has a grey moustache, and an elaborate head of grey hair: as if he had been taken out of a hairdresser's window and cast into the furnace. There he is: a most grotesque and hideously comic old soul: for ever blistering in the real sun, and melting in the mimic fire, for the gratification and improvement (and the contributions) of the poor Genoese.

They are not a very joyous people, and are seldom seen to dance on their holidays: the staple places of entertainment among the women, being the churches and the public walks. They are very good-tempered, obliging, and industrious. Industry has not made them clean, for their habitations are extremely filthy, and their usual occupation on a fine Sunday morning, is to sit at their doors, hunting in each other's heads. But their dwellings are so close and confined that if those parts of the city had been beaten down by Massena in the time of the terrible Blockade, it would have at least occasioned one public benefit among many misfortunes.

The Peasant Women, with naked feet and legs, are so constantly washing clothes, in the public tanks, and in every stream and ditch, that one cannot help wondering, in the midst of all this dirt, who wears them when they are clean. The custom is to lay the wet linen which is being operated upon, on a smooth stone, and hammer away at it, with a flat wooden mallet. This they do, as furiously as if they were revenging themselves on dress in general for being connected with the Fall of Mankind.

It is not unusual to see, lying on the edge of the tank at these times, or on another flat stone, an unfortunate baby, tightly swathed up, arms and legs and all, in an enormous quantity of wrapper, so that it is unable to move a toe or finger. This custom (which we often see represented in old pictures) is universal among the common people. A child is left anywhere, without the possibility of crawling away, or is accidentally knocked off a shelf, or tumbled out of bed, or is hung up to a hook now and then, and left dangling like a doll at an English rag-shop, without the least inconvenience to anybody.

I was sitting, one Sunday, soon after my arrival, in the little country church of San Martino, a couple of miles from the city, while a baptism took place. I saw the priest, and an attendant with a large taper, and a man, and a woman, and some others; but I had no more idea, until the ceremony was all over, that it was a baptism, or that the curious little stiff instrument, that was passed from one to another, in the course of the ceremony, by the handle—like a short poker—

was a child, than I had that it was my own christening.
I borrowed the child afterwards, for a minute or two (it was
lying across the font then), and found it very red in the face
but perfectly quiet, and not to be bent on any terms. The number of cripples in the streets, soon ceased to surprise me.

There are plenty of Saints' and Virgin's Shrines, of course;
generally at the corners of streets. The favourite memento
to the Faithful, about Genoa, is a painting, representing
a peasant on his knees, with a spade and some other agri-
cultural implements beside him; and the Madonna, with
the Infant Saviour in her arms, appearing to him in a cloud.
This is the legend of the Madonna della Guardia: a chapel
on a mountain within a few miles, which is in high repute.
It seems that this peasant lived all alone by himself, tilling
some land atop of the mountain, where, being a devout man,
he daily said his prayers to the Virgin in the open air; for
his hut was a very poor one. Upon a certain day, the
Virgin appeared to him, as in the picture, and said, "Why
do you pray in the open air, and without a priest?" The
peasant explained because there was neither priest nor
church at hand—a very uncommon complaint indeed in
Italy. "I should wish, then," said the Celestial Visitor,
"to have a chapel built here, in which the prayers of the
Faithful may be offered up." "But, Santissima Madonna,"
said the peasant, "I am a poor man; and chapels cannot be
built without money. They must be supported, too, Santissima; for to have a chapel and not support it liberally, is
a wickedness—a deadly sin." This sentiment gave great
satisfaction to the visitor. "Go!" said she. "There is
such a village in the valley on the left, and such another
village in the valley on the right, and such another village
elsewhere, that will gladly contribute to the building of
a chapel. Go to them! Relate what you have seen; and do
not doubt that sufficient money will be forthcoming to erect
my chapel, or that it will, afterwards, be handsomely maintained." All of which (miraculously) turned out to be quite
true. And in proof of this prediction and revelation, there
is the chapel of the Madonna della Guardia, rich and flourishing at this day.

The splendour and variety of the Genoese churches, can
hardly be exaggerated. The church of the Annunciata
especially: built, like many of the others, at the cost of one
noble family, and now in slow progress of repair: from the

outer door to the utmost height of the high cupola, is so elaborately painted and set in gold, that it looks (as SIMOND describes it, in his charming book on Italy) like a great enamelled snuff-box. Most of the richer churches contain some beautiful pictures, or other embellishments of great price, almost universally set, side by side, with sprawling effigies of maudlin monks, and the veriest trash and tinsel ever seen.

It may be a consequence of the frequent direction of the popular mind, and pocket, to the souls in Purgatory, but there is very little tenderness for the *bodies* of the dead here. For the very poor, there are, immediately outside one angle of the walls, and behind a jutting point of the fortification, near the sea, certain common pits—one for every day in the year—which all remain closed up, until the turn of each comes for its daily reception of dead bodies. Among the troops in the town, there are usually some Swiss: more or less. When any of these die, they are buried out of a fund maintained by such of their countrymen as are resident in Genoa. Their providing coffins for these men is matter of great astonishment to the authorities.

Certainly, the effect of this promiscuous and indecent splashing down of dead people in so many wells, is bad. It surrounds Death with revolting associations, that insensibly become connected with those whom Death is approaching. Indifference and avoidance are the natural result; and all the softening influences of the great sorrow are harshly disturbed.

There is a ceremony when an old Cavalière or the like, expires, of erecting a pile of benches in the cathedral, to represent his bier; covering them over with a pall of black velvet; putting his hat and sword on the top; making a little square of seats about the whole; and sending out formal invitations to his friends and acquaintances to come and sit there, and hear Mass: which is performed at the principal Altar, decorated with an infinity of candles for that purpose.

When the better kind of people die, or are at the point of death, their nearest relations generally walk off: retiring into the country for a little change, and leaving the body to be disposed of, without any superintendence from them. The procession is usually formed, and the coffin borne, and the funeral conducted, by a body of persons called a Con-

fratérnita, who, as a kind of voluntary penance, undertake
to perform these offices, in regular rotation, for the dead ;
but who, mingling something of pride with their humility,
are dressed in a loose garment covering their whole person,
and wear a hood concealing the face ; with breathing-holes
and apertures for the eyes. The effect of this costume is
very ghastly : especially in the case of a certain Blue Con-
fratérnita belonging to Genoa, who, to say the least of them,
are very ugly customers, and who look—suddenly encountered in their pious ministration in the streets—as if they
were Ghoules or Demons, bearing off the body for themselves.

Although such a custom may be liable to the abuse
attendant on many Italian customs, of being recognised as
a means of establishing a current account with Heaven, on
which to draw, too easily, for future bad actions, or as an
expiation for past misdeeds, it must be admitted to be a good
one, and a practical one, and one involving unquestionably
good works. A voluntary service like this, is surely better
than the imposed penance (not at all an infrequent one)
of giving so many licks to such and such a stone in the
pavement of the cathedral ; or than a vow to the Madonna
to wear nothing but blue for a year or two. This is supposed to give great delight above ; blue being (as is well
known) the Madonna's favourite colour. Women who have
devoted themselves to this act of Faith, are very commonly
seen walking in the streets.

There are three theatres in the city, besides an old one
now rarely opened. The most important—the Carlo Felice :
the opera-house of Genoa—is a very splendid, commodious,
and beautiful theatre. A company of comedians were acting
there, when we arrived : and soon after their departure,
a second-rate opera company came. The great season is not
until the carnival time—in the spring. Nothing impressed
me, so much, in my visits here (which were pretty numerous)
as the uncommonly hard and cruel character of the audience,
who resent the slightest defect, take nothing good-humouredly,
seem to be always lying in wait for an opportunity to hiss,
and spare the actresses as little as the actors. But, as there
is nothing else of a public nature at which they are allowed
to express the least disapprobation, perhaps they are resolved
to make the most of this opportunity.

There are a great number of Piedmontese officers too, who

are allowed the privilege of kicking their heels in the pit,
for next to nothing: gratuitous, or cheap accommodation for
these gentlemen being insisted on, by the Governor, in all
public or semi-public entertainments. They are lofty critics
in consequence, and infinitely more exacting than if they
made the unhappy manager's fortune.

The TEATRO DIURNO, or Day Theatre, is a covered stage
in the open air, where the performances take place by daylight, in the cool of the afternoon; commencing at four or
five o'clock, and lasting some three hours. It is curious,
sitting among the audience, to have a fine view of the
neighbouring hills and houses, and to see the neighbours
at their windows looking on, and to hear the bells of the
churches and convents ringing at most complete cross-
purposes with the scene. Beyond this, and the novelty of
seeing a play in the fresh pleasant air, with the darkening
evening closing in, there is nothing very exciting or characteristic in the performances. The actors are indifferent; and
though they sometimes represent one of Goldoni's comedies,
the staple of the Drama is French. Anything like nationality
is dangerous to despotic governments, and Jesuit-beleaguered
kings.

The Theatre of Puppets, or Marionetti—a famous company
from Milan—is, without any exception, the drollest exhibi
tion I ever beheld in my life. I never saw anything so
exquisitely ridiculous. They *look* between four and five feet
high, but are really much smaller; for when a musician in
the orchestra happens to put his hat on the stage, it becomes
alarmingly gigantic, and almost blots out an actor. They
usually play a comedy, and a ballet. The comic man in the
comedy I saw one summer night, is a waiter in an hotel.
There never was such a locomotive actor, since the world began.
Great pains are taken with him. He has extra joints in his
legs: and a practical eye, with which he winks at the pit,
in a manner that is absolutely insupportable to a stranger,
but which the initiated audience, mainly composed of the
common people, receive (so they do everything else) quite as
a matter of course, and as if he were a man. His spirits are
prodigious. He continually shakes his legs, and winks his
eye. And there is a heavy father with grey hair, who sits
down on the regular conventional stage-bank, and blesses
his daughter in the regular conventional way, who is tremendous. No one would suppose it possible that anything

short of a real man could be so tedious.   It is the triumph
of art.

In the ballet, an Enchanter runs away with the Bride, in
the very hour of her nuptials.   He brings her to his cave,
and tries to soothe her.   They sit down on a sofa (the
regular sofa ! in the regular place, O. P. Second Entrance !)
and a procession of musicians enters ; one creature playing
a drum, and knocking himself off his legs at every blow.
These failing to delight her, dancers appear.   Four first ;
then two ; *the* two ; the flesh-coloured two.   The way in
which they dance ; the height to which they spring ; the
impossible and inhuman extent to which they pirouette ; the
revelation of their preposterous legs ; the coming down with
a pause, on the very tips of their toes, when the music
requires it ; the gentleman's retiring up, when it is the lady's
turn ; and the lady's retiring up, when it is the gentleman's
turn ; the final passion of a pas-de-deux ; and the going off
with a bound !—I shall never see a real ballet, with a composed countenance again.

I went, another night, to see these Puppets act a play
called "St. Helena, or the Death of Napoleon."   It began by
the disclosure of Napoleon, with an immense head, seated on
a sofa in his chamber at St. Helena ; to whom his valet
entered with this obscure announcement :

"Sir Yew ud se on Low ? " (the *ow*, as in cow).

Sir Hudson (that you could have seen his regimentals !)
was a perfect mammoth of a man, to Napoleon ; hideously
ugly ; with a monstrously disproportionate face, and a great
clump for the lower jaw, to express his tyrannical and
obdurate nature.   He began his system of persecution, by
calling his prisoner "General Buonaparte ; " to which the
latter replied, with the deepest tragedy, "Sir Yew ud se on
Low, call me not thus.   Repeat that phrase and leave me !
I am Napoleon, Emperor of France ! "   Sir Yew ud se on,
nothing daunted, proceeded to entertain him with an ordi-
nance of the British Government, regulating the state he
should preserve, and the furniture of his rooms : and limiting
his attendants to four or five persons.   "Four or five for
me ! " said Napoleon.   "Me !   One hundred thousand men
were lately at my sole command ; and this English officer
talks of four or five for *me !* "   Throughout the piece,
Napoleon (who talked very like the real Napoleon, and was,
for ever, having small soliloquies by himself) was very bitter

on "these English officers," and "these English soldiers;"
to the great satisfaction of the audience, who were perfectly
delighted to have Low bullied; and who, whenever Low
said "General Buonaparte" (which he always did: always
receiving the same correction), quite execrated him. It would
be hard to say why; for Italians have little cause to sym-
pathise with Napoleon, Heaven knows.

There was no plot at all, except that a French officer, dis-
guised as an Englishman, came to propound a plan of escape ;
and being discovered, but not before Napoleon had magnani-
mously refused to steal his freedom, was immediately ordered
off by Low to be hanged. In two very long speeches, which
Low made memorable, by winding up with "Yas!"—to
show that he was English—which brought down thunders
of applause. Napoleon was so affected by this catastrophe,
that he fainted away on the spot, and was carried out by
two other puppets. Judging from what followed, it would
appear that he never recovered the shock; for the next
act showed him, in a clean shirt, in his bed (curtains
crimson and white), where a lady, prematurely dressed in
mourning, brought two little children, who kneeled down by
the bedside, while he made a decent end; the last word on
his lips being "Vatterlo."

It was unspeakably ludicrous. Buonaparte's boots were
so wonderfully beyond control, and did such marvellous
things of their own accord: doubling themselves up, and
getting under tables, and dangling in the air, and sometimes
skating away with him, out of all human knowledge, when
he was in full speech—mischances which were not rendered
the less absurd, by a settled melancholy depicted in his face.
To put an end to one conference with Low, he had to go to
a table, and read a book: when it was the finest spectacle I
ever beheld, to see his body bending over the volume, like a
boot-jack, and his sentimental eyes glaring obstinately into
the pit. He was prodigiously good, in bed, with an immense
collar to his shirt, and his little hands outside the coverlet. So
was Dr. Antommarchi, represented by a puppet with long lank
hair, like Mawworm's, who, in consequence of some derangement of his wires, hovered about the couch like a vulture, and
gave medical opinions in the air. He was almost as good
as Low, though the latter was great at all times—a decided
brute and villain, beyond all possibility of mistake. Low
was especially fine at the last, when, hearing the doctor and

the valet say, "The Emperor is dead!" he pulled out his watch, and wound up the piece (not the watch) by exclaiming, with characteristic brutality, "Ha! ha! Eleven minutes to six! The General dead! and the spy hanged!" This brought the curtain down, triumphantly.

There is not in Italy, they say (and I believe them), a lovelier residence than the Palazzo Peschiere, or Palace of the Fishponds, whither we removed as soon as our three months' tenancy of the Pink Jail at Albaro had ceased and determined.

It stands on a height within the walls of Genoa, but aloof from the town : surrounded by beautiful gardens of its own, adorned with statues, vases, fountains, marble basins, terraces, walks of orange-trees and lemon-trees, groves of roses and camellias. All its apartments are beautiful in their proportions and decorations ; but the great hall, some fifty feet in height, with three large windows at the end, overlooking the whole town of Genoa, the harbour, and the neighbouring sea, affords one of the most fascinating and delightful prospects in the world. Any house more cheerful and habitable than the great rooms are, within, it would be difficult to conceive : and certainly nothing more delicious than the scene without, in sunshine or in moonlight, could be imagined. It is more like an enchanted place in an Eastern story than a grave and sober lodging.

How you may wander on, from room to room, and never tire of the wild fancies on the walls and ceilings, as bright in their fresh colouring as if they had been painted yesterday ; or how one floor, or even the great hall which opens on eight other rooms, is a spacious promenade ; or how there are corridors and bedchambers above, which we never use and rarely visit, and scarcely know the way through ; or how there is a view of a perfectly different character on each of the four sides of the building ; matters little. But that prospect from the hall is like a vision to me. I go back to it, in fancy, as I have done in calm reality a hundred times a day ; and stand there, looking out, with the sweet scents from the garden rising up about me, in a perfect dream of happiness.

There lies all Genoa, in beautiful confusion, with its many churches, monasteries, and convents, pointing up into the sunny sky ; and down below me, just where the roofs begin, a solitary convent parapet, fashioned like a gallery, with an iron across at the end, where sometimes early in the morning, I have seen a little group of dark-veiled nuns gliding sorrowfully to and fro, and stopping now and then to peep down upon the waking world in which they have no part. Old Monte Faccio, brightest of hills in good weather, but sulkiest when storms are coming on, is here, upon the left. The Fort within the walls (the good King built it to command the town, and beat the houses of the Genoese about their ears, in case they should be discontented) commands that height upon the right. The broad sea lies beyond, in front there; and that line of coast, beginning by the lighthouse, and tapering away, a mere speck in the rosy distance, is the beautiful coast road that leads to Nice. The garden near at hand, among the roofs and houses: all red with roses and fresh with little fountains: is the Acqua Sola—a public promenade, where the military band plays gaily, and the white veils cluster thick, and the Genoese nobility ride round, and round, and round, in state-clothes and coaches at least, if not in absolute wisdom. Within a stone's-throw, as it seems, the audience of the Day Theatre sit: their faces turned this way. But as the stage is hidden, it is very odd, without a knowledge of the cause, to see their faces changed so suddenly from earnestness to laughter; and odder still, to hear the rounds upon rounds of applause, rattling in the evening air, to which the curtain falls. But, being Sunday night, they act their best and most attractive play. And now, the sun is going down, in such magnificent array of red, and green, and golden light, as neither pen nor pencil could depict; and to the ringing of the vesper bells, darkness sets in at once. without a twilight. Then, lights begin to shine in Genoa, and on the country road; and the revolving lantern out at sea there, flashing, for an instant, on this palace front and portico, illuminates it as if there were a bright moon bursting from behind a cloud; then, merges it in deep obscurity. And this, so far as I know, is the only reason why the Genoese avoid it after dark, and think it haunted.

My memory will haunt it, many nights, in time to come; but nothing worse, I will engage. The same Ghost will occasionally sail away, as I did one pleasant autumn evening, into the bright prospect, and snuff the morning air at Marseilles.

The corpulent hairdresser was still sitting in his slippers

outside his shop-door there, but the twirling ladies in the window, with the natural inconstancy of their sex, had ceased to twirl, and were languishing, stock still, with their beautiful faces addressed to blind corners of the establishment, where it was impossible for admirers to penetrate.

The steamer had come from Genoa in a delicious run of eighteen hours, and we were going to run back again by the Cornice road from Nice : not being satisfied to have seen only the outsides of the beautiful towns that rise in picturesque white clusters from among the olive woods, and rocks, and hills, upon the margin of the Sea.

The Boat which started for Nice that night, at eight o'clock, was very small, and so crowded with goods that there was scarcely room to move ; neither was there anything to eat on board, except bread ; nor to drink, except coffee. But being due at Nice at about eight or so in the morning, this was of no consequence : so when we began to wink at the bright stars, in involuntary acknowledgment of their winking at us, we turned into our berths, in a crowded, but cool little cabin, and slept soundly till morning.

The Boat, being as dull and dogged a little boat as ever was built, it was within an hour of noon when we turned into Nice Harbour, where we very little expected anything but breakfast. But we were laden with wool. Wool must not remain in the Custom-house at Marseilles more than twelve months at a stretch, without paying duty. It is the custom to make fictitious removals of unsold wool to evade this law ; to take it somewhere when the twelve months are nearly out ; bring it straight back again ; and warehouse it, as a new cargo, for nearly twelve months longer. This wool of ours, had come originally from some place in the East. It was recognised as Eastern produce, the moment we entered the harbour. Accordingly, the gay little Sunday boats, full of holiday people, which had come off to greet us, were warned away by the authorities ; we were declared in quarantine ; and a great flag was solemnly run up to the mast-head on the wharf, to make it known to all the town.

It was a very hot day indeed. We were unshaved, unwashed, undressed, unfed, and could hardly enjoy the absurdity of lying blistering in a lazy harbour, with the town looking on from a respectful distance, all manner of whiskered men in cocked hats discussing our fate at a remote guard-house, with gestures (we looked very hard at them

through telescopes) expressive of a week's detention at least:
and nothing whatever the matter all the time. But even in
this crisis the brave Courier achieved a triumph. He telegraphed somebody (*I* saw nobody) either naturally connected
with the hotel, or put *en rapport* with the establishment for
that occasion only. The telegraph was answered, and in
half an hour or less, there came a loud shout from the
guard-house. The captain was wanted. Everybody helped
the captain into his boat. Everybody got his luggage, and
said we were going. The captain rowed away, and disappeared behind a little jutting corner of the Galley-slaves'
Prison: and presently came back with something, very sulkily.
The brave Courier met him at the side, and received the
something as its rightful owner. It was a wicker basket,
folded in a linen cloth; and in it were two great bottles of
wine, a roast fowl, some salt fish chopped with garlic, a great
loaf of bread, a dozen or so of peaches, and a few other
trifles. When we had selected our own breakfast, the brave
Courier invited a chosen party to partake of these refreshments, and assured them that they need not be deterred by
motives of delicacy, as he would order a second basket to be
furnished at their expense. Which he did—no one knew
how—and by-and-by, the captain being again summoned,
again sulkily returned with another something; over which
my popular attendant presided as before: carving with a
clasp-knife, his own personal property, something smaller
than a Roman sword.

The whole party on board were made merry by these unexpected supplies; but none more so than a loquacious little
Frenchman, who got drunk in five minutes, and a sturdy
Cappuccino Friar, who had taken everybody's fancy mightily,
and was one of the best friars in the world, I verily believe.

He had a free, open countenance; and a rich brown,
flowing beard; and was a remarkably handsome man, of
about fifty. He had come up to us, early in the morning,
and inquired whether we were sure to be at Nice by eleven;
saying that he particularly wanted to know, because if we
reached it by that time he would have to perform Mass, and
must deal with the consecrated wafer, fasting; whereas, if
there were no chance of his being in time, he would immediately breakfast. He made this communication, under the
idea that the brave Courier was the captain; and indeed he
looked much more like it than anybody else on board. Being

assured that we should arrive in good time, he fasted, and talked, fasting, to everybody, with the most charming good humour; answering jokes at the expense of friars, with other jokes at the expense of laymen, and saying that, friar as he was, he would engage to take up the two strongest men on board, one after the other, with his teeth, and carry them along the deck. Nobody gave him the opportunity, but I dare say he could have done it; for he was a gallant, noble figure of a man, even in the Cappuccíno dress, which is the ugliest and most ungainly that can well be.

All this had given great delight to the loquacious Frenchman, who gradually patronised the Friar very much, and seemed to commiserate him as one who might have been born a Frenchman himself, but for an unfortunate destiny. Although his patronage was such as a mouse might bestow upon a lion, he had a vast opinion of its condescension; and in the warmth of that sentiment, occasionally rose on tiptoe, to slap the Friar on the back.

When the baskets arrived : it being then too late for Mass: the Friar went to work bravely: eating prodigiously of the cold meat and bread, drinking deep draughts of the wine, smoking cigars, taking snuff, sustaining an uninterrupted conversation with all hands, and occasionally running to the boat's side and hailing somebody on shore with the intelligence that we *must* be got out of this quarantine somehow or other, as he had to take part in a great religious procession in the afternoon. After this, he would come back, laughing lustily from pure good humour: while the Frenchman wrinkled his small face into ten thousand creases, and said how droll it was, and what a brave boy was that Friar! At length the heat of the sun without, and the wine within, made the Frenchman sleepy. So, in the noontide of his patronage of his gigantic protégé, he lay down among the wool, and began to snore.

It was four o'clock before we were released; and the Frenchman, dirty and woolly, and snuffy, was still sleeping when the Friar went ashore. As soon as we were free, we all hurried away, to wash and dress, that we might make a decent appearance at the procession; and I saw no more of the Frenchman until we took up our station in the main street to see it pass, when he squeezed himself into a front place, elaborately renovated; threw back his little coat, to show a broad-barred velvet waistcoat, sprinkled all over with stars; then adjusted himself and his cane so as utterly to bewilder and transfix the Friar, when he should appear.

The procession was a very long one, and included an immense number of people divided into small parties; each party chanting nasally, on its own account, without reference to any other, and producing a most dismal result. There were angels, crosses, Virgins carried on flat boards surrounded by Cupids, crowns, saints, missals, infantry, tapers, monks, nuns, relics, dignitaries of the church in green hats, walking under crimson parasols: and, here and there, a species of sacred street-lamp hoisted on a pole. We looked out anxiously for the Cappuccíni, and presently their brown robes and corded girdles were seen coming on, in a body.

I observed the little Frenchman chuckle over the idea that when the Friar saw him in the broad-barred waistcoat, he would mentally exclaim, "Is that my Patron! *That* distinguished man!" and would be covered with confusion. Ah! never was the Frenchman so deceived. As our friend the Cappuccíno advanced, with folded arms, he looked straight into the visage of the little Frenchman, with a bland, serene, composed abstraction, not to be described. There was not the faintest trace of recognition or amusement on his features; not the smallest consciousness of bread and meat, wine, snuff, or cigars. "C'est lui-même," I heard the little Frenchman say, in some doubt. Oh yes, it was himself. It was not his brother or his nephew, very like him. It was he. He walked in great state; being one of the Superiors of the Order: and looked his part to admiration. There never was anything so perfect of its kind as the contemplative way in which he allowed his placid gaze to rest on us, his late companions, as if he had never seen us in his life and didn't see us then. The Frenchman, quite humbled, took off his hat at last, but the Friar still passed on, with the same imperturbable serenity; and the broad-barred waistcoat, fading into the crowd, was seen no more.

The procession wound up with a discharge of musketry that shook all the windows in the town. Next afternoon we started for Genoa, by the famed Cornice road.

The half-French, half-Italian Vetturíno, who undertook, with his little rattling carriage and pair, to convey us thither in three days, was a careless, good-looking fellow, whose light-heartedness and singing propensities knew no bounds as long as we went on smoothly. So long, he had a word and a smile, and a flick of his whip, for all the peasant girls, and odds and ends of the Sonnambula for all the echoes. So long, he went jingling through every little village, with bells on his horses and rings in his ears: a very meteor of gallantry and cheerfulness. But, it was highly characteristic to see him under a slight reverse of circumstances, when, in one part of the journey, we came to a narrow place where a waggon had broken down and stopped up the road. His hands were twined in his hair immediately, as if a combination of all the direst accidents in life had suddenly fallen on his devoted head. He swore in French, prayed in Italian, and went up and down, beating his feet on the ground in a very ecstasy of despair. There were various carters and mule-drivers assembled round the broken waggon, and at last some man of an original turn of mind, proposed that a general and joint effort should be made to get things to rights again, and clear the way—an idea which I verily believe would never have presented itself to our friend, though we had remained there until now. It was done at no great cost of labour ; but at every pause in the doing, his hands were wound in his hair again, as if there were no ray of hope to lighten his misery. The moment he was on his box once more, and clattering briskly down hill, he returned to the Sonnambula and the peasant girls, as if it were not in the power of misfortune to depress him.

Much of the romance of the beautiful towns and villages on this beautiful road, disappears when they are entered, for many of them are very miserable. The streets are narrow, dark, and dirty; the inhabitants lean and squalid ; and the withered old women, with their wiry grey hair twisted up into a knot on the top of the head, like a pad to carry loads on, are so intensely ugly, both along the Riviera, and in Genoa, too, that, seen straggling about in dim doorways with their spindles, or crooning together in by-corners, they are like a population of Witches—except that they certainly are not to be suspected of brooms or any other instrument of cleanliness. Neither are the pig-skins, in common use to hold wine, and hung out in the sun in all directions, by any means ornamental, as they always preserve the form of very bloated pigs, with their heads and legs cut off, dangling upside-down by their own tails.

These towns, as they are seen in the approach, however: nestling, with their clustering roofs and towers, among trees on steep hill-sides, or built upon the brink of noble bays: are charming. The vegetation is, everywhere, luxuriant and beautiful, and the Palm-tree makes a novel feature in the novel scenery. In one town, San Remo—a most extraordinary place, built on gloomy open arches, so that one might ramble underneath the whole town—there are pretty terrace gardens; in other towns, there is the clang of shipwrights' hammers, and the building of small vessels on the beach. In some of the broad bays, the fleets of Europe might ride at anchor. In every case, each little group of houses presents, in the distance, some enchanting confusion of picturesque and fanciful shapes.

The road itself—now high above the glittering sea, which breaks against the foot of the precipice: now turning inland to sweep the shore of a bay: now crossing the stony bed of a mountain stream: now low down on the beach: now winding among riven rocks of many forms and colours: now chequered by a solitary ruined tower, one of a chain of towers built, in old time, to protect the coast from the invasions of the Barbary Corsairs—presents new beauties every moment. When its own striking scenery is passed, and it trails on through a long line of suburb, lying on the flat seashore, to Genoa, then, the changing glimpses of that noble city and its harbour, awaken a new source of interest; freshened by every huge, unwieldy, half-inhabited old house in its outskirts: and coming to its climax when the city gate is reached, and all Genoa with its beautiful harbour, and neighbouring hills, bursts proudly on the view.

TO PARMA, MODENA, AND BOLOGNA

I STROLLED away from Genoa on the 6th of November, bound
for a good many places (England among them), but first for
Piacenza; for which town I started in the *coupé* of a machine
something like a travelling caravan, in company with the brave
Courier, and a lady with a large dog, who howled dolefully,
at intervals, all night. It was very wet, and very cold; very
dark, and very dismal; we travelled at the rate of barely
four miles an hour, and stopped nowhere for refreshment.
At ten o'clock next morning, we changed coaches at
Alessandria, where we were packed up in another coach
(the body whereof would have been small for a fly), in
company with a very old priest; a young Jesuit, his companion—who carried their breviaries and other books, and
who, in the exertion of getting into the coach, had made
a gash of pink leg between his black stocking and his
black knee-shorts, that reminded one of Hamlet in Ophelia's
closet, only it was visible on both legs—a provincial Avvocáto;
and a gentleman with a red nose that had an uncommon and
singular sheen upon it, which I never observed in the human
subject before.   In this way we travelled on, until four
o'clock in the afternoon; the roads being still very heavy,
and the coach very slow. To mend the matter, the old
priest was troubled with cramps in his legs, so that he had
to give a terrible yell every ten minutes or so, and be hoisted
out by the united efforts of the company; the coach always
stopping for him, with great gravity. This disorder, and the
roads, formed the main subject of conversation. Finding, in
the afternoon, that the *coupé* had discharged two people, and
had only one passenger inside—a monstrous ugly Tuscan,
with a great purple moustache, of which no man could see
the ends when he had his hat on—I took advantage of its
better accommodation, and in company with this gentleman
(who was very conversational and good-humoured) travelled
on, until nearly eleven o'clock at night, when the driver

reported that he couldn't think of going any farther, and we accordingly made a halt at a place called Stradella.

The inn was a series of strange galleries surrounding a yard; where our coach, and a waggon or two, and a lot of fowls, and firewood, were all heaped up together, higgledy-piggledy; so that you didn't know, and couldn't have taken your oath, which was a fowl and which was a cart. We followed a sleepy man with a flaring torch, into a great, cold room, where there were two immensely broad beds, on what looked like two immensely broad deal dining-tables; another deal table of similar dimensions in the middle of the bare floor; four windows; and two chairs. Somebody said it was my room; and I walked up and down it, for half an hour or so, staring at the Tuscan, the old priest, the young priest, and the Avvocáto (Red-Nose lived in the town, and had gone home), who sat upon their beds, and stared at me in return.

The rather dreary whimsicality of this stage of the proceedings, is interrupted by an announcement from the Brave (he has been cooking) that supper is ready; and to the priest's chamber (the next room and the counterpart of mine) we all adjourn. The first dish is a cabbage, boiled with a great quantity of rice in a tureen full of water, and flavoured with cheese. It is so hot, and we are so cold, that it appears almost jolly. The second dish is some little bits of pork, fried with pigs' kidneys. The third, two red fowls. The fourth, two little red turkeys. The fifth, a huge stew of garlic and truffles, and I don't know what else; and this concludes the entertainment.

Before I can sit down in my own chamber, and think it of the dampest, the door opens, and the Brave comes moving in, in the middle of such a quantity of fuel that he looks like Birnam Wood taking a winter walk. He kindles this heap in a twinkling, and produces a jorum of hot brandy and water; for that bottle of his keeps company with the seasons, and now holds nothing but the purest *eau de vie.* When he has accomplished this feat, he retires for the night; and I hear him, for an hour afterwards, and indeed until I fall asleep, making jokes in some outhouse (apparently under the pillow), where he is smoking cigars with a party of confidential friends. He never was in the house in his life before; but he knows everybody everywhere, before he has been anywhere five minutes; and is certain to have attracted to himself, in the meantime, the enthusiastic devotion of the whole establishment.

This is at twelve o'clock at night. At four o'clock next morning, he is up again, fresher than a new-blown rose; making blazing fires without the least authority from the landlord; producing mugs of scalding coffee when nobody else can get anything but cold water; and going out into the dark streets, and roaring for fresh milk, on the chance of somebody with a cow getting up to supply it. While the horses are "coming," I stumble out into the town too. It seems to be all one little Piazza, with a cold damp wind blowing in and out of the arches, alternately, in a sort of pattern. But it is profoundly dark, and raining heavily; and I shouldn't know it to-morrow, if I were taken there to try. Which Heaven forbid.

The horses arrive in about an hour. In the interval, the driver swears; sometimes Christian oaths, sometimes Pagan oaths. Sometimes, when it is a long, compound oath, he begins with Christianity and merges into Paganism. Various messengers are dispatched; not so much after the horses, as after each other; for the first messenger never comes back, and all the rest imitate him. At length the horses appear, surrounded by all the messengers; some kicking them, and some dragging them, and all shouting abuse to them. Then, the old priest, the young priest, the Avvocáto, the Tuscan, and all of us, take our places; and sleepy voices proceeding from the doors of extraordinary hutches in divers parts of the yard, cry out "Addio corrière mio! Buon' viággio, corrière!" Salutations which the courier, with his face one monstrous grin, returns in like manner as we go jolting and wallowing away, through the mud.

At Piacenza, which was four or five hours' journey from the inn at Stradella, we broke up our little company before the hotel door, with divers manifestations of friendly feeling on all sides. The old priest was taken with the cramp again, before he had got half-way down the street; and the young priest laid the bundle of books on a doorstep, while he dutifully rubbed the old gentleman's legs. The client of the Avvocáto was waiting for him at the yard-gate, and kissed him on each cheek, with such a resounding smack, that I am afraid he had either a very bad case, or a scantily-furnished purse. The Tuscan, with a cigar in his mouth, went loitering off, carrying his hat in his hand that he might the better trail up the ends of his dishevelled moustache. And the brave Courier, as he and I strolled away to look about us, began immediately to entertain me with the private histories and family affairs of the whole party.

A brown, decayed, old town, Piacenza is. A deserted, solitary, grass-grown place, with ruined ramparts ; half-filled-up trenches, which afford a frowzy pasturage to the lean kine that wander about them ; and streets of stern houses, moodily frowning at the other houses over the way. The sleepiest and shabbiest of soldiery go wandering about, with the double curse of laziness and poverty, uncouthly wrinkling their mis-fitting regimentals ; the dirtiest of children play with their impromptu toys (pigs and mud) in the feeblest of gutters ; and the gauntest of dogs trot in and out of the dullest of archways, in perpetual search of something to eat, which they never seem to find. A mysterious and solemn Palace, guarded by two colossal statues, twin Genii of the place, stands gravely in the midst of the idle town ; and the king with the marble legs, who flourished in the time of the thousand and one Nights, might live contentedly inside of it, and never have the energy, in his upper half of flesh and blood, to want to come out.

What a strange, half-sorrowful and half-delicious doze it is, to ramble through these places gone to sleep and basking in the sun! Each, in its turn, appears to be, of all the mouldy, dreary, God-forgotten towns in the wide world, the chief. Sitting on this hillock where a bastion used to be, and where a noisy fortress was, in the time of the old Roman station here, I became aware that I have never known till now, what it is to be lazy. A dormouse must surely be in very much the same condition before he retires under the wool in his cage ; or a tortoise before he buries himself. I feel that I am getting rusty. That any attempt to think, would be accompanied with a creaking noise. That there is nothing, anywhere, to be done, or needing to be done. That there is no more human progress, motion, effort, or advance-ment, of any kind beyond this. That the whole scheme stopped here centuries ago, and laid down to rest until the Day of Judgment.

Never while the brave Courier lives ! Behold him jing-ling out of Piacenza, and staggering this way, in the tallest posting-chaise ever seen, so that he looks out of the front window as if he were peeping over a garden wall ; while the postillion, concentrated essence of all the shabbiness of Italy, pauses for a moment in his animated conversation, to touch his hat to a blunt-nosed little Virgin, hardly less shabby than himself, enshrined in a plaster Punch's show outside the town.

In Genoa, and thereabouts, they train the vines on trellis-work, supported on square clumsy pillars, which, in themselves, are anything but picturesque. But, here, they twine them around trees, and let them trail among the hedges; and the vineyards are full of trees, regularly planted for this purpose, each with its own vine twining and clustering about it. Their leaves are now of the brightest gold and deepest red; and never was anything so enchantingly graceful and full of beauty. Through miles of these delightful forms and colours, the road winds its way. The wild festoons, the elegant wreaths, and crowns, and garlands of all shapes; the fairy nets flung over great trees, and making them prisoners in sport; the tumbled heaps and mounds of exquisite shapes upon the ground; how rich and beautiful they are! And every now and then, a long, long line of trees, will be all bound and garlanded together: as if they had taken hold of one another, and were coming dancing down the field!

Parma has cheerful, stirring streets, for an Italian town; and consequently is not so characteristic as many places of less note. Always excepting the retired Piazza, where the Cathedral, Baptistery, and Campanile—ancient buildings, of a sombre brown, embellished with innumerable grotesque monsters and dreamy-looking creatures carved in marble and red stone—are clustered in a noble and magnificent repose. Their silent presence was only invaded, when I saw them, by the twittering of the many birds that were flying in and out of the crevices in the stones and little nooks in the architecture, where they had made their nests. They were busy, rising from the cold shade of Temples made with hands, into the sunny air of Heaven. Not so the worshippers within, who were listening to the same drowsy chaunt, or kneeling before the same kinds of images and tapers, or whispering, with their heads bowed down, in the selfsame dark confessionals, as I had left in Genoa and everywhere else.

The decayed and mutilated paintings with which this church is covered, have, to my thinking, a remarkably mournful and depressing influence. It is miserable to see great works of art—something of the Souls of Painters—

perishing and fading away, like human forms. This cathedral is odorous with the rotting of Correggio's frescoes in the Cupola. Heaven knows how beautiful they may have been at one time. Connoisseurs fall into raptures with them now ; but such a labyrinth of arms and legs : such heaps of foreshortened limbs, entangled and involved and jumbled together : no operative surgeon, gone mad, could imagine in his wildest delirium.

There is a very interesting subterranean church here : the roof supported by marble pillars, behind each of which there seemed to be at least one beggar in ambush : to say nothing of the tombs and secluded altars. From every one of these lurking-places, such crowds of phantom-looking men and women, leading other men and women with twisted limbs or chattering jaws, or paralytic gestures, or idiotic heads, or some other sad infirmity, came hobbling out to beg, that if the ruined frescoes in the cathedral above, had been suddenly animated, and had retired to this lower church, they could hardly have made a greater confusion, or exhibited a more confounding display of arms and legs.

There is Petrarch's Monument, too ; and there is the Baptistery, with its beautiful arches and immense font ; and there is a gallery containing some very remarkable pictures, whereof a few were being copied by hairy-faced artists, with little velvet caps more off their heads than on. There is the Farnese Palace, too ; and in it one of the dreariest spectacles of decay that ever was seen—a grand, old, gloomy theatre, mouldering away.

It is a large wooden structure, of the horse-shoe shape ; the lower seats arranged upon the Roman plan, but above them, great heavy chambers, rather than boxes, where the Nobles sat, remote in their proud state. Such desolation as has fallen on this theatre, enhanced in the spectator's fancy by its gay intention and design, none but worms can be familiar with. A hundred and ten years have passed, since any play was acted here. The sky shines in through the gashes in the roof ; the boxes are dropping down, wasting away, and only tenanted by rats ; damp and mildew smear the faded colours, and make spectral maps upon the panels ; lean rags are dangling down where there were gay festoons on the Proscenium ; the stage has rotted so, that a narrow wooden gallery is thrown across it, or it would sink beneath the tread, and bury the visitor in the gloomy depth beneath.

The desolation and decay impress themselves on all the senses. The air has a mouldering smell, and an earthy taste; any stray outer sounds that straggle in with some lost sunbeam, are muffled and heavy; and the worm, the maggot, and the rot have changed the surface of the wood beneath the touch, as time will seam and roughen a smooth hand. If ever Ghosts act plays, they act them on this ghostly stage.

It was most delicious weather, when we came into Modena, where the darkness of the sombre colonnades over the footways skirting the main street on either side, was made refreshing and agreeable by the bright sky, so wonderfully blue. I passed from all the glory of the day, into a dim cathedral, where High Mass was performing, feeble tapers were burning, people were kneeling in all directions before all manner of shrines, and officiating priests were crooning the usual chant, in the usual, low, dull, drawling, melancholy tone.

Thinking how strange it was, to find, in every stagnant town, this same Heart beating with the same monotonous pulsation, the centre of the same torpid, listless system, I came out by another door, and was suddenly scared to death by a blast from the shrillest trumpet that ever was blown. Immediately, came tearing round the corner, an equestrian company from Paris: marshalling themselves under the walls of the church, and flouting, with their horses' heels, the griffins, lions, tigers, and other monsters in stone and marble, decorating its exterior. First, there came a stately nobleman with a great deal of hair, and no hat, bearing an enormous banner, on which was inscribed, MAZEPPA! TO-NIGHT! Then, a Mexican chief, with a great pear-shaped club on his shoulder, like Hercules. Then, six or eight Roman chariots: each with a beautiful lady in extremely short petticoats, and unnaturally pink tights, erect within: shedding beaming looks upon the crowd, in which there was a latent expression of discomposure and anxiety, for which I couldn't account, until, as the open back of each chariot presented itself, I saw the immense difficulty with which the pink legs maintained their perpendicular, over the uneven pavement of the town: which gave me quite a new idea of the ancient Romans and Britons. The procession was brought to a close, by some dozen indomitable warriors of different nations, riding two and two, and haughtily surveying the tame population of Modena: among whom, however, they occasionally

condescended to scatter largesse in the form of a few handbills. After caracolling among the lions and tigers, and proclaiming that evening's entertainments with blast of trumpet,
it then filed off, by the other end of the square, and left a
new and greatly increased dulness behind.

When the procession had so entirely passed away, that the
shrill trumpet was mild in the distance, and the tail of the
last horse was hopelessly round the corner, the people who
had come out of the church to stare at it, went back again.
But one old lady, kneeling on the pavement within, near the
door, had seen it all, and had been immensely interested,
without getting up; and this old lady's eye, at that juncture,
I happened to catch : to our mutual confusion. She cut our
embarrassment very short, however, by crossing herself devoutly, and going down, at full length, on her face, before
a figure in a fancy petticoat and a gilt crown ; which was so
like one of the procession-figures, that perhaps at this hour
she may think the whole appearance a celestial vision.
Anyhow, I must certainly have forgiven her her interest in
the Circus, though I had been her Father Confessor.

There was a little fiery-eyed old man with a crooked
shoulder, in the cathedral, who took it very ill that I made
no effort to see the bucket (kept in an old tower) which the
people of Modena took away from the people of Bologna in
the fourteenth century, and about which there was war
made and a mock-heroic poem by TASSONE, too. Being quite
content, however, to look at the outside of the tower, and
feast, in imagination, on the bucket within ; and preferring
to loiter in the shade of the tall Campanile, and about the
cathedral ; I have no personal knowledge of this bucket, even
at the present time.

Indeed, we were at Bologna, before the little old man (or
the Guide-Book) would have considered that we had half
done justice to the wonders of Modena. But it is such a
delight to me to leave new scenes behind, and still go on,
encountering newer scenes—and, moreover, I have such a
perverse disposition in respect of sights that are cut, and
dried, and dictated—that I fear I sin against similar authorities in every place I visit.

Be this as it may, in the pleasant Cemetery at Bologna,
I found myself walking next Sunday morning, among the
stately marble tombs and colonnades, in company with a
crowd of Peasants, and escorted by a little Cicerone of that

M

town, who was excessively anxious for the honour of the place, and most solicitous to divert my attention from the bad monuments: whereas he was never tired of extolling the good ones. Seeing this little man (a good-humoured little man he was, who seemed to have nothing in his face but shining teeth and eyes) looking wistfully at a certain plot of grass, I asked him who was buried there. "The poor people, Signore," he said, with a shrug and a smile, and stopping to look back at me—for he always went on a little before, and took off his hat to introduce every new monument. "Only the poor, Signore! It's very cheerful. It's very lively. How green it is, how cool! It's like a meadow! There are five," —holding up all the fingers of his right hand to express the number, which an Italian peasant will always do, if it be within the compass of his ten fingers,—"there are five of my little children buried there, Signore; just there; a little to the right. Well! Thanks to God! It's very cheerful. How green it is, how cool it is! It's quite a meadow!"

He looked me very hard in the face, and seeing I was sorry for him, took a pinch of snuff (every Cicerone takes snuff), and made a little bow; partly in deprecation of his having alluded to such a subject, and partly in memory of the children and of his favourite saint. It was as unaffected and as perfectly natural a little bow, as ever man made. Immediately afterwards, he took his hat off altogether, and begged to introduce me to the next monument; and his eyes and his teeth shone brighter than before.

THROUGH BOLOGNA AND FERRARA

THERE was such a very smart official in attendance at the Cemetery where the little Cicerone had buried his children, that when the little Cicerone suggested to me, in a whisper, that there would be no offence in presenting this officer, in return for some slight extra service, with a couple of pauls (about tenpence, English money), I looked incredulously at his cocked hat, wash-leather gloves, well-made uniform, and dazzling buttons, and rebuked the little Cicerone with a grave shake of the head. For, in splendour of appearance, he was at least equal to the Deputy Usher of the Black Rod; and the idea of his carrying, as Jeremy Diddler would say, "such a thing as tenpence" away with him, seemed monstrous. He took it in excellent part, however, when I made bold to give it him, and pulled off his cocked hat with a flourish that would have been a bargain at double the money.

It seemed to be his duty to describe the monuments to the people—at all events he was doing so; and when I compared him, like Gulliver in Brobdingnag, "with the Institutions of my own beloved country, I could not refrain from tears of pride and exultation." He had no pace at all; no more than a tortoise. He loitered as the people loitered, that they might gratify their curiosity; and positively allowed them, now and then, to read the inscriptions on the tombs. He was neither shabby, nor insolent, nor churlish, nor ignorant. He spoke his own language with perfect propriety, and seemed to consider himself, in his way, a kind of teacher of the people, and to entertain a just respect both for himself and them. They would no more have such a man for a Verger in Westminster Abbey, than they would let the people in (as they do at Bologna) to see the monuments for nothing [1].

[1] A far more liberal and just recognition of the public has arisen in Westminster Abbey since this was written.

Again, an ancient sombre town, under the brilliant sky; with heavy arcades over the footways of the older streets, and lighter and more cheerful archways in the newer portions of the town. Again, brown piles of sacred buildings, with more birds flying in and out of chinks in the stones ; and more snarling monsters for the bases of the pillars. Again, rich churches, drowsy Masses, curling incense, tinkling bells, priests in bright vestments: pictures, tapers, laced altar cloths, crosses, images, and artificial flowers.

There is a grave and learned air about the city, and a pleasant gloom upon it, that would leave it, a distinct and separate impression in the mind, among a crowd of cities, though it were not still further marked in the traveller's remembrance by the two brick leaning towers (sufficiently unsightly in themselves, it must be acknowledged), inclining cross-wise as if they were bowing stiffly to each other—a most extraordinary termination to the perspective of some of the narrow streets. The colleges, and churches too, and palaces : and above all the academy of Fine Arts, where there are a host of interesting pictures, especially by Guido, Domenichino, and Ludovico Caracci: give it a place of its own in the memory. Even though these were not, and there were nothing else to remember it by, the great Meridian on the pavement of the church of San Petronio, where the sunbeams mark the time among the kneeling people, would give it a fanciful and pleasant interest.

Bologna being very full of tourists, detained there by an inundation which rendered the road to Florence impassable, I was quartered up at the top of an hotel, in an out-of-the-way room which I never could find : containing a bed, big enough for a boarding-school, which I couldn't fall asleep in. The chief among the waiters who visited this lonely retreat, where there was no other company but the swallows in the broad eaves over the window, was a man of one idea in connexion with the English ; and the subject of this harmless monomania, was Lord Byron. I made the discovery by accidentally remarking to him, at breakfast, that the matting with which the floor was covered, was very comfortable at that season, when he immediately replied that Milor Beeron had been much attached to that kind of matting. Observing, at the same moment, that I took no milk, he exclaimed with enthusiasm, that Milor Beeron had never touched it. At first, I took it for granted, in my innocence, that he had

been one of the Beeron servants; but no, he said, no, he was
in the habit of speaking about my Lord, to English gentlemen; that was all. He knew all about him, he said. In
proof of it, he connected him with every possible topic, from
the Monte Pulciano wine at dinner (which was grown on
an estate he had owned), to the big bed itself, which was
the very model of his. When I left the inn, he coupled with
his final bow in the yard, a parting assurance that the road
by which I was going, had been Milor Beeron's favourite
ride; and before the horses' feet had well begun to clatter
on the pavement, he ran briskly upstairs again, I dare say
to tell some other Englishman in some other solitary room
that the guest who had just departed was Lord Beeron's
living image.

I had entered Bologna by night—almost midnight—and
all along the road thither, after our entrance into the Papal
territory: which is not, in any part, supremely well governed,
Saint Peter's keys being rather rusty now; the driver had so
worried about the danger of robbers in travelling after dark,
and had so infected the brave Courier, and the two had been
so constantly stopping and getting up and down to look after
a portmanteau which was tied on behind, that I should have
felt almost obliged to any one who would have had the goodness to take it away. Hence it was stipulated, that, whenever we left Bologna, we should start so as not to arrive at
Ferrara later than eight at night; and a delightful afternoon
and evening journey it was, albeit through a flat district
which gradually became more marshy from the overflow of
brooks and rivers in the recent heavy rains.

At sunset, when I was walking on alone, while the horses
rested, I arrived upon a little scene, which, by one of those
singular mental operations of which we are all conscious,
seemed perfectly familiar to me, and which I see distinctly
now. There was not much in it. In the blood red light,
there was a mournful sheet of water, just stirred by the
evening wind; upon its margin a few trees. In the fore-
ground was a group of silent peasant girls leaning over the
parapet of a little bridge, and looking, now up at the sky,
now down into the water; in the distance, a deep bell; the
shade of approaching night on everything. If I had been
murdered there, in some former life, I could not have seemed
to remember the place more thoroughly, or with a more
emphatic chilling of the blood; and the mere remembrance

of it acquired in that minute, is so strengthened by the imaginary recollection, that I hardly think I could forget it.

More solitary, more depopulated, more deserted, old Ferrara, than any city of the solemn brotherhood! The grass so grows up in the silent streets, that any one might make hay there, literally, while the sun shines. But the sun shines with diminished cheerfulness in grim Ferrara; and the people are so few who pass and repass through the places, that the flesh of its inhabitants might be grass indeed, and growing in the squares.

I wonder why the head coppersmith in an Italian town, always lives next door to the Hotel, or opposite: making the visitor feel as if the beating hammers were his own heart, palpitating with a deadly energy! I wonder why jealous corridors surround the bedroom on all sides, and fill it with unnecessary doors that can't be shut, and will not open, and abut on pitchy darkness! I wonder why it is not enough that these distrustful genii stand agape at one's dreams all night, but there must also be round open portholes, high in the wall, suggestive, when a mouse or rat is heard behind the wainscot, of a somebody scraping the wall with his toes, in his endeavours to reach one of these portholes and look in! I wonder why the faggots are so constructed, as to know of no effect but an agony of heat when they are lighted and replenished, and an agony of cold and suffocation at all other times! I wonder, above all, why it is the great feature of domestic architecture in Italian inns, that all the fire goes up the chimney, except the smoke!

The answer matters little. Coppersmiths, doors, portholes, smoke, and faggots, are welcome to me. Give me the smiling face of the attendant, man or woman; the courteous manner; the amiable desire to please and to be pleased; the lighthearted, pleasant, simple air—so many jewels set in dirt—and I am theirs again to-morrow!

Ariosto's house, Tasso's prison, a rare old Gothic cathedral, and more churches of course, are the sights of Ferrara. But the long silent streets, and the dismantled palaces, where ivy waves in lieu of banners, and where rank weeds are slowly creeping up the long-untrodden stairs, are the best sights of all.

The aspect of this dreary town, half an hour before sunrise one fine morning, when I left it, was as picturesque as it seemed unreal and spectral. It was no matter that the people were not yet out of bed; for if they had all been up and busy, they would have made but little difference in that desert of a place. It was best to see it, without a single figure in the picture; a city of the dead, without one solitary survivor. Pestilence might have ravaged streets, squares, and market-places; and sack and siege have ruined the old houses, battered down their doors and windows, and made breaches in their roofs. In one part, a great tower rose into the air; the only landmark in the melancholy view. In another, a prodigious castle, with a moat about it, stood aloof: a sullen city in itself. In the black dungeons of this castle, Parisina and her lover were beheaded in the dead of night. The red light, beginning to shine when I looked back upon it, stained its walls without, as they have, many a time, been stained within, in old days; but for any sign of life they gave, the castle and the city might have been avoided by all human creatures, from the moment when the axe went down upon the last of the two lovers: and might have never vibrated to another sound

> Beyond the blow that to the block
> Pierced through with forced and sullen shock.

Coming to the Po, which was greatly swollen, and running fiercely, we crossed it by a floating bridge of boats, and so came into the Austrian territory, and resumed our journey: through a country of which, for some miles, a great part was under water. The brave Courier and the soldiery had first quarrelled, for half an hour or more, over our eternal passport. But this was a daily relaxation with the Brave, who was always stricken deaf when shabby functionaries in uniform came, as they constantly did come, plunging out of wooden boxes to look at it—or in other words to beg—and who, stone deaf to my entreaties that the man might have a trifle given him, and we resume our journey in peace, was wont to sit reviling the functionary in broken English: while the unfortunate man's face was a portrait of mental agony framed in the coach window, from his perfect ignorance of what was being said to his disparagement.

There was a postillion, in the course of this day's journey, as wild and savagely good-looking a vagabond as you would desire to see. He was a tall, stout-made, dark-complexioned fellow, with a profusion of shaggy black hair hanging all over his face, and great black whiskers stretching down his throat. His dress was a torn suit of rifle green, garnished here and there with red ; a steeple-crowned hat, innocent of nap, with a broken and bedraggled feather stuck in the band ; and a flaming red neckerchief hanging on his shoulders. He was not in the saddle, but reposed, quite at his ease, on a sort of low foot-board in front of the postchaise, down amongst the horses' tails—convenient for having his brains kicked out, at any moment. To this Brigand, the brave Courier, when we were at a reasonable trot, happened to suggest the practicability of going faster. He received the proposal with a perfect yell of derision ; brandished his whip about his head (such a whip! it was more like a home-made bow) ; flung up his heels, much higher than the horses ; and disappeared, in a paroxysm, somewhere in the neigh-bourhood of the axletree. I fully expected to see him lying in the road, a hundred yards behind, but up came the steeple-crowned hat again, next minute, and he was seen reposing, as on a sofa, entertaining himself with the idea, and crying, "Ha ha ! what next ! Oh the devil ! Faster too ! Shoo—hoo—o—o !" (This last ejaculation, an inexpressibly defiant hoot.) Being anxious to reach our immediate des-tination that night, I ventured, by-and-by, to repeat the experiment on my own account. It produced exactly the same effect. Round flew the whip with the same scornful flourish, up came the heels, down went the steeple-crowned hat, and presently he reappeared, reposing as before and saying to himself, "Ha ha ! what next ! Faster too ! Oh the devil ! Shoo—hoo—o—o !"

AN ITALIAN DREAM

I HAD been travelling, for some days; resting very little in the night, and never in the day. The rapid and unbroken succession of novelties that had passed before me, came back like half-formed dreams; and a crowd of objects wandered in the greatest confusion through my mind, as I travelled on, by a solitary road. At intervals, some one among them would stop, as it were, in its restless flitting to and fro, and enable me to look at it, quite steadily, and behold it in full distinctness. After a few moments, it would dissolve, like a view in a magic-lantern; and while I saw some part of it quite plainly, and some faintly, and some not at all, would show me another of the many places I had lately seen, lingering behind it, and coming through it. This was no sooner visible than, in its turn, it melted into something else.

At one moment, I was standing again, before the brown old rugged churches of Modena. As I recognised the curious pillars with grim monsters for their bases, I seemed to see them, standing by themselves in the quiet square at Padua, where there were the staid old University, and the figures, demurely gowned, grouped here and there in the open space about it. Then, I was strolling in the outskirts of that pleasant city, admiring the unusual neatness of the dwelling-houses, gardens, and orchards, as I had seen them a few hours before. In their stead arose, immediately, the two towers of Bologna; and the most obstinate of all these objects, failed to hold its ground, a minute, before the monstrous moated castle of Ferrara, which, like an illustration to a wild romance, came back again in the red sunrise, lording it over the solitary, grass-grown, withered town. In short, I had that incoherent but delightful jumble in my brain, which travellers are apt to have, and are indolently willing to encourage. Every shake of the coach in which I sat, half dozing in the dark, appeared to jerk some new recollection out of its place, and to jerk some other new recollection into it; and in this state I fell asleep.

I was awakened after some time (as I thought) by the stopping of the coach. It was now quite night, and we were at the water-side. There lay here, a black boat, with a little house or cabin in it of the same mournful colour. When I had taken my seat in this, the boat was paddled, by two men, towards a great light, lying in the distance on the sea.

Ever and again, there was a dismal sigh of wind. It ruffled the water, and rocked the boat, and sent the dark clouds flying before the stars. I could not but think how strange it was, to be floating away at that hour: leaving the land behind, and going on, towards this light upon the sea. It soon began to burn brighter; and from being one light became a cluster of tapers, twinkling and shining out of the water, as the boat approached towards them by a dreamy kind of track, marked out upon the sea by posts and piles.

We had floated on, five miles or so, over the dark water, when I heard it rippling in my dream, against some obstruction near at hand. Looking out attentively, I saw, through the gloom, a something black and massive—like a shore, but lying close and flat upon the water, like a raft—which we were gliding past. The chief of the two rowers said it was a burial-place.

Full of the interest and wonder which a cemetery lying out there, in the lonely sea, inspired, I turned to gaze upon it as it should recede in our path, when it was quickly shut out from my view. Before I knew by what, or how, I found that we were gliding up a street—a phantom street; the houses rising on both sides, from the water, and the black boat gliding on beneath their windows. Lights were shining from some of these casements, plumbing the depth of the black stream with their reflected rays, but all was profoundly silent.

So we advanced into this ghostly city, continuing to hold our course through narrow streets and lanes, all filled and flowing with water. Some of the corners where our way branched off, were so acute and narrow, that it seemed impossible for the long slender boat to turn them; but the rowers, with a low melodious cry of warning, sent it skimming on without a pause. Sometimes, the rowers of another black boat like our own, echoed the cry, and slackening their speed (as I thought we did ours) would come flitting past us like a dark shadow. Other boats, of the same sombre hue, were lying moored, I thought, to painted pillars, near to dark mysterious doors that opened straight upon the water. Some of these were empty; in some, the rowers lay asleep; towards one, I saw some figures coming down a gloomy archway from the interior of a palace: gaily dressed, and attended by torch-bearers. It was but a glimpse I had of them; for a bridge, so low and close upon the boat that it seemed ready to fall down and crush us: one of the many bridges that perplexed the Dream: blotted them out, instantly. On we went, floating towards the heart of this strange place—with water all about us where never water was elsewhere—clusters of houses, churches, heaps of stately buildings growing out of it —and, everywhere, the same extraordinary silence. Presently, we shot across a broad and open stream; and passing, as I thought, before a spacious paved quay, where the bright lamps with which it was illuminated showed long rows of arches and pillars, of ponderous construction and great strength, but as light to the eye as garlands of hoar-frost or gossamer—and where, for the first time, I saw people walking —arrived at a flight of steps leading from the water to a large mansion, where, having passed through corridors and galleries innumerable, I lay down to rest; listening to the black boats stealing up and down the window on the rippling water, till I fell asleep.

The glory of the day that broke upon me in this Dream; its freshness, motion, buoyancy; its sparkles of the sun in water; its clear blue sky and rustling air; no waking words can tell. But, from my window, I looked down on boats and barks; on masts, sails, cordage, flags; on groups of busy sailors, working at the cargoes of these vessels; on wide quays, strewn with bales, casks, merchandise of many kinds; on great ships, lying near at hand in stately indolence; on islands, crowned with gorgeous domes and turrets: and where golden crosses glittered in the light, atop of wondrous churches, springing from the sea! Going down upon the margin of the green sea, rolling on before the door, and filling all the streets, I came upon a place of such surpassing beauty, and such grandeur, that all the rest was poor and faded, in comparison with its absorbing loveliness.

It was a great Piazza, as I thought; anchored, like all the rest, in the deep ocean. On its broad bosom, was a Palace, more majestic and magnificent in its old age, than all the buildings of the earth, in the high prime and fulness of their youth. Cloisters and galleries: so light, they might have

been the work of fairy hands: so strong that centuries had
battered them in vain: wound round and round this palace,
and enfolded it with a Cathedral, gorgeous in the wild
luxuriant fancies of the East. At no great distance from its
porch, a lofty tower, standing by itself, and rearing its proud
head, alone, into the sky, looked out upon the Adriatic Sea.
Near to the margin of the stream, were two ill-omened pillars
of red granite ; one having on its top, a figure with a sword
and shield; the other, a winged lion. Not far from these
again, a second tower : richest of the rich in all its decorations : even here, where all was rich : sustained aloft, a great
orb, gleaming with gold and deepest blue : the Twelve Signs
painted on it, and a mimic sun revolving in its course around
them : while above, two bronze giants hammered out the
hours upon a sounding bell. An oblong square of lofty
houses of the whitest stone, surrounded by a light and
beautiful arcade, formed part of this enchanted scene ; and,
here and there, gay masts for flags rose, tapering, from the
pavement of the unsubstantial ground.

I thought I entered the Cathedral, and went in and out
among its many arches: traversing its whole extent. A
grand and dreamy structure, of immense proportions ; golden
with old mosaics ; redolent of perfumes ; dim with the smoke
of incense ; costly in treasure of precious stones and metals,
glittering through iron bars ; holy with the bodies of deceased
saints ; rainbow-hued with windows of stained glass ; dark
with carved woods and coloured marbles; obscure in its
vast heights, and lengthened distances ; shining with silver
lamps and winking lights ; unreal, fantastic, solemn, inconceivable throughout. I thought I entered the old palace ;
pacing silent galleries and council-chambers, where the old
rulers of this mistress of the waters looked sternly out, in
pictures, from the walls, and where her high-prowed galleys,
still victorious on canvas, fought and conquered as of old.
I thought I wandered through its halls of state and triumph
—bare and empty now !—and musing on its pride and might,
extinct : for that was past ; all past : heard a voice say,
" Some tokens of its ancient rule and some consoling reasons
for its downfall, may be traced here, yet ! "

I dreamed that I was led on, then, into some jealous rooms,
communicating with a prison near the palace ; separated from
it by a lofty bridge crossing a narrow street; and called, I
dreamed, The Bridge of Sighs.

But first I passed two jagged slits in a stone wall; the lions' mouths—now toothless—where, in the distempered horror of my sleep, I thought denunciations of innocent men to the old wicked Council, had been dropped through, many a time, when the night was dark. So, when I saw the council-room to which such prisoners were taken for examination, and the door by which they passed out, when they were condemned—a door that never closed upon a man with life and hope before him—my heart appeared to die within me.

It was smitten harder though, when, torch in hand, I descended from the cheerful day into two ranges, one below another, of dismal, awful, horrible stone cells. They were quite dark. Each had a loop-hole in its massive wall, where, in the old time, every day, a torch was placed—I dreamed—to light the prisoner within, for half an hour. The captives, by the glimmering of these brief rays, had scratched and cut inscriptions in the blackened vaults. I saw them. For their labour with a rusty nail's point, had outlived their agony and them, through many generations.

One cell, I saw, in which no man remained for more than four-and-twenty hours; being marked for dead before he entered it. Hard by, another, and a dismal one, whereto, at midnight, the confessor came—a monk brown-robed, and hooded—ghastly in the day, and free bright air, but in the midnight of that murky prison, Hope's extinguisher, and Murder's herald. I had my foot upon the spot, where, at the same dread hour, the shriven prisoner was strangled; and struck my hand upon the guilty door—low-browed and stealthy—through which the lumpish sack was carried out into a boat, and rowed away, and drowned where it was death to cast a net.

Around this dungeon stronghold, and above some part of it: licking the rough walls without, and smearing them with damp and slime within: stuffing dank weeds and refuse into chinks and crevices, as if the very stones and bars had mouths to stop: furnishing a smooth road for the removal of the bodies of the secret victims of the State—a road so ready that it went along with them, and ran before them, like a cruel officer—flowed the same water that filled this Dream of mine, and made it seem one, even at the time.

Descending from the palace by a staircase, called, I thought, the Giant's—I had some imaginary recollection of an old man abdicating, coming, more slowly and more feebly, down it, when he heard the bell, proclaiming his successor—I glided off, in one of the dark boats, until we came to an old arsenal guarded by four marble lions. To make my Dream more monstrous and unlikely, one of these had words and sentences upon its body, inscribed there, at an unknown time, and in an unknown language; so that their purport was a mystery to all men.

There was little sound of hammers in this place for building ships, and little work in progress; for the greatness of the city was no more, as I have said. Indeed, it seemed a very wreck found drifting on the sea; a strange flag hoisted in its honourable stations, and strangers standing at its helm. A splendid barge in which its ancient chief had gone forth, pompously, at certain periods, to wed the ocean, lay here, I thought, no more; but, in its place, there was a tiny model, made from recollection like the city's greatness; and it told of what had been (so are the strong and weak confounded in the dust) almost as eloquently as the massive pillars, arches, roofs, reared to overshadow stately ships that had no other shadow now, upon the water or the earth.

An armoury was there yet. Plundered and despoiled; but an armoury. With a fierce standard taken from the Turks, drooping in the dull air of its cage. Rich suits of mail worn by great warriors were hoarded there; crossbows and bolts; quivers full of arrows; spears; swords, daggers, maces, shields, and heavy-headed axes. Plates of wrought steel and iron, to make the gallant horse a monster cased in metal scales; and one spring-weapon (easy to be carried in the breast) designed to do its office noiselessly, and made for shooting men with poisoned darts.

One press or case I saw, full of accursed instruments of torture: horribly contrived to cramp, and pinch, and grind and crush men's bones, and tear and twist them with the torment of a thousand deaths. Before it, were two iron helmets, with breast-pieces: made to close up tight and smooth upon the heads of living sufferers; and fastened on to each, was a small knob or anvil, where the directing devil could repose his elbow at his ease, and listen, near the walled-up ear, to the lamentations and confessions of the wretch within. There was that grim resemblance in them to the human shape—they were such moulds of sweating faces, pained and cramped—that it was difficult to think them empty; and terrible distortions lingering within them, seemed to follow me, when, taking to my boat again, I rowed off to a kind of garden or public walk in the sea, where there were grass and trees. But I forgot them when I stood upon its farthest brink—I stood there, in my dream—and looked, along the ripple, to the setting sun; before me, in the sky and on the deep, a crimson flush; and behind me the whole city resolving into streaks of red and purple, on the water.

In the luxurious wonder of so rare a dream, I took but little heed of time, and had but little understanding of its flight. But there were days and nights in it; and when the sun was high, and when the rays of lamps were crooked in the running water, I was still afloat, I thought: plashing the slippery walls and houses with the cleavings of the tide, as my black boat, borne upon it, skimmed along the streets.

Sometimes, alighting at the doors of churches and vast palaces, I wandered on, from room to room, from aisle to aisle, through labyrinths of rich altars, ancient monuments; decayed apartments where the furniture, half awful, half grotesque, was mouldering away. Pictures were there, replete with such enduring beauty and expression: with such passion, truth and power: that they seemed so many young and fresh realities among a host of spectres. I thought these, often intermingled with the old days of the city: with its beauties, tyrants, captains, patriots, merchants, courtiers, priests: nay, with its very stones, and bricks, and public places; all of which lived again, about me, on the walls. Then, coming down some marble staircase where the water lapped and oozed against the lower steps, I passed into my boat again, and went on in my dream.

Floating down narrow lanes, where carpenters, at work with plane and chisel in their shops, tossed the light shaving straight upon the water, where it lay like weed, or ebbed away before me in a tangled heap. Past open doors, decayed and rotten from long steeping in the wet, through which some scanty patch of vine shone green and bright, making unusual shadows on the pavement with its trembling leaves. Past quays and terraces, where women, gracefully veiled, were passing and repassing, and where idlers were reclining in the sunshine, on flag-stones and on flights of steps. Past bridges, where there were idlers too; loitering and looking over. Below stone balconies, erected at a giddy height, before the loftiest windows of the loftiest houses.

Past plots of garden, theatres, shrines, prodigious piles of architecture—Gothic—Saracenic—fanciful with all the fancies of all times and countries. Past buildings that were high, and low, and black, and white, and straight, and crooked; mean and grand, crazy and strong. Twining among a tangled lot of boats and barges, and shooting out at last into a Grand Canal! There, in the errant fancy of my dream, I saw old Shylock passing to and fro upon a bridge, all built upon with shops and humming with the tongues of men; a form I seemed to know for Desdemona's, leaned down through a latticed blind to pluck a flower. And, in the dream, I thought that Shakespeare's spirit was abroad upon the water somewhere: stealing through the city.

At night, when two votive lamps burnt before an image of the Virgin, in a gallery outside the great cathedral, near the roof, I fancied that the great piazza of the Winged Lion was a blaze of cheerful light, and that its whole arcade was thronged with people; while crowds were diverting themselves in splendid coffee-houses opening from it—which were never shut, I thought, but open all night long. When the bronze giants struck the hour of midnight on the bell, I thought the life and animation of the city were all centred here; and as I rowed away, abreast the silent quays, I only saw them dotted, here and there, with sleeping boatmen wrapped up in their cloaks, and lying at full length upon the stones.

But close about the quays and churches, palaces and prisons: sucking at their walls, and welling up into the secret places of the town: crept the water always. Noiseless and watchful: coiled round and round it, in its many folds, like an old serpent: waiting for the time, I thought, when people should look down into its depths for any stone of the old city that had claimed to be its mistress.

Thus it floated me away, until I awoke in the old market-place at Verona. I have, many and many a time, thought since, of this strange Dream upon the water: half-wondering if it lie there yet, and if its name be VENICE.

BY VERONA, MANTUA, AND MILAN, ACROSS THE PASS OF THE SIMPLON INTO SWITZERLAND

I HAD been half afraid to go to Verona, lest it should at all put me out of conceit with Romeo and Juliet. But, I was no sooner come into the old market-place, than the misgiving vanished. It is so fanciful, quaint, and picturesque a place, formed by such an extraordinary and rich variety of fantastic buildings, that there could be nothing better at the core of even this romantic town : scene of one of the most romantic and beautiful of stories.

It was natural enough, to go straight from the Market-place, to the House of the Capulets, now degenerated into a most miserable little inn. Noisy vetturíni and muddy market-carts were disputing possession of the yard, which was ankle-deep in dirt, with a brood of splashed and be-spattered geese; and there was a grim-visaged dog, viciously panting in a doorway, who would certainly have had Romeo by the leg, the moment he put it over the wall, if he had existed and been at large in those times. The orchard fell into other hands, and was parted off many years ago; but there used to be one attached to the house— or at all events there may have been,—and the hat (Cappéllo) the ancient cognizance of the family, may still be seen, carved in stone, over the gateway of the yard. The geese, the market-carts, their drivers, and the dog, were somewhat in the way of the story, it must be confessed; and it would have been pleasanter to have found the house empty, and to have been able to walk through the disused rooms. But the hat was unspeakably comfortable; and the place where the garden used to be, hardly less so. Besides, the house is a distrust-ful, jealous-looking house as one would desire to see, though of a very moderate size. So I was quite satisfied with it, as the veritable mansion of old Capulet, and was correspond-ingly grateful in my acknowledgments to an extremely un-sentimental middle-aged lady, the Padrona of the Hotel, who was lounging on the threshold looking at the geese; and who at least resembled the Capulets in the one particular of being very great indeed in the "Family" way.

From Juliet's home, to Juliet's tomb, is a transition as natural to the visitor, as to fair Juliet herself, or to the proudest Juliet that ever has taught the torches to burn bright in any time. So, I went off, with a guide, to an old, old garden, once belonging to an old, old convent, I suppose; and being admitted, at a shattered gate, by a bright-eyed woman who was washing clothes, went down some walks where fresh plants and young flowers were prettily growing among fragments of old wall, and ivy-coloured mounds; and was shown a little tank, or water-trough, which the bright-eyed woman—drying her arms upon her 'kerchief, called "La tomba di Giulietta la sfortunáta." With the best disposition in the world to believe, I could do no more than believe that the bright-eyed woman believed; so I gave her that much credit, and her customary fee in ready money. It was a pleasure, rather than a disappointment, that Juliet's resting-place was forgotten. However consolatory it may have been to Yorick's Ghost, to hear the feet upon the pavement overhead, and, twenty times a day, the repetition of his name, it is better for Juliet to lie out of the track of tourists, and to have no visitors but such as come to graves in spring-rain, and sweet air, and sunshine.

Pleasant Verona! With its beautiful old palaces, and charming country in the distance, seen from terrace walks, and stately, balustraded galleries. With its Roman gates, still spanning the fair street, and casting, on the sunlight of to-day, the shade of fifteen hundred years ago. With its marble-fitted churches, lofty towers, rich architecture, and quaint old quiet thoroughfares, where shouts of Montagues and Capulets once resounded,

> And made Verona's ancient citizens
> Cast by their grave, beseeming ornaments,
> To wield old partizans.

With its fast-rushing river, picturesque old bridge, great castle, waving cypresses, and prospect so delightful, and so cheerful! Pleasant Verona!

In the midst of it, in the Piazza di Brá—a spirit of old time among the familiar realities of the passing hour—is the great Roman Amphitheatre. So well preserved, and carefully maintained, that every row of seats is there, unbroken.

Over certain of the arches, the old Roman numerals may yet be seen; and there are corridors, and staircases, and subterranean passages for beasts, and winding ways, above ground and below, as when the fierce thousands hurried in and out, intent upon the bloody shows of the arena. Nestling in some of the shadows and hollow places of the walls, now, are smiths with their forges, and a few small dealers of one kind or other; and there are green weeds, and leaves, and grass, upon the parapet. But little else is greatly changed.

When I had traversed all about it, with great interest, and had gone up to the topmost round of seats, and turning from the lovely panorama closed in by the distant Alps, looked down into the building, it seemed to lie before me like the inside of a prodigious hat of plaited straw, with an enormously broad brim and a shallow crown; the plaits being represented by the four-and-forty rows of seats. The comparison is a homely and fantastic one, in sober remembrance and on paper, but it was irresistibly suggested at the moment, nevertheless.

An equestrian troop had been there, a short time before— the same troop, I dare say, that appeared to the old lady in the church at Modena—and had scooped out a little ring at one end of the area; where their performances had taken place, and where the marks of their horses' feet were still fresh. I could not but picture to myself, a handful of spectators gathered together on one or two of the old stone seats, and a spangled Cavalier being gallant, or a Policinello funny, with the grim walls looking on. Above all, I thought how strangely those Roman mutes would gaze upon the favourite comic scene of the travelling English, where a British nobleman (Lord John), with a very loose stomach: dressed in a blue-tailed coat down to his heels, bright yellow breeches, and a white hat: comes abroad, riding double on a rearing horse, with an English lady (Lady Betsy) in a straw bonnet and green veil, and a red spencer; and who always carries a gigantic reticule, and a put-up parasol.

I walked through and through the town all the rest of the day, and could have walked there until now, I think. In one place, there was a very pretty modern theatre, where they had just performed the opera (always popular in Verona) of Romeo and Juliet. In another there was a collection, under a colonnade, of Greek, Roman, and Etruscan remains,

presided over by an ancient man who might have been an
Etruscan relic himself; for he was not strong enough to
open the iron gate, when he had unlocked it, and had neither
voice enough to be audible when he described the curiosities,
nor sight enough to see them: he was so very old. In another
place, there was a gallery of pictures: so abominably bad,
that it was quite delightful to see them mouldering away.
But anywhere: in the churches, among the palaces, in the
streets, on the bridge, or down beside the river: it was
always pleasant Verona, and in my remembrance always
will be.

I read Romeo and Juliet in my own room at the inn that
night—of course, no Englishman had ever read it there,
before—and set out for Mantua next day at sunrise, repeating to myself (in the *coupé* of an omnibus, and next to the
conductor, who was reading the Mysteries of Paris),

> There is no world without Verona's walls
> But purgatory, torture, hell itself.
> Hence-banished is banished from the world,
> And world's exile is death——

which reminded me that Romeo was only banished five-and-
twenty miles after all, and rather disturbed my confidence
in his energy and boldness.

Was the way to Mantua as beautiful, in his time, I wonder!
Did it wind through pasture land as green, bright with
the same glancing streams, and dotted with fresh clumps
of graceful trees! Those purple mountains lay on the horizon, then, for certain; and the dresses of these peasant girls,
who wear a great, knobbed, silver pin like an English "life-
preserver" through their hair behind, can hardly be much
changed. The hopeful feeling of so bright a morning, and
so exquisite a sunrise, can have been no stranger, even to an
exiled lover's breast; and Mantua itself must have broken
on him in the prospect, with its towers, and walls, and
water, pretty much as on a common-place and matrimonial
omnibus. He made the same sharp twists and turns, perhaps, over two rumbling drawbridges; passed through the
like long, covered, wooden bridge; and leaving the marshy
water behind, approached the rusty gate of stagnant Mantua.

If ever a man were suited to his place of residence, and his
place of residence to him, the lean Apothecary and Mantua
came together in a perfect fitness of things. It may have
been more stirring then, perhaps. If so, the Apothecary

was a man in advance of his time, and knew what Mantua would be, in eighteen hundred and forty-four. He fasted much, and that assisted him in his foreknowledge.

I put up at the Hotel of the Golden Lion, and was in my own room arranging plans with the brave Courier, when there came a modest little tap at the door, which opened on an outer gallery surrounding a court-yard; and an intensely shabby little man looked in, to inquire if the gentleman would have a Cicerone to show the town. His face was so very wistful and anxious, in the half-opened doorway, and there was so much poverty expressed in his faded suit and little pinched hat, and in the threadbare worsted glove with which he held it—not expressed the less, because these were evidently his genteel clothes, hastily slipped on—that I would as soon have trodden on him as dismissed him. I engaged him on the instant, and he stepped in directly.

While I finished the discussion in which I was engaged, he stood, beaming by himself in a corner, making a feint of brushing my hat with his arm. If his fee had been as many napoleons as it was francs, there could not have shot over the twilight of his shabbiness such a gleam of sun, as lighted up the whole man, now that he was hired.

"Well!" said I, when I was ready, "shall we go out now?"

"If the gentleman pleases. It is a beautiful day. A little fresh, but charming; altogether charming. The gentleman will allow me to open the door. This is the Inn Yard. The court-yard of the Golden Lion! The gentleman will please to mind his footing on the stairs."

We were now in the street.

"This is the street of the Golden Lion. This, the outside of the Golden Lion. The interesting window up there, on the first *piano*, where the pane of glass is broken, is the window of the gentleman's chamber!"

Having viewed all these remarkable objects, I inquired if there were much to see in Mantua.

"Well! Truly, no. Not much! So, so," he said, shrugging his shoulders apologetically.

"Many churches?"

"No. Nearly all suppressed by the French."

"Monasteries or convents?"

"No. The French again! Nearly all suppressed by Napoleon."

"Much business?"

"Very little business."

"Many strangers?"

"Ah Heaven!"

I thought he would have fainted.

"Then, when we have seen the two large churches yonder,
what shall we do next?" said I.

He looked up the street, and down the street, and rubbed
his chin timidly; and then said, glancing in my face as if a
light had broken on his mind, yet with a humble appeal to
my forbearance that was perfectly irresistible:

"We can take a little turn about the town, Signore!"
(Si può far' un piccolo giro della città).

It was impossible to be anything but delighted with the
proposal, so we set off together in great good-humour.   In
the relief of his mind, he opened his heart, and gave up as
much of Mantua as a Cicerone could.

"One must eat," he said; "but, bah! it was a dull place,
without doubt!"

He made as much as possible of the Basilica of Santa
Andrea—a noble church—and of an inclosed portion of the
pavement, about which tapers were burning, and a few people
kneeling, and under which is said to be preserved the San-
greal of the old Romances.   This church disposed of, and
another after it (the cathedral of San Pietro), we went to the
Museum, which was shut up.   "It was all the same," he
said, "Bah!   There was not much inside!"   Then, we
went to see the Piazza del Diavolo, built by the Devil (for no
particular purpose) in a single night; then, the Piazza Vir-
giliana; then, the statue of Virgil—*our* Poet, my little friend
said, plucking up a spirit, for the moment, and putting his
hat a little on one side.   Then, we went to a dismal sort of
farm-yard, by which a picture-gallery was approached.   The
moment the gate of this retreat was opened, some five hundred geese came waddling round us, stretching out their
necks, and clamouring in the most hideous manner, as if
they were ejaculating, "Oh! here's somebody come to see
the Pictures!   Don't go up!   Don't go up!"   While we
went up, they waited very quietly about the door in a crowd,
cackling to one another occasionally, in a subdued tone; but the
instant we appeared again, their necks came out like telescopes,
and setting up a great noise, which meant, I have no doubt,
"What, you would go, would you?   What do you think of

it ? How do you like it ?" they attended us to the outer
gate, and cast us forth, derisively, into Mantua.

The geese who saved the Capitol, were, as compared to
these, Pork to the learned Pig. What a gallery it was!
I would take their opinion on a question of art, in preference
to the discourses of Sir Joshua Reynolds.

Now that we were standing in the street, after being thus
ignominiously escorted thither, my little friend was plainly
reduced to the "piccolo giro," or little circuit of the town, he
had formerly proposed. But my suggestion that we should
visit the Palazzo Tè (of which I had heard a great deal, as
a strange wild place) imparted new life to him, and away
we went.

The secret of the length of Midas's ears, would have been
more extensively known, if that servant of his, who whispered
it to the reeds, had lived in Mantua, where there are reeds
and rushes enough to have published it to all the world. The
Palazzo Tè stands in a swamp, among this sort of vegetation;
and is, indeed, as singular a place as I ever saw.

Not for its dreariness, though it is very dreary. Nor for
its dampness, though it is very damp. Nor for its desolate
condition, though it is as desolate and neglected as house can
be. But chiefly for the unaccountable nightmares with which
its interior has been decorated (among other subjects of more
delicate execution), by Giulio Romano. There is a leering
Giant over a certain chimneypiece, and there are dozens of
Giants (Titans warring with Jove) on the walls of another
room, so inconceivably ugly and grotesque, that it is marvellous how any man can have imagined such creatures. In the
chamber in which they abound, these monsters, with swollen
faces and cracked cheeks, and every kind of distortion of look
and limb, are depicted as staggering under the weight of
falling buildings, and being overwhelmed in the ruins; up-
heaving masses of rock, and burying themselves beneath;
vainly striving to sustain the pillars of heavy roofs that
topple down upon their heads; and, in a word, undergoing
and doing every kind of mad and demoniacal destruction.
The figures are immensely large, and exaggerated to the
utmost pitch of uncouthness; the colouring is harsh and disagreeable; and the whole effect more like (I should imagine)
a violent rush of blood to the head of the spectator, than any
real picture set before him by the hand of an artist. This
apoplectic performance was shown by a sickly-looking woman,

whose appearance was referable, I dare say, to the bad air of
the marshes; but it was difficult to help feeling as if she were
too much haunted by the Giants, and they were frightening
her to death, all alone in that exhausted cistern of a Palace,
among the reeds and rushes, with the mists hovering about
outside, and stalking round and round it continually.

Our walk through Mantua showed us, in almost every street,
some suppressed church: now used for a warehouse, now for
nothing at all: all as crazy and dismantled as they could be,
short of tumbling down bodily. The marshy town was so
intensely dull and flat, that the dirt upon it seemed not to
have come there in the ordinary course, but to have settled
and mantled on its surface as on standing water. And yet
there were some business-dealings going on, and some profits
realising; for there were arcades full of Jews, where those
extraordinary people were sitting outside their shops, contemplating their stores of stuffs, and woollens, and bright
handkerchiefs, and trinkets: and looking, in all respects, as
wary and business-like, as their brethren in Houndsditch,
London.

Having selected a Vetturíno from among the neighbouring
Christians, who agreed to carry us to Milan in two days and
a half, and to start, next morning, as soon as the gates were
opened, I returned to the Golden Lion, and dined luxuriously
in my own room, in a narrow passage between two bedsteads:
confronted by a smoky fire, and backed up by a chest of
drawers. At six o'clock next morning, we were jingling in
the dark through the wet cold mist that enshrouded the
town; and, before noon, the driver (a native of Mantua, and
sixty years of age or thereabouts) began *to ask the way* to
Milan.

It lay through Bozzolo; formerly a little republic, and now
one of the most deserted and poverty-stricken of towns:
where the landlord of the miserable inn (God bless him! it
was his weekly custom) was distributing infinitesimal coins
among a clamorous herd of women and children, whose rags
were fluttering in the wind and rain outside his door, where
they were gathered to receive his charity. It lay through
mist, and mud, and rain, and vines trained low upon the
ground, all that day and the next; the first sleeping-place
being Cremona, memorable for its dark brick churches, and
immensely high tower, the Torrazzo—to say nothing of its
violins, of which it certainly produces none in these degenerate

days; and the second, Lodi. Then we went on, through more mud, mist, and rain, and marshy ground: and through such a fog, as Englishmen, strong in the faith of their own grievances, are apt to believe is nowhere to be found but in their own country, until we entered the paved streets of Milan.

The fog was so dense here, that the spire of the far-famed Cathedral might as well have been at Bombay, for anything that could be seen of it at that time. But as we halted to refresh, for a few days then, and returned to Milan again next summer, I had ample opportunities of seeing the glorious structure in all its majesty and beauty.

All Christian homage to the saint who lies within it! There are many good and true saints in the calendar, but San Carlo Borromeo has—if I may quote Mrs. Primrose on such a subject—"my warm heart." A charitable doctor to the sick, a munificent friend to the poor, and this, not in any spirit of blind bigotry, but as the bold opponent of enormous abuses in the Romish church, I honour his memory. I honour it none the less, because he was nearly slain by a priest, suborned, by priests, to murder him at the altar: in acknowledgment of his endeavours to reform a false and hypocritical brotherhood of monks. Heaven shield all imitators of San Carlo Borromeo as it shielded him! A reforming Pope would need a little shielding, even now.

The subterranean chapel in which the body of San Carlo Borromeo is preserved, presents as striking and as ghastly a contrast, perhaps, as any place can show. The tapers which are lighted down there, flash and gleam on alti-rilievi in gold and silver, delicately wrought by skilful hands, and representing the principal events in the life of the saint. Jewels, and precious metals, shine and sparkle on every side. A windlass slowly removes the front of the altar; and, within it, in a gorgeous shrine of gold and silver, is seen, through alabaster, the shrivelled mummy of a man: the pontifical robes with which it is adorned, radiant with diamonds, emeralds, rubies: every costly and magnificent gem. The shrunken heap of poor earth in the midst of this great glitter, is more pitiful than if it lay upon a dunghill. There is not a ray of imprisoned light in all the flash and fire of jewels, but seems to mock the dusty holes where eyes were, once. Every thread of silk in the rich vestments seems only a provision from the worms that spin, for the behoof of worms that propagate in sepulchres.

In the old refectory of the dilapidated Convent of Santa Maria delle Grazie, is the work of art, perhaps, better known than any other in the world : the Last Supper, by Leonardo da Vinci—with a door cut through it by the intelligent Dominican friars, to facilitate their operations at dinner-time.

I am not mechanically acquainted with the art of painting, and have no other means of judging of a picture than as I see it resembling and refining upon nature, and presenting graceful combinations of forms and colours. I am, therefore, no authority whatever, in reference to the "touch" of this or that master ; though I know very well (as anybody may, who chooses to think about the matter) that few very great masters can possibly have painted, in the compass of their lives, one-half of the pictures that bear their names, and that are recognised by many aspirants to a reputation for taste, as undoubted originals. But this, by the way. Of the Last Supper, I would simply observe, that in its beautiful composition and arrangement, there it is, at Milan, a wonderful picture ; and that, in its original colouring, or in its original expression of any single face or feature, there it is not. Apart from the damage it has sustained from damp, decay, or neglect, it has been (as Barry shows) so retouched upon, and repainted, and that so clumsily, that many of the heads are, now, positive deformities, with patches of paint and plaster sticking upon them like wens, and utterly distorting the expression. Where the original artist set that impress of his genius on a face, which, almost in a line or touch, separated him from meaner painters and made him what he was, succeeding bunglers, filling up, or painting across seams and cracks, have been quite unable to imitate his hand ; and putting in some scowls, or frowns, or wrinkles, of their own, have blotched and spoiled the work. This is so well established as an historical fact, that I should not repeat it, at the risk of being tedious, but for having observed an English gentleman before the picture, who was at great pains to fall into what I may describe as mild convulsions, at certain minute details of expression which are not left in it. Whereas, it would be comfortable and rational for travellers and critics to arrive at a general understanding that it cannot fail to have been a work of extraordinary merit, once : when, with so few of its original beauties remaining, the grandeur of the general design is yet sufficient to sustain it, as a piece replete with interest and dignity.

We achieved the other sights of Milan, in due course, and a fine city it is, though not so unmistakably Italian as to possess the characteristic qualities of many towns far less important in themselves. The Corso, where the Milanese gentry ride up and down in carriages, and rather than not do which, they would half starve themselves at home, is a most noble public promenade, shaded by long avenues of trees. In the splendid theatre of La Scala, there was a ballet of action performed after the opera, under the title of Prometheus: in the beginning of which, some hundred or two of men and women represented our mortal race before the refinements of the arts and sciences, and loves and graces, came on earth to soften them. I never saw anything more effective. Generally speaking, the pantomimic action of the Italians is more remarkable for its sudden and impetuous character than for its delicate expression; but, in this case, the drooping monotony: the weary, miserable, listless, moping life: the sordid passions and desires of human creatures, destitute of those elevating influences to which we owe so much, and to whose promoters we render so little: were expressed in a manner really powerful and affecting. I should have thought it almost impossible to present such an idea so strongly on the stage, without the aid of speech.

Milan soon lay behind us, at five o'clock in the morning; and before the golden statue on the summit of the cathedral spire was lost in the blue sky, the Alps, stupendously confused in lofty peaks and ridges, clouds and snow, were towering in our path.

Still, we continued to advance toward them until nightfall; and, all day long, the mountain tops presented strangely shifting shapes, as the road displayed them in different points of view. The beautiful day was just declining, when we came upon the Lago Maggiore, with its lovely islands. For however fanciful and fantastic the Isola Bella may be, and is, it still is beautiful. Anything springing out of that blue water, with that scenery around it, must be.

It was ten o'clock at night when we got to Domo d'Ossola, at the foot of the Pass of the Simplon. But as the moon was shining brightly, and there was not a cloud in the starlit sky, it was no time for going to bed, or going anywhere but on. So, we got a little carriage, after some delay, and began the ascent.

It was late in November; and the snow lying four or five

feet thick in the beaten road on the summit (in other parts the new drift was already deep), the air was piercing cold. But, the serenity of the night, and the grandeur of the road, with its impenetrable shadows, and deep glooms, and its sudden turns into the shining of the moon and its incessant roar of falling water, rendered the journey more and more sublime at every step.

Soon leaving the calm Italian villages below us, sleeping in the moonlight, the road began to wind among dark trees, and after a time emerged upon a barer region, very steep and toilsome, where the moon shone bright and high.   By degrees, the roar of water grew louder ; and the stupendous track, after crossing the torrent by a bridge, struck in between two massive perpendicular walls of rock that quite shut out the moonlight, and only left a few stars shining in the narrow strip of sky above.   Then, even this was lost, in the thick darkness of a cavern in the rock, through which the way was pierced ; the terrible cataract thundering and roaring close below it, and its foam and spray hanging, in a mist, about the entrance.   Emerging from this cave, and coming again into the moonlight, and across a dizzy bridge, it crept and twisted upward, through the Gorge of Gondo, savage and grand beyond description, with smooth-fronted precipices, rising up on either hand, and almost meeting overhead.   Thus we went, climbing on our rugged way, higher and higher all night, without a moment's weariness : lost in the contemplation of the black rocks, the tremendous heights and depths, the fields of smooth snow lying, in the clefts and hollows, and the fierce torrents thundering head-long down the deep abyss.

Towards daybreak, we came among the snow, where a keen wind was blowing fiercely.   Having, with some trouble, awakened the inmates of a wooden house in this solitude : round which the wind was howling dismally, catching up the snow in wreaths and hurling it away : we got some breakfast in a room built of rough timbers, but well warmed by a stove, and well contrived (as it had need to be) for keeping out the bitter storms.   A sledge being then made ready, and four horses harnessed to it, we went, ploughing, through the snow.   Still upward, but now in the cold light of morning, and with the great white desert on which we travelled, plain and clear.

We were well upon the summit of the mountain : and had

before us the rude cross of wood, denoting its greatest altitude above the sea: when the light of the rising sun, struck, all at once, upon the waste of snow, and turned it a deep red. The lonely grandeur of the scene, was then at its height.

As we went sledging on, there came out of the Hospice founded by Napoleon, a group of Peasant travellers, with staves and knapsacks, who had rested there last night: attended by a Monk or two, their hospitable entertainers, trudging slowly forward with them, for company's sake. It was pleasant to give them good morning, and pretty, looking back a long way after them, to see them looking back at us, and hesitating presently, when one of our horses stumbled and fell, whether or no they should return and help us. But he was soon up again, with the assistance of a rough waggoner whose team had stuck fast there too; and when we had helped him out of his difficulty, in return, we left him slowly ploughing towards them, and went softly and swiftly forward, on the brink of a steep precipice, among the mountain pines.

Taking to our wheels again, soon afterwards, we began rapidly to descend; passing under everlasting glaciers, by means of arched galleries, hung with clusters of dripping icicles; under and over foaming waterfalls; near places of refuge, and galleries of shelter against sudden danger; through caverns over whose arched roofs the avalanches slide, in spring, and bury themselves in the unknown gulf beneath. Down, over lofty bridges, and through horrible ravines: a little shifting speck in the vast desolation of ice and snow, and monstrous granite rocks; down through the deep Gorge of the Saltine, and deafened by the torrent plunging madly down, among the riven blocks of rock, into the level country, far below. Gradually down, by zig-zag roads, lying between an upward and a downward precipice, into warmer weather, calmer air, and softer scenery, until there lay before us, glittering like gold or silver in the thaw and sunshine, the metal-covered, red, green, yellow, domes and church-spires of a Swiss town.

The business of these recollections being with Italy, and my business, consequently, being to scamper back thither as fast as possible, I will not recall (though I am sorely tempted) how the Swiss villages, clustered at the feet of Giant mountains, looked like playthings; or how confusedly the houses were heaped and piled together; or how there were very narrow streets to shut the howling winds out in the winter-time; and broken bridges, which the impetuous torrents, suddenly released in spring, had swept away. Or how there were peasant women here, with great round fur caps: looking, when they peeped out of casements and only their heads were seen, like a population of Sword-bearers to the Lord Mayor of London; or how the town of Vevay, lying on the smooth lake of Geneva, was beautiful to see; or how the statue of Saint Peter in the street at Fribourg, grasps the largest key that ever was beheld; or how Fribourg is illustrious for its two suspension bridges, and its grand cathedral organ.

Or how, between that town and Bâle, the road meandered among thriving villages of wooden cottages, with overhanging thatched roofs, and low protruding windows, glazed with small round panes of glass like crown-pieces; or how, in every little Swiss homestead, with its cart or waggon carefully stowed away beside the house, its little garden, stock of poultry, and groups of red-cheeked children, there was an air of comfort, very new and very pleasant after Italy; or how the dresses of the women changed again, and there were no more sword-bearers to be seen; and fair white stomachers, and great black, fan-shaped, gauzy-looking caps, prevailed instead.

Or how the country by the Jura mountains, sprinkled with snow, and lighted by the moon, and musical with falling water, was delightful; or how, below the windows of the great hotel of the Three Kings at Bâle, the swollen Rhine ran fast and green; or how, at Strasbourg, it was quite as fast but not as green: and was said to be foggy lower down: and, at that late time of the year, was a far less certain means of progress, than the highway road to Paris.

Or how Strasbourg itself, in its magnificent old Gothic Cathedral, and its ancient houses with their peaked roofs and gables, made a little gallery of quaint and interesting views; or how a crowd was gathered inside the cathedral at noon, to see the famous mechanical clock in motion, striking twelve. How, when it struck twelve, a whole army of puppets went through many ingenious evolutions; and, among them, a huge puppet-cock, perched on the top, crowed twelve times, loud and clear. Or how it was wonderful to see this cock at great pains to clap its wings, and strain its throat; but obviously

The Chiffonier

having no connexion whatever with its own voice; which was deep within the clock, a long way down.

Or how the road to Paris, was one sea of mud, and thence to the coast, a little better for a hard frost. Or how the cliffs of Dover were a pleasant sight, and England was so wonderfully neat—though dark, and lacking colour on a winter's day, it must be conceded.

Or how, a few days afterwards, it was cool, re-crossing the channel, with ice upon the decks, and snow lying pretty deep in France. Or how the Malle Poste scrambled through the snow, headlong, drawn in the hilly parts by any number of stout horses at a canter; or how there were, outside the Post-office Yard in Paris, before daybreak, extraordinary adventurers in heaps of rags, groping in the snowy streets with little rakes, in search of odds and ends.

Or how, between Paris and Marseilles, the snow being then exceeding deep, a thaw came on, and the mail waded rather than rolled for the next three hundred miles or so; breaking springs on Sunday nights, and putting out its two passengers to warm and refresh themselves pending the repairs, in miserable billiard-rooms, where hairy company, collected about stoves, were playing cards; the cards being very like themselves—extremely limp and dirty.

Or how there was detention at Marseilles from stress of weather; and steamers were advertised to go, which did not go; or how the good Steam-packet Charlemagne at length put out, and met such weather that now she threatened to run into Toulon, and now into Nice, but, the wind moderating, did neither, but ran on into Genoa harbour instead, where the familiar Bells rang sweetly in my ear. Or how there was a travelling party on board, of whom one member was very ill in the cabin next to mine, and being ill was cross, and therefore declined to give up the Dictionary, which he kept under his pillow; thereby obliging his companions to come down to him, constantly, to ask what was the Italian for a lump of sugar—a glass of brandy and water—what's o'clock? and so forth: which he always insisted on looking out, with his own sea-sick eyes, declining to entrust the book to any man alive.

Like GRUMIO, I might have told you, in detail, all this and something more—but to as little purpose—were I not deterred by the remembrance that my business is with Italy. Therefore, like GRUMIO's story, "it shall die in oblivion."

N

TO ROME BY PISA AND SIENA

THERE is nothing in Italy, more beautiful to me, than the coast-road between Genoa and Spezzia. On one side: sometimes far below, sometimes nearly on a level with the road, and often skirted by broken rocks of many shapes: there is the free blue sea, with here and there a picturesque felucca gliding slowly on; on the other side are lofty hills, ravines besprinkled with white cottages, patches of dark olive woods, country churches with their light open towers, and country houses gaily painted. On every bank and knoll by the wayside, the wild cactus and aloe flourish in exuberant profusion; and the gardens of the bright villages along the road, are seen, all blushing in the summer-time with clusters of the Belladonna, and are fragrant in the autumn and winter with golden oranges and lemons.

Some of the villages are inhabited, almost exclusively, by fishermen; and it is pleasant to see their great boats hauled up on the beach, making little patches of shade, where they lie asleep, or where the women and children sit romping and looking out to sea, while they mend their nets upon the shore. There is one town, Camoglia, with its little harbour on the sea, hundreds of feet below the road; where families of mariners live, who, time out of mind, have owned coasting-vessels in that place, and have traded to Spain and elsewhere. Seen from the road above, it is like a tiny model on the margin of the dimpled water, shining in the sun. Descended into, by the winding mule-tracks, it is a perfect miniature of a primitive seafaring town; the saltest, roughest, most piratical little place that ever was seen. Great rusty iron rings and mooring-chains, capstans, and fragments of old masts and spars, choke up the way; hardy rough-weather boats, and seamen's clothing, flutter in the little harbour or are drawn out on the sunny stones to dry; on the parapet of the rude pier, a few amphibious-looking fellows lie asleep, with their legs dangling over the wall, as though earth or water were all one to them, and if they slipped in, they

would float away, dozing comfortably among the fishes; the
church is bright with trophies of the sea, and votive offerings, in commemoration of escape from storm and shipwreck.
The dwellings not immediately abutting on the harbour are
approached by blind low archways, and by crooked steps, as
if in darkness and in difficulty of access they should be like
holds of ships, or inconvenient cabins under water; and
everywhere, there is a smell of fish, and sea-weed, and old
rope.

The coast-road whence Camoglia is descried so far below,
is famous, in the warm season, especially in some parts near
Genoa, for fire-flies. Walking there on a dark night, I have
seen it made one sparkling firmament by these beautiful
insects: so that the distant stars were pale against the flash
and glitter that spangled every olive wood and hill-side, and
pervaded the whole air.

It was not in such a season, however, that we traversed
this road on our way to Rome. The middle of January was
only just past, and it was very gloomy and dark weather;
very wet besides. In crossing the fine pass of Bracco, we
encountered such a storm of mist and rain, that we travelled
in a cloud the whole way. There might have been no
Mediterranean in the world, for anything that we saw of it
there, except when a sudden gust of wind, clearing the mist
before it, for a moment, showed the agitated sea at a great
depth below, lashing the distant rocks, and spouting up its
foam furiously. The rain was incessant; every brook and
torrent was greatly swollen; and such a deafening leaping,
and roaring, and thundering of water, I never heard the like
of in my life.

Hence, when we came to Spezzia, we found that the Magra,
an unbridged river on the high-road to Pisa, was too high
to be safely crossed in the Ferry Boat, and were fain to wait
until the afternoon of next day, when it had, in some degree,
subsided. Spezzia, however, is a good place to tarry at; by
reason, firstly, of its beautiful bay; secondly, of its ghostly
Inn; thirdly, of the head-dress of the women, who wear, on
one side of their head, a small doll's straw hat, stuck on to
the hair; which is certainly the oddest and most roguish
head-gear that ever was invented.

The Magra safely crossed in the Ferry Boat—the passage
is not by any means agreeable, when the current is swollen
and strong—we arrived at Carrara, within a few hours. In

good time next morning, we got some ponies, and went out
to see the marble quarries.

They are four or five great glens, running up into a range
of lofty hills, until they can run no longer, and are stopped
by being abruptly strangled by Nature. The quarries, "or
caves," as they call them there, are so many openings, high
up in the hills, on either side of these passes, where they
blast and excavate for marble : which may turn out good or
bad : may make a man's fortune very quickly, or ruin him
by the great expense of working what is worth nothing.
Some of these caves were opened by the ancient Romans,
and remain as they left them to this hour. Many others
are being worked at this moment ; others are to be begun
to-morrow, next week, next month ; others are unbought,
unthought of ; and marble enough for more ages than have
passed since the place was resorted to, lies hidden everywhere : patiently awaiting its time of discovery.

As you toil and clamber up one of these steep gorges
(having left your pony soddening his girths in water, a mile
or two lower down) you hear, every now and then, echoing
among the hills, in a low tone, more silent than the previous
silence, a melancholy warning bugle,—a signal to the miners
to withdraw. Then, there is a thundering, and echoing from
hill to hill, and perhaps a splashing up of great fragments
of rock into the air ; and on you toil again until some other
bugle sounds, in a new direction, and you stop directly, lest
you should come within the range of the new explosion.

There were numbers of men, working high up in these
hills—on the sides—clearing away, and sending down the
broken masses of stone and earth, to make way for the blocks
of marble that had been discovered. As these came rolling
down from unseen hands into the narrow valley, I could
not help thinking of the deep glen (just the same sort of
glen) where the Roc left Sindbad the Sailor ; and where the
merchants from the heights above, flung down great pieces
of meat for the diamonds to stick to. There were no eagles
here, to darken the sun in their swoop, and pounce upon
them ; but it was as wild and fierce as if there had been
hundreds.

But the road, the road down which the marble comes,
however immense the blocks ! The genius of the country,
and the spirit of its institutions, pave that road : repair it,
watch it, keep it going ! Conceive a channel of water running

over a rocky bed, beset with great heaps of stone of all
shapes and sizes, winding down the middle of this valley;
and *that* being the road—because it was the road five hundred years ago! Imagine the clumsy carts of five hundred
years ago, being used to this hour, and drawn, as they used
to be, five hundred years ago, by oxen, whose ancestors were
worn to death five hundred years ago, as their unhappy descendants are now, in twelve months, by the suffering and
agony of this cruel work! Two pair, four pair, ten pair,
twenty pair, to one block, according to its size; down it
must come, this way. In their struggling from stone to
stone, with their enormous loads behind them, they die frequently upon the spot; and not they alone; for their pas-
sionate drivers, sometimes tumbling down in their energy,
are crushed to death beneath the wheels. But it was good
five hundred years ago, and it must be good now: and a
railroad down one of these steeps (the easiest thing in the
world) would be flat blasphemy.

When we stood aside, to see one of these cars drawn by
only a pair of oxen (for it had but one small block of marble
on it), coming down, I hailed, in my heart, the man who sat
upon the heavy yoke, to keep it on the neck of the poor
beasts—and who faced backwards: not before him—as the
very Devil of true despotism. He had a great rod in his
hand, with an iron point; and when they could plough and
force their way through the loose bed of the torrent no
longer, and came to a stop, he poked it into their bodies,
beat it on their heads, screwed it round and round in their
nostrils, got them on a yard or two, in the madness of intense
pain; repeated all these persuasions, with increased intensity
of purpose, when they stopped again; got them on, once
more; forced and goaded them to an abrupter point of the
descent; and when their writhing and smarting, and the
weight behind them, bore them plunging down the precipice
in a cloud of scattered water, whirled his rod above his head,
and gave a great whoop and hallo, as if he had achieved
something, and had no idea that they might shake him off,
and blindly mash his brains upon the road, in the noon-tide
of his triumph.

Standing in one of the many studii of Carrara, that afternoon—for it is a great workshop, full of beautifully-finished
copies in marble, of almost every figure, group, and bust,
we know—it seemed, at first, so strange to me that those

exquisite shapes, replete with grace, and thought, and delicate repose, should grow out of all this toil, and sweat, and
torture! But I soon found a parallel to it, and an explanation of it, in every virtue that springs up in miserable ground,
and every good thing that has its birth in sorrow and distress. And, looking out of the sculptor's great window, upon
the marble mountains, all red and glowing in the decline of
day, but stern and solemn to the last, I thought, my God!
how many quarries of human hearts and souls, capable of
far more beautiful results, are left shut up and mouldering
away: while pleasure-travellers through life, avert their faces,
as they pass, and shudder at the gloom and ruggedness that
conceal them!

The then reigning Duke of Modena, to whom this territory in part belonged, claimed the proud distinction of being
the only sovereign in Europe who had not recognised Louis-
Philippe as King of the French! He was not a wag, but
quite in earnest. He was also much opposed to railroads;
and if certain lines in contemplation by other potentates, on
either side of him, had been executed, would have probably
enjoyed the satisfaction of having an omnibus plying to and
fro across his not very vast dominions, to forward travellers
from one terminus to another.

Carrara, shut in by great hills, is very picturesque and
bold. Few tourists stay there; and the people are nearly all
connected, in one way or other, with the working of marble.
There are also villages among the caves, where the workmen
live. It contains a beautiful little Theatre, newly built;
and it is an interesting custom there, to form the chorus of
labourers in the marble quarries, who are self-taught and
sing by ear. I heard them in a comic opera, and in an act
of "Norma;" and they acquitted themselves very well; unlike the common people of Italy generally, who (with some
exceptions among the Neapolitans) sing vilely out of tune,
and have very disagreeable singing voices.

From the summit of a lofty hill beyond Carrara, the first
view of the fertile plain in which the town of Pisa lies—with
Leghorn, a purple spot in the flat distance—is enchanting.
Nor is it only distance that lends enchantment to the view;
for the fruitful country, and rich woods of olive-trees through
which the road subsequently passes, render it delightful.

The moon was shining when we approached Pisa, and for
a long time we could see, behind the wall, the leaning Tower,

all awry in the uncertain light; the shadowy original of the old pictures in school-books, setting forth "The Wonders of the World." Like most things connected in their first associations with school-books and school-times, it was too small. I felt it keenly. It was nothing like so high above the wall as I had hoped. It was another of the many deceptions practised by Mr. Harris, Bookseller, at the corner of St. Paul's Churchyard, London. *His* Tower was a fiction, but this was a reality—and, by comparison, a short reality. Still, it looked very well, and very strange, and was quite as much out of the perpendicular as Harris had represented it to be. The quiet air of Pisa too; the big guard-house at the gate, with only two little soldiers in it; the streets with scarcely any show of people in them; and the Arno, flowing quaintly through the centre of the town; were excellent. So, I bore no malice in my heart against Mr. Harris (remembering his good intentions), but forgave him before dinner, and went out, full of confidence, to see the Tower next morning.

I might have known better; but, somehow, I had expected to see it, casting its long shadow on a public street where people came and went all day. It was a surprise to me to find it in a grave retired place, apart from the general resort, and carpeted with smooth green turf. But, the group of buildings, clustered on and about this verdant carpet: comprising the Tower, the Baptistery, the Cathedral, and the Church of the Campo Santo : is perhaps the most remarkable and beautiful in the whole world ; and from being clustered there, together, away from the ordinary transactions and details of the town, they have a singularly venerable and impressive character. It is the architectural essence of a rich old city, with all its common life and common habitations pressed out, and filtered away.

SIMOND compares the Tower to the usual pictorial representations in children's books of the Tower of Babel. It is a happy simile, and conveys a better idea of the building than chapters of laboured description. Nothing can exceed the grace and lightness of the structure ; nothing can be more remarkable than its general appearance. In the course of the ascent to the top (which is by an easy staircase), the inclination is not very apparent ; but, at the summit, it becomes so, and gives one the sensation of being in a ship that has heeled over, through the action of an ebb-tide. The effect *upon the low side*, so to speak—looking over from the

gallery, and seeing the shaft recede to its base—is very startling ; and I saw a nervous traveller hold on to the Tower
involuntarily, after glancing down, as if he had some idea of
propping it up.   The view within, from the ground—looking
up, as through a slanted tube—is also very curious.   It
certainly inclines as much as the most sanguine tourist could
desire.   The natural impulse of ninety-nine people out of a
hundred, who were about to recline upon the grass below
it, to rest, and contemplate the adjacent buildings, would
probably be, not to take up their position under the leaning
side ; it is so very much aslant.

The manifold beauties of the Cathedral and Baptistery
need no recapitulation from me ; though in this case, as in a
hundred others, I find it difficult to separate my own delight
in recalling them, from your weariness in having them
recalled.   There is a picture of St. Agnes, by Andrea del
Sarto, in the former, and there are a variety of rich columns
in the lattter, that tempt me strongly.

It is, I hope, no breach of my resolution not to be tempted
into elaborate descriptions, to remember the Campo Santo ;
where grass-grown graves are dug in earth brought more
than six hundred years ago, from the Holy Land; and where
there are, surrounding them, such cloisters, with such playing
lights and shadows falling through their delicate tracery on
the stone pavement, as surely the dullest memory could
never forget.   On the walls of this solemn and lovely place,
are ancient frescoes, very much obliterated and decayed, but
very curious.   As usually happens in almost any collection
of paintings, of any sort, in Italy, where there are many
heads, there is, in one of them, a striking accidental likeness
of Napoleon.   At one time, I used to please my fancy with
the speculation whether these old painters, at their work,
had a foreboding knowledge of the man who would one day
arise to wreak such destruction upon art : whose soldiers
would make targets of great pictures, and stable their horses
among triumphs of architecture.   But the same Corsican
face is so plentiful in some parts of Italy at this day, that
a more commonplace solution of the coincidence is una-
voidable.

If Pisa be the seventh wonder of the world in right of its
Tower, it may claim to be, at least, the second or third in
right of its beggars.   They waylay the unhappy visitor at
every turn, escort him to every door he enters at, and lie in

wait for him, with strong reinforcements, at every door by which they know he must come out. The grating of the portal on its hinges is the signal for a general shout, and the moment he appears, he is hemmed in, and fallen on, by heaps of rags and personal distortions. The beggars seem to embody all the trade and enterprise of Pisa. Nothing else is stirring, but warm air. Going through the streets, the fronts of the sleepy houses look like backs. They are all so still and quiet, and unlike houses with people in them, that the greater part of the city has the appearance of a city at daybreak, or during a general siesta of the population. Or it is yet more like those backgrounds of houses in common prints, or old engravings, where windows and doors are squarely indicated, and one figure (a beggar of course) is seen walking off by itself into illimitable perspective.

Not so Leghorn (made illustrious by SMOLLETT's grave), which is a thriving, business-like, matter-of-fact place, where idleness is shouldered out of the way by commerce. The regulations observed there, in reference to trade and merchants, are very liberal and free; and the town, of course, benefits by them. Leghorn had a bad name in connexion with stabbers, and with some justice it must be allowed; for, not many years ago, there was an assassination club there, the members of which bore no ill-will to anybody in particular, but stabbed people (quite strangers to them) in the streets at night, for the pleasure and excitement of the recreation. I think the president of this amiable society was a shoemaker. He was taken, however, and the club was broken up. It would, probably, have disappeared in the natural course of events, before the railroad between Leghorn and Pisa, which is a good one, and has already begun to astonish Italy with a precedent of punctuality, order, plain dealing, and improvement—the most dangerous and heretical astonisher of all. There must have been a slight sensation, as of earthquake, surely, in the Vatican, when the first Italian railroad was thrown open.

Returning to Pisa, and hiring a good-tempered Vetturíno, and his four horses, to take us on to Rome, we travelled through pleasant Tuscan villages and cheerful scenery all day. The roadside crosses in this part of Italy are numerous and curious. There is seldom a figure on the cross, though there is sometimes a face; but they are remarkable for being garnished with little models in wood, of every possible object

that can be connected with the Saviour's death. The cock
that crowed when Peter had denied his Master thrice, is
usually perched on the tip-top; and an ornithological phe-
nomenon he generally is. Under him, is the inscription.
Then, hung on to the cross-beam, are the spear, the reed
with the sponge of vinegar and water at the end, the coat
without seam for which the soldiers cast lots, the dice-box
with which they threw for it, the hammer that drove in the
nails, the pincers that pulled them out, the ladder which was
set against the cross, the crown of thorns, the instrument of
flagellation, the lantern with which Mary went to the tomb
(I suppose), and the sword with which Peter smote the servant
of the high priest,—a perfect toy-shop of little objects, repeated
at every four or five miles, all along the highway.

On the evening of the second day from Pisa, we reached
the beautiful old city of Siena. There was what they called
a Carnival, in progress; but, as its secret lay in a score or
two of melancholy people walking up and down the principal
street in common toy-shop masks, and being more melancholy,
if possible, than the same sort of people in England, I say
no more of it. We went off, betimes next morning, to see
the Cathedral, which is wonderfully picturesque inside and
out, especially the latter—also the market-place, or great
Piazza, which is a large square, with a great broken-nosed
fountain in it: some quaint Gothic houses: and a high square
brick tower; *outside* the top of which—a curious feature in
such views in Italy—hangs an enormous bell. It is like
a bit of Venice, without the water. There are some curious
old Palazzi in the town, which is very ancient; and without
having (for me) the interest of Verona, or Genoa, it is very
dreamy and fantastic, and most interesting.

We went on again, as soon as we had seen these things,
and going over a rather bleak country (there had been nothing
but vines until now: mere walking-sticks at that season of
the year), stopped, as usual, between one and two hours in
the middle of the day, to rest the horses; that being a part
of every Vetturíno contract. We then went on again, through
a region gradually becoming bleaker and wilder, until it
became as bare and desolate as any Scottish moors. Soon
after dark, we halted for the night, at the osteria of La
Scala: a perfectly lone house, where the family were sitting
round a great fire in the kitchen, raised on a stone platform
three or four feet high, and big enough for the roasting of

an ox. On the upper, and only other floor of this hotel, there was a great wild rambling sála, with one very little window in a by-corner, and four black doors opening into four black bedrooms in various directions. To say nothing of another large black door, opening into another large black sála, with the staircase coming abruptly through a kind of trap-door in the floor, and the rafters of the roof looming above: a suspicious little press skulking in one obscure corner: and all the knives in the house lying about in various directions. The fireplace was of the purest Italian architecture, so that it was perfectly impossible to see it for the smoke. The waitress was like a dramatic brigand's wife, and wore the same style of dress upon her head. The dogs barked like mad; the echoes returned the compliments bestowed upon them; there was not another house within twelve miles; and things had a dreary, and rather a cut-throat, appearance.

They were not improved by rumours of robbers having come out, strong and boldly, within a few nights; and of their having stopped the mail very near that place. They were known to have waylaid some travellers not long before, on Mount Vesuvius itself, and were the talk at all the road-side inns. As they were no business of ours, however (for we had very little with us to lose), we made ourselves merry on the subject, and were very soon as comfortable as need be. We had the usual dinner in this solitary house; and a very good dinner it is, when you are used to it. There is something with a vegetable or some rice in it, which is a sort of shorthand or arbitrary character for soup, and which tastes very well, when you have flavoured it with plenty of grated cheese, lots of salt, and abundance of pepper. There is the half fowl of which this soup has been made. There is a stewed pigeon, with the gizzards and livers of himself and other birds stuck all round him. There is a bit of roast beef, the size of a small French roll. There are a scrap of Parmesan cheese, and five little withered apples, all huddled together on a small plate, and crowding one upon the other, as if each were trying to save itself from the chance of being eaten. Then there is coffee; and then there is bed. You don't mind brick floors; you don't mind yawning doors, nor banging windows; you don't mind your own horses being stabled under the bed: and so close, that every time a horse coughs or sneezes, he wakes you. If you are good-humoured to the people about you, and speak pleasantly, and look cheerful, take my word for it you may be well entertained in the very worst Italian Inn, and always in the most obliging manner, and may go from one end of the country to the other (despite all stories to the contrary) without any great trial of your patience anywhere. Especially, when you get such wine in flasks, as the Orvieto, and the Monte Pulciano.

It was a bad morning when we left this place; and we went, for twelve miles, over a country as barren, as stony, and as wild, as Cornwall in England, until we came to Radicofani, where there is a ghostly, goblin inn: once a hunting-seat, belonging to the Dukes of Tuscany. It is full of such rambling corridors, and gaunt rooms, that all the murdering and phantom tales that ever were written might have originated in that one house. There are some horrible old Palazzi in Genoa: one in particular, not unlike it, outside: but there is a winding, creaking, wormy, rustling, door-opening, foot-on-staircase-falling character about this Radicofani Hotel, such as I never saw, anywhere else. The town, such as it is, hangs on a hill-side above the house, and in front of it. The inhabitants are all beggars; and as soon as they see a carriage coming, they swoop down upon it, like so many birds of prey.

When we got on the mountain pass, which lies beyond this place, the wind (as they had forewarned us at the inn) was so terrific, that we were obliged to take my other half out of the carriage, lest she should be blown over, carriage and all, and to hang to it, on the windy side (as well as we could for laughing), to prevent its going, Heaven knows where. For mere force of wind, this land-storm might have competed with an Atlantic gale, and had a reasonable chance of coming off victorious. The blast came sweeping down great gullies in a range of mountains on the right: so that we looked with positive awe at a great morass on the left, and saw that there was not a bush or twig to hold by. It seemed as if, once blown from our feet, we must be swept out to sea, or away into space. There was snow, and hail, and rain, and lightning, and thunder; and there were rolling mists, travelling with incredible velocity. It was dark, awful, and solitary to the last degree; there were mountains above mountains, veiled in angry clouds; and there was such a wrathful, rapid, violent, tumultuous hurry, everywhere, as rendered the scene unspeakably exciting and grand.

It was a relief to get out of it, notwithstanding; and to cross even the dismal dirty Papal Frontier. After passing through two little towns; in one of which, Acquapendente, there was also a "Carnival" in progress: consisting of one man dressed and masked as a woman, and one woman dressed and masked as a man, walking ankle-deep, through the muddy streets, in a very melancholy manner: we came, at dusk, within sight of the Lake of Bolsena, on whose bank there is a little town of the same name, much celebrated for malaria. With the exception of this poor place, there is not a cottage on the banks of the lake, or near it (for nobody dare sleep there); not a boat upon its waters; not a stick or stake to break the dismal monotony of seven-and-twenty watery miles. We were late in getting in, the roads being very bad from heavy rains; and, after dark, the dulness of the scene was quite intolerable.

We entered on a very different, and a finer scene of desolation, next night, at sunset. We had passed through Montefiaschone (famous for its wine) and Viterbo (for its fountains): and after climbing up a long hill of eight or ten miles' extent, came suddenly upon the margin of a solitary lake: in one part very beautiful, with a luxuriant wood; in another, very barren, and shut in by bleak volcanic hills. Where this lake flows, there stood, of old, a city. It was swallowed up one day; and in its stead, this water rose. There are ancient traditions (common to many parts of the world) of the ruined city having been seen below, when the water was clear; but however that may be, from this spot of earth it vanished. The ground came bubbling up above it; and the water too; and here they stand, like ghosts on whom the other world closed suddenly, and who have no means of getting back again. They seem to be waiting the course of ages, for the next earthquake in that place; when they will plunge below the ground, at its first yawning, and be seen no more. The unhappy city below, is not more lost and dreary, than these fire-charred hills and the stagnant water, above. The red sun looked strangely on them, as with the knowledge that they were made for caverns and darkness; and the melancholy water oozed and sucked the mud, and crept quietly among the marshy grass and reeds, as if the overthrow of all the ancient towers and house-tops, and the death of all the ancient people born and bred there, were yet heavy on its conscience.

A short ride from this lake, brought us to Ronciglione; a little town like a large pig-sty, where we passed the night. Next morning at seven o'clock, we started for Rome.

As soon as we were out of the pig-sty, we entered on the Campagne Romana; an undulating flat (as you know), where few people can live; and where, for miles and miles, there is nothing to relieve the terrible monotony and gloom. Of all kinds of country that could, by possibility, lie outside the gates of Rome, this is the aptest and fittest burial-ground for the Dead City. So sad, so quiet, so sullen; so secret in its covering up of great masses of ruin, and hiding them; so like the waste places into which the men possessed with devils used to go and howl, and rend themselves, in the old days of Jerusalem. We had to traverse thirty miles of this Campagna; and for two-and-twenty we went on and on, seeing nothing but now and then a lonely house, or a villainous-looking shepherd: with matted hair all over his face, and himself wrapped to the chin in a frowzy brown mantle, tending his sheep. At the end of that distance, we stopped to refresh the horses, and to get some lunch, in a common malaria-shaken, despondent little public-house, whose every inch of wall and beam, inside, was (according to custom) painted and decorated in a way so miserable that every room looked like the wrong side of another room, and, with its wretched imitation of drapery, and lop-sided little daubs of lyres, seemed to have been plundered from behind the scenes of some travelling circus.

When we were fairly going off again, we began, in a perfect fever, to strain our eyes for Rome; and when, after another mile or two, the Eternal City appeared, at length, in the distance; it looked like—I am half afraid to write the word —like LONDON!!! There it lay, under a thick cloud, with innumerable towers, and steeples, and roofs of houses, rising up into the sky, and high above them all, one Dome. I swear, that keenly as I felt the seeming absurdity of the comparison, it was so like London, at that distance, that if you could have shown it me, in a glass, I should have taken it for nothing else.

ROME

WE entered the Eternal City, at about four o'clock in the afternoon, on the thirtieth of January, by the Porta del Popolo, and came immediately—it was a dark, muddy day, and there had been heavy rain—on the skirts of the Carnival. We did not, then, know that we were only looking at the fag end of the masks, who were driving slowly round and round the Piazza until they could find a promising opportunity for falling into the stream of carriages, and getting, in good time, into the thick of the festivity; and coming among them so abruptly, all travel-stained and weary, was not coming very well prepared to enjoy the scene.

We had crossed the Tiber by the Ponte Molle two or three miles before. It had looked as yellow as it ought to look, and hurrying on between its worn-away and miry banks, had a promising aspect of desolation and ruin. The masquerade dresses on the fringe of the Carnival, did great violence to this promise. There were no great ruins, no solemn tokens of antiquity, to be seen;—they all lie on the other side of the city. There seemed to be long streets of commonplace shops and houses, such as are to be found in any European town; there were busy people, equipages, ordinary walkers to and fro; a multitude of chattering strangers. It was no more *my* Rome: the Rome of anybody's fancy, man or boy; degraded and fallen and lying asleep in the sun among a heap of ruins: than the Place de la Concorde in Paris is. A cloudy sky, a dull cold rain, and muddy streets, I was prepared for, but not for this: and I confess to having gone to bed, that night, in a very indifferent humour, and with a very considerably quenched enthusiasm.

Immediately on going out next day, we hurried off to St. Peter's. It looked immense in the distance, but distinctly and decidedly small, by comparison, on a near approach. The beauty of the Piazza, on which it stands, with its clusters of exquisite columns, and its gushing fountains—so fresh, so broad, and free, and beautiful—nothing can exaggerate. The first burst of the interior, in all its expansive majesty and glory : and, most of all, the looking up into the Dome : is a sensation never to be forgotten. But, there were preparations for a Festa ; the pillars of stately marble were swathed in some impertinent frippery of red and yellow ; the altar, and entrance to the subterranean chapel : which is before it : in the centre of the church : were like a goldsmith's shop, or one of the opening scenes in a very lavish pantomime. And though I had as high a sense of the beauty of the building (I hope) as it is possible to entertain, I felt no very strong emotion. I have been infinitely more affected in many English cathedrals when the organ has been playing, and in many English country churches when the congregation have been singing. I had a much greater sense of mystery and wonder, in the Cathedral of San Mark at Venice.

When we came out of the church again (we stood nearly an hour staring up into the dome : and would not have " gone over " the Cathedral then, for any money), we said to the coachman, " Go to the Coliseum." In a quarter of an hour or so, he stopped at the gate, and we went in.

It is no fiction, but plain, sober, honest Truth, to say : so suggestive and distinct is it at this hour : that, for a moment —actually in passing in—they who will, may have the whole great pile before them, as it used to be, with thousands of eager faces staring down into the arena, and such a whirl of strife, and blood, and dust going on there, as no language can describe. Its solitude, its awful beauty, and its utter desolation, strike upon the stranger the next moment, like a softened sorrow ; and never in his life, perhaps, will he be so moved and overcome by any sight, not immediately connected with his own affections and afflictions.

To see it crumbling there, an inch a year ; its walls and arches overgrown with green ; its corridors open to the day ; the long grass growing in its porches ; young trees of yesterday, springing up on its ragged parapets, and bearing fruit : chance produce of the seeds dropped there by the birds who build their nests within its chinks and crannies : to see its Pit of Fight filled up with earth, and the peaceful Cross planted in the centre ; to climb into its upper halls, and look down on ruin, ruin, ruin, all about it ; the triumphal arches of Constantine, Septimus Severus, and Titus ; the Roman Forum ; the Palace of the Cæsars ; the temples of the old religion, fallen down and gone ; is to see the ghost of old

The Colosseum of Rome

Rome, wicked wonderful old city, haunting the very ground on which its people trod. It is the most impressive, the most stately, the most solemn, grand, majestic, mournful sight, conceivable. Never, in its bloodiest prime, can the sight of the gigantic Coliseum, full and running over with the lustiest life, have moved one heart, as it must move all who look upon it now, a ruin. GOD be thanked: a ruin!

As it tops the other ruins: standing there, a mountain among graves: so do its ancient influences outlive all other remnants of the old mythology and old butchery of Rome, in the nature of the fierce and cruel Roman people. The Italian face changes as the visitor approaches the city; its beauty becomes devilish; and there is scarcely one countenance in a hundred, among the common people in the streets, that would not be at home and happy in a renovated Coliseum to-morrow.

Here was Rome indeed at last; and such a Rome as no one can imagine in its full and awful grandeur! We wandered out upon the Appian Way, and then went on, through miles of ruined tombs and broken walls, with here and there a desolate and uninhabited house: past the Circus of Romulus, where the course of the chariots, the stations of the judges, competitors, and spectators, are yet as plainly to be seen as in old time: past the tomb of Cecilia Metella: past all inclosure, hedge, or stake, wall or fence: away upon the open Campagna, where on that side of Rome, nothing is to be beheld but Ruin. Except where the distant Apennines bound the view upon the left, the whole wide prospect is one field of ruin. Broken aqueducts, left in the most picturesque and beautiful clusters of arches; broken temples; broken tombs. A desert of decay, sombre and desolate beyond all expression; and with a history in every stone that strews the ground.

On Sunday, the Pope assisted in the performance of High Mass at St. Peter's. The effect of the Cathedral on my mind, on that second visit, was exactly what it was at first, and what it remains after many visits. It is not religiously impressive or affecting. It is an immense edifice, with no one point for the mind to rest upon; and it tires itself with wandering round and round. The very purpose of the place, is not expressed in anything you see there, unless you examine its details—and all examination of details is incompatible with the place itself. It might be a Pantheon, or a Senate House, or a great architectural trophy, having no other object than an architectural triumph. There is a black statue of St. Peter, to be sure, under a red canopy; which is larger than life, and which is constantly having its great toe kissed by good Catholics. You cannot help seeing that: it is so very prominent and popular. But it does not heighten the effect of the temple, as a work of art; and it is not expressive—to me at least—of its high purpose.

A large space behind the altar, was fitted up with boxes, shaped like those at the Italian Opera in England, but in their decoration much more gaudy. In the centre of the kind of theatre thus railed off, was a canopied dais with the Pope's chair upon it. The pavement was covered with a carpet of the brightest green; and what with this green, and the intolerable reds and crimsons, and gold borders of the hangings, the whole concern looked like a stupendous Bonbon. On either side of the altar, was a large box for lady strangers. These were filled with ladies in black dresses and black veils. The gentlemen of the Pope's guard, in red coats, leather breeches, and jack-boots, guarded all this reserved space, with drawn swords that were very flashy in every sense; and from the altar all down the nave, a broad lane was kept clear by the Pope's Swiss guard, who wear a quaint striped surcoat, and striped tight legs, and carry halberds like those which are usually shouldered by those theatrical supernumeraries, who never *can* get off the stage fast enough, and who may be generally observed to linger in the enemy's camp after the open country, held by the opposite forces, has been split up the middle by a convulsion of Nature.

I got upon the border of the green carpet, in company with a great many other gentlemen, attired in black (no other passport is necessary), and stood there at my ease, during the performance of Mass. The singers were in a crib of wirework (like a large meat-safe or bird-cage) in one corner; and sang most atrociously. All about the green carpet, there was a slowly moving crowd of people: talking to each other: staring at the Pope through eye-glasses; defrauding one another, in moments of partial curiosity, out of precarious seats on the bases of pillars: and grinning hideously at the ladies. Dotted here and there, were little knots of friars (Francescáni, or Cappuccíni, in their coarse brown dresses and peaked hoods) making a strange contrast to the gaudy ecclesiastics of higher degree, and having their humility gratified to the utmost, by being shouldered about, and elbowed right and left, on all sides. Some of these had muddy sandals and umbrellas, and stained garments : having trudged in from the country. The faces of the greater part were as coarse and heavy as their dress ; their dogged, stupid, monotonous stare at all the glory and splendour, having something in it, half miserable, and half ridiculous.

Upon the green carpet itself, and gathered round the altar, was a perfect army of cardinals and priests, in red, gold, purple, violet, white, and fine linen. Stragglers from these, went to and fro among the crowd, conversing two and two, or giving and receiving introductions, and exchanging salutations ; other functionaries in black gowns, and other functionaries in court-dresses, were similarly engaged. In the midst of all these, and stealthy Jesuits creeping in and out, and the extreme restlessness of the Youth of England, who were perpetually wandering about, some few steady persons in black cassocks, who had knelt down with their faces to the wall, and were poring over their missals, became, unintentionally, a sort of humane man-traps, and with their own devout legs, tripped up other people's by the dozen.

There was a great pile of candles lying down on the floor near me, which a very old man in a rusty black gown with an open-work tippet, like a summer ornament for a fireplace in tissue-paper, made himself very busy in dispensing to all the ecclesiastics : one a-piece. They loitered about with these for some time, under their arms like walking-sticks, or in their hands like truncheons. At a certain period of the ceremony, however, each carried his candle up to the Pope, laid it across his two knees to be blessed, took it back again, and filed off. This was done in a very attenuated procession, as you may suppose, and occupied a long time. Not because it takes long to bless a candle through and through, but because there were so many candles to be blessed. At last they were all blessed ; and then they were all lighted ; and then the Pope was taken up, chair and all, and carried round the church.

I must say, that I never saw anything, out of November, so like the popular English commemoration of the fifth of that month. A bundle of matches and a lantern, would have made it perfect. Nor did the Pope, himself, at all mar the resemblance, though he has a pleasant and venerable face ; for, as

this part of the ceremony makes him giddy and sick, he shuts
his eyes when it is performed : and having his eyes shut and
a great mitre on his head, and his head itself wagging to
and fro as they shook him in carrying, he looked as if his
mask were going to tumble off. The two immense fans which
are always borne, one on either side of him, accompanied
him, of course, on this occasion. As they carried him along,
he blessed the people with the mystic sign ; and as he passed
them, they kneeled down. When he had made the round
of the church, he was brought back again, and if I am not
mistaken, this performance was repeated, in the whole, three
times. There was, certainly, nothing solemn or effective in
it ; and certainly very much that was droll and tawdry. But
this remark applies to the whole ceremony, except the raising
of the Host, when every man in the guard dropped on one
knee instantly, and dashed his naked sword on the ground ;
which had a fine effect.

The next time I saw the cathedral, was some two or three
weeks afterwards, when I climbed up into the ball; and
then, the hangings being taken down, and the carpet taken
up, but all the framework left, the remnants of these decorations looked like an exploded cracker.

The Friday and Saturday having been solemn Festa days,
and Sunday being always a *dies non* in carnival proceedings,
we had looked forward, with some impatience and curiosity, to
the beginning of the new week : Monday and Tuesday being
the two last and best days of the Carnival.

On the Monday afternoon at one or two o'clock, there
began to be a great rattling of carriages into the court-yard
of the hotel ; a hurrying to and fro of all the servants in it ;
and, now and then, a swift shooting across some doorway or
balcony, of a straggling stranger in a fancy dress : not yet
sufficiently well used to the same, to wear it with confidence,
and defy public opinion. All the carriages were open, and
had the linings carefully covered with white cotton or calico,
to prevent their proper decorations from being spoiled by
the incessant pelting of sugar-plums ; and people were packing and cramming into every vehicle as it waited for its
occupants, enormous sacks and baskets full of these confétti,
together with such heaps of flowers, tied up in little nosegays, that some carriages were not only brimful of flowers,
but literally running over : scattering, at every shake and jerk

of the springs, some of their abundance on the ground. Not to be behindhand in these essential particulars, we caused two very respectable sacks of sugar-plums (each about three feet high) and a large clothes-basket full of flowers to be conveyed into our hired barouche, with all speed. And from our place of observation, in one of the upper balconies of the hotel, we contemplated these arrangements with the liveliest satisfaction. The carriages now beginning to take up their company, and move away, we got into ours, and drove off too, armed with little wire masks for our faces; the sugarplums, like Falstaff's adulterated sack, having lime in their composition.

The Corso is a street a mile long; a street of shops, and palaces, and private houses, sometimes opening into a broad piazza. There are verandahs and balconies, of all shapes and sizes, to almost every house—not on one story alone, but often to one room or another on every story—put there in general with so little order or regularity, that if, year after year, and season after season, it had rained balconies, hailed balconies, snowed balconies, blown balconies, they could scarcely have come into existence in a more disorderly manner.

This is the great fountain-head and focus of the Carnival. But all the streets in which the Carnival is held, being vigilantly kept by dragoons, it is necessary for carriages, in the first instance, to pass, in line, down another thoroughfare, and so come into the Corso at the end remote from the Piázza del Popolo; which is one of its terminations. Accordingly, we fell into the string of coaches, and, for some time, jogged on quietly enough; now crawling on at a very slow walk; now trotting half-a-dozen yards; now backing fifty; and now stopping altogether: as the pressure in front obliged us. If any impetuous carriage dashed out of the rank and clattered forward, with the wild idea of getting on faster, it was suddenly met, or overtaken, by a trooper on horseback, who, deaf as his own drawn sword to all remonstrances, immediately escorted it back to the very end of the row, and made it a dim speck in the remotest perspective. Occasionally, we interchanged a volley of confétti with the carriage next in front, or the carriage next behind; but as yet, this capturing of stray and errant coaches by the military, was the chief amusement.

Presently, we came into a narrow street, where, besides one

line of carriages going, there was another line of carriages returning. Here the sugar-plums and the nosegays began to fly about, pretty smartly; and I was fortunate enough to observe one gentleman attired as a Greek warrior, catch a light-whiskered brigand on the nose (he was in the very act of tossing up a bouquet to a young lady in a first-floor window) with a precision that was much applauded by the bystanders. As this victorious Greek was exchanging a facetious remark with a stout gentleman in a doorway—one-half black and one-half white, as if he had been peeled up the middle—who had offered him his congratulations on this achievement, he received an orange from a house-top, full on his left ear, and was much surprised, not to say discomfited. Especially, as he was standing up at the time; and in consequence of the carriage moving on suddenly, at the same moment, staggered ignominiously, and buried himself among his flowers.

Some quarter of an hour of this sort of progress, brought us to the Corso; and anything so gay, so bright, and lively as the whole scene there, it would be difficult to imagine. From all the innumerable balconies: from the remotest and highest, no less than from the lowest and nearest: hangings of bright red, bright green, bright blue, white and gold, were fluttering in the brilliant sunlight. From windows, and from parapets, and tops of houses, streamers of the richest colours, and draperies of the gaudiest and most sparkling hues, were floating out upon the street. The buildings seemed to have been literally turned inside out, and to have all their gaiety towards the highway. Shop-fronts were taken down, and the windows filled with company, like boxes at a shining theatre; doors were carried off their hinges, and long tapestried groves, hung with garlands of flowers and evergreens, displayed within; builder's scaffoldings were gorgeous temples, radiant in silver, gold, and crimson; and in every nook and corner, from the pavement to the chimney-tops, where women's eyes could glisten, there they danced, and laughed, and sparkled, like the light in water. Every sort of bewitching madness of dress was there. Little preposterous scarlet jackets; quaint old stomachers, more wicked than the smartest bodices; Polish pelisses, strained and tight as ripe gooseberries; tiny Greek caps, all awry, and clinging to the dark hair, Heaven knows how; every wild, quaint, bold, shy, pettish, madcap fancy had its illustration in a dress; and every fancy was as dead forgotten by its owner, in the tumult of merriment, as if the three old aqueducts that still remain entire had brought Lethe into Rome, upon their sturdy arches, that morning.

The carriages were now three abreast; in broader places four; often stationary for a long time together; always one close mass of variegated brightness; showing, the whole streetful, through the storm of flowers, like flowers of a larger growth themselves. In some, the horses were richly caparisoned in magnificent trappings; in others they were decked from head to tail, with flowing ribbons. Some were driven by coachmen with enormous double faces: one face leering at the horses: the other cocking its extraordinary eyes into the carriage: and both rattling again, under the hail of sugar-plums. Other drivers were attired as women, wearing long ringlets and no bonnets, and looking more ridiculous in any real difficulty with the horses (of which, in such a concourse, there were a great many) than tongue can tell, or pen describe. Instead of sitting *in* the carriages, upon the seats, the handsome Roman women, to see and to be seen the better, sit in the heads of the barouches, at this time of general licence, with their feet upon the cushions—and oh the flowing skirts and dainty waists, the blessed shapes and laughing faces, the free, good-humoured, gallant figures that they make! There were great vans, too, full of handsome girls—thirty, or more together, perhaps—and the broadsides that were poured into, and poured out of, these fairy fire-shops, splashed the air with flowers and bon-bons for ten minutes at a time. Carriages, delayed long in one place, would begin a deliberate engagement with other carriages, or with people at the lower windows; and the spectators at some upper balcony or window, joining in the fray, and attacking both parties, would empty down great bags of confétti, that descended like a cloud, and in an instant made them white as millers. Still, carriages on carriages, dresses on dresses, colours on colours, crowds upon crowds, without end. Men and boys clinging to the wheels of coaches, and holding on behind, and following in their wake, and diving in among the horses' feet to pick up scattered flowers to sell again; maskers on foot (the drollest generally) in fantastic exaggerations of court-dresses, surveying the throng through enormous eye-glasses, and always transported with an ecstasy of love, on the discovery of any particularly old lady at a window; long strings of Policinelli, laying about them with blown bladders at the ends of sticks;

a waggonful of madmen, screaming and tearing to the life ;
a coachful of grave Mamelukes, with their horse-tail standard
set up in the midst ; a party of gipsy-women engaged in
terrific conflict with a shipful of sailors ; a man-monkey on a
pole, surrounded by strange animals with pigs' faces, and
lions' tails, carried under their arms, or worn gracefully over
their shoulders ; carriages on carriages, dresses on dresses,
colours on colours, crowds upon crowds, without end.   Not
many actual characters sustained, or represented, perhaps,
considering the number dressed, but the main pleasure of
the scene consisting in its perfect good temper ; in its bright,
and infinite, and flashing variety ; and in its entire abandonment to the mad humour of the time—an abandonment
so perfect, so contagious, so irresistible, that the steadiest
foreigner fights up to his middle in flowers and sugar-plums,
like the wildest Roman of them all, and thinks of nothing
else till half-past four o'clock, when he is suddenly reminded
(to his great regret) that this is not the whole business of his
existence, by hearing the trumpets sound, and seeing the
dragoons begin to clear the street.

How it ever *is* cleared for the race that takes place at five,
or how the horses ever go through the race, without going
over the people, is more than I can say.   But the carriages
get out into the by-streets, or up into the Piázza del Popolo,
and some people sit in temporary galleries in the latter place,
and tens of thousands line the Corso on both sides, when the
horses are brought out into the Piázza—to the foot of that
same column which, for centuries, looked down upon the
games and chariot-races in the Circus Maximus.

At a given signal they are started off.   Down the live lane,
the whole length of the Corso, they fly like the wind : rider-
less, as all the world knows : with shining ornaments upon
their backs, and twisted in their plaited manes : and with
heavy little balls stuck full of spikes, dangling at their sides,
to goad them on.   The jingling of these trappings, and the
rattling of their hoofs upon the hard stones ; the dash and
fury of their speed along the echoing street ; nay, the very
cannon that are fired—these noises are nothing to the roaring
of the multitude : their shouts : the clapping of their hands.
But it is soon over—almost instantaneously.   More cannon
shake the town.   The horses have plunged into the carpets
put across the street to stop them ; the goal is reached ; the
prizes are won (they are given, in part, by the poor Jews, as a

compromise for not running foot-races themselves); and there is an end to that day's sport.

But if the scene be bright, and gay, and crowded, on the last day but one, it attains, on the concluding day, to such a height of glittering colour, swarming life, and frolicsome uproar, that the bare recollection of it makes me giddy at this moment. The same diversions, greatly heightened and intensified in the ardour with which they are pursued, go on until the same hour. The race is repeated; the cannon are fired; the shouting and clapping of hands are renewed; the cannon are fired again; the race is over; and the prizes are won. But the carriages: ankle-deep with sugar-plums within, and so be-flowered and dusty without, as to be hardly recognisable for the same vehicles that they were, three hours ago: instead of scampering off in all directions, throng into the Corso, where they are soon wedged together in a scarcely moving mass. For the diversion of the Moccoletti, the last gay madness of the Carnival, is now at hand; and sellers of little tapers like what are called Christmas candles in England, are shouting lustily on every side, "Moccoli, Moccoli! Ecco Moccoli!"—a new item in the tumult; quite abolishing that other item of "Ecco Fiòri! Ecco Fior—r—r!" which has been making itself audible over all the rest, at intervals, the whole day through.

As the bright hangings and dresses are all fading into one dull, heavy, uniform colour in the decline of the day, lights begin flashing, here and there: in the windows, on the house-tops, in the balconies, in the carriages, in the hands of the foot-passengers: little by little: gradually, gradually: more and more: until the whole long street is one great glare and blaze of fire. Then, everybody present has but one engrossing object; that is, to extinguish other people's candles, and to keep his own alight; and everybody: man, woman, or child, gentleman or lady, prince or peasant, native or foreigner: yells and screams, and roars incessantly, as a taunt to the subdued, "Senza Moccolo, Senza Moccolo!" (Without a light! Without a light!) until nothing is heard but a gigantic chorus of those two words, mingled with peals of laughter.

The spectacle, at this time, is one of the most extraordinary that can be imagined. Carriages coming slowly by, with everybody standing on the seats or on the box, holding up their lights at arms' length, for greater safety; some in paper shades; some with a bunch of undefended little tapers, kindled altogether; some with blazing torches; some with feeble little candles; men on foot, creeping along, among the wheels, watching their opportunity, to make a spring at some particular light, and dash it out; other people climbing up into carriages, to get hold of them by main force; others, chasing some unlucky wanderer, round and round his own coach, to blow out the light he has begged or stolen somewhere, before he can ascend to his own company, and enable them to light their extinguished tapers; others, with their hats off, at a carriage-door, humbly beseeching some kind-hearted lady to oblige them with a light for a cigar, and when she is in the fulness of doubt whether to comply or no, blowing out the candle she is guarding so tenderly with her little hand; other people at the windows, fishing for candles with lines and hooks, or letting down long willow-wands with handkerchiefs at the end, and flapping them out, dexterously, when the bearer is at the height of his triumph; others, biding their time in corners, with immense extinguishers like halberds, and suddenly coming down upon glorious torches; others, gathered round one coach, and sticking to it; others, raining oranges and nosegays at an obdurate little lantern, or regularly storming a pyramid of men, holding up one man among them, who carries one feeble little wick above his head, with which he defies them all! Senza Moccolo! Senza Moccolo! Beautiful women, standing up in coaches, pointing in derision at extinguished lights, and clapping their hands, as they pass on crying, "Senza Moccolo! Senza Moccolo!" low balconies full of lovely faces and gay dresses, struggling with assailants in the streets; some repressing them as they climb up, some bending down, some leaning over, some shrinking back— delicate arms and bosoms—graceful figures—glowing lights, fluttering dresses, Senza Moccolo, Senza Moccoli, Senza Mocco-lo-o-o-o!—when in the wildest enthusiasm of the cry, and fullest ecstasy of the sport, the Ave Maria rings from the church steeples, and the Carnival is over in an instant—put out like a taper, with a breath!

There was a masquerade at the theatre at night, as dull and senseless as a London one, and only remarkable for the summary way in which the house was cleared at eleven o'clock: which was done by a line of soldiers forming along the wall, at the back of the stage, and sweeping the whole company out before them, like a broad broom. The game of the Moccoletti (the word, in the singular, Moccoletto, is the diminutive of Moccolo, and means a little lamp or candle-snuff) is supposed by some to be a ceremony of burlesque mourning for the death of the Carnival: candles being indispensable to Catholic grief. But whether it be so, or be a remnant of the ancient Saturnalia, or an incorporation of both, or have its origin in anything else, I shall always remember it, and the frolic, as a brilliant and most captivating sight: no less remarkable for the unbroken good-humour of all concerned, down to the very lowest (and among those who scaled the carriages, were many of the commonest men and boys), than for its innocent vivacity. For, odd as it may seem to say so, of a sport so full of thoughtlessness and personal display, it is as free from any taint of immodesty as any general mingling of the two sexes can possibly be ; and there seems to prevail, during its progress, a feeling of general, almost childish, simplicity and confidence, which one thinks of with a pang, when the Ave Maria has rung it away, for a whole year.

Availing ourselves of a part of the quiet interval between the termination of the Carnival and the beginning of the Holy Week: when everybody had run away from the one, and few people had yet begun to run back again for the other : we went conscientiously to work, to see Rome. And, by dint of going out early every morning, and coming back late every evening, and labouring hard all day, I believe we made acquaintance with every post and pillar in the city, and the country round; and, in particular, explored so many churches, that I abandoned that part of the enterprise at last, before it was half finished, lest I should never, of my own accord, go to church again, as long as I lived. But, I managed, almost every day, at one time or other, to get back to the Coliseum, and out upon the open Campagna, beyond the Tomb of Cecilia Metella.

We often encountered, in these expeditions, a company of English Tourists, with whom I had an ardent, but ungratified longing, to establish a speaking acquaintance. They were one Mr. Davis, and a small circle of friends. It was impossible not to know Mrs. Davis's name, from her being always in great request among her party, and her party being every-where. During the Holy Week, they were in every part of every scene of every ceremony. For a fortnight or three weeks before it, they were in every tomb, and every church, and every ruin, and every Picture Gallery ; and I hardly ever

observed Mrs. Davis to be silent for a moment.   Deep underground, high up in St. Peter's, out on the Campagna, and
stifling in the Jews' quarter, Mrs. Davis turned up, all the
same.   I don't think she ever saw anything, or ever looked
at anything; and she had always lost something out of a
straw hand-basket, and was trying to find it, with all her
might and main, among an immense quantity of English
halfpence, which lay, like sands upon the sea-shore, at the
bottom of it.   There was a professional Cicerone always
attached to the party (which had been brought over from
London, fifteen or twenty strong, by contract), and if he so
much as looked at Mrs. Davis, she invariably cut him short
by saying, "There, God bless the man, don't worrit me!   I
don't understand a word you say, and shouldn't if you was
to talk till you was black in the face!"   Mr. Davis always
had a snuff-coloured great-coat on, and carried a great green
umbrella in his hand, and had a slow curiosity constantly
devouring him, which prompted him to do extraordinary
things, such as taking the covers off urns in tombs, and
looking in at the ashes as if they were pickles—and tracing
out inscriptions with the ferrule of his umbrella, and saying,
with intense thoughtfulness, "Here's a B you see, and there's
a R, and this is the way we goes on in; is it?"   His anti-
quarian habits occasioned his being frequently in the rear of
the rest; and one of the agonies of Mrs. Davis, and the
party in general, was an ever-present fear that Davis would
be lost.   This caused them to scream for him, in the strangest
places, and at the most improper seasons.   And when he
came, slowly emerging out of some sepulchre or other, like a
peaceful Ghoul, saying "Here I am!" Mrs. Davis invariably
replied, "You'll be buried alive in a foreign country, Davis,
and it's no use trying to prevent you!"

Mr. and Mrs. Davis, and their party, had, probably, been
brought from London in about nine or ten days.   Eighteen
hundred years ago, the Roman legions under Claudius, protested against being led into Mr. and Mrs. Davis's country,
urging that it lay beyond the limits of the world.

Among what may be called the Cubs or minor Lions of
Rome, there was one that amused me mightily.   It is always
to be found there; and its den is on the great flight of steps
that lead from the Piazza di Spágna, to the church of Trínita
del Monte.   In plainer words, these steps are the great place
of resort for the artists' "Models," and there they are con-

stantly waiting to be hired. The first time I went up there, I could not conceive why the faces seemed familiar to me; why they appeared to have beset me, for years, in every possible variety of action and costume; and how it came to pass that they started up before me, in Rome, in the broad day, like so many saddled and bridled nightmares. I soon found that we had made acquaintance, and improved it, for several years, on the walls of various Exhibition Galleries. There is one old gentleman, with long white hair and an immense beard, who, to my knowledge, has gone half through the catalogue of the Royal Academy. This is the venerable, or patriarchal model. He carries a long staff; and every knot and twist in that staff I have seen, faithfully delineated, innumerable times. There is another man in a blue cloak, who always pretends to be asleep in the sun (when there is any), and who, I need but say, is always very wide awake, and very attentive to the disposition of his legs. This is the *dolce far' niente* model. There is another man in a brown cloak, who leans against a wall, with his arms folded in his mantle, and looks out of the corners of his eyes; which are just visible beneath his broad slouched hat. This is the assassin model. There is another man, who constantly looks over his own shoulder, and is always going away, but never does. This is the haughty, or scornful model. As to Domestic Happiness, and Holy Families, they should come very cheap, for there are lumps of them, all up the steps; and the cream of the thing is, that they are all the falsest vagabonds in the world, especially made up for the purpose, and having no counterparts in Rome or any other part of the habitable globe.

My recent mention of the Carnival, reminds me of its being said to be a mock mourning (in the ceremony with which it closes), for the gaieties and merry-makings before Lent; and this again reminds me of the real funerals and mourning processions of Rome, which, like those in most other parts of Italy, are rendered chiefly remarkable to a Foreigner, by the indifference with which the mere clay is universally regarded, after life has left it. And this is not from the survivors having had time to dissociate the memory of the dead from their well-remembered appearance and form on earth; for the interment follows too speedily after death, for that: almost always taking place within four-and-twenty hours, and, sometimes, within twelve.

At Rome, there is the same arrangement of Pits in a great, bleak, open, dreary space, that I have already described as existing in Genoa. When I visited it, at noonday, I saw a solitary coffin of plain deal: uncovered by any shroud or pall, and so slightly made, that the hoof of any wandering mule would have crushed it in : carelessly tumbled down, all on one side, on the door of one of the pits—and there left, by itself, in the wind and sunshine. "How does it come to be left here ? " I asked the man who showed me the place. "It was brought here half an hour ago, Signore," he said. I remembered to have met the procession, on its return: straggling away at a good round pace. "When will it be put in the pit ? " I asked him. "When the cart comes, and it is opened to-night," he said. "How much does it cost to be brought here in this way, instead of coming in the cart ? " I asked him. "Ten scudi," he said (about two pounds, two-and-sixpence, English). "The other bodies, for whom nothing is paid, are taken to the church of the Santa Maria della Consolázione," he continued, "and brought here altogether, in the cart at night." I stood, a moment, looking at the coffin, which had two initial letters scrawled upon the top ; and turned away, with an expression in my face, I suppose, of not much liking its exposure in that manner: for he said, shrugging his shoulders with great vivacity, and giving a pleasant smile, " But he's dead, Signore, he's dead. Why not ? "

Among the innumerable churches, there is one I must select for separate mention. It is the church of the Ara Cœli, supposed to be built on the site of the old Temple of Jupiter Feretrius ; and approached, on one side, by a long steep flight of steps, which seem incomplete without some group of bearded soothsayers on the top. It is remarkable for the possession of a miraculous Bambíno, or wooden doll, representing the Infant Saviour ; and I first saw this miraculous Bambíno, in legal phrase, in manner following, that is to say:

We had strolled into the church one afternoon, and were looking down its long vista of gloomy pillars (for all these ancient churches built upon the ruins of old temples, are dark and sad), when the Brave came running in, with a grin upon his face that stretched it from ear to ear, and implored us to follow him, without a moment's delay, as they were going to show the Bambíno to a select party. We accord·

ingly hurried off to a sort of chapel, or sacristy, hard by the chief altar, but not in the church itself, where the select party, consisting of two or three Catholic gentlemen and ladies (not Italians), were already assembled: and where one hollow-cheeked young monk was lighting up divers candles, while another was putting on some clerical robes over his coarse brown habit. The candles were on a kind of altar, and above it were two delectable figures, such as you would see at any English fair, representing the Holy Virgin, and Saint Joseph, as I suppose, bending in devotion over a wooden box, or coffer; which was shut.

The hollow-cheeked monk, number One, having finished lighting the candles, went down on his knees, in a corner, before this set-piece; and the monk number Two, having put on a pair of highly ornamented and gold-bespattered gloves, lifted down the coffer, with great reverence, and set it on the altar. Then, with many genuflexions, and muttering certain prayers, he opened it, and let down the front, and took off sundry coverings of satin and lace from the inside. The ladies had been on their knees from the commencement; and the gentlemen now dropped down devoutly, as he exposed to view a little wooden doll, in face very like General Tom Thumb, the American Dwarf: gorgeously dressed in satin and gold lace, and actually blazing with rich jewels. There was scarcely a spot upon its little breast, or neck, or stomach, but was sparkling with the costly offerings of the Faithful. Presently, he lifted it out of the box, and carrying it round among the kneelers, set its face against the forehead of every one, and tendered its clumsy foot to them to kiss—a ceremony which they all performed down to a dirty little ragamuffin of a boy who had walked in from the street. When this was done, he laid it in the box again: and the company, rising, drew near, and commended the jewels in whispers. In good time, he replaced the coverings, shut up the box, put it back in its place, locked up the whole concern (Holy Family and all) behind a pair of folding-doors; took off his priestly vestments; and received the customary "small charge," while his companion, by means of an extinguisher fastened to the end of a long stick, put out the lights, one after another. The candles being all extinguished, and the money all collected, they retired, and so did the spectators.

I met this same Bambíno, in the street a short time afterwards, going, in great state, to the house of some sick person.

O

It is taken to all parts of Rome for this purpose, constantly;
but, I understand that it is not always as successful as could
be wished ; for, making its appearance at the bedside of weak
and nervous people in extremity, accompanied by a numerous
escort, it not unfrequently frightens them to death.   It is
most popular in cases of childbirth, where it has done such
wonders, that if a lady be longer than usual in getting
through her difficulties, a messenger is dispatched, with all
speed, to solicit the immediate attendance of the Bambino.
It is a very valuable property, and much confided in—
especially by the religious body to whom it belongs.

I am happy to know that it is not considered immaculate,
by some who are good Catholics, and who are behind the
scenes, from what was told me by the near relation of a
Priest, himself a Catholic, and a gentleman of learning and
intelligence.   This Priest made my informant promise that
he would, on no account, allow the Bambino to be borne
into the bedroom of a sick lady, in whom they were both
interested.   "For," said he, "if they (the monks) trouble her
with it, and intrude themselves into her room, it will certainly
kill her."   My informant accordingly looked out of the window
when it came ; and, with many thanks, declined to open the
door.   He endeavoured, in another case of which he had no
other knowledge than such as he gained as a passer-by at
the moment, to prevent its being carried into a small unwholesome chamber, where a poor girl was dying.   But, he
strove against it unsuccessfully, and she expired while the
crowd were pressing round her bed.

Among the people who drop into St. Peter's at their
leisure, to kneel on the pavement, and say a quiet prayer,
there are certain schools and seminaries, priestly and otherwise, that come in, twenty or thirty strong.   These boys
always kneel down in single file, one behind the other, with
a tall grim master in a black gown, bringing up the rear:
like a pack of cards arranged to be tumbled down at a touch,
with a disproportionately large Knave of clubs at the end.
When they have had a minute or so at the chief altar, they
scramble up, and filing off to the chapel of the Madonna, or
the sacrament, flop down again in the same order ; so that
if anybody *did* stumble against the master, a general and
sudden overthrow of the whole line must inevitably ensue.

The scene in all the churches is the strangest possible.
The same monotonous, heartless, drowsy chaunting, always

going on; the same dark building, darker from the brightness of the street without; the same lamps dimly burning; the self-same people kneeling here and there; turned towards you, from one altar or other, the same priest's back, with the same large cross embroidered on it; however different in size, in shape, in wealth, in architecture, this church is from that, it is the same thing still. There are the same dirty beggars stopping in their muttered prayers to beg; the same miserable cripples exhibiting their deformity at the doors; the same blind men, rattling little pots like kitchen pepper-castors: their depositories for alms; the same preposterous crowns of silver stuck upon the painted heads of single saints and Virgins in crowded pictures, so that a little figure on a mountain has a head-dress bigger than the temple in the fore-ground, or adjacent miles of landscape; the same favourite shrine or figure, smothered with little silver hearts and crosses, and the like: the staple trade and show of all the jewellers; the same odd mixture of respect and indecorum, faith and phlegm: kneeling on the stones, and spitting on them, loudly; getting up from prayers to beg a little, or to pursue some other worldly matter: and then kneeling down again, to resume the contrite supplication at the point where it was interrupted. In one church, a kneeling lady got up from her prayer, for a moment, to offer us her card, as a teacher of Music; and in another, a sedate gentleman with a very thick walking-staff, arose from his devotions to belabour his dog, who was growling at another dog: and whose yelps and howls resounded through the church, as his master quietly relapsed into his former train of meditation—keeping his eye upon the dog, at the same time, nevertheless.

Above all, there is always a receptacle for the contributions of the Faithful, in some form or other. Sometimes, it is a money-box, set up between the worshipper, and the wooden life-size figure of the Redeemer; sometimes, it is a little chest for the maintenance of the Virgin; sometimes, an appeal on behalf of a popular Bambíno; sometimes, a bag at the end of a long stick, thrust among the people here and there, and vigilantly jingled by an active Sacristan; but there it always is, and, very often, in many shapes in the same church, and doing pretty well in all. Nor, is it wanting in the open air —the streets and roads—for, often as you are walking along, thinking about anything rather than a tin canister, that object pounces out upon you from a little house by the wayside;

and on its top is painted, " For the Souls in Purgatory ; " an appeal which the bearer repeats a great many times, as he rattles it before you, much as Punch rattles the cracked bell which his sanguine disposition makes an organ of.

And this reminds me that some Roman altars of peculiar sanctity, bear the inscription, " Every Mass performed at this altar frees a soul from Purgatory." I have never been able to find out the charge for one of these services, but they should needs be expensive. There are several Crosses in Rome too, the kissing of which, confers indulgences for varying terms. That in the centre of the Coliseum, is worth a hundred days ; and people may be seen kissing it from morning to night. It is curious that some of these crosses seem to acquire an arbitrary popularity: this very one among them. In another part of the Coliseum there is a cross upon a marble slab, with the inscription, " Who kisses this cross shall be entitled to Two hundred and forty days' indulgence." But I saw no one person kiss it, though, day after day, I sat in the arena, and saw scores upon scores of peasants pass it, on their way to kiss the other.

To single out details from the great dream of Roman Churches, would be the wildest occupation in the world. But St. Stefano Rotondo, a damp, mildewed vault of an old church in the outskirts of Rome, will always struggle upper-most in my mind, by reason of the hideous paintings with which its walls are covered. These represent the martyrdoms of saints and early Christians ; and such a panorama of horror and butchery no man could imagine in his sleep, though he were to eat a whole pig raw, for supper. Grey-bearded men being boiled, fried, grilled, crimped, singed, eaten by wild beasts, worried by dogs, buried alive, torn asunder by horses, chopped up small with hatchets : women having their breasts torn with iron pinchers, their tongues cut out, their ears screwed off, their jaws broken, their bodies stretched upon the rack, or skinned upon the stake, or crackled up and melted in the fire : these are among the mildest subjects. So insisted on, and laboured at, besides, that every sufferer gives you the same occasion for wonder as poor old Duncan awoke, in Lady Macbeth, when she mar-velled at his having so much blood in him.

There is an upper chamber in the Mamertine prisons, over what is said to have been—and very possibly may have been —the dungeon of St. Peter. This chamber is now fitted up as an oratory, dedicated to that saint; and it lives, as a distinct and separate place, in my recollection, too. It is very small and low-roofed; and the dread and gloom of the ponderous, obdurate old prison are on it, as if they had come up in a dark mist through the floor. Hanging on the walls, among the clustered votive offerings, are objects, at once strangely in keeping, and strangely at variance, with the place—rusty daggers, knives, pistols, clubs, divers instruments of violence and murder, brought here, fresh from use, and hung up to propitiate offended Heaven: as if the blood upon them would drain off in consecrated air, and have no voice to cry with. It is all so silent and so close, and tomb-like; and the dungeons below are so black and stealthy, and stagnant, and naked; that this little dark spot becomes a dream within a dream: and in the vision of great churches which come rolling past me like a sea, it is a small wave by itself, that melts into no other wave, and does not flow on with the rest.

It is an awful thing to think of the enormous caverns that are entered from some Roman churches, and undermine the city. Many churches have crypts and subterranean chapels of great size, which, in the ancient time, were baths, and secret chambers of temples, and what not; but I do not speak of them. Beneath the church of St. Giovanni and St. Paolo, there are the jaws of a terrific range of caverns, hewn out of the rock, and said to have another outlet underneath the Coliseum—tremendous darknesses of vast extent, half-buried in the earth and unexplorable, where the dull torches, flashed by the attendants, glimmer down long ranges of distant vaults branching to the right and left, like streets in a city of the dead; and show the cold damp stealing down the walls, drip-drop, drip-drop, to join the pools of water that lie here and there, and never saw, or never will see, one ray of the sun. Some accounts make these the prisons of the wild beasts destined for the amphitheatre; some the prisons of the condemned gladiators; some, both. But the legend most appalling to the fancy is, that in the upper range (for there are two stories of these caves) the Early Christians destined to be eaten at the Coliseum Shows, heard the wild beasts, hungry for them, roaring down below; until, upon the night and solitude of their captivity, there burst the sudden noon and life of the vast theatre crowded to the parapet, and of these, their dreaded neighbours, bounding in!

Below the church of San Sebastiano, two miles beyond the gate of San Sebastiano, on the Appian Way, is the entrance to the catacombs of Rome—quarries in the old time, but afterwards the hiding-places of the Christians. These ghastly passages have been explored for twenty miles; and form a chain of labyrinths, sixty miles in circumference.

A gaunt Franciscan friar, with a wild bright eye, was our only guide, down into this profound and dreadful place. The narrow ways and openings hither and thither, coupled with the dead and heavy air, soon blotted out, in all of us, any recollection of the track by which we had come: and I could not help thinking "Good Heaven, if, in a sudden fit of madness, he should dash the torches out, or if he should be seized with a fit, what would become of us!" On we wandered, among martyrs' graves: passing great subterranean vaulted roads, diverging in all directions, and choked up with heaps of stones, that thieves and murderers may not take refuge there, and form a population under Rome, even worse than that which lives between it and the sun. Graves, graves, graves; Graves of men, of women, of their little children, who ran crying to the persecutors, "We are Christians! We are Christians!" that they might be murdered with their parents; Graves with the palm of martyrdom roughly cut into their stone boundaries, and little niches, made to hold a vessel of the martyrs' blood; Graves of some who lived down here, for years together, ministering to the rest, and preaching truth, and hope, and comfort, from the rude altars, that bear witness to their fortitude at this hour; more roomy graves, but far more terrible, where hundreds, being surprised, were hemmed in and walled up: buried before Death, and killed by slow starvation.

"The Triumphs of the Faith are not above ground in our splendid churches," said the friar, looking round upon us, as we stopped to rest in one of the low passages, with bones and dust surrounding us on every side. "They are here! Among the Martyrs' Graves!" He was a gentle, earnest man, and said it from his heart; but when I thought how Christian men have dealt with one another; how, perverting our most merciful religion, they have hunted down and tortured, burnt and beheaded, strangled, slaughtered, and oppressed each other; I pictured to myself an agony surpassing any that this Dust had suffered with the breath of life yet lingering in it, and how these great and constant hearts

In the Catacombs

would have been shaken—how they would have quailed and drooped—if a foreknowledge of the deeds that professing Christians would commit in the Great Name for which they died, could have rent them with its own unutterable anguish, on the cruel wheel, and bitter cross, and in the fearful fire.

Such are the spots and patches in my dream of churches, that remain apart, and keep their separate identity. I have a fainter recollection, sometimes of the relics; of the fragments of the pillar of the Temple that was rent in twain; of the portion of the table that was spread for the Last Supper; of the well at which the woman of Samaria gave water to Our Saviour; of two columns from the house of Pontius Pilate; of the stone to which the Sacred hands were bound, when the scourging was performed; of the gridiron of Saint Lawrence, and the stone below it, marked with the frying of his fat and blood; these set a shadowy mark on some cathedrals, as an old story, or a fable might, and stop them for an instant, as they flit before me. The rest is a vast wilderness of consecrated buildings of all shapes and fancies, blending one with another; of battered pillars of old Pagan temples, dug up from the ground, and forced, like giant captives, to support the roofs of Christian churches; of pictures, bad, and wonderful, and impious, and ridiculous; of kneeling people, curling incense, tinkling bells, and sometimes (but not often) of a swelling organ: of Madonne, with their breasts stuck full of swords, arranged in a half-circle like a modern fan; of actual skeletons of dead saints, hideously attired in gaudy satins, silks, and velvets trimmed with gold: their withered crust of skull adorned with precious jewels, or with chaplets of crushed flowers; sometimes, of people gathered round the pulpit, and a monk within it stretching out the crucifix, and preaching fiercely: the sun just streaming down through some high window on the sail-cloth stretched above him and across the church, to keep his high-pitched voice from being lost among the echoes of the roof. Then my tired memory comes out upon a flight of steps, where knots of people are asleep, or basking in the light; and strolls away, among the rags, and smells, and palaces, and hovels, of an old Italian street.

On one Saturday morning (the eighth of March), a man was beheaded here. Nine or ten months before, he had waylaid a Bavarian countess, travelling as a pilgrim to Rome—

alone and on foot, of course—and performing, it is said, that
act of piety for the fourth time.   He saw her change a piece
of gold at Viterbo, where he lived ; followed her ; bore her
company on her journey for some forty miles or more, on the
treacherous pretext of protecting her ; attacked her, in the
fulfilment of his unrelenting purpose, on the Campagna,
within a very short distance of Rome, near to what is called
(but what is not) the Tomb of Nero ; robbed her ; and beat
her to death with her own pilgrim's staff.   He was newly
married, and gave some of her apparel to his wife : saying
that he had bought it at a fair.   She, however, who had
seen the pilgrim-countess passing through their town, recognised some trifle as having belonged to her.   Her husband
then told her what he had done.   She, in confession, told
a priest ; and the man was taken, within four days after the
commission of the murder.

There are no fixed times for the administration of justice,
or its execution, in this unaccountable country ; and he had
been in prison ever since.   On the Friday, as he was dining
with the other prisoners, they came and told him he was to
be beheaded next morning, and took him away.   It is very
unusual to execute in Lent ; but his crime being a very bad
one, it was deemed advisable to make an example of him at
that time, when great numbers of pilgrims were coming
towards Rome, from all parts, for the Holy Week.   I heard
of this on the Friday evening, and saw the bills up at the
churches, calling on the people to pray for the criminal's soul.
So, I determined to go, and see him executed.

The beheading was appointed for fourteen and a-half
o'clock, Roman time : or a quarter before nine in the forenoon.   I had two friends with me ; and as we did not know
but that the crowd might be very great, we were on the
spot by half-past seven.   The place of execution was near the
church of San Giovanni decolláto (a doubtful compliment to
Saint John the Baptist) in one of the impassable back streets
without any footway, of which a great part of Rome is composed—a street of rotten houses, which do not seem to belong
to anybody, and do not seem to have ever been inhabited,
and certainly were never built on any plan, or for any particular purpose, and have no window-sashes, and are a little
like deserted breweries, and might be warehouses but for
having nothing in them.   Opposite to one of these, a white
house, the scaffold was built.   An untidy, unpainted, uncouth,

crazy-looking thing of course : some seven feet high, perhaps :
with a tall, gallows-shaped frame rising above it, in which
was the knife, charged with a ponderous mass of iron, all
ready to descend, and glittering brightly in the morning sun,
whenever it looked out, now and then, from behind a cloud.

There were not many people lingering about; and these
were kept at a considerable distance from the scaffold, by
parties of the Pope's dragoons.   Two or three hundred foot-
soldiers were under arms, standing at ease in clusters here
and there ; and the officers were walking up and down in
twos and threes, chatting together, and smoking cigars.

At the end of the street, was an open space, where there
would be a dust-heap, and piles of broken crockery, and
mounds of vegetable refuse, but for such things being thrown
anywhere and everywhere in Rome, and favouring no particular sort of locality.   We got into a kind of wash-house,
belonging to a dwelling-house on this spot; and standing
there in an old cart, and on a heap of cart-wheels piled
against the wall, looked, through a large grated window, at
the scaffold, and straight down the street beyond it, until, in
consequence of its turning off abruptly to the left, our perspective was brought to a sudden termination, and had a
corpulent officer, in a cocked hat, for its crowning feature.

Nine o'clock struck, and ten o'clock struck, and nothing
happened.   All the bells of all the churches rang as usual.
A little parliament of dogs assembled in the open space, and
chased each other, in and out among the soldiers.   Fierce-
looking Romans of the lowest class, in blue cloaks, russet
cloaks, and rags uncloaked, came and went, and talked
together.   Women and children fluttered, on the skirts of
the scanty crowd.   One large muddy spot was left quite bare,
like a bald place on a man's head.   A cigar-merchant, with
an earthen pot of charcoal ashes in one hand, went up and
down, crying his wares.   A pastry-merchant divided his
attention between the scaffold and his customers.   Boys tried
to climb up walls, and tumbled down again.   Priests and
monks elbowed a passage for themselves among the people,
and stood on tiptoe for a sight of the knife : then went
away.   Artists, in inconceivable hats of the middle-ages, and
beards (thank Heaven !) of no age at all, flashed picturesque
scowls about them from their stations in the throng.   One
gentleman (connected with the fine arts, I presume) went up
and down in a pair of Hessian-boots, with a red beard hang-

ing down on his breast, and his long and bright red hair, plaited into two tails, one on either side of his head, which fell over his shoulders in front of him, very nearly to his waist, and were carefully entwined and braided!

Eleven o'clock struck; and still nothing happened. A rumour got about, among the crowd, that the criminal would not confess; in which case, the priests would keep him until the Ave Maria (sunset); for it is their merciful custom never finally to turn the crucifix away from a man at that pass, as one refusing to be shriven, and consequently a sinner abandoned of the Saviour, until then. People began to drop off. The officers shrugged their shoulders and looked doubtful. The dragoons, who came riding up below our window, every now and then, to order an unlucky hackney-coach or cart away, as soon as it had comfortably established itself, and was covered with exulting people (but never before), became imperious, and quick-tempered. The bald place hadn't a straggling hair upon it; and the corpulent officer, crowning the perspective, took a world of snuff.

Suddenly, there was a noise of trumpets. "Attention!" was among the foot-soldiers instantly. They were marched up to the scaffold and formed round it. The dragoons galloped to their nearer stations too. The guillotine became the centre of a wood of bristling bayonets and shining sabres. The people closed round nearer, on the flank of the soldiery. A long straggling stream of men and boys, who had accompanied the procession from the prison, came pouring into the open space. The bald spot was scarcely distinguishable from the rest. The cigar and pastry-merchants resigned all thoughts of business, for the moment, and abandoning themselves wholly to pleasure, got good situations in the crowd. The perspective ended, now, in a troop of dragoons. And the corpulent officer, sword in hand, looked hard at a church close to him, which he could see, but we, the crowd, could not.

After a short delay, some monks were seen approaching to the scaffold from this church; and above their heads, coming on slowly and gloomily, the effigy of Christ upon the cross, canopied with black. This was carried round the foot of the scaffold, to the front, and turned towards the criminal, that he might see it to the last. It was hardly in its place, when he appeared on the platform, bare-footed; his hands bound; and with the collar and neck of his shirt cut away, almost to the shoulder. A young man—six-and-twenty—vigorously made, and well-shaped. Face pale; small dark moustache; and dark brown hair.

He had refused to confess, it seemed, without first having his wife brought to see him; and they had sent an escort for her, which had occasioned the delay.

He immediately kneeled down, below the knife. His neck fitting into a hole, made for the purpose, in a cross plank, was shut down, by another plank above; exactly like the pillory. Immediately below him was a leathern bag. And into it his head rolled instantly.

The executioner was holding it by the hair, and walking with it round the scaffold, showing it to the people, before one quite knew that the knife had fallen heavily, and with a rattling sound.

When it had travelled round the four sides of the scaffold, it was set upon a pole in front—a little patch of black and white, for the long street to stare at, and the flies to settle on. The eyes were turned upward, as if he had avoided the sight of the leathern bag, and looked to the crucifix. Every tinge and hue of life had left it in that instant. It was dull, cold, livid, wax. The body also.

There was a great deal of blood. When we left the window, and went close up to the scaffold, it was very dirty; one of the two men who were throwing water over it, turning to help the other lift the body into a shell, picked his way as through mire. A strange appearance was the apparent annihilation of the neck. The head was taken off so close, that it seemed as if the knife had narrowly escaped crushing the jaw, or shaving off the ear; and the body looked as if there were nothing left above the shoulder.

Nobody cared, or was at all affected. There was no manifestation of disgust, or pity, or indignation, or sorrow. My empty pockets were tried, several times, in the crowd immediately below the scaffold, as the corpse was being put into its coffin. It was an ugly, filthy, careless, sickening spectacle; meaning nothing but butchery beyond the momentary interest, to the one wretched actor. Yes! Such a sight has one meaning and one warning. Let me not forget it. The speculators in the lottery, station themselves at favourable points for counting the gouts of blood that spirt out, here or there; and buy that number. It is pretty sure to have a run upon it.

The body was carted away in due time, the knife cleansed,

the scaffold taken down, and all the hideous apparatus
removed. The executioner : an outlaw *ex officio* (what a satire
on the Punishment !) who dare not, for his life, cross the
Bridge of St. Angelo but to do his work : retreated to his
lair, and the show was over.

At the head of the collections in the palaces of Rome, the
Vatican, of course, with its treasures of art, its enormous
galleries, and staircases, and suites upon suites of immense
chambers, ranks highest and stands foremost. Many most
noble statues, and wonderful pictures, are there ; nor is it
heresy to say that there is a considerable amount of rubbish
there, too. When any old piece of sculpture dug out of the
ground, finds a place in a gallery because it is old, and
without any reference to its intrinsic merits : and finds
admirers by the hundred, because it is there, and for no other
reason on earth : there will be no lack of objects, very indifferent in the plain eyesight of any one who employs so
vulgar a property, when he may wear the spectacles of Cant
for less than nothing, and establish himself as a man of taste
for the mere trouble of putting them on.
     I unreservedly confess, for myself, that I cannot leave my
natural perception of what is natural and true, at a palace-
door, in Italy or elsewhere, as I should leave my shoes if
I were travelling in the East. I cannot forget that there are
certain expressions of face, natural to certain passions, and
as unchangeable in their nature as the gait of a lion, or the
flight of an eagle. I cannot dismiss from my certain knowledge, such commonplace facts as the ordinary proportion
of men's arms, and legs, and heads ; and when I meet with
performances that do violence to these experiences and
recollections, no matter where they may be, I cannot honestly
admire them, and think it best to say so ; in spite of high
critical advice that we should sometimes feign an admiration,
though we have it not.
     Therefore, I freely acknowledge that when I see a Jolly
young Waterman representing a cherubim, or a Barclay and
Perkins's Drayman depicted as an Evangelist, I see nothing
to commend or admire in the performance, however great its
reputed Painter. Neither am I partial to libellous Angels,
who play on fiddles and bassoons, for the edification of sprawling monks apparently in liquor. Nor to those Monsieur
Tonsons of galleries, Saint Francis and Saint Sebastian ; both

of whom I submit should have very uncommon and rare merits, as works of art, to justify their compound multiplication by Italian Painters.

It seems to me, too, that the indiscriminate and determined raptures in which some critics indulge, is incompatible with the true appreciation of the really great and transcendent works. I cannot imagine, for example, how the resolute champion of undeserving pictures can soar to the amazing beauty of Titian's great picture of the Assumption of the Virgin at Venice; or how the man who is truly affected by the sublimity of that exquisite production, or who is truly sensible of the beauty of Tintoretto's great picture of the Assembly of the Blessed in the same place, can discern in Michael Angelo's Last Judgment, in the Sistine chapel, any general idea, or one pervading thought, in harmony with the stupendous subject. He who will contemplate Raphael's masterpiece, the Transfiguration, and will go away into another chamber of that same Vatican, and contemplate another design of Raphael, representing (in incredible caricature) the miraculous stopping of a great fire by Leo the Fourth—and who will say that he admires them both, as works of extraordinary genius—must, as I think, be wanting in his powers of perception in one of the two instances, and, probably, in the high and lofty one.

It is easy to suggest a doubt, but I have a great doubt whether, sometimes, the rules of art are not too strictly observed, and whether it is quite well or agreeable that we should know beforehand, where this figure will be turning round, and where that figure will be lying down, and where there will be drapery in folds, and so forth. When I observe heads inferior to the subject, in pictures of merit, in Italian galleries, I do not attach that reproach to the Painter, for I have a suspicion that these great men, who were, of necessity, very much in the hands of monks and priests, painted monks and priests a great deal too often. I frequently see, in pictures of real power, heads quite below the story and the painter: and I invariably observe that those heads are of the Convent stamp, and have their counterparts among the Convent inmates of this hour; so, I have settled with myself that, in such cases, the lameness was not with the painter, but with the vanity and ignorance of certain of his employers, who would be apostles—on canvas, at all events.

The exquisite grace and beauty of Canova's statues; the

wonderful gravity and repose of many of the ancient works
in sculpture, both in the Capitol and the Vatican; and the
strength and fire of many others; are, in their different ways,
beyond all reach of words.   They are especially impressive
and delightful, after the works of Bernini and his disciples,
in which the churches of Rome, from St. Peter's downward,
abound; and which are, I verily believe, the most detestable
class of productions in the wide world.   I would infinitely
rather (as mere works of art) look upon the three deities of
the Past, the Present, and the Future, in the Chinese Collection, than upon the best of these breezy maniacs; whose
every fold of drapery is blown inside-out; whose smallest
vein, or artery, is as big as an ordinary forefinger; whose
hair is like a nest of lively snakes; and whose attitudes put
all other extravagance to shame.   Insomuch that I do
honestly believe, there can be no place in the world, where
such intolerable abortions, begotten of the sculptor's chisel,
are to be found in such profusion, as in Rome.

There is a fine collection of Egyptian antiquities, in the
Vatican; and the ceilings of the rooms in which they are
arranged, are painted to represent a starlight sky in the
Desert.   It may seem an odd idea, but it is very effective.
The grim, half-human monsters from the temples, look more
grim and monstrous underneath the deep dark blue; it sheds
a strange uncertain gloomy air on everything—a mystery
adapted to the objects; and you leave them, as you find them,
shrouded in a solemn night.

In the private places, pictures are seen to the best advantage.   There are seldom so many in one place that the attention need become distracted, or the eye confused.   You see
them very leisurely; and are rarely interrupted by a crowd of
people.   There are portraits innumerable, by Titian, and
Rembrandt, and Vandyke; heads by Guido, and Domenichino, and Carlo Dolci; various subjects by Correggio, and
Murillo, and Raphael, and Salvator Rosa, and Spagnoletto—
many of which it would be difficult, indeed, to praise too
highly, or to praise enough; such is their tenderness and
grace; their noble elevation, purity, and beauty.

The portrait of Beatrice di Cenci, in the Palazzo Berberini,
is a picture almost impossible to be forgotten.   Through the
transcendent sweetness and beauty of the face, there is a
something shining out, that haunts me.   I see it now, as I
see this paper, or my pen.   The head is loosely draped in

white; the light hair falling down below the linen folds. She has turned suddenly towards you; and there is an expression in the eyes—although they are very tender and gentle—as if the wildness of a momentary terror, or distraction, had been struggled with and overcome, that instant; and nothing but a celestial hope, and a beautiful sorrow, and a desolate earthly helplessness remained. Some stories say that Guido painted it, the night before her execution; some other stories, that he painted it from memory, after having seen her, on her way to the scaffold. I am willing to believe that, as you see her on his canvas, so she turned towards him, in the crowd, from the first sight of the axe, and stamped upon his mind a look which he has stamped on mine as though I had stood beside him in the concourse. The guilty palace of the Cenci: blighting a whole quarter of the town, as it stands withering away by grains: had that face, to my fancy, in its dismal porch, and at its black blind windows, and flitting up and down its dreary stairs, and growing out of the darkness of the ghostly galleries. The History is written in the Painting; written, in the dying girl's face, by Nature's own hand. And oh! how in that one touch she puts to flight (instead of making kin) the puny world that claim to be related to her, in right of poor conventional forgeries!

I saw in the Palazzo Spada, the statue of Pompey; the statue at whose base Cæsar fell. A stern, tremendous figure! I imagined one of greater finish: of the last refinement: full of delicate touches: losing its distinctness, in the giddy eyes of one whose blood was ebbing before it, and settling into some such rigid majesty as this, as Death came creeping over the upturned face.

The excursions in the neighbourhood of Rome are charming, and would be full of interest were it only for the changing views they afford, of the wild Campagna. But, every inch of ground, in every direction, is rich in associations, and in natural beauties. There is Albano, with its lovely lake and wooded shore, and with its wine, that certainly has not improved since the days of Horace, and in these times hardly justifies his panegyric. There is squalid Tivoli, with the river Anio, diverted from its course, and plunging down, headlong, some eighty feet in search of it. With its picturesque Temple of the Sibyl, perched high on a crag; its minor waterfalls glancing and sparkling in the sun; and one good cavern yawning darkly, where the river takes a

fearful plunge and shoots on, low down under beetling rocks.
There, too, is the Villa d'Este, deserted and decaying among
groves of melancholy pine and cypress trees, where it seems
to lie in state. Then, there is Frascati, and, on the steep
above it, the ruins of Tusculum, where Cicero lived, and
wrote, and adorned his favourite house (some fragments of
it may yet be seen there), and where Cato was born. We
saw its ruined amphitheatre on a grey dull day, when a shrill
March wind was blowing, and when the scattered stones of
the old city lay strewn about the lonely eminence, as desolate
and dead as the ashes of a long-extinguished fire.

One day we walked out, a little party of three, to Albano,
fourteen miles distant ; possessed by a great desire to go
there by the ancient Appian way, long since ruined and overgrown. We started at half-past seven in the morning, and
within an hour or so were out upon the open Campagna. For
twelve miles we went climbing on, over an unbroken succession of mounds, and heaps, and hills, of ruin. Tombs and
temples, overthrown and prostrate ; small fragments of
columns, friezes, pediments ; great blocks of granite and
marble ; mouldering arches, grass-grown and decayed ; ruin
enough to build a spacious city from ; lay strewn about us.
Sometimes, loose walls, built up from these fragments by
the shepherds, came across our path ; sometimes, a ditch
between two mounds of broken stones, obstructed our progress ; sometimes, the fragments themselves, rolling from
beneath our feet, made it a toilsome matter to advance ; but
it was always ruin. Now, we tracked a piece of the old road,
above the ground ; now traced it, underneath a grassy covering, as if that were its grave ; but all the way was ruin. In
the distance, ruined aqueducts went stalking on their giant
course along the plain ; and every breath of wind that swept
towards us, stirred early flowers and grasses, springing up,
spontaneously, on miles of ruin. The unseen larks above
us, who alone disturbed the awful silence, had their nests in
ruin ; and the fierce herdsmen, clad in sheepskins, who now
and then scowled out upon us from their sleeping nooks,
were housed in ruin. The aspect of the desolate Campagna
in one direction, where it was most level, reminded me of
an American prairie ; but what is the solitude of a region
where men have never dwelt, to that of a Desert, where a
mighty race have left their footprints in the earth from which
they have vanished ; where the resting-places of their Dead,

have fallen like their Dead; and the broken hour-glass of Time is but a heap of idle dust! Returning, by the road, at sunset! and looking, from the distance, on the course we had taken in the morning, I almost feel (as I had felt when I first saw it, at that hour) as if the sun would never rise again, but looked its last, that night, upon a ruined world.

To come again on Rome, by moonlight, after such an expedition, is a fitting close to such a day. The narrow streets, devoid of footways, and choked, in every obscure corner, by heaps of dunghill-rubbish, contrast so strongly, in their cramped dimensions, and their filth, and darkness, with the broad square before some haughty church: in the centre of which, a hieroglyphic-covered obelisk, brought from Egypt in the days of the Emperors, looks strangely on the foreign scene about it; or perhaps an ancient pillar, with its honoured statue overthrown, supports a Christian saint: Marcus Aurelius giving place to Paul, and Trajan to St. Peter. Then, there are the ponderous buildings reared from the spoliation of the Coliseum, shutting out the moon, like mountains: while here and there, are broken arches and rent walls, through which it gushes freely, as the life comes pouring from a wound. The little town of miserable houses, walled, and shut in by barred gates, is the quarter where the Jews are locked up nightly, when the clock strikes eight—a miserable place, densely populated, and reeking with bad odours, but where the people are industrious and money-getting. In the daytime, as you make your way along the narrow streets, you see them all at work; upon the pavement, oftener than in their dark and frowzy shops: furbishing old clothes, and driving bargains.

Crossing from these patches of thick darkness, out into the moon once more, the fountain of Trevi, welling from a hundred jets, and rolling over mimic rocks, is silvery to the eye and ear. In the narrow little throat of street, beyond, a booth, dressed out with flaring lamps, and boughs of trees, attracts a group of sulky Romans round its smoky coppers of hot broth, and cauliflower stew; its trays of fried fish, and its flasks of wine. As you rattle round the sharply-twisting corner, a lumbering sound is heard. The coachman stops abruptly, and uncovers, as a van comes slowly by, preceded by a man who bears a large cross; by a torch-bearer; and a priest: the latter chaunting as he goes. It is the Dead Cart, with the bodies of the poor, on their way to burial in

the Sacred Field outside the walls, where they will be thrown
into the pit that will be covered with a stone to-night, and
sealed up for a year.

But whether, in this ride, you pass by obelisks, or columns:
ancient temples, theatres, houses, porticoes, or forums: it is
strange to see, how every fragment, whenever it is possible,
has been blended into some modern structure, and made
to serve some modern purpose—a wall, a dwelling-place,
a granary, a stable—some use for which it never was designed,
and associated with which it cannot otherwise than lamely
assort. It is stranger still, to see how many ruins of the old
mythology: how many fragments of obsolete legend and
observance: have been incorporated into the worship of
Christian altars here; and how, in numberless respects, the
false faith and the true are fused into a monstrous union.

From one part of the city, looking out beyond the walls,
a squat and stunted pyramid (the burial-place of Caius
Cestius) makes an opaque triangle in the moonlight. But,
to an English traveller, it serves to mark the grave of Shelley
too, whose ashes lie beneath a little garden near it. Nearer
still, almost within its shadow, lie the bones of Keats, "whose
name is writ in water," that shines brightly in the landscape
of a calm Italian night.

The Holy Week in Rome is supposed to offer great attractions to all visitors; but, saving for the sights of Easter
Sunday, I would counsel those who go to Rome for its own
interest, to avoid it at that time. The ceremonies, in general,
are of the most tedious and wearisome kind; the heat and
crowd at every one of them, painfully oppressive; the noise,
hubbub, and confusion, quite distracting. We abandoned
the pursuit of these shows, very early in the proceedings,
and betook ourselves to the Ruins again. But, we plunged
into the crowd for a share of the best of the sights; and
what we saw, I will describe to you.

At the Sistine chapel, on the Wednesday, we saw very
little, for by the time we reached it (though we were early)
the besieging crowd had filled it to the door, and overflowed
into the adjoining hall, where they were struggling, and
squeezing, and mutually expostulating, and making great
rushes every time a lady was brought out faint, as if at least
fifty people could be accommodated in her vacant standing-
room. Hanging in the doorway of the chapel, was a heavy

curtain, and this curtain, some twenty people nearest to it, in their anxiety to hear the chaunting of the Miserere, were continually plucking at, in opposition to each other, that it might not fall down and stifle the sound of the voices. The consequence was, that it occasioned the most extraordinary confusion, and seemed to wind itself about the unwary, like a Serpent. Now, a lady was wrapped up in it, and couldn't be unwound. Now, the voice of a stifling gentleman was heard inside it, beseeching to be let out. Now, two muffled arms, no man could say of which sex, struggled in it as in a sack. Now, it was carried by a rush, bodily overhead into the chapel, like an awning. Now, it came out the other way, and blinded one of the Pope's Swiss Guard, who had arrived, that moment, to set things to rights.

Being seated at a little distance, among two or three of the Pope's gentlemen, who were very weary and counting the minutes—as perhaps his Holiness was too— we had better opportunities of observing this eccentric entertainment, than of hearing the Miserere. Sometimes, there was a swell of mournful voices that sounded very pathetic and sad, and died away, into a low strain again ; but that was all we heard.

At another time, there was the Exhibition of Relics in St. Peter's, which took place at between six and seven o'clock in the evening, and was striking from the cathedral being dark and gloomy, and having a great many people in it. The place into which the relics were brought, one by one, by a party of three priests, was a high balcony near the chief altar. This was the only lighted part of the church. There are always a hundred and twelve lamps burning near the altar, and there were two tall tapers, besides, near the black statue of St. Peter ; but these were nothing in such an immense edifice. The gloom, and the general upturning of faces to the balcony, and the prostration of true believers on the pavement, as shining objects, like pictures or looking-glasses, were brought out and shown, had something effective in it, despite the very preposterous manner in which they were held up for the general edification, and the great eleva-tion at which they were displayed ; which one would think rather calculated to diminish the comfort derivable from a full conviction of their being genuine.

On the Thursday, we went to see the Pope convey the Sacrament from the Sistine chapel, to deposit it in the Capella Paolina, another chapel in the Vatican ; – a ceremony emblematical of the entombment of the Saviour before His Resurrection. We waited in a great gallery with a great crowd of people (three-fourths of them English) for an hour or so, while they were chaunting the Miserere, in the Sistine chapel again. Both chapels opened out of the gallery ; and the general attention was concentrated on the occasional opening and shutting of the door of the one for which the Pope was ultimately bound. None of these openings disclosed anything more tremendous than a man on a ladder, lighting a great quantity of candles ; but at each and every opening, there was a terrific rush made at this ladder and this man, something like (I should think) a charge of the heavy British cavalry at Waterloo. The man was never brought down, however, nor the ladder ; for it performed the strangest antics in the world among the crowd—where it was carried by the man, when the candles were all lighted ; and finally it was stuck up against the gallery wall, in a very disorderly manner, just before the opening of the other chapel, and the commencement of a new chaunt, announced the approach of his Holiness. At this crisis, the soldiers of the guard, who had been poking the crowd into all sorts of shapes, formed down the gallery : and the procession came up, between the two lines they made.

There were a few choristers, and then a great many priests, walking two and two, and carrying—the good-looking priests at least—their lighted tapers, so as to throw the light with a good effect upon their faces : for the room was darkened. Those who were not handsome, or who had not long beards, carried *their* tapers anyhow, and abandoned themselves to spiritual contemplation. Meanwhile, the chaunting was very monotonous and dreary. The procession passed on, slowly, into the chapel, and the drone of voices went on, and came on, with it, until the Pope himself appeared, walking under a white satin canopy, and bearing the covered Sacrament in both hands ; cardinals and canons clustered round him, making a brilliant show. The soldiers of the guard knelt down as he passed ; all the bystanders bowed ; and so he passed on into the chapel : the white satin canopy being removed from over him at the door, and a white satin parasol hoisted over his poor old head, in place of it. A few more couples brought up the rear, and passed into the chapel also. Then, the chapel door was shut ; and it was all over ; and everybody hurried off headlong, as for life or death, to see something else, and say it wasn't worth the trouble.

I think the most popular and most crowded sight (excepting those of Easter Sunday and Monday, which are open to all classes of people) was the Pope washing the feet of Thirteen men, representing the twelve apostles, and Judas Iscariot. The place in which this pious office is performed, is one of the chapels of St. Peter's, which is gaily decorated for the occasion; the thirteen sitting, "all of a row," on a very high bench, and looking particularly uncomfortable, with the eyes of Heaven knows how many English, French, Americans, Swiss, Germans, Russians, Swedes, Norwegians, and other foreigners, nailed to their faces all the time. They are robed in white; and on their heads they wear a stiff white cap, like a large English porter-pot, without a handle. Each carries in his hand, a nosegay, of the size of a fine cauliflower; and two of them, on this occasion, wore spectacles; which, remembering the characters they sustained, I thought a droll appendage to the costume. There was a great eye to character. St. John was represented by a good-looking young man. St. Peter, by a grave-looking old gentleman, with a flowing brown beard; and Judas Iscariot by such an enormous hypocrite (I could not make out, though, whether the expression of his face was real or assumed) that if he had acted the part to the death and had gone away and hanged himself, he would have left nothing to be desired.

As the two large boxes, appropriated to ladies at this sight, were full to the throat, and getting near was hopeless, we posted off, along with a great crowd, to be in time at the Table, where the Pope, in person, waits on these Thirteen; and after a prodigious struggle at the Vatican staircase, and several personal conflicts with the Swiss guard, the whole crowd swept into the room. It was a long gallery hung with drapery of white and red, with another great box for ladies (who are obliged to dress in black at these ceremonies, and to wear black veils), a royal box for the King of Naples and his party; and the table itself, which, set out like a ball supper, and ornamented with golden figures of the real apostles, was arranged on an elevated platform on one side of the gallery. The counterfeit apostles' knives and forks were laid out on that side of the table which was nearest to the wall, so that they might be stared at again, without let or hindrance.

The body of the room was full of male strangers; the crowd immense; the heat very great; and the pressure sometimes frightful. It was at its height, when the stream came pouring in, from the feet-washing; and then there were such shrieks and outcries, that a party of Piedmontese dragoons went to the rescue of the Swiss guard, and helped them to calm the tumult.

The ladies were particularly ferocious, in their struggles for places. One lady of my acquaintance was seized round the waist, in the ladies' box, by a strong matron, and hoisted out of her place; and there was another lady (in a back row in the same box) who improved her position by sticking a large pin into the ladies before her.

The gentlemen about me were remarkably anxious to see what was on the table; and one Englishman seemed to have embarked the whole energy of his nature in the determination to discover whether there was any mustard. "By Jupiter there's vinegar!" I heard him say to his friend, after he had stood on tiptoe an immense time, and had been crushed and beaten on all sides. "And there's oil! I saw them distinctly, in cruets! Can any gentleman, in front there, see mustard on the table? Sir, will you oblige me? *Do* you see a Mustard-Pot?"

The apostles and Judas appearing on the platform, after much expectation, were marshalled, in line, in front of the table, with Peter at the top; and a good long stare was taken at them by the company, while twelve of them took a long smell at their nosegays, and Judas—moving his lips very obtrusively—engaged in inward prayer. Then, the Pope, clad in a scarlet robe, and wearing on his head a skull-cap of white satin, appeared in the midst of a crowd of Cardinals and other dignitaries, and took in his hand a little golden ewer, from which he poured a little water over one of Peter's hands, while one attendant held a golden basin; a second, a fine cloth; a third, Peter's nosegay, which was taken from him during the operation. This his Holiness performed, with considerable expedition, on every man in the line (Judas, I observed to be particularly overcome by his condescension); and then the whole Thirteen sat down to dinner. Grace said by the Pope. Peter in the chair.

There was white wine, and red wine: and the dinner looked very good. The courses appeared in portions, one for each apostle : and these being presented to the Pope, by Cardinals upon their knees, were by him handed to the Thirteen. The manner in which Judas grew more white-livered over his victuals, and languished, with his head on one side, as if he had no appetite, defies all description. Peter was a good, sound, old man, and went in, as the saying is, "to win;" eating everything that was given him (he got the best : being first in the row) and saying nothing to anybody. The dishes appeared to be chiefly composed of fish and vegetables. The Pope helped the Thirteen to wine also ; and, during the whole dinner, somebody read something aloud, out of a large book —the Bible, I presume—which nobody could hear, and to which nobody paid the least attention. The Cardinals, and other attendants, smiled to each other, from time to time, as if the thing were a great farce ; and if they thought so, there is little doubt they were perfectly right. His Holiness did what he had to do, as a sensible man gets through a troublesome ceremony, and seemed very glad when it was all over.

The Pilgrims' Suppers: where lords and ladies waited on the Pilgrims, in token of humility, and dried their feet when they had been well washed by deputy: were very attractive. But, of all the many spectacles of dangerous reliance on outward observances, in themselves mere empty forms, none struck me half so much as the Scala Santa, or Holy Staircase, which I saw several times, but to the greatest advantage, or disadvantage, on Good Friday.

This holy staircase is composed of eight-and-twenty steps, said to have belonged to Pontius Pilate's house, and to be the identical stairs on which Our Saviour trod, in coming down from the judgment-seat. Pilgrims ascend it, only on their knees. It is steep ; and, at the summit, is a chapel, reported to be full of relics ; into which they peep through some iron bars, and then come down again, by one of two side staircases, which are not sacred, and may be walked on.

On Good Friday, there were, on a moderate computation, a hundred people, slowly shuffling up these stairs, on their knees, at one time ; while others, who were going up, or had come down—and a few who had done both, and were going up again for the second time—stood loitering in the porch below, where an old gentleman in a sort of watch-box, rattled a tin canister, with a slit in the top, incessantly, to remind them that he took the money. The majority were country-

people, male and female. There were four or five Jesuit
priests, however, and some half-dozen well-dressed women.
A whole school of boys, twenty at least, were about half-way
up—evidently enjoying it very much. They were all wedged
together, pretty closely; but the rest of the company gave
the boys as wide a berth as possible, in consequence of their
betraying some recklessness in the management of their
boots.

I never, in my life, saw anything at once so ridiculous,
and so unpleasant, as this sight—ridiculous in the absurd
incidents inseparable from it; and unpleasant in its senseless
and unmeaning degradation. There are two steps to begin
with, and then a rather broad landing. The more rigid
climbers went along this landing on their knees, as well as
up the stairs; and the figures they cut, in their shuffling
progress over the level surface, no description can paint.
Then, to see them watch their opportunity from the porch,
and cut in where there was a place next the wall! And to
see one man with an umbrella (brought on purpose, for it
was a fine day) hoisting himself, unlawfully, from stair to
stair! And to observe a demure lady of fifty-five or so,
looking back, every now and then, to assure herself that her
legs were properly disposed!

There were such odd differences in the speed of different
people, too. Some got on as if they were doing a match
against time; others stopped to say a prayer on every step.
This man touched every stair with his forehead, and kissed
it; that man scratched his head all the way. The boys got
on brilliantly, and were up and down again before the old
lady had accomplished her half-dozen stairs. But most of
the penitents came down, very sprightly and fresh, as having
done a real good substantial deed which it would take a good
deal of sin to counterbalance; and the old gentleman in the
watch-box was down upon them with his canister while they
were in this humour, I promise you.

As if such a progress were not in its nature inevitably droll
enough, there lay, on the top of the stairs, a wooden figure
on a crucifix, resting on a sort of great iron saucer: so rickety
and unsteady, that whenever an enthusiastic person kissed the
figure, with more than usual devotion, or threw a coin into
the saucer, with more than common readiness (for it served
in this respect as a second or supplementary canister), it gave
a great leap and rattle, and nearly shook the attendant lamp

out: horribly frightening the people further down, and
throwing the guilty party into unspeakable embarrassment.

On Easter Sunday, as well as on the preceding Thursday,
the Pope bestows his benediction on the people, from the
balcony in front of St. Peter's. This Easter Sunday was a
day so bright and blue: so cloudless, balmy, wonderfully
bright: that all the previous bad weather vanished from
the recollection in a moment. I had seen the Thursday's
Benediction dropping damply on some hundreds of umbrellas,
but there was not a sparkle then, in all the hundred fountains
of Rome—such fountains as they are!—and on this Sunday
morning they were running diamonds. The miles of miserable streets through which we drove (compelled to a certain
course by the Pope's dragoons: the Roman police on such
occasions) were so full of colour, that nothing in them was
capable of wearing a faded aspect. The common people
came out in their gayest dresses; the richer people in their
smartest vehicles; Cardinals rattled to the church of the
Poor Fishermen in their state carriages; shabby magnificence
flaunted its threadbare liveries and tarnished cocked hats, in
the sun; and every coach in Rome was put in requisition for
the Great Piazza of St. Peter's.

One hundred and fifty thousand people were there at least!
Yet there was ample room. How many carriages were there,
I don't know; yet there was room for them too, and to spare.
The great steps of the church were densely crowded. There
were many of the Contadini, from Albano (who delight in
red), in that part of the square, and the mingling of bright
colours in the crowd was beautiful. Below the steps the
troops were ranged. In the magnificent proportions of the
place they looked like a bed of flowers. Sulky Romans, lively
peasants from the neighbouring country, groups of pilgrims
from distant parts of Italy, sight-seeing foreigners of all
nations, made a murmur in the clear air, like so many insects;
and high above them all, plashing and bubbling, and making
rainbow colours in the light, the two delicious fountains welled
and tumbled bountifully.

A kind of bright carpet was hung over the front of the
balcony; and the sides of the great window were bedecked
with crimson drapery. An awning was stretched, too, over
the top, to screen the old man from the hot rays of the sun.
As noon approached, all eyes were turned up to this window.
In due time, the chair was seen approaching to the front,

with the gigantic fans of peacock's feathers, close behind. The doll within it (for the balcony is very high) then rose up, and stretched out its tiny arms, while all the male spectators in the square uncovered, and some, but not by any means the greater part, kneeled down. The guns upon the ramparts of the Castle of St. Angelo proclaimed, next moment, that the benediction was given ; drums beat ; trumpets sounded; arms clashed ; and the great mass below, suddenly breaking into smaller heaps, and scattering here and there in rills, was stirred like parti-coloured sand.

What a bright noon it was, as we rode away ! The Tiber was no longer yellow, but blue.   There was a blush on the old bridges, that made them fresh and hale again.   The Pantheon, with its majestic front, all seamed and furrowed like an old face, had summer light upon its battered walls. Every squalid and desolate hut in the Eternal City (bear witness every grim old palace, to the filth and misery of the plebeian neighbour that elbows it, as certain as Time has laid its grip on its patrician head !) was fresh and new with some ray of the sun.   The very prison in the crowded street, a whirl of carriages and people, had some stray sense of the day, dropping through its chinks and crevices : and dismal prisoners who could not wind their faces round the barricading of the blocked-up windows, stretched out their hands, and clinging to the rusty bars, turned *them* towards the overflowing street : as if it were a cheerful fire, and could be shared in that way.

But, when the night came on, without a cloud to dim the full moon, what a sight it was to see the Great Square full once more, and the whole church, from the cross to the ground, lighted with innumerable lanterns, tracing out the architecture, and winking and shining all round the colonnade of the piazza ! And what a sense of exultation, joy, delight, it was, when the great bell struck half-past seven—on the instant—to behold one bright red mass of fire, soar gallantly from the top of the cupola to the extremest summit of the cross, and the moment it leaped into its place, become the signal of a bursting out of countless lights, as great, and red, and blazing as itself, from every part of the gigantic church ; so that every cornice, capital, and smallest ornament of stone, expressed itself in fire : and the black solid groundwork of the enormous dome seemed to grow transparent as an egg-shell !

A train of gunpowder, an electric chain—nothing could be fired, more suddenly and swiftly, than this second illumination; and when we had got away, and gone upon a distant height, and looked towards it two hours afterwards, there it still stood, shining and glittering in the calm night like a jewel! Not a line of its proportions wanting; not an angle blunted; not an atom of its radiance lost.

The next night—Easter Monday—there was a great display of fireworks from the Castle of St. Angelo. We hired a room in an opposite house, and made our way, to our places, in good time, through a dense mob of people choking up the square in front, and all the avenues leading to it; and so loading the bridge by which the castle is approached, that it seemed ready to sink into the rapid Tiber below. There are statues on this bridge (execrable works), and, among them, great vessels full of burning tow were placed: glaring strangely on the faces of the crowd, and not less strangely on the stone counterfeits above them.

The show began with a tremendous discharge of cannon; and then, for twenty minutes or half an hour, the whole castle was one incessant sheet of fire, and labyrinth of blazing wheels of every colour, size, and speed: while rockets streamed into the sky, not by ones or twos, or scores, but hundreds at a time. The concluding burst—the Girandola—was like the blowing up into the air of the whole massive castle, without smoke or dust.

In half an hour afterwards, the immense concourse had dispersed: the moon was looking calmly down upon her wrinkled image in the river; and half-a-dozen men and boys, with bits of lighted candle in their hands: moving here and there, in search of anything worth having, that might have been dropped in the press: had the whole scene to themselves.

By way of contrast we rode out into old ruined Rome, after all this firing and booming, to take our leave of the Coliseum. I had seen it by moonlight before (I could never get through a day without going back to it), but its tremendous solitude that night is past all telling. The ghostly pillars in the Forum; the Triumphal Arches of Old Emperors; those enormous masses of ruins which were once their palaces; the grass-grown mounds that mark the graves of ruined temples; the stones of the Via Sacra, smooth with the tread of feet in ancient Rome; even these were dimmed, in their transcendent melancholy, by the dark ghost of its bloody holidays, erect and grim; haunting the old scene; despoiled by pillaging Popes and fighting Princes, but not laid; wringing wild hands of weed, and grass, and bramble; and lamenting to the night in every gap and broken arch— the shadow of its awful self, immovable!

As we lay down on the grass of the Campagna, next day, on our way to Florence, hearing the larks sing, we saw that a little wooden cross had been erected on the spot where the poor Pilgrim Countess was murdered. So, we piled some loose stones about it, as the beginning of a mound to her memory, and wondered if we should ever rest there again, and look back at Rome.

A RAPID DIORAMA

WE are bound for Naples! And we cross the threshold of the Eternal City at yonder gate, the Gate of San Giovanni Laterano, where the two last objects that attract the notice of a departing visitor, and the two first objects that attract the notice of an arriving one, are a proud church and a decaying ruin—good emblems of Rome.

Our way lies over the Campagna, which looks more solemn on a bright blue day like this, than beneath a darker sky; the great extent of ruin being plainer to the eye: and the sunshine through the arches of the broken aqueducts, showing other broken arches shining through them in the melancholy distance. When we have traversed it, and look back from Albano, its dark undulating surface lies below us like a stagnant lake, or like a broad dull Lethe flowing round the walls of Rome, and separating it from all the world! How often have the Legions, in triumphant march, gone glittering across that purple waste, so silent and unpeopled now! How often has the train of captives looked, with sinking hearts, upon the distant city, and beheld its population pouring out, to hail the return of their conqueror! What riot, sensuality and murder, have run mad in the vast palaces now heaps of brick and shattered marble! What glare of fires, and roar of popular tumult, and wail of pestilence and famine, have come sweeping over the wild plain where nothing is now heard but the wind, and where the solitary lizards gambol unmolested in the sun!

The train of wine-carts going into Rome, each driven by a shaggy peasant reclining beneath a little gipsy-fashioned canopy of sheepskin, is ended now, and we go toiling up into a higher country where there are trees. The next day brings us on the Pontine Marshes, wearily flat and lonesome, and overgrown with brushwood, and swamped with water, but with a fine road made across them, shaded by a long, long avenue. Here and there, we pass a solitary guard-house; here and there a hovel, deserted, and walled up. Some herdsmen loiter on the banks of the stream beside the road, and sometimes a flat-bottomed boat, towed by a man, comes rippling idly along it. A horseman passes occasionally, carrying a long gun cross-wise on the saddle before him, and attended by fierce dogs; but there is nothing else astir save the wind and the shadows, until we come in sight of Terracina.

How blue and bright the sea, rolling below the windows of the inn so famous in robber stories! How picturesque the great crags and points of rock overhanging to-morrow's narrow road, where galley-slaves are working in the quarries above, and the sentinels who guard them lounge on the sea-shore! All night there is the murmur of the sea beneath the stars; and, in the morning, just at daybreak, the prospect suddenly becoming expanded, as if by a miracle, reveals —in the far distance, across the sea there!—Naples with its islands, and Vesuvius spouting fire! Within a quarter of an hour, the whole is gone as if it were a vision in the clouds, and there is nothing but the sea and sky.

The Neapolitan frontier crossed, after two hours' travelling; and the hungriest of soldiers and custom-house officers with difficulty appeased; we enter, by a gateless portal, into the first Neapolitan town—Fondi. Take note of Fondi, in the name of all that is wretched and beggarly.

A filthy channel of mud and refuse meanders down the centre of the miserable streets, fed by obscene rivulets that trickle from the abject houses. There is not a door, a window, or a shutter; not a roof, a wall, a post, or a pillar, in all Fondi, but is decayed, and crazy, and rotting away. The wretched history of the town, with all its sieges and pillages by Barbarossa and the rest, might have been acted last year. How the gaunt dogs that sneak about the miserable streets, come to be alive, and undevoured by the people, is one of the enigmas of the world.

A hollow-cheeked and scowling people they are! All beggars; but that's nothing. Look at them as they gather round. Some, are too indolent to come downstairs, or are too wisely mistrustful of the stairs, perhaps, to venture: so stretch out their lean hands from upper windows, and howl; others, come flocking about us, fighting and jostling one another, and demanding, incessantly, charity for the love of God, charity for the love of the Blessed Virgin, charity for the love of all the Saints. A group of miserable children, almost naked, screaming forth the same petition, discover that they can see themselves reflected in the varnish of the carriage, and begin to dance and make grimaces, that they may have the pleasure of seeing their antics repeated in this mirror. A crippled idiot, in the act of striking one of them who drowns his clamorous demand for charity, observes his angry counterpart in the panel, stops short, and thrusting out his tongue, begins to wag his head and chatter. The shrill cry raised at this, awakens half-a-dozen wild creatures wrapped in frowzy brown cloaks, who are lying on the church-steps with pots and pans for sale. These, scrambling up, approach, and beg defiantly. "I am hungry. Give me something. Listen to me, Signor. I am hungry!" Then, a ghastly old woman, fearful of being too late, comes hobbling down the street, stretching out one hand, and scratching herself all the way with the other, and screaming, long before she can be heard, "Charity, charity! I'll go and pray for you directly, beautiful lady, if you'll give me charity!" Lastly, the members of a brotherhood for burying the dead : hideously masked, and attired in shabby black robes, white at the skirts, with the splashes of many muddy winters : escorted by a dirty priest, and a congenial cross-bearer : come hurrying past. Surrounded by this motley concourse, we move out of Fondi: bad bright eyes glaring at us, out of the darkness of every crazy tenement, like glistening fragments of its filth and putrefaction.

A noble mountain-pass, with the ruins of a fort on a strong eminence, traditionally called the Fort of Fra Diavolo; the old town of Itrí, like a device in pastry, built up, almost perpendicularly, on a hill, and approached by long steep flights of steps ; beautiful Mola di Gaëta, whose wines, like those of Albano, have degenerated since the days of Horace, or his taste for wine was bad : which is not likely of one who enjoyed it so much, and extolled it so well ; another night upon the road at St. Agatha ; a rest next day at Capua, which is picturesque, but hardly so seductive to a traveller now, as the soldiers of Prætorian Rome were wont to find the ancient city of that name ; a flat road among vines festooned and looped from tree to tree ; and Mount Vesuvius close at hand at last!—its cone and summit whitened with snow ; and its smoke hanging over it, in the heavy atmosphere of the day, like a dense cloud. So we go, rattling down hill, into Naples.

A funeral is coming up the street, towards us. The body, on an open bier, borne on a kind of palanquin, covered with a gay cloth of crimson and gold. The mourners, in white gowns and masks. If there be death abroad, life is well represented too, for all Naples would seem to be out of doors, and tearing to and fro in carriages. Some of these, the common Vetturíno vehicles, are drawn by three horses abreast, decked with smart trappings and great abundance of brazen ornament, and always going very fast. Not that their loads are light; for the smallest of them has at least six people inside, four in front, four or five more hanging on behind, and two or three more, in a net or bag below the axle-tree, where they lie half-suffocated with mud and dust. Exhibitors of Punch, buffo singers with guitars, reciters of poetry, reciters of stories, a row of cheap exhibitions with clowns and showmen, drums, and trumpets, painted cloths representing the wonders within, and admiring crowds assembled without, assist the whirl and bustle. Ragged lazzaroni lie asleep in doorways, archways, and kennels; the gentry, gaily dressed, are dashing up and down in carriages on the Chiaja, or walking in the Public Gardens; and quiet letter-writers, perched behind their little desks and inkstands under the Portico of the Great Theatre of San Carlo, in the public street, are waiting for clients.

Here is a galley-slave in chains, who wants a letter written to a friend. He approaches a clerkly-looking man, sitting under the corner arch, and makes his bargain. He has obtained permission of the sentinel who guards him : who stands near, leaning against the wall and cracking nuts. The galley-slave dictates in the ear of the letter-writer, what he desires to say; and as he can't read writing, looks intently in his face, to read there whether he sets down faithfully what he is told. After a time, the galley-slave becomes discursive—incoherent. The secretary pauses and rubs his chin. The galley-slave is voluble and energetic. The secretary, at length, catches the idea, and with the air of a man who knows how to word it, sets it down ; stopping, now and then, to glance back at his text admiringly. The galley-slave is silent. The soldier stoically cracks his nuts. Is there anything more to say? inquires the letter-writer. No more. Then listen, friend of mine. He reads it through. The galley-slave is quite enchanted. It is folded, and addressed, and given to him, and he pays the fee. The secretary falls back indolently in his chair, and takes a book. The galley-slave gathers up an empty sack. The sentinel throws away a handful of nut-shells, shoulders his musket, and away they go together.

Why do the beggars rap their chins constantly, with their right hands, when you look at them? Everything is done in pantomime in Naples, and that is the conventional sign for hunger. A man who is quarrelling with another, yonder, lays the palm of his right hand on the back of his left, and shakes the two thumbs—expressive of a donkey's ears—whereat his adversary is goaded to desperation. Two people bargaining for fish, the buyer empties an imaginary waistcoat pocket when he is told the price, and walks away without a word : having thoroughly conveyed to the seller that he considers it too dear. Two people in carriages, meeting, one touches his lips, twice or thrice, holding up the five fingers of his right hand, and gives a horizontal cut in the air with the palm. The other nods briskly, and goes his way. He has been invited to a friendly dinner at half-past five o'clock, and will certainly come.

All over Italy, a peculiar shake of the right hand from the wrist, with the forefinger stretched out, expresses a negative—the only negative beggars will ever understand. But, in Naples, those five fingers are a copious language.

All this, and every other kind of out-door life and stir, and maccaroni-eating at sunset, and flower-selling all day long, and begging and stealing everywhere and at all hours, you see upon the bright sea-shore, where the waves of the bay sparkle merrily. But, lovers and hunters of the picturesque, let us not keep too studiously out of view the miserable depravity, degradation, and wretchedness, with which this gay Neapolitan life is inseparably associated ! It is not well to find Saint Giles's so repulsive, and the Porta Capuana so attractive. A pair of naked legs and a ragged red scarf, do not make *all* the difference between what is interesting and what is coarse and odious? Painting and poetising for ever, if you will, the beauties of this most beautiful and lovely spot of earth, let us, as our duty, try to associate a new picturesque with some faint recognition of man's destiny and capabilities ; more hopeful, I believe, among the ice and snow of the North Pole, than in the sun and bloom of Naples.

Capri—once made odious by the deified beast Tiberius—

Ischia, Procida, and the thousand distant beauties of the Bay,
lie in the blue sea yonder, changing in the mist and sunshine
twenty times a-day: now close at hand, now far off, now
unseen.   The fairest country in the world, is spread about
us.   Whether we turn towards the Miseno shore of the
splendid watery amphitheatre, and go by the Grotto of
Posilipo to the Grotto del Cane and away to Baiæ : or take
the other way, towards Vesuvius and Sorrento, it is one
succession of delights.   In the last-named direction, where,
over doors and archways, there are countless little images of
San Gennaro, with his Canute's hand stretched out, to check
the fury of the Burning Mountain, we are carried pleasantly,
by a railroad on the beautiful Sea Beach, past the town of
Torre del Greco, built upon the ashes of the former town
destroyed by an eruption of Vesuvius, within a hundred
years ; and past the flat-roofed houses, granaries, and
maccaroni manufactories ; to Castel-a-Mare, with its ruined
castle, now inhabited by fishermen, standing in the sea upon
a heap of rocks.   Here, the railroad terminates ; but, hence
we may ride on, by an unbroken succession of enchanting
bays, and beautiful scenery, sloping from the highest summit
of Saint Angelo, the highest neighbouring mountain, down
to the water's edge—among vineyards, olive-trees, gardens of
oranges and lemons, orchards, heaped-up rocks, green gorges
in the hills—and by the bases of snow-covered heights, and
through small towns with handsome, dark-haired women at
the doors—and past delicious summer villas—to Sorrento,
where the Poet Tasso drew his inspiration from the beauty
surrounding him.   Returning, we may climb the heights
above Castel-a-Mare, and looking down among the boughs
and leaves, see the crisp water glistening in the sun ; and
clusters of white houses in distant Naples, dwindling, in the
great extent of prospect, down to dice.   The coming back to
the city, by the beach again, at sunset : with the glowing
sea on one side, and the darkening mountain, with its smoke
and flame, upon the other: is a sublime conclusion to the
glory of the day.

    That church by the Porta Capuana—near the old fisher-
market in the dirtiest quarter of dirty Naples, where the
revolt of Masaniello began—is memorable for having been
the scene of one of his earliest proclamations to the people,
and is particularly remarkable for nothing else, unless it be
its waxen and bejewelled Saint in a glass case, with two odd

hands; or the enormous number of beggars who are constantly rapping their chins there, like a battery of castanets. The cathedral with the beautiful door, and the columns of African and Egyptian granite that once ornamented the temple of Apollo, contains the famous sacred blood of San Gennaro or Januarius : which is preserved in two phials in a silver tabernacle, and miraculously liquefies three times a-year, to the great admiration of the people. At the same moment, the stone (distant some miles) where the Saint suffered martyrdom, becomes faintly red. It is said that the officiating priests turn faintly red also, sometimes, when these miracles occur.

The old, old men who live in hovels at the entrance of these ancient catacombs, and who, in their age and infirmity. seem waiting here, to be buried themselves, are members of a curious body, called the Royal Hospital, who are the official attendants at funerals. Two of these old spectres totter away, with lighted tapers, to show the caverns of death—as unconcerned as if they were immortal. They were used as burying-places for three hundred years ; and, in one part, is a large pit full of skulls and bones, said to be the sad remains of a great mortality occasioned by a plague. In the rest there is nothing but dust. They consist, chiefly, of great wide corridors and labyrinths, hewn out of the rock. At the end of some of these long passages, are unexpected glimpses of the daylight, shining down from above. It looks as ghastly and as strange : among the torches, and the dust, and the dark vaults : as if it, too, were dead and buried.

The present burial-place lies out yonder, on a hill between the city and Vesuvius. The old Campo Santo with its three hundred and sixty-five pits, is only used for those who die in hospitals, and prisons, and are unclaimed by their friends. The graceful new cemetery, at no great distance from it, though yet unfinished, has already many graves among its shrubs and flowers, and airy colonnades. It might be reasonably objected elsewhere, that some of the tombs are meretricious and too fanciful; but the general brightness seems to justify it here ; and Mount Vesuvius, separated from them by a lovely slope of ground, exalts and saddens the scene.

If it be solemn to behold from this new City of the Dead. with its dark smoke hanging in the clear sky, how much more awful and impressive is it, viewed from the ghostly ruins of Herculaneum and Pompeii !

Stand at the bottom of the great market-place of Pompeii, and look up the silent streets, through the ruined temples of Jupiter and Isis, over the broken houses with their inmost sanctuaries open to the day, away to Mount Vesuvius, bright and snowy in the peaceful distance ; and lose all count of time, and heed of other things, in the strange and melancholy sensation of seeing the Destroyed and the Destroyer making this quiet picture in the sun.   Then, ramble on, and see, at every turn, the little familiar tokens of human habitation and every-day pursuits ; the chafing of the bucket-rope in the stone rim of the exhausted well ; the track of carriage-wheels in the pavement of the street ; the marks of drinking-vessels on the stone counter of the wine-shop ; the amphoræ in private cellars, stored away so many hundred years ago, and undisturbed to this hour—all rendering the solitude and deadly lonesomeness of the place, ten thousand times more solemn, than if the volcano, in its fury, had swept the city from the earth, and sunk it in the bottom of the sea.

After it was shaken by the earthquake which preceded the eruption, workmen were employed in shaping out, in stone, new ornaments for temples and other buildings that had suffered.   Here lies their work, outside the city gate, as if they would return to-morrow.

In the cellar of Diomede's house, where certain skeletons were found huddled together, close to the door, the impression of their bodies on the ashes, hardened with the ashes, and became stamped and fixed there, after they had shrunk, inside, to scanty bones.   So, in the theatre of Herculaneum, a comic mask, floating on the stream when it was hot and liquid, stamped its mimic features in it as it hardened into stone ; and now, it turns upon the stranger the fantastic look it turned upon the audiences in that same theatre two thousand years ago.

Next to the wonder of going up and down the streets, and in and out of the houses, and traversing the secret chambers of the temples of a religion that has vanished from the earth, and finding so many fresh traces of remote antiquity : as if the course of Time had been stopped after this desolation, and there had been no nights and days, months, years, and centuries, since : nothing is more impressive and terrible than the many evidences of the searching nature of the ashes, as bespeaking their irresistible power, and the impossibility of escaping them.   In the wine-cellars, they forced their way

The Street of the Tombs: Pompeii

into the earthen vessels: displacing the wine and choking them, to the brim, with dust. In the tombs, they forced the ashes of the dead from the funeral urns, and rained new ruin even into them. The mouths, and eyes, and skulls of all the skeletons, were stuffed with this terrible hail. In Herculaneum, where the flood was of a different and a heavier kind, it rolled in, like a sea. Imagine a deluge of water turned to marble, at its height—and that is what is called "the lava" here.

Some workmen were digging the gloomy well on the brink of which we now stand, looking down, when they came on some of the stone benches of the theatre—those steps (for such they seem) at the bottom of the excavation—and found the buried city of Herculaneum. Presently going down, with lighted torches, we are perplexed by great walls of monstrous thickness, rising up between the benches, shutting out the stage, obtruding their shapeless forms in absurd places, confusing the whole plan, and making it a disordered dream. We cannot, at first, believe, or picture to ourselves, that THIS came rolling in, and drowned the city; and that all that is not here, has been cut away, by the axe, like solid stone. But this perceived and understood, the horror and oppression of its presence are indescribable.

Many of the paintings on the walls in the roofless chambers of both cities, or carefully removed to the museum at Naples, are as fresh and plain, as if they had been executed yesterday. Here are subjects of still life, as provisions, dead game, bottles, glasses, and the like; familiar classical stories, or mythological fables, always forcibly and plainly told; conceits of cupids, quarrelling, sporting, working at trades; theatrical rehearsals; poets reading their productions to their friends; inscriptions chalked upon the walls; political squibs, advertisements, rough drawings by schoolboys; everything to people and restore the ancient cities, in the fancy of their wondering visitor. Furniture, too, you see, of every kind—lamps, tables, couches; vessels for eating, drinking, and cooking; workmen's tools, surgical instruments, tickets for the theatre, pieces of money, personal ornaments, bunches of keys found clenched in the grasp of skeletons, helmets of guards and warriors; little household bells, yet musical with their old domestic tones.

The least among these objects, lends its aid to swell the interest of Vesuvius, and invest it with a perfect fascination.

The looking, from either ruined city, into the neighbouring grounds overgrown with beautiful vines and luxuriant trees ; and remembering that house upon house, temple on temple, building after building, and street after street, are still lying underneath the roots of all the quiet cultivation, waiting to be turned up to the light of day ; is something so wonderful, so full of mystery, so captivating to the imagination, that one would think it would be paramount, and yield to nothing else.   To nothing but Vesuvius ; but the mountain is the genius of the scene.   From every indication of the ruin it has worked, we look, again, with an absorbing interest to where its smoke is rising up into the sky.   It is beyond us, as we thread the ruined streets : above us, as we stand upon the ruined walls ; we follow it through every vista of broken columns, as we wander through the empty court-yards of the houses ; and through the garlandings and interlacings of every wanton vine.   Turning away to Pæstum yonder, to see the awful structures built, the least aged of them, hundreds of years before the birth of Christ, and standing yet, erect in lonely majesty, upon the wild, malaria-blighted plain—we watch Vesuvius as it disappears from the prospect, and watch for it again, on our return, with the same thrill of interest : as the doom and destiny of all this beautiful country, biding its terrible time.

It is very warm in the sun, on this early spring-day, when we return from Pæstum, but very cold in the shade : insomuch, that although we may lunch, pleasantly, at noon, in the open air, by the gate of Pompeii, the neighbouring rivulet supplies thick ice for our wine.   But, the sun is shining brightly ; there is not a cloud or speck of vapour in the whole blue sky, looking down upon the bay of Naples ; and the moon will be at the full to-night.   No matter that the snow and ice lie thick upon the summit of Vesuvius, or that we have been on foot all day at Pompeii, or that croakers maintain that strangers should not be on the mountain by night, in such an unusual season.   Let us take advantage of the fine weather ; make the best of our way to Resina, the little village at the foot of the mountain ; prepare ourselves, as well as we can, on so short a notice, at the guide's house ; ascend at once, and have sunset half-way up, moon-light at the top, and midnight to come down in !

At four o'clock in the afternoon, there is a terrible uproar in the little stable-yard of Signor Salvatore, the recognised head-guide, with the gold band round his cap; and thirty under-guides who are all scuffling and screaming at once, are preparing half-a-dozen saddled ponies, three litters, and some stout staves, for the journey. Every one of the thirty, quarrels with the other twenty-nine, and frightens the six ponies; and as much of the village as can possibly squeeze itself into the little stable-yard, participates in the tumult, and gets trodden on by the cattle.

After much violent skirmishing, and more noise than would suffice for the storming of Naples, the procession starts. The head-guide, who is liberally paid for all the attendants, rides a little in advance of the party; the other thirty guides proceed on foot. Eight go forward with the litters that are to be used by-and-by; and the remaining two-and-twenty beg.

We ascend, gradually, by stony lanes like rough broad flights of stairs, for some time. At length, we leave these, and the vineyards on either side of them, and emerge upon a bleak bare region where the lava lies confusedly, in enormous rusty masses: as if the earth had been ploughed up by burning thunderbolts. And now, we halt to see the sun set. The change that falls upon the dreary region, and on the whole mountain, as its red light fades, and the night comes on—and the unutterable solemnity and dreariness that reign around, who that has witnessed it, can ever forget!

It is dark, when after winding, for some time, over the broken ground, we arrive at the foot of the cone: which is extremely steep, and seems to rise, almost perpendicularly, from the spot where we dismount. The only light is reflected from the snow, deep, hard, and white, with which the cone is covered. It is now intensely cold, and the air is piercing. The thirty-one have brought no torches, knowing that the moon will rise before we reach the top. Two of the litters are devoted to the two ladies; the third, to a rather heavy gentleman from Naples, whose hospitality and good-nature have attached him to the expedition, and determined him to assist in doing the honours of the mountain. The rather heavy gentleman is carried by fifteen men; each of the ladies by half-a-dozen. We who walk, make the best use of our staves; and so the whole party begin to labour upward over the snow,—as if they were toiling to the summit of an ante-diluvian Twelfth-cake.

We are a long time toiling up; and the head-guide looks oddly about him when one of the company—not an Italian,

though an habitué of the mountain for many years: whom
we will call, for our present purpose, Mr. Pickle of Portici—
suggests that, as it is freezing hard, and the usual footing of
ashes is covered by the snow and ice, it will surely be difficult
to descend.   But the sight of the litters above, tilting up and
down, and jerking from this side to that, as the bearers continually slip and tumble, diverts our attention; more especially
as the whole length of the rather heavy gentleman is, at that
moment, presented to us alarmingly foreshortened, with his
head downwards.

The rising of the moon soon afterwards, revives the flagging
spirits of the bearers.   Stimulating each other with their
usual watchword, "Courage, friend! It is to eat maccaroni!"
they press on, gallantly, for the summit.

From tingeing the top of the snow above us, with a band
of light, and pouring it in a stream through the valley below,
while we have been ascending in the dark, the moon soon
lights the whole white mountain-side, and the broad sea down
below, and tiny Naples in the distance, and every village in
the country round.   The whole prospect is in this lovely state,
when we come upon the platform on the mountain-top—the
region of Fire—an exhausted crater formed of great masses of
gigantic cinders, like blocks of stone from some tremendous
waterfall, burnt up; from every chink and crevice of which,
hot, sulphurous smoke is pouring out: while, from another
conical-shaped hill, the present crater, rising abruptly from
this platform at the end, great sheets of fire are streaming
forth: reddening the night with flame, blackening it with
smoke, and spotting it with red-hot stones and cinders, that
fly up into the air like feathers, and fall down like lead.
What words can paint the gloom and grandeur of this
scene!

The broken ground; the smoke; the sense of suffocation
from the sulphur; the fear of falling down through the
crevices in the yawning ground; the stopping, every now and
then, for somebody who is missing in the dark (for the dense
smoke now obscures the moon); the intolerable noise of the
thirty; and the hoarse roaring of the mountain; make it a
scene of such confusion, at the same time, that we reel again.
But, dragging the ladies through it, and across another
exhausted crater to the foot of the present Volcano, we
approach close to it on the windy side, and then sit down
among the hot ashes at its foot, and look up in silence;

faintly estimating the action that is going on within, from its being full a hundred feet higher, at this minute, than it was six weeks ago.

There is something in the fire and roar, that generates an irresistible desire to get nearer to it. We cannot rest long, without starting off, two of us, on our hands and knees, accompanied by the head-guide, to climb to the brim of the flaming crater, and try to look in. Meanwhile, the thirty yell, as with one voice, that it is a dangerous proceeding, and call to us to come back ; frightening the rest of the party out of their wits.

What with their noise, and what with the trembling of the thin crust of ground, that seems about to open underneath our feet and plunge us in the burning gulf below (which is the real danger, if there be any); and what with the flashing of the fire in our faces, and the shower of red-hot ashes that is raining down, and the choking smoke and sulphur ; we may well feel giddy and irrational, like drunken men. But, we contrive to climb up to the brim, and look down, for a moment, into the Hell of boiling fire below. Then, we all three come rolling down ; blackened, and singed, and scorched, and hot, and giddy: and each with his dress alight in half-a-dozen places.

You have read, a thousand times, that the usual way of descending, is, by sliding down the ashes : which, forming a gradually-increasing ledge below the feet, prevent too rapid a descent. But, when we have crossed the two exhausted craters on our way back, and are come to this precipitous place, there is (as Mr. Pickle has foretold) no vestige of ashes to be seen ; the whole being a smooth sheet of ice.

In this dilemma, ten or a dozen of the guides cautiously join hands, and make a chain of men ; of whom the foremost beat, as well as they can, a rough track with their sticks, down which we prepare to follow. The way being fearfully steep, and none of the party: even of the thirty : being able to keep their feet for six paces together, the ladies are taken out of their litters, and placed, each between two careful persons ; while others of the thirty hold by their skirts, to prevent their falling forward — a necessary precaution, tending to the immediate and hopeless dilapidation of their apparel. The rather heavy gentleman is adjured to leave his litter too, and be escorted in a similar manner ; but he resolves to be brought down as he was brought up, on the principle that his fifteen bearers are not likely to tumble all at once, and that he is safer so, than trusting to his own legs.

In this order, we begin the descent: sometimes on foot, sometimes shuffling on the ice: always proceeding much more quietly and slowly, than on our upward way: and constantly alarmed by the falling among us of somebody from behind, who endangers the footing of the whole party, and clings pertinaciously to anybody's ankles. It is impossible for the litter to be in advance, too, as the track has to be made; and its appearance behind us, overhead—with some one or other of the bearers always down, and the rather heavy gentleman with his legs always in the air—is very threatening and frightful. We have gone on thus, a very little way, painfully and anxiously, but quite merrily, and regarding it as a great success—and have all fallen several times, and have all been stopped, somehow or other, as we were sliding away—when Mr. Pickle of Portici, in the act of remarking on these uncommon circumstances as quite beyond his experience, stumbles, falls, disengages himself, with quick presence of mind, from those about him, plunges away head foremost, and rolls, over and over, down the whole surface of the cone!

Sickening as it is to look, and be so powerless to help him, I see him there, in the moonlight—I have had such a dream often—skimming over the white ice, like a cannon-ball. Almost at the same moment, there is a cry from behind; and a man who has carried a light basket of spare cloaks on his head, comes rolling past, at the same frightful speed, closely followed by a boy. At this climax of the chapter of accidents, the remaining eight-and-twenty vociferate to that degree, that a pack of wolves would be music to them!

Giddy, and bloody, and a mere bundle of rags, is Pickle of Portici when we reach the place where we dismounted, and where the horses are waiting; but, thank God, sound in limb! And never are we likely to be more glad to see a man alive and on his feet, than to see him now—making light of it too, though sorely bruised and in great pain. The boy is brought into the Hermitage on the Mountain, while we are at supper, with his head tied up; and the man is heard of, some hours afterwards. He too is bruised and stunned, but has broken no bones; the snow having, fortunately, covered all the larger blocks of rock and stone, and rendered them harmless.

After a cheerful meal, and a good rest before a blazing

fire, we again take horse, and continue our descent to Salvatore's house—very slowly, by reason of our bruised friend
being hardly able to keep the saddle, or endure the pain of
motion.   Though it is so late at night, or early in the morning, all the people of the village are waiting about the little
stable-yard when we arrive, and looking up the road by which
we are expected.   Our appearance is hailed with a great
clamour of tongues, and a general sensation for which in our
modesty we are somewhat at a loss to account, until, turning
into the yard, we find that one of a party of French gentlemen who were on the mountain at the same time is lying
on some straw in the stable, with a broken limb : looking
like Death, and suffering great torture ; and that we were
confidently supposed to have encountered some worse
accident.

So "well returned, and Heaven be praised ! " as the cheerful
Vetturíno, who has borne us company all the way from Pisa,
says, with all his heart !   And away with his ready horses,
into sleeping Naples !

It wakes again to Policinelli and pickpockets, buffo singers
and beggars, rags, puppets, flowers, brightness, dirt, and
universal degradation ; airing its Harlequin suit in the sunshine, next day and every day ; singing, starving, dancing,
gaming, on the sea-shore ; and leaving all labour to the
burning mountain, which is ever at its work.

Our English dilettanti would be very pathetic on the
subject of the national taste, if they could hear an Italian
opera half as badly sung in England as we may hear the
Foscari performed, to-night, in the splendid theatre of San
Carlo.   But, for astonishing truth and spirit in seizing and
embodying the real life about it, the shabby little San Carlino
Theatre—the rickety house one story high, with a staring
picture outside : down among the drums and trumpets, and
the tumblers, and the lady conjurer—is without a rival anywhere.

There is one extraordinary feature in the real life of
Naples, at which we may take a glance before we go—the
Lotteries.

They prevail in most parts of Italy, but are particularly
obvious, in their effects and influences, here.   They are drawn
every Saturday.   They bring an immense revenue to the
Government ; and diffuse a taste for gambling among the
poorest of the poor, which is very comfortable to the coffers

of the State, and very ruinous to themselves. The lowest
stake is one grain ; less than a farthing. One hundred
numbers—from one to a hundred, inclusive—are put into
a box. Five are drawn. Those are the prizes. I buy three
numbers. If one of them come up, I win a small prize. If
two, some hundreds of times my stake. If three, three
thousand five hundred times my stake. I stake (or play as
they call it) what I can upon my numbers, and buy what
numbers I please. The amount I play, I pay at the lottery
office, where I purchase the ticket ; and it is stated on the
ticket itself.

Every lottery office keeps a printed book, an Universal
Lottery Diviner, where every possible accident and circumstance is provided for, and has a number against it. For
instance, let us take two carlini—about sevenpence. On our
way to the lottery office, we run against a black man. When
we get there, we say gravely, " The Diviner." It is handed
over the counter, as a serious matter of business. We look
at black man. Such a number. " Give us that." We look
at running against a person in the street. " Give us that."
We look at the name of the street itself. " Give us that."
Now, we have our three numbers.

If the roof of the theatre of San Carlo were to fall in, so
many people would play upon the numbers attached to such
an accident in the Diviner, that the Government would soon
close those numbers, and decline to run the risk of losing
any more upon them. This often happens. Not long ago,
when there was a fire in the King's Palace, there was such
a desperate run on fire, and king, and palace, that further
stakes on the numbers attached to those words in the Golden
Book were forbidden. Every accident or event, is supposed,
by the ignorant populace, to be a revelation to the beholder,
or party concerned, in connexion with the lottery. Certain
people who have a talent for dreaming fortunately, are much
sought after ; and there are some priests who are constantly
favoured with visions of the lucky numbers.

I heard of a horse running away with a man, and dashing
him down, dead, at the corner of a street. Pursuing the
horse with incredible speed, was another man, who ran so
fast, that he came up, immediately after the accident. He
threw himself upon his knees beside the unfortunate rider,
and clasped his hand with an expression of the wildest grief.
" If you have life," he said, " speak one word to me ! If you

have one gasp of breath left, mention your age for Heaven's sake, that I may play that number in the lottery."

It is four o'clock in the afternoon, and we may go to see our lottery drawn. The ceremony takes place every Saturday, in the Tribunale, or Court of Justice—this singular, earthy-smelling room, or gallery, as mouldy as an old cellar, and as damp as a dungeon. At the upper end is a platform, with a large horse-shoe table upon it; and a President and Council sitting round—all Judges of the Law. The man on the little stool behind the President, is the Capo Lazzarone, a kind of tribune of the people, appointed on their behalf to see that all is fairly conducted: attended by a few personal friends. A ragged, swarthy fellow he is: with long matted hair hanging down all over his face: and covered, from head to foot, with most unquestionably genuine dirt. All the body of the room is filled with the commonest of the Neapolitan people: and between them and the platform, guarding the steps leading to the latter, is a small body of soldiers.

There is some delay in the arrival of the necessary number of judges; during which, the box, in which the numbers are being placed, is a source of the deepest interest. When the box is full, the boy who is to draw the numbers out of it becomes the prominent feature of the proceedings. He is already dressed for his part, in a tight brown Holland coat, with only one (the left) sleeve to it, which leaves his right arm bared to the shoulder, ready for plunging down into the mysterious chest.

During the hush and whisper that pervade the room, all eyes are turned on this young minister of fortune. People begin to inquire his age, with a view to the next lottery; and the number of his brothers and sisters; and the age of his father and mother; and whether he has any moles or pimples upon him; and where, and how many; when the arrival of the last judge but one (a little old man, universally dreaded as possessing the Evil Eye) makes a slight diversion, and would occasion a greater one, but that he is immediately deposed, as a source of interest, by the officiating priest, who advances gravely to his place, followed by a very dirty little boy, carrying his sacred vestments, and a pot of Holy Water.

Here is the last judge come at last, and now he takes his place at the horse-shoe table.

There is a murmur of irrepressible agitation. In the midst

of it, the priest puts his head into the sacred vestments, and pulls the same over his shoulders. Then he says a silent prayer; and dipping a brush into the pot of Holy Water, sprinkles it over the box and over the boy, and gives them a double-barrelled blessing, which the box and the boy are both hoisted on the table to receive. The boy remaining on the table, the box is now carried round the front of the platform, by an attendant, who holds it up and shakes it lustily all the time; seeming to say, like the conjurer, "There is no deception, ladies and gentlemen; keep your eyes upon me, if you please!"

At last, the box is set before the boy; and the boy, first holding up his naked arm and open hand, dives down into the hole (it is made like a ballot-box) and pulls out a number, which is rolled up, round something hard, like a bonbon. This he hands to the judge next him, who unrolls a little bit, and hands it to the President, next to whom he sits. The President unrolls it, very slowly. The Capo Lazzarone leans over his shoulder. The President holds it up, unrolled, to the Capo Lazzarone. The Capo Lazzarone, looking at it eagerly, cries out, in a shrill loud voice, "Sessantadue!" (sixty-two), expressing the two upon his fingers, as he calls it out. Alas! the Capo Lazzarone himself has not staked on sixty-two. His face is very long, and his eyes roll wildly.

As it happens to be a favourite number, however, it is pretty well received, which is not always the case. They are all drawn with the same ceremony, omitting the blessing. One blessing is enough for the whole multiplication-table. The only new incident in the proceedings, is the gradually deepening intensity of the change in the Capo Lazzarone, who has, evidently, speculated to the very utmost extent of his means; and who, when he sees the last number, and finds that it is not one of his, clasps his hands, and raises his eyes to the ceiling before proclaiming it, as though remonstrating, in a secret agony, with his patron saint, for having committed so gross a breach of confidence. I hope the Capo Lazzarone may not desert him for some other member of the Calendar, but he seems to threaten it.

Where the winners may be, nobody knows. They certainly are not present; the general disappointment filling one with pity for the poor people. They look: when we stand aside, observing them, in their passage through the court-yard down below: as miserable as the prisoners in the jail (it forms a part of the building), who are peeping down upon them, from between their bars; or, as the fragments of human heads which are still dangling in chains outside, in memory of the good old times, when their owners were strung up there, for the popular edification.

Away from Naples in a glorious sunrise, by the road to Capua, and then on a three days' journey along by-roads, that we may see, on the way, the monastery of Monte Cassino, which is perched on the steep and lofty hill above the little town of San Germano, and is lost on a misty morning in the clouds.

So much the better, for the deep sounding of its bell, which, as we go winding up, on mules, towards the convent, is heard mysteriously in the still air, while nothing is seen but the grey mist, moving solemnly and slowly, like a funeral procession. Behold, at length the shadowy pile of building close before us: its grey walls and towers dimly seen, though so near and so vast: and the raw vapour rolling through its cloisters heavily.

There are two black shadows walking to and fro in the quadrangle, near the statues of the Patron Saint and his sister; and hopping on behind them, in and out of the old arches, is a raven, croaking in answer to the bell, and uttering, at intervals, the purest Tuscan. How like a Jesuit he looks! There never was a sly and stealthy fellow so at home as is this raven, standing now at the refectory door, with his head on one side, and pretending to glance another way, while he is scrutinizing the visitors keenly, and listening with fixed attention. What a dull-headed monk the porter becomes in comparison!

"He speaks like us!" says the porter: "quite as plainly." Quite as plainly, Porter. Nothing could be more expressive than his reception of the peasants who are entering the gate with baskets and burdens. There is a roll in his eye, and a chuckle in his throat, which should qualify him to be chosen Superior of an Order of Ravens. He knows all about it. "It's all right," he says. "We know what we know. Come along, good people. Glad to see you!"

How was this extraordinary structure ever built in such a situation, where the labour of conveying the stone and iron, and marble, so great a height, must have been prodigious? "Caw!" says the raven, welcoming the peasants. How. being despoiled by plunder, fire and earthquake, has it risen from its ruins, and been again made what we now see it, with its church so sumptuous and magnificent? " Caw ! " says the raven, welcoming the peasants. These people have a miserable appearance, and (as usual) are densely ignorant, and all beg, while the monks are chaunting in the chapel. " Caw ! " says the raven, " Cuckoo ! "

So we leave him, chuckling and rolling his eye at the convent gate, and wind slowly down again through the cloud. At last emerging from it, we come in sight of the village far below, and the flat green country intersected by rivulets ; which is pleasant and fresh to see after the obscurity and haze of the convent—no disrespect to the raven, or the holy friars.

Away we go again, by muddy roads, and through the most shattered and tattered of villages, where there is not a whole window among all the houses, or a whole garment among all the peasants, or the least appearance of anything to eat, in any of the wretched hucksters' shops. The women wear a bright red bodice laced before and behind, a white skirt, and the Neapolitan head-dress of square folds of linen, primitively meant to carry loads on. The men and children wear any- thing they can get. The soldiers are as dirty and rapacious as the dogs. The inns are such hobgoblin places, that they are infinitely more attractive and amusing than the best hotels in Paris. Here is one near Valmontone (that is Val- montone, the round, walled town on the mount opposite), which is approached by a quagmire almost knee-deep. There is a wild colonnade below, and a dark yard full of empty stables and lofts, and a great long kitchen with a great long bench and a great long form, where a party of travellers, with two priests among them, are crowding round the fire while their supper is cooking. Above stairs, is a rough brick gallery to sit in, with very little windows with very small patches of knotty glass in them, and all the doors that open from it (a dozen or two) off their hinges, and a bare board on trestles for a table, at which thirty people might dine easily, and a fireplace large enough in itself for a breakfast-parlour, where, as the faggots blaze and crackle, they illuminate the ugliest and grimmest of faces, drawn in charcoal on the whitewashed chimney-sides by previous travellers. There is a flaring country lamp on the table ; and, hovering about it, scratching her thick black hair continually, a yellow dwarf of a woman, who stands on tiptoe to arrange the hatchet

knives, and takes a flying leap to look into the water-jug.
The beds in the adjoining rooms are of the liveliest kind.
There is not a solitary scrap of looking-glass in the house,
and the washing apparatus is identical with the cooking
utensils. But the yellow dwarf sets on the table a good flask
of excellent wine, holding a quart at least; and produces,
among half-a-dozen other dishes, two-thirds of a roasted kid,
smoking hot. She is as good-humoured, too, as dirty, which
is saying a great deal. So here's long life to her, in the flask
of wine, and prosperity to the establishment.

Rome gained and left behind, and with it the Pilgrims
who are now repairing to their own homes again—each with
his scallop shell and staff, and soliciting alms for the love
of God—we come, by a fair country, to the Falls of Terni,
where the whole Velino river dashes, headlong, from a rocky
height, amidst shining spray and rainbows. Perugia, strongly
fortified by art and nature, on a lofty eminence, rising
abruptly from the plain where purple mountains mingle with
the distant sky, is glowing, on its market-day, with radiant
colours. They set off its sombre but rich Gothic buildings
admirably. The pavement of its market-place is strewn with
country goods. All along the steep hill leading from the
town, under the town wall, there is a noisy fair of calves,
lambs, pigs, horses, mules, and oxen. Fowls, geese, and
turkeys, flutter vigorously among their very hoofs; and
buyers, sellers, and spectators, clustering everywhere, block
up the road as we come shouting down upon them.

Suddenly, there is a ringing sound among our horses. The
driver stops them. Sinking in his saddle, and casting up
his eyes to Heaven, he delivers this apostrophe, "Oh Jove
Omnipotent! here is a horse has lost his shoe!"

Notwithstanding the tremendous nature of this accident,
and the utterly forlorn look and gesture (impossible in any
one but an Italian Vetturíno) with which it is announced, it
is not long in being repaired by a mortal Farrier, by whose
assistance we reach Castiglione the same night, and Arezzo
next day. Mass is, of course, performing in its fine cathedral,
where the sun shines in among the clustered pillars, through
rich stained-glass windows: half revealing, half concealing
the kneeling figures on the pavement, and striking out paths
of spotted light in the long aisles.

But, how much beauty of another kind is here, when, on
a fair clear morning, we look, from the summit of a hill, on

Florence! See where it lies before us in a sun-lighted valley, bright with the winding Arno, and shut in by swelling hills; its domes, and towers, and palaces, rising from the rich country in a glittering heap, and shining in the sun like gold!

Magnificently stern and sombre are the streets of beautiful Florence; and the strong old piles of building make such heaps of shadow, on the ground and in the river, that there is another and a different city of rich forms and fancies, always lying at our feet. Prodigious palaces, constructed for defence, with small distrustful windows heavily barred, and walls of great thickness formed of huge masses of rough stone, frown, in their old sulky state, on every street. In the midst of the city—in the Piazza of the Grand Duke, adorned with beautiful statues and the Fountain of Neptune—rises the Palazzo Vecchio, with its enormous overhanging battlements, and the Great Tower that watches over the whole town. In its court-yard—worthy of the Castle of Otranto in its ponderous gloom—is a massive staircase that the heaviest waggon and the stoutest team of horses might be driven up. Within it, is a Great Saloon, faded and tarnished in its stately decorations, and mouldering by grains, but recording yet, in pictures on its walls, the triumphs of the Medici and the wars of the old Florentine people. The prison is hard by, in an adjacent court-yard of the building—a foul and dismal place, where some men are shut up close, in small cells like ovens; and where others look through bars and beg; where some are playing draughts, and some are talking to their friends, who smoke, the while, to purify the air; and some are buying wine and fruit of women-vendors; and all are squalid, dirty, and vile to look at. "They are merry enough, Signor," says the Jailer. "They are all blood-stained here," he adds, indicating, with his hand, three-fourths of the whole building. Before the hour is out, an old man, eighty years of age, quarrelling over a bargain with a young girl of seventeen, stabs her dead, in the market-place full of bright flowers; and is brought in prisoner, to swell the number.

Among the four old bridges that span the river, the Ponte Vecchio—that bridge which is covered with the shops of Jewellers and Goldsmiths—is a most enchanting feature in the scene. The space of one house, in the centre, being left open, the view beyond is shown as in a frame; and that precious glimpse of sky, and water, and rich buildings, shining so quietly among the huddled roofs and gables on the bridge, is exquisite. Above it, the Gallery of the Grand Duke crosses the river. It was built to connect the two Great Palaces by a secret passage ; and it takes its jealous course among the streets and houses, with true despotism : going where it lists, and spurning every obstacle away, before it.

The Grand Duke has a worthier secret passage through the streets, in his black robe and hood, as a member of the Compagnia della Misericordia, which brotherhood includes all ranks of men. If an accident take place, their office is, to raise the sufferer, and bear him tenderly to the Hospital. If a fire break out, it is one of their functions to repair to the spot, and render their assistance and protection. It is, also, among their commonest offices, to attend and console the sick ; and they neither receive money, nor eat, nor drink, in any house they visit for this purpose. Those who are on duty for the time, are all called together, on a moment's notice, by the tolling of the great bell of the Tower ; and it is said that the Grand Duke has been seen, at this sound, to rise from his seat at table, and quietly withdraw to attend the summons.

In this other large Piazza, where an irregular kind of market is held, and stores of old iron and other small merchandise are set out on stalls, or scattered on the pavement, are grouped together the Cathedral with its great Dome, the beautiful Italian Gothic Tower the Campanile, and the Baptistery with its wrought bronze doors. And here, a small untrodden square in the pavement, is "the Stone of DANTE," where (so runs the story) he was used to bring his stool, and sit in contemplation. I wonder was he ever, in his bitter exile, withheld from cursing the very stones in the streets of Florence the ungrateful, by any kind remembrance of this old musing-place, and its association with gentle thoughts of little Beatrice ?

The chapel of the Medici, the Good and Bad Angels of Florence ; the church of Santa Croce where Michael Angelo lies buried, and where every stone in the cloisters is eloquent on great men's deaths ; innumerable churches, often masses of unfinished heavy brickwork externally, but solemn and serene within ; arrest our lingering steps, in strolling through the city.

In keeping with the tombs among the cloisters, is the Museum of Natural History, famous through the world for its preparations in wax; beginning with models of leaves, seeds, plants, inferior animals; and gradually ascending, through separate organs of the human frame, up to the whole structure of that wonderful creation, exquisitely presented, as in recent death. Few admonitions of our frail mortality can be more solemn and more sad, or strike so home upon the heart, as the counterfeits of Youth and Beauty that are lying there, upon their beds, in their last sleep.

Beyond the walls, the whole sweet Valley of the Arno, the convent at Fiesole, the Tower of Galileo, BOCCACCIO's house, old villas and retreats; innumerable spots of interest, all glowing in a landscape of surpassing beauty steeped in the richest light; are spread before us. Returning from so much brightness, how solemn and how grand the streets again, with their great, dark, mournful palaces, and many legends: not of siege, and war, and might, and Iron Hand alone, but of the triumphant growth of peaceful Arts and Sciences.

What light is shed upon the world, at this day, from amidst these rugged Palaces of Florence! Here, open to all comers, in their beautiful and calm retreats, the ancient Sculptors are immortal, side by side with Michael Angelo, Canova, Titian, Rembrandt, Raphael, Poets, Historians, Philosophers —those illustrious men of history, beside whom its crowned heads and harnessed warriors show so poor and small, and are so soon forgotten. Here, the imperishable part of noble minds survives, placid and equal, when strongholds of assault and defence are overthrown; when the tyranny of the many, or the few, or both, is but a tale; when Pride and Power are so much cloistered dust. The fire within the stern streets, and among the massive Palaces and Towers, kindled by rays from Heaven, is still burning brightly, when the flickering of war is extinguished and the household fires of generations have decayed; as thousands upon thousands of faces, rigid with the strife and passion of the hour, have faded out of the old Squares and public haunts, while the nameless Florentine Lady, preserved from oblivion by a Painter's hand, yet lives on, in enduring grace and youth.

Let us look back on Florence while we may, and when its shining Dome is seen no more, go travelling through cheerful Tuscany, with a bright remembrance of it; for Italy will be the fairer for the récollection. The summer-time being come: and Genoa, and Milan, and the Lake of Como lying far behind us: and we resting at Faido, a Swiss village, near the

And let us not remember Italy the less regardfully, because, in every fragment of her fallen Temples, and every stone of her deserted palaces and prisons, she helps to inculcate the lesson that the wheel of Time is rolling for an end, and that the world is, in all great essentials, better, gentler, more forbearing, and more hopeful, as it rolls!

THE END.

Vineyard Scene. A page from the first edition, 1846

awful rocks and mountains, the everlasting snows and roaring cataracts, of the Great Saint Gothard : hearing the Italian tongue for the last time on this journey : let us part from Italy, with all its miseries and wrongs, affectionately, in our admiration of the beauties, natural and artificial, of which it is full to overflowing, and in our tenderness towards a people, naturally well-disposed, and patient, and sweet-tempered. Years of neglect, oppression, and misrule, have been at work, to change their nature and reduce their spirit ; miserable jealousies, fomented by petty Princes to whom union was destruction, and division strength, have been a canker at their root of nationality, and have barbarized their language ; but the good that was in them ever, is in them yet, and a noble people may be, one day, raised up from these ashes. Let us entertain that hope ! And let us not remember Italy the less regardfully, because, in every fragment of her fallen Temples, and every stone of her deserted palaces and prisons, she helps to inculcate the lesson that the wheel of Time is rolling for an end, and that the world is, in all great essentials, better, gentler, more forbearing, and more hopeful, as it rolls !

THE END